LAR CRIME

# WHITE-COLLAR CRIME

## OFFENSES IN BUSINESS, POLITICS, AND THE PROFESSIONS

*Edited, with Introduction and Notes, by Gilbert Geis and Robert F. Meier*

Revised Edition

**THE FREE PRESS**
*A Division of Macmillan Publishing Co., Inc.*
NEW YORK

Collier Macmillan Publishers
LONDON

The Free Press
A Division of Macmillan Publishing Co., Inc.
866 Third Avenue, New York, N.Y. 10022

Collier Macmillan Canada, Ltd.

Library of Congress Catalog Card Number: 76–27223

Printed in the United States of America

printing number
       3  4  5  6  7  8  9  10

Library of Congress Cataloging in Publication Data

Geis, Gilbert, comp.
   White-collar crime.

   First ed. published in 1968 under title:  White-collar
criminal.
   Bibliography:  p.
   Includes index.
   1.  White collar crimes--United States--Addresses,
essays, lectures.  I.  Meier, Robert Frank
II.  Title.
HV6635.G35  1977      364.1      76-27223
ISBN 0-02-911590-6
ISBN 0-02-911600-7 pbk.

This is a revision of the edition published in 1968 by Atherton Press as *White-Collar
Criminal: The Offender in Business and the Professions*, edited by Gilbert Geis.

*For Robley and Lee*

# CONTENTS

# PREFACE

In the first edition of this book, which appeared in 1968, it was predicted that studies of white-collar crime were about to proliferate at a rapid rate. In one sense, this has been true. The work of consumer advocates, such as Ralph Nader and his colleagues, and the explosion of Watergate have focused public attention on criminal activities in the upper echelons of the social system. In another sense, however, the prediction went astray, for social scientists have been relatively inactive in their investigation of white-collar crime. Throughout the volume we offer explanations for this state of affairs and suggestions as to how it might be overcome.

The challenge offered by white-collar crime, therefore, has continued to be unanswered. We still know relatively little about the social, economic, and legal dynamics that contribute to its appearance and form. The growing number of undergraduate and law school courses focusing directly on this subject, however, is encouraging. This volume, we believe, conveys the present state of our knowledge of white-collar crime. We have included the classic materials as well as more recent discussions of white-collar crime in the political arena. In addition, several selections offer opposing views on controversial matters relating to white-collar crime, such as questions of definition and public policy.

A number of people have helped us with substantive advice or technical assistance. We would like to express our thanks to Roe Gruber, Bob Harrington, Paul Jesilow, Anne Simoneau, John G. Munns, Betty Trusty, and Terry Plotkin. A special expression of gratitude is due Jennifer and Chrissy Meier for all those intangible contributions that, in the final analysis, make it all especially exciting.

# INTRODUCTION

I

More than a third of a century has gone by since Edwin H. Sutherland, speaking as president of the American Sociological Society, introduced the term "white-collar crime" into the language of social science. Sutherland's ground-breaking examination of criminal activity in corporate, commercial, professional, and political life opened up a new and exciting realm of scholarly inquiry. Much of the major research on white-collar crime appeared relatively soon after Sutherland's foray into the field. Published studies from this period—all of which are presented in this volume—constitute the "classic" core of white-collar-crime investigation. In large measure, these early studies are empirical inquiries on rather divergent subjects, which grope toward some kind of theoretical integration and cumulative insight. Further advance toward these goals has not, however, been very rapid in recent years. It is noteworthy, for instance, that less than a third of the material in this book represents work published since the first edition appeared in 1968.

But this state of affairs may change soon. For one thing, the appearance of a more militant consumer constituency is likely to encourage criminological research regarding white-collar crime. Certainly, in the past, the intense concentration by criminologists on traditional forms of law-breaking activity, such as property offenses, crimes of violence, and, most notably, juvenile delinquency, was spurred by deep public concern with such behavior and the concomitant appearance of government and private foundation funds for their investigation and, presumably, control.

There are other indications as well of forthcoming legislative and social revolt against exploitative business and political practices which could bring in their wake a shift in criminological emphasis toward white-collar crime. A recent survey of fifty-one persons noted for their work in the field of criminal justice, for instance, posed the following question: "In your opinion, what new crime categories will be added to the criminal codes by 1980?" The responses named white-collar crime as the arena most likely to be entered by legislatures. Twenty respondents predicted new statutes regarding environmental pollution, six thought that new crimes would be created to protect consumers more adequately, and five suggested that business crimes would be an area of forthcoming statutory concern. Thirteen of the remaining respondents indicated a belief that no major law changes would take place, while five thought that gun-possession laws would come onto the books by 1980.[1]

Similarly, Joseph Coates of the National Science Foundation, attempting to forecast the future of crime in the United States from the 1970s to the year 2000, thought that "[t]here may be greater recognition of a new class of crimes: the crime with the multi-victims and the uncertain victims." Coates noted further:

> Pollution of the environment, whether it is water, air, or the acoustic or aesthetic environment, may become a greater subject for regulation and penalty as the significance and assessment of pollution become clearer. While it is unlikely that we ever will have effective anti-litter or "don't spit on the sidewalk" legislation, there is every likelihood that we can enforce with a new seriousness the sanctions against business and business-men who fail to heed the law on industrial pollution, and against those public officials who fail to enforce the law.[2]

A third indicator of a changing emphasis in public policy of the kind that might herald a shift in scholarly investigation appeared early in 1975 when the Department of Justice directed the Federal Bureau of Investigation to focus time and energy on white-collar offenses. The new directive moved the FBI in the direction suggested by the guidelines that had been set for it when it was first established in 1908[3] and away from the "gang-buster" image it later cultivated. It was summarized in the following terms by an antitrust official:

> The typical FBI agent does not wake up in the morning thinking antitrust. We are trying to make them more conscious of the fact that price-fixing is a criminal violation just like financial fraud or kidnapping.[4]

The relative absence to date of a large body of scholarly work on white-collar crime seems to be traceable to, among other things, the extraordinarily complex nature of the subject matter. Most white-collar crimes are not defined in the conventional criminal codes but are "hidden" in civil and administrative laws and involve rather complex matters of legal protocol. In addition, etiological explanation, an enterprise accorded high status in social-science work, is very difficult in regard to white-collar crime. Standard kinds of correlative research (involving such variables as age, socioeconomic background, and race) are not particularly useful for understanding white-collar offenders and offenses. Psychopathy and/or an inability to defer gratification do not provide much insight into antitrust violations and the pollution of navigable waters. Labeling theory, which concentrates on the social processes leading to the criminalization of certain behaviors and on the consequences of such processes, seems awkward when brought to bear upon white-collar crime. White-collar offenders are often labeled. A General Electric official, for instance, complained that he was exposed to "relentless publicity"[5] and that the newspapers "used some terms which I don't think are necessary—they don't use the term 'price-fixing.' It's always 'price rigging' or trying to make it as sensational as possible."[6] But the labeling seems not to produce the dire consequences alleged for it when it is brought to bear upon certain traditional kinds of offenders.

In addition, white-collar crime sanctums such as corporate board-rooms are generally impervious to firsthand observation; even the Mafia (whatever that group is) seems to abide more by the spirit of the Freedom of Information Act than does the corporate world. Nobody is tapping the telephone at General Motors and making the transcripts available to a prurient public. And neither the FBI nor the CIA is employing undercover agents to infiltrate the Chrysler Corporation or Alcoa to discover what alleged conspiracies are being hatched in violation of the criminal law.

The information on white-collar crime that becomes available to social scientists from congressional committee investigations or court cases tends to be fragmentary and rather impressionistic in regard to fine points of criminological theorizing. Corporations often plead *nolo contendere* to those criminal charges which are brought, a luxury not generally made available to robbers and burglars (but one afforded former Vice President Agnew on a charge of income-tax evasion). Such pleas stifle opportunities to accumulate trial information, always a rich source of data. Those few white-collar criminals who are sentenced to correctional facilities tend to be long gone from their cells before the sociological researcher, with questionnaire in hand, locates them. White-collar criminals, too, especially those from the corporate and political worlds, are quite as skillful and adept as researchers are, so that they can sidestep adroitly the kinds of invidious inquiries that often mark studies of traditional criminals.

It is not that there is a dearth of hypotheses to be investigated in the area of white-collar crime. Sutherland himself threw out hunches with almost profligate abandon. He hypothesized, for instance, that white-collar offenders are scornful of government officials and processes, that they share the social and economic views held by judges and prosecuting officials, that they are treated tenderly by the mass media as compared with other kinds of offenders, that the insistence of upper executives that they are unaware of lawbreaking beneath them is nothing more than an alibi similar to those offered by other kinds of offenders. Other ideas worth pursuing appear like overripe fruit in the scholarly vineyard of white-collar crime. In this volume, for instance, Quinney suggests that the attitudes of professionals about their work might predict their behavior in regard to the legal constraints under which it is carried on. Lane offers a number of ideas about the structure of companies and their tendency to violate the law. Aubert suggests that researchers might profitably concentrate upon legislation and the public's interpretation of it when attempting to understand white-collar crime. Ball puts forward the idea that the investigation of objective circumstances and subjective responses to such circumstances might be informative in regard to the emergence of criminal offenses such as violations of rent-control laws.

In the long run, studies of white-collar crime will have to be incorporated into the mainstream of behavioral-science research, drawing intellectual nourishment from the diverse disciplines that enter into the study of criminal behavior. In the short run, though, there is a pressing need for accumulation of case studies, for hypothesis development and testing, and for the kind of research that moves forward by careful, additive processes. Current concern with white-collar crime seems to indicate a renaissance of this kind. It is part of the more general drive for social equity, involving such things as welfare rights, convict organizations, and community control of educational facilities and activities. No reputable scholar today, for example, would be likely to say, as Ernest Burgess did in 1950, that "a criminal is a person who regards himself as a criminal and is so regarded by society,"[7] and that, therefore, it is unacceptable to define violators of laws regulating commerce and corporate activity as criminals.

## II

Behavior duplicating in form and spirit what is now regarded as white-collar crime can be found throughout recorded history. Nonetheless, a large number of offenses currently prominent in the inventory of white-collar crime could not have come into existence before the appearance of social arrangements permitting their performance; corporate crime, for instance, could obviously not take place until the emergence of the corporation as a business and social form.

The triumph of laissez-faire capitalism in the nineteenth century saw the entrenchment of doctrines establishing the supremacy of property rights. Writers of this period employ terms from the criminal law to defend what they regard as the right of capitalists to make unchecked use of their holdings. Thus Lord Gainford wrote that it was nothing other than "sheer robbery" to limit the profit on coal mines,[8] and Lord Hugh Cecil, in a book on conservatism, insisted that, even if private property was employed mischievously, society could not interfere because to do so would be "theft."[9]

The attitude which prevailed at this time, and which continues today, though perhaps to a lesser extent, has been characterized by R. H. Tawney as follows:

> The secret of industrialism's triumph is obvious. . . . It concentrates attention upon the right of those who possess or can acquire power to make the fullest use of it for their own self-advancement. By fixing men's minds, not upon the discharge of social obligations, which restricts their energy . . . but upon the exercise of the right to pursue their own self-interest, it offers unlimited scope for the acquisition of riches, and therefore gives free play to one of the most powerful of human instincts. To the strong it promises unfettered freedom for the exercise of their strength; to the weak the hope that they too one day may be strong. Before the eyes of both it suspends a golden prize, which not all can attain, but for which each may strive, the enchanting vision of infinite expansion. It assures men that there are no ends other than their own ends, no law other than their desires, no limit other than that which they think advisable. . . . It relieves communities of te necessity of discriminating . . . between enterprise and avarice, energy and unscrupulous greed, property which is legitimate and property which is theft . . . because it treats all economic activities as standing upon the same level, and suggests that excess or defect, waste or superfluidity, require no conscious effort of social will to avert them.[10]

In the 1920s, however, the tide began to turn slightly, following a crusade against the more glaring abuses of big business by the muckrakers, a fervent and articulate group of writers including Ida Tarbell, Lincoln Steffens, and, in the realm of fiction, Frank Norris, Upton Sinclair, and Sinclair Lewis.[11]

Muckraking, the antecedent of later studies of white-collar crime,[12] had begun as a coherent enterprise about 1902, though its aims had received their major statement before the turn of the century in two books that penetrated deeply into American awareness: Lord Bryce's *The American Comonwealth* (1888) and Henry Demarest Lloyd's *Wealth Against Commonwealth* (1894). Well-documented findings of corruption in American politics and business underlay Bryce's conclusion that democracy in America, then just a dozen years past its centennial, had not altered the human traits and the conditions that foster white-collar crime. Lloyd also lashed out at the predators he saw infesting the commercial and political structure of American society. The following accusation was typical:

> In an incredible number of the necessaries and luxuries of life, from meat to tombstones, some inner circle of the "fittest" has sought, and very often obtained, the sweet power which Judge Barrett found the sugar trust had: It "can close every refinery at will, close some and open others, limit the purchases of raw material, artificially limit the production of raw sugar, enhance the price to enrich themselves and their associates at public expense, and depress the price when necessary to crush out and impoverish a foolhardy rival."[13]

The control of political life by corporate enterprise came in for scathing denunciation by Lloyd. The Standard Oil Company, he noted sarcastically, "has done everything with the Pennsylvania legislature except to refine it."[14]

During the first decade of the twentieth century, the muckrakers assiduously and effectively plowed the fields laid out by Bryce and Lloyd. A growing tendency toward sensationalism for its own sake, however, soon earned them the label given them by President Theodore Roosevelt, recalling the man in Bunyan's *Pilgrim's Progress* who could "look no way but downward, with a muckrake in his hands; who was offered a celestial crown for his muckrake, but who would neither look up nor regard the crown he was offered, but continued to rake to himself the filth on the floor."[15] Roosevelt himself, however, voiced a plaint often echoed today in writings about white-collar crime; though the roster of offenses may differ, the essential problem remains:

> Swindling in stocks, corrupting legislatures, making fortunes by the inflation of securities, by wrecking railroads, by destroying competitors by rebates—these forms of wrongdoing in the capitalist are far more infamous than any ordinary form of embezzlement or forgery; yet it is a matter of extreme difficulty to secure punishments of the men most guilty of them, most responsible for them.[16]

Rather subtly, however, the function performed by novelists and other social commentators in the United States began to be assumed by sociologists, members of a newly emerging academic discipline. Writers of fiction moved toward clinical dissection of individual motivation and toward portraiture of their protagonists—people responding to given social conditions which, however deplorable they might be, nonetheless demanded their due and, failing to exact it, took their psychic and social toll.

The early sociological scholars came from a wide diversity of backgrounds, but few could miss the strong ministerial tone that pervaded their ranks. They were persons of evangelical bent who believed that they had found the resolution of human difficulties in a moral fervor buttressed by the dictates and the metaphors of science. They were marked by a devotion to principles that can best be called "quasi-empirical," and by an insistent thrust to the roots of society where they intended to work their will, fortified by the tools of their trade and the trappings of their academic positions.

In 1896, when sociology was barely out of swaddling clothes, Edward A. Ross, author of the first significant sociological statement about white-collar crime (reprinted as the initial reading in this volume), insisted that sociology was a field that does not "meekly sidle in among the established sciences dealing with the various aspects of life"; it "aspires to nothing less than suzerainty."[17] Lester F. Ward, the American Sociological Society's first president (1906–1907), explained how the new science would operate. American society, he wrote, "should not drift aimlessly to and fro, backwards and forwards, without guidance. Rather, the group should carefully study its situations, comprehend the aims it desires to accomplish, study scientifically the best methods for attainment of these, and then concentrate social energy to the task set before it."[18] In these terms, Ward found agencies such as legislatures well on their way toward senescence. Perhaps they would have to be maintained, he noted, "but more and more they will become merely a formal way of putting the final sanction of society on decisions that have been worked out in the . . . sociological laboratory."[19] For Albion W. Small, a third pioneering sociologist, even the question of social values was readily susceptible to resolution by means of science. "The most reliable criterion of human values which science can propose," Small wrote, "would be the consensus of councils of scientists representing the largest possible variety of human interest, and cooperating to reduce their special judgments to a scale which would render their due to each of the interests of the total calculation."[20]

The early reformist zeal and zest in sociological work gave way in time to a devotion to scientism: the attempt by social scientists to operate as value-free, neutral observers of the passing social scene. The earlier sociologists, like the muckrakers, came to be ridiculed for turning their minds to "sex, sin, and sewage."[21] High respect was now accorded to the work of those later caricatured by David Riesman as pedants who, "with no philosophical training, consume their time affixing exact degrees of significance to insignificant correlations and never get around to discovering anything new about society."[22]

This was the social-science scene onto which Sutherland dropped his ideas about white-collar crime, and it explains why at the time Sutherland felt so strongly impelled to insist that he was concerned not with social reform but rather with the advancement of theoretical explanations of criminal behavior. The gradual return of American social science to matters of social importance began with the conclusion of World War II[23] and was sharply accelerated during the social upheavals of the late 1960s. The new "radical" sociology of this period,[24] drawing sustenance from the work of C. Wright Mills,[25] in some ways corresponded to the original, old sociology of Ward, Ross, and Small. Criminology too has experienced a renewal of earlier concerns, although new villains have been established to replace the old ones. In earlier days it was the lower classes, and particularly the second-generation immigrant robbers and burglars, who were seen as the progenitors of social pathology; nowadays malaise is likely to be traced to the machinations of the police, the courts, and the legislatures.[26] All these currents and cross-currents, as well as the eddies from adjacent social and intellectual streams, must be considered when attempting to understand the amount and nature of work in the area of white-collar crime.

## III

It is important to realize initially that Sutherland, by virtue of his position in American sociology, by the attractiveness of his terminology and of the illustrations he employed to support his views, broadened the horizons of criminological research well beyond their traditional limits. The tendency to generalize about crime and criminals on the basis of the more readily visible forms of criminal activity, such as murder, assault, and robbery, was irreversibly affected by Sutherland's analysis that the propensity to violate the law is not confined to the stereotyped "criminal." In his foreword to the 1961 edition of *White Collar Crime*, Donald R. Cressey also observes, "The lasting merit of this book . . . is its demonstration that a pattern of crime can be found to exist outside both the focus of popular preoccupation with crime and the focus of scientific investigation of crime and criminality."[27] For Cressey, a paramount problem is determining why white-collar crime was able to remain beyond popular and criminological purview for so long.

Justice Oliver Wendell Holmes provided an approach to this issue when he pointed out that matters which a society chooses to study and acts which it desires to proscribe are telling indications of fundamental values. "It is perfectly proper to regard and study law simply as a great anthropological document," Holmes noted, continuing:

It is proper to resort to [law] to discover what ideals of society have been strong enough to reach that final form of expression, or what have been the changes in dominant ideas from century to century. It is proper to study it as an exercise in the morphology and transformation of human ideas. The study pursued for such ends becomes science in its strictest sense.[28]

Few scholars have directed their attention to the charting of circumstances giving rise to statutes designed to discourage and punish certain derelictions by members of the more powerful and entrenched segments of the society, though many have noted the striking increase in such rules and have marked signposts along the way. Holmes, for example, observed:

> When we read in the old books that it is the duty of one exercising a common calling to do his work upon demand and do it with reasonable skill, we shall see that the gentleman is in the saddle and means to have the common people kept up to the mark for his convenience. We recognize the imperative tone which in our day has changed sides, and is oftener to be heard from the hotel clerk than from the guest.[29]

The growing concentration of statutory law on principles such as *caveat vendor* ("let the seller beware") undoubtably represents a function of, among other things, population growth, the development of cities, greater life expectancy, and enhanced technology, the last rich in its potential and awesome in its threat. As Pound has noted, "The points at which the claims and desires of each individual and those of his fellows conflict or overlap have increased enormously. Likewise, new agencies of menace to the general security have developed in profusion."[30]

Two dominant motifs mark the history of response to acts now considered white-collar crime. On the one hand, throughout time there has been a broad sweep of denunciation based almost exclusively on moral principles, usually deemed self-evident and part of a natural, immutable code. Witness, for example, the diatribes of the Biblical prophets, such as Micah, the yeoman farmer of the eighth century before Christ who bespoke the doom of Judah because of its low ethical level;[31] note, too, the uncompromising verdict of the Book of Ecclesiastes regarding commercial activities:

> A merchant shall hardly keep himself from doing wrong, and a huckster shall not be freed from sin. . . . As a nail sticketh between the joinings of the stones, so doth sin stick close to buying and selling.[32]

On the other hand, there has been a rambling and variegated response in the law to conditions such as those denounced in Biblical writings. Part of the explanation for the discrepancy between moral and legal codes can be found in the function of law. Law, for instance, may be employed to maintain the status quo as well as to establish new ground rules. Also, a reading of the legal record cannot merely involve rote perusal of provisions with the presumption that absence equals indifference. Failure to outlaw certain behavior may represent espousal of goals likely to be compromised if lesser aims are accentuated. Legal statements may also stand for quite fanciful positions, and the gap between the law on the books and the law in fact may be substantial. Moreover, the oft-repeated dictum that the law tends to be a reflection, however belated, of customary conditions fails to do justice to the basic question of *whose* customary ways will prevail and for what reason.

In such terms, a major thesis regarding white-collar crime is that the legal delineation of such offenses can be said to represent (though not in a direct or simple manner) social views that, for complex reasons, have come to be embodied in official codes. One facet of this development may be briefly summarized by reference to the extension of the law of theft into white-collar-crime realms.

Anthropological evidence makes it clear that a sense of rightful possession of private property is far from an innate human characteristic. Sociologists have suggested that for Western civilization the doctrine of predestination, arising with notable intensity in countries persuaded to Calvinistic dogma, became translated into a belief that material possessions indicated divine approval, manifest in their bestowal.[33] Extratheological precepts also obviously contributed to a belief in the sovereignty of ownership. In the United States, the early entrenchment of this thesis is marked in the ringing words of John Adams, the country's second president:

> Property is surely a right of mankind as really as liberty. . . . The moment the idea is admitted into society, that property is not as sacred as the laws of God, and that there is not a force of law and public justice to protect it, anarchy and tyranny commence.[34]

It was from such an ideological perspective that the law of fraud, fundamental in white-collar crime, emerged. In his meticulous tracing of this development in *Theft, Law and Society,* Jerome Hall concentrates initially upon the decision in the Carrier's case in 1473, a decision which for the first time included within the definition of theft the appropriation of goods by an intermediary. Prior to 1473 virtually all theft involved cattle, and the law covered only direct acts. By the time of the Carrier's case, however, manufacturing had begun to replace the old feudal system. The new middle class had started to take shape, and its trade interests coincided with those of the Crown. In addition, the Carrier's case probably involved wool and textile products, and these goods had recently become England's most significant exports. It was these conditions that coalesced in 1473 to change the Anglo-Saxon definition of theft.[35]

The slow, erratic, but nonetheless inexorable expansion of the concept of commercial fraud during the half-millennium since the Carrier's case provides fascinating material on the interplay between two groups: (1) those seeking to protect goods in their possession and to place themselves in a position to acquire more, and (2) other groups seeking their own advantage; the state remains between these two groups, attempting to set rules by which the game will be played.

A few landmarks along the way may be noted briefly.[36] The thirteenth-century English courts, for example, provided that there was to be "no remedy for that man who to his damage had trusted the word of a liar."[37] Even in the eighteenth century, a British chief justice could ask rhetorically: "When A got money from B by pretending that C had sent for it, shall we indict one man for making a fool of another?"[38] It was only in 1757 that a statutory provision for the punishment of "mere private cheating" was placed into the English law. It was such judicial sentiments which led Jonathan Swift to locate an ancient Hebrew tradition in a land visited by Gulliver:

> The Lilliputians look upon fraud as a greater crime than theft, and therefore seldom fail to punish it with death; for they allege that care and vigilance, with a very common understanding, may preserve a man's goods from theft, but honesty has no defense against superior cunning.[39]

In the United States, development of the law of fraud was fought each step of the way by those who held the view, expressed in the words of Chief Justice Stone, that "any interference with the operation of the natural laws of greed" was "subversive of liberty."[40] Some of the underlying factors that encouraged state interference with commerce provide keys to present enactments in the area of white-collar crime. Hermann Mannheim noted some of these items: (1) movement from an agricultural to a commercial and industrial society; (2) increasing inequality in the distribution of property, and the amassing of great wealth by the few; (3) the growing need to leave property in the hands of other persons; (4) transformation of ownership of visible property into intangible powers and rights, such as corporate shares, including a system of social security in the place of ownership of goods; and (5) passage of property from private to corporate ownership.[41]

The pressure to regulate economic activity, which crystallized during the nineteenth century, arose in particular from fears over the consequences of economic monopolization. The attempts to check monopoly power, however, often resulted in laws which presented a façade of control, but sidestepped measures that might be most effective. In particular, many of the new regulations were located in civil and administrative codes rather than being enacted as criminal laws. Location of the statutes in the non-criminal codes would later influence public beliefs about the relative seriousness of the economic behaviors and dictate the kinds of penalties meted out to many white-collar offenders.

Illustrations of this process are offered by several scholars, including Gabriel Kolko, who documents the role of the major railroads in "helping" congressional officials draft legislation which conceded peripheral points (often with the goal of keeping less powerful competitors in their place), but allowed the railroads to proceed unimpeded in many kinds of economic activity that clearly seemed to be against the public interest. Involvement of the railroads in the actual drafting of legislation that was supposed to control them was a consequence, it was said, of their presumed expertise regarding the matters under consideration.[42]

## IV

No consideration of white-collar crime would be complete without reference to the work of Ralph Nader and his associates. Nader's efforts have directly intersected those of the criminological establishment only once, when he briefly reviewed the work of the President's Commission on Law Enforcement and Administration of Justice[43] in regard to the "few words on business crime" that were "tucked away in the ninth and final Task Force Report." Nader used the contents of the report as a springboard for one of his favorite themes: that there ought to be more, and more severe, criminal penalties for white-collar criminals.[44]

There is a particularly interesting sentence in the Nader piece on the Crime Commission's efforts: "Scratch the image of any industry and unsavory practices become visible."[45] The Nader statement is strikingly similar to a much-quoted observation of Sutherland: "White-collar criminality is found in every occupation, as can be discovered readily in casual conversation with a representative of an occupation by asking him, 'What crooked practices are found in your occupation?' "[46] The parallel between Nader and Sutherland is, in fact, much more fundamental. Nader, like Sutherland, is strongly opposed to what he regards as the trend in the United States toward "corporate socialism," a condition in which vital decisions about the welfare of the country are made secretly and together by corporate powers.

Unlike Sutherland, however, Nader feels no obligation to search for theoretical insights; indeed, he has been scornful of such efforts, as when he talks about "the leisure of the theory class."[47] Nader's underlying philosophy is preeminently clear. Like Lord Acton, he believes that power tends to corrupt and absolute power to corrupt absolutely. The duty of the citizen, as Nader views it, is to see to it that a keen eye is kept upon government, business, and the professions, the major locales of power, so that they fulfill their public obligations.

Investigation of the work of the Food and Drug Administration (FDA) by a Nader study group demonstrates how Nader and his colleagues come to grips with white-collar offenses. They rely primarily upon (1) research; (2) use of legal processes; and (3) publicity. The legal process is employed, along with other methods, to make certain that the investigators are accorded access to relevant materials. Research undergirds their case, and publicity hits at the upperworld's special sensitivity to notoriety.[48]

The Nader team, as noted, work on the premise that industry will take advantage of virtually any opportunity to exploit the consuming public, and will desist from such exploitation only when forced to do so by government organizations goaded into action by the pressure of public opinion. The focus of the Nader work, therefore, has been on documentation of the failure of federal and state regulatory agencies to control practices which Congress gave them the power to regulate.

The Nader survey of the FDA, for instance, begins with an overview of the food industry, which, according to Nader, has become concentrated into "fewer and fewer corporate hands," with the following result:

> The competition, such as it is, has focused heavily on massive promotional expenditures (between 16 and 18 percent of gross revenues), on brand-name identification, wasteful nonprice competition, and other marketing expenses that do not provide added value for the consumer but simply increase food prices. In addition, the food companies have one of the tiniest research budgets (for nutrition and food quality) of any United States industry.[49]

The probe into the work of the FDA, conducted largely by college students and recent graduates, found that, rather than launch campaigns against major firms that routinely break the law, the FDA pursues small and inconsequential violators, so as to give the appearance of activity with a record of successful prosecution, while allowing major depredators to proceed unmolested. Even when successful, as in the following case, the FDA is hampered by an archaic penalty structure:

> In 1958 the FDA became involved in a complicated legal battle with the Caltec Citrus Company after having staked out the company's warehouse and observed sugar, vitamin C, and other substances not allowed in pure orange juice being carried in a back door. It was estimated that the watering and adulterating practices of the company cost consumers $1 million in lost value—$1 million of pure company profits. The outcome of the case . . . was a total fine of $6,000, and a suspended sentence for the violators. A man who could return $1 million on a $6,000 investment would be considered brilliant in any business circle.[50]

Nonetheless, the Nader team was not convinced that limited enforcement power was the primary handicap of the FDA; if the agency allowed the public to be bilked, the cause was its own apathy and indifference. "As long as the FDA believes that the food industry wishes to provide the safest, highest-quality food possible to the American people," the team concluded, "no amount of legislation, manpower, or money will turn the agency into an effective food regulator." The Nader group found the FDA's faith in industrial self-regulation "ludicrous, if not tragic." The food industry, it insisted, "has vigorously set about its task of making profits."

Therefore, it was time that the FDA set about *"its* assigned task of insuring that profits made by the food industry are not the result of fraud, deception, adulteration, or misbranding." Otherwise, the public interest will continue to be mauled by the food industry's "callousness, ignorance, and greed."[51]

Nader's work is instructive for criminologists. For one thing, it demonstrates the possibility of acquiring substantial data on government and business practices, if enough doggedness goes into the effort. It indicates, too, how the locus and structure of academic criminology in the United States have often been responsible for the direction and tone of its work. Note might be made, for example, that virtually all of the leading criminologists in the United States have been Midwesterners located at the Big Ten land-grant universities—men such as George Vold at Minnesota, Sutherland at Indiana, John Gillin at Wisconsin, Donald Taft at Illinois. Yet the centers of power in the United States are Washington, D.C., and New York City. Washington proper has no major university. In New York City, scholars at so prestigious an institution as Columbia University barely deign to work in the field of crime. Robert K. Merton, for instance, Columbia's leading sociologist, has been publicly critical of what he saw in himself in the earlier part of his career as a "slum-encouraged provincialism of thinking that the primary subject-matter of sociology was centered on such peripheral problems of social life as divorce and juvenile delinquency."[52]

Nader, working in Washington, has access to records, officials, agencies, and similar on-site sources of information about criminal activity of a white-collar nature. The American criminologists who set the framework for the field more often than not had to be satisfied with studies of prisoners—penal institutions were in the hinterlands too—and with relating criminal behavior to such things as race, sex, age, and urban–rural locale.

Like Sutherland, Nader is a muckraker, with a command of vibrant language and an incessant drive to draw parallels between traditional and white-collar crime. "Smogging" is compared to "mugging," for instance, and is said to have taken on the proportions of a "massive crime wave" which has been neglected in federal and state compilations on lawbreaking.[53] Typical of Nader's approach is the following juxtaposition of the response of official agencies to diverse behaviors:

The Chicago Seven kept twelve lawyers busy in the Justice Department. I've yet to hear of *one* of Attorney General Mitchell's lawyers concerning himself with the Detroit Four. GM and Ford are criminals. This is serious enough to hand over to Vice President Agnew for action—but before he becomes interested we'll have to find polluters who wear beards and sandals.[54]

V

Most causal explanations of white-collar crime derive from an "evil causes evil" view based on the belief that only deplorable conditions of person or place can give rise to criminal behavior. There is neglect of the fact that perfectly adequate human beings and perfectly adequate social situations, judged by reasonable criteria, may produce untoward consequences, in the manner that both kindness and murder kill.

One of the earliest and hardiest explanations of white-collar crime is suggested by Aristotle in *Politics*. "Men may desire superfluities in order to enjoy pleasure unaccompanied with pain, and therefore they commit crimes," he noted. "The greatest crimes are caused by excess and not by necessity."[55] Sutherland, however, in perhaps the most telling of his observations on crime causation, laid to rest the Aristotelian postulate and its contemporary kin. "Though criminal behavior is an expression of general needs and values," he emphasized, "it is not explained by those general needs and values, since non-criminal behavior is an expression of the same needs and values."[56] The financially pressed male corporate executive, Sutherland's view points out, may embezzle, or he may move to a cheaper house, send his wife to work, himself take a weekend job, or borrow money from an uncle. Each of these alternatives may be able to satisfy his necessity adequately. The need alone, shared by untold numbers of other individuals who resolve it both legally and illegally, or not at all, offers little clue to the precise method that may be selected for its satisfaction.

Sutherland's focus was on the enunciation of a theory to explain all crime. In an article on corporate violations, for instance, he noted mockingly that General Motors does not have an inferiority complex, United States Steel does not suffer from an unresolved Oedipus problem, and the DuPonts do not desire to return to the womb. It was a clever piece of invective, designed to demolish the position of clinical theorists in criminology. "The assumption that an offender may have some such pathological distortion of the intellect seems to me absurd," Sutherland wrote, "and if it is absurd regarding the crimes of businessmen, it is equally absurd regarding the crimes of persons in the lower economic classes."[57]

To substitute for partial explanations and for psychological theses regarding criminal behavior, Sutherland advanced his own hypothesis which, "for reasons of economy, simplicity, and logic," was to be used to explain both white-collar and lower-class criminality. This was his theory of differential association. "Criminality is learned," the theory started in part, "in direct or indirect association with those who already practice the behavior." Since criminality is so learned, Sutherland observed, it can be and is learned at all social levels.[58]

It is important to realize that no one, of course, had ever maintained that General Motors or its management personnel suffered from an inferiority complex, any more than any serious scholar would have taken the position that all criminals, of either the lower or upper class, are driven by an unrequited yearning to return to the womb. Sutherland was flailing a theoretical nonesuch, and it was, in fact, Sutherland himself who, in one vital respect, came nearest to the theories he was belaboring, with his insistence that all criminals could, and should, be analyzed in terms of a single theoretical construct.

It was this commitment that inevitably tended to blur distinctions for Sutherland. As Merton has noted, "the decision to encompass a great variety of behaviors under one heading naturally leads us to look for an all-encompassing set of propositions which will account for the entire range of behavior." "This is not too remote," Merton points out, "from the assumption of a John Brown or a Benjamin Rush that there must be *a* theory of disease, rather than distinct theories of disease—of tuberculosis and of arthritis, of typhoid and syphilis—theories which are diverse rather than single."[59]

The matter noted by Merton does not relate to the accuracy of an all-embracing theoretical postulate such as that advanced by Sutherland. It is, after all, accurate to maintain that the "real" cause of crime is the enactment of legal statutes; without the statutes, there could be no crime. The problem with such a statement (though it has its use in focusing attention on the legislative process) is that it is not as powerful an interpretative approach as other explanations seem apt to be for providing deeper understanding of crime. The task is to locate the theory that offers the best insight into the processes being examined and provides the best leads for further work and, if desired, for social action. A Freudian approach may be satisfactory in some instances as a base for understanding therapeutic intervention in regard to some sex offenses; a Marxist interpretation of property offenses may serve as a basis for social action. Neither approach, however, is apt to fit all of the facts; qualifications will have to be made. In time, the qualifications may be so significant that it appears best to abandon the particular theoretical base and press forward toward another, more useful approach.

A major difficulty in the search for explanation and understanding concerns the determination of behaviors that are to be regarded as homogeneous and those that are to be seen as heterogeneous; that is, what things are to be viewed as similar and what as different. In making certain kinds of distinctions, we may destroy the base upon which the most sophisticated understanding can be built. Hirschi provides a fine illustration of this point with his observation that typologists, persons who believe in grouping behaviors which have the appearance of similarity, may be engaged in self-defeating behavior. "They would have us believe," Hirschi notes, "that it is 'patently absurd' to attempt to explain with a single theory such diverse phenomena as the movement of the tides, the erect posture of trees, and the difficulty of writing on the ceiling with a ballpoint pen."[60] Hirschi is suggesting that perhaps some day criminologists may be able to discover a law such as the law of gravity, which explains all of the phenomena listed in the foregoing quotation. Nonetheless, the Hirschi illustration too must be qualified. Categorization of some kind is the essence of all understanding and communication. The need is to make distinctions with care and with a certain tentativeness, always examining carefully the roots and consequences of particular kinds of groupings.

## VI

Where do we stand and where are we likely to be heading in regard to the study of white-collar crime? Several matters may be noted in conclusion:

(1) There is a need for a wider variety of theoretical perspectives to be brought to bear upon the analysis of white-collar crime. The materials on white-collar crime to date have tended to concentrate on determination of public perceptions of white-collar crime, on the nature of judicial response to white-collar criminals, and on matters concerning the proper definition of the behavior. Aside from Sutherland's use of the differential association perspective, and a brief article by Sherwin, in which he applied some of the concepts derived from Merton's notion of anomie to white-collar crime,[61] much of the work is atheoretical. Questions such as the following remain unanswered: What are the implications of labeling theory[62] for white-collar crime? How do the concepts of inadequate socialization, criminal subculture, and criminal motivation apply to white-collar crime? There also appears to be a need for case studies, statistical comparisons, personality profiles, and historical analyses of industrial growth and concentration. These approaches have provided considerable insight into other forms of criminal behavior; if they are not appropriate for the investigation of white-collar crime, this ought to be made known; if they are, they ought to be employed.

(2) There is a need to express openly the value premises that underlie work on white-collar crime, and to confront directly some striking differences between the manner in which scholars in the field seem to view traditional offenses and white-collar offenses. There is some support today for the view that traditional prisoners are victims of the political process; as "political prisoners" they are seen as having little, if any, control over their social condition and the acts of law violation in which they indulge.[63] Why, then, is it alleged that white-collar offenders should be held totally responsible for their acts, and why should they be regarded as nefarious

and dangerous enemies of society when, perhaps, they have as little control over the wellsprings of their behavior as do traditional offenders? Or, alternatively, if it is suggested that white-collar criminals deserve to be incarcerated because of what they have done, why should it not also be held that traditional offenders merit the same fate? Hollander has put the matter well in regard to what often happens:

> [S]ocial determinism (sympathetically applied to those who are perceived to be the underdogs) becomes suspended when judging the behavior of other groups, such as the military brass, FBI agents, policemen, politicians, corporation executives, Southern "rednecks" or Northern construction workers. In short, the bad guys have a choice but the good ones don't.[64]

It is not that these inconsistencies cannot be resolved, but that few attempts have been made to do so. The idea that the rich ought to be held to higher standards than the poor offers one possible resolution. Another resolution might lie in the view that the amount of free will (and, thus, responsibility) is directly related to the wherewithal an individual possesses. A third possible approach is to maintain that white-collar crime causes more social disruption than traditional crime, and that therefore white-collar offenders deserve to be treated differently. Whether these rationales will hold up when scrutinized carefully remains an open question.

(3) Scholars studying white-collar crime may have to cover some of the same areas already examined by Ralph Nader, but they will have to do so with more theoretical sophistication than Nader has shown. Nader has demonstrated clearly that the data are there to be gathered by the diligent and aggressive researcher; but he does not do the kind of work needed for a theoretically sophisticated social science of criminal behavior. In fact, persons concerned with white-collar crime might well examine Nader's operations in an attempt to understand the roots of his success to date and the aspects of his work which might appear to undermine continuing achievement. Will Nader become a transient figure on the political scene, more and more ignored as his message appears to be redundant and stereotypic, or will he be able to continue to score points against established ways, bringing along with him a new and dedicated group of young persons who buy into his mission?

White-collar crime, we are saying, is an area of study in which much material remains to be mined. It is an area of study which may be able to throw light on some of the most significant aspects of contemporary life. Among the criminological topics which further work on white-collar crime may illuminate, the following seem notable:

1. White-collar crime challenges the more banal kinds of explanations of criminal activity. To say that poverty "causes" crime, for instance, fails

utterly to account for widespread lawbreaking by persons who are extraordinarily affluent.

2. White-collar crime indicates the distribution of power in our society. An examination of the statute books shows what kinds of occupational acts have come to be included within the criminal code and what kind go unproscribed. The enactment of laws curbing the activities of certain persons demonstrates that, at least for a moment, other persons with other interests had the power to prevail legislatively.

3. White-collar crime portrays the manner in which power is exercised in our society. A review of upperworld violations and the manner in which they are prosecuted and punished tells who is able to control what in American society and indicates the extent to which such control is effective.

4. White-collar crime provides an indication of the degree of hypocrisy present in a society. Such hypocrisy may be seen as leverage by means of which the society may be forced toward congruence between its verbal commitments and its actual conduct, much as Myrdal insisted that the "dilemma" in the United States between conduct toward minorities and democratic values exerted incessant pressure for a reconciliation along the lines of the values.[65] In regard to white-collar crime, hypocrisy exists when fraud among the lower classes is viewed with distaste and punished, while upper-class deception is countenanced and defined as nothing more malevolent than "shrewd business practice."

5. White-collar crime illustrates changes in social and business life. Thus, the old-time grocer, weighing merchandise by hand and dealing with customers on a personal basis, probably had less inclination and less opportunity to defraud. Today's supermarkets, engaged essentially in the rental of shelf space to manufacturers, epitomize impersonality, with consequences for the emergence of a new form of crime, that involving consumer fraud.

6. White-collar crime furnishes material helpful for an understanding of changes in social values. Recent laws demanding that foods be uncontaminated and that pollution be controlled reflect an emerging ethos insisting that persons be accorded every reasonable opportunity to remain alive and healthy until cut down by uncontrollable forces. In the future, if support grows for enunciation of the right of each human being to achieve his or her full potential, new forms of white-collar crime will be legislated.

These postulates, as well as those noted earlier, constitute the kinds of general propositions that may emerge in greater detail—with additional refinements or with negating counterstatements—if white-collar crime comes to be investigated as rapidly as many traditional crime forms are now being explored.

*Notes*

1. H. Joo Shin, *Criminal Justice in 1980* (Albany, N.Y.: School of Criminal Justice, State University of New York at Albany, 1973).

2. Joseph F. Coates, "The Future of Crime in the United States from Now to the Year 2000," *Policy Sciences*, 3 (1972), p. 40.

3. See Max Lowenthal, *The Federal Bureau of Investigation* (New York: Sloane, 1950).

4. Edwin L. Dale, "F.B.I. to Aid Fight on Price-Fixers," *New York Times*, January 2, 1975, p. 9.

5. *New York Times*, March 17, 1961.

6. Quoted in Gilbert Geis, "The Heavy Electrical Equipment Antitrust Cases of 1961," in Marshall B. Clinard and Richard Quinney, eds., *Criminal Behavior Systems* (New York: Holt, Rinehart and Winston, 1967) p. 149. See pp. 117–132 below.

7. Ernest W. Burgess, "Comment," *American Journal of Sociology* 56 (July, 1950), p. 33.

8. Quoted in R. H. Tawney, *The Acquisitive Society* (New York: Harcourt, Brace, 1920), p. 26.

9. *Ibid.*, p. 23.

10. *Ibid.*, pp. 30–31.

11. Ida M. Tarbell, *The History of the Standard Oil Company* (New York: Macmillan, 1904); Lincoln Steffens, *The Shame of the Cities* (New York: McClure, Phillips, 1904); Frank Norris, *The Pit* (New York: Doubleday and Page, 1903), and *The Octopus* (New York: Doubleday and Page, 1901); Upon Sinclair, *The Jungle* (New York: Doubleday and Page, 1906); Sinclair Lewis, *Main Street* (New York: Harcourt, Brace, 1920), and *Babbitt* (New York: Harcourt Brace, 1922).

12. See, generally, David M. Chalmers, *Social and Political Ideas of Muckrakers* (New York: Citadel Press, 1964); Arthur Weinberg, *The Muckrakers* (New York: Simon and Schuster, 1961); Harvey Swados, ed., *Years of Conscience: The Muckrakers* (Cleveland: World Publishing Company, 1962).

13. Henry D. Lloyd, *Wealth Against Commonwealth* (New York: Harper and Brothers, 1904), p. 4. The jurist was George C. Barrett of the New York Supreme Court, the case *People v. North River Sugar refining Co.*, N.Y. Supplement, 3 (January 9, 1889), p. 413.

14. *Ibid.*, p. 315.

15. John Bunyan, *Pilgrim's Progress* (1678) (New York: Revell, 1903), p. 207.

16. Theodore Roosevelt, *The Roosevelt Policy* (New York: Current Literature Publishing Company, 1908), 2:687.

17. Edward A. Ross, *Foundations of Sociology*, 5th ed. (New York: Macmillan, 1926), p. 8.

18. Quoted in James Quayle Dealey, "Lester Frank Ward," in Howard W. Odum, ed., *American Masters of Social Science* (New York: Holt, 1927), p. 82.

19. Lester F. Ward, *Applied Sociology* (Boston: Ginn, 1906), pp. 338–339.

20. Albion W. Small, *The Meaning of Social Science* (Chicago: University of Chicago Press, 1910), p. 242.

21. Howard Becker, "Anthropology and Sociology," in John Gillin, ed., *For a Science of Man* (New York: Macmillan, 1954), p. 145.

22. David Riesman, *Thorstein Veblen: A Critical Interpretation* (New York: Scribner, 1953), p. 48.

23. Louis Wirth, quoted in Leon Bramson, *The Political Context of Sociology* (Princeton, N.J.: Princeton University Press, 1961), pp. 93–94.

24. See, for example, Irving L. Horowitz, ed., *The New Sociology* (New York: Oxford University Press, 1965).

25. C. Wright Mills, *The Power Elite* (New York: Oxford University Press, 1956) and *idem, Sociological Imagination* (New York: Oxford University Press, 1959).

26. Robert F. Meier, Review of Ian Taylor, Paul Walton and Jock Young, *The New Criminology* in *Journal of Criminal Justice* 2 (Winter, 1974), pp. 365–368. See

also *idem*, "The New Criminology: Continuity in Criminological Theory," *Journal of Criminal Law and Criminology*, forthcoming (December, 1976 or March, 1977), and Gresham Sykes, "The Rise of Critical Criminology," *Journal of Criminal Law and Criminology* 65 (June, 1974), pp. 206–213.

27. Donald R. Cressey, "Foreword" to Edwin H. Sutherland, *White Collar Crime* (New York: Holt, Rinehart and Winston, 1961), p. xii.

28. Oliver Wendell Holmes, "Law in Science and Science in Law," in *Collected Legal Papers* (New York: Harcourt, Brace, 1921), p. 212.

29. *Ibid.*, pp. 213–214.

30. Roscoe Pound, *Criminal Justice in America* (New York: Holt, 1930), p. 12.

31. Micah 1:1–16 and 2:1–12.

32. Ecclesiastes 27:2.

33. Max Weber, *The Protestant Ethic and the Spirit of Capitalism*, trans. Talcott Parsons (London: George Allen, 1930).

34. John Adams, *Works* (Boston: Little, Brown, 1853) 6:8–9.

35. Jerome Hall, *Theft, Law and Society*, 2nd ed. (Indianapolis: Bobbs-Merrill, 1952), pp. 1–33.

36. Much of this material is drawn from Hermann Mannheim, *Criminal Justice and Social Reconstruction* (London: Routledge, 1946), section 3, and *idem*, *Comparative Criminology* (Boston: Houghton Mifflin, 1967), chapter 21.

37. Frederick Pollock and Frederic W. Maitland, *History of English Law* (Boston: Little, Brown, 1909), 2:535.

38. Quoted in Mannheim, *Criminal Justice, op. cit.*, p. 121.

39. Jonathan Swift, "A Voyage to Lilliput," in *Gulliver's Travels*, Pt. 1, chapter 6 (1735).

40. Alpheus T. Mason, *Harlan Fiske Stone* (New York: Viking, 1956), p. 380.

41. Mannheim, *Criminal Justice, op. cit.*, p. 380.

42. Gabriel Kolko, *Railroads and Regulation, 1877–1916* (Princeton, N.J.: Princeton University Press, 1965). See also William J. Chambliss, "The State, The Law, and the Definition of Behavior as Criminal, or Delinquent," in Daniel Glaser, ed., *Handbook of Criminology* (Chicago: Rand McNally, 1974), pp. 7–43.

43. President's Commission on Law Enforcement and Administration of Justice, *Task Force Report: Crime and Its Impact; An Assessment* (Washington, D.C.: U.S. Government Printing Office, 1967), chapter 8.

44. Ralph Nader, "Business Crime," in David Sanford, ed., *Hot War on the Consumer* (New York: Pitman, 1969), pp. 138–140.

45. *Ibid.*, p. 140.

46. Edwin H. Sutherland, "White-Collar Criminality," *American Sociological Review*, 5 (February, 1940), p. 3.

47. Quoted in Charles McCarry, *Citizen Nader* (New York: Saturday Review Press, 1972), p. 216.

48. See, generally, Francis E. Rourke, "Law Enforcement Through Publicity," *University of Chicago Law Review*, 24 (Winter, 1957), pp. 225–255.

49. Ralph Nader, "Foreword" to James S. Turner, *The Chemical Feast* (New York: Grossman, 1970), p. vii.

50. Turner, *op. cit.*, p. 63.

51. *Ibid.*, pp. 85–86.

52. Robert K. Merton, *Social Theory and Social Structure* (New York: Free Press, 1957), p. 17.

53. Ralph Nader, "Foreword" to John C. Esposito, *The Vanishing Air* (New York: Grossman, 1970), p. viii.

54. McCarry, *op. cit.*, p. 306.

55. Aristotle, *Politics*, trans. J. E. C. Welldon (London: Macmillan, 1932), Book II, chapter 7, p. 65.

56. Edwin H. Sutherland and Donald R. Cressey, *Principles of Criminology*, 7th ed. (Philadelphia: Lippincott, 1966), p. 82.

57. Edwin H. Sutherland, "Crimes of Corporations," in Albert Cohen, Alfred Lindesmith, and Karl Schuessler, eds., *The Sutherland Papers* (Bloomington: Indiana University Press, 1956), p. 96.

58. See Sutherland and Cressey, *op. cit.*, chapter 4.

59. Robert K. Merton, in Helen L. Witmer and Ruth Kotinsky, eds., *New Perspectives for Research on Juvenile Delinquency* (Washington D.C.: Children's Bureau Publication No. 356, 1956), p. 27.

60. Travis Hirschi, "Procedural Rules and the Study of Deviant Behavior," *Social Problems*, 21 (Fall, 1973), p. 168, note 18.

61. Robert Sherwin, "White-Collar Crime, Conventional Crime and Merton's Deviant Behavior Theory," *Wisconsin Sociologist*, 2 (Spring, 1963), pp. 7–10.

62. See, for example, Edwin M. Lemert, *Social Pathology* (New York: McGraw-Hill, 1951); Lemert, *Human Deviance, Social Problems and Social Control*, 2nd ed. (Englewood Cliffs, N.J.: Prentice-Hall, 1972); Howard Becker, *Outsiders* (New York: Free Press, 1963); John I. Kitsuse, "Societal Reaction to Deviant Behavior: Problems of Theory and Method," *Social Problems*, 9 (Winter, 1962), pp. 247–256; Kitsuse, "Deviance, Deviant Behavior, and Deviants: Some Conceptual Issues," in William J. Filstead, ed., *An Introduction to Deviance* (Chicago: Markham, 1972), pp. 233–243; Edwin H. Schur, *Labeling Deviant Behavior* (New York: Harper and Row, 1971); and Jack P. Gibbs, "Issues in Defining Deviant Behavior," in Robert A. Scott and Jack D. Douglas, eds. *Theoretical Prespectives on Deviant Behavior* (New York: Basic Books, 1972), pp. 39–68.

63. See, for example, Stuart A. Brody, "The Political Prisoner Syndrome," *Crime and Delinquency* 20 (April, 1974), pp. 97–106.

64. Paul Hollander, "Sociology, Selective Determinism, and the Rise of Expectations," *American Sociologist*, 8 (November, 1973), p. 149.

65. Gunnar Myrdal, *An American Dilemma* (New York: Harper and Brothers, 1944).

# WHAT IS "WHITE-COLLAR CRIME"?

What exactly is meant by the term "white-collar crime"? The three readings in this section offer partial answers, though at times they are more teasing than intellectually satisfying. The first article, by Edward A. Ross (1866–1951), stands as the earliest major statement by a sociologist regarding the kinds of behavior which later would come to be classified as "white-collar crime." The initial public use of the term itself was by Edwin H. Sutherland (1883–1950) in his presidential address to the American Sociological Society in 1939;[1] this talk is reprinted as the second selection. The final article in the section, by Donald J. Newman, reviews some of the major contributions to the ongoing debate about the most satisfactory definition and most meaningful boundaries for the category of "white-collar crime."

Ross's piece is a fine example of much early writing in the newly emergent field of sociology. Until his time, Ross had found sociology to be a "turgid mass of stale metaphysics, dark sayings, random historical allusions, and mawkish ethical raptures."[2] Now, by his work, Ross intended to make the discipline count in the "real" world. Indeed, perhaps the most lasting testament to Ross's desire to be involved in important political events is found in the opening line of John Reed's *Ten Days That Shook the World*, the classic chronicle of the Russian Revolution, in which Reed notes the presence in Moscow of an unnamed sociologist (it was Ross) during the early days of the upheaval.[3] In the same manner, Ross's book *Social Control* was read in 1906 by Justice Oliver Wendell Holmes who communicated his enthusiasm to President Theodore Roosevelt who, also apparently excited by the book, conveyed his appreciation to Ross.[4] Perhaps Ross's attitudes are best suggested by his statement that, "suckled on the practicalism of Lester F. Ward,"* he wouldn't give "a snap of my fingers for the 'pussyfooting' sociologists."[5]

Physically imposing (he stood 6 feet, 6 inches tall and weighed more than 250 pounds), Ross was, in the words of a former student, "always a person whom one held in awe," and "to have been associated with him was a supremely choice life experience."[6] Ross's extraordinary erudition, with its classical roots, and the unusual force and grace of his language, even with its old-fashioned ring, permeate his article on "The Criminaloid."

A major difference between Sutherland and Ross lies in their expressed attitudes toward their material. Ross reveled in exposing to public view the illegal acts of supposedly respectable business and political figures. Sutherland, on the other hand, always maintained that his work represented a disengaged, scholarly effort, intended to reform criminological theory and not to influence legislation, judicial administration, or business ethics. The very first two sentences of Sutherland's *White Collar Crime* (1949) read: "This book is a study of the theory of criminal behavior. It is an attempt to reform the theory of criminal behavior, not to reform anything else."[7] Nonetheless, no contemporary reader of Sutherland's work is apt to regard such statements as other than a patent disingenuousness, rather similar to the disclaimers of eighteenth-century satirists faced with ostracism or excommunication were their professional heresies to become manifest. Sutherland, it must be appreciated, was writing at a time when sociology yearned to be regarded as a "pure science," a value-free, impersonal, passionless enterprise.

Aside from this difference between Ross and Sutherland, the backgrounds of the two men were remarkably similar.[8] Both were the product of rural Midwestern parents, and both were raised in intensely religious atmospheres. Sutherland's father was a Baptist minister, Ross's grandfather a well-known Presbyterian clergyman. Both men grew up in milieus that exhibited great populist concern over the increasing dominance of business and the rising concentration of economic power and wealth. Both regarded with nostalgia and regret the shift in the United States from the personal, close-knit, interdependent relationship of the "community" to the more anonymous and more formal relationships of the "society," a change designated by the German scholar Ferdinand Tonnies as one from a *gemeinschaft* to a *gesellschaft* form of social existence.[9] It should also be appreciated, as Jon Snodgrass observed in a study of American criminologists, that Sutherland resembles "much more the old-time

* Ward, by profession a government geologist and paleobotanist, was Ross's uncle my marriage and in 1906 became the first president of the American Sociological Society.

prophet" than the political revolutionary. Sutherland was not interested in reforms such as the rearrangement of wealth or the restructuring of social classes. He believed that white-collar crime undermined basic American principles of economic competition and free trade, and he was concerned that all criminals, regardless of their position in society, be apprehended and punished.[10]

Sutherland's work on white-collar crime was clearly influenced by his earlier investigation of professional theft.[11] He came to regard white-collar criminals as the upperworld counterparts of the professional thieves. In both groups, Sutherland maintained, illegal activity was an integral part of occupational efforts, and for both groups there was no loss of prestige among colleagues because of criminal activity. Both sets of activities also required considerable training, tutelage, and specialized skill. A significant difference between professional theft and white-collar crime, Sutherland thought, lay in the self-conception of the violators. "Professional thieves, when they speak honestly, admit that they are thieves," Sutherland observed, while white-collar criminals "think of themselves as honest men."[12] It becomes evident that in some ways Sutherland came to admire and to glamorize the professional thief and to loathe the white-collar offender, a loathing that translated into his claim that businessmen are the most subversive force in America and his equating of the advertising tactics of the power and light utilities with the propaganda of the German Nazis.[13]

A second major influence on Sutherland's work in the area of white-collar crime appears to lie in his advisory role in connection with Thorstein Sellin's monograph *Culture Conflict and Crime* (1938).[14] Sutherland and Sellin maintained a lengthy correspondence as the monograph took shape, with Sellin supporting the view that violations of conduct norms, whether or not they are formally defined as criminal, ought to be embraced within the boundaries of criminological investigation. Sutherland explicitly rejected this thesis,[15] but it certainly seems to have contributed to the rather haphazard array of illustrations he employed in his book-length study to illustrate the behavior of white-collar crime. At one point, for instance, he describes the perfectly legal shenanigans of a graduate student who worked as a shoe salesman to indicate characteristics of white-collar crime.[16]

Sutherland was fifty-seven years old at the time he delivered the paper reprinted in this section, and it was his first published statement on white-collar crime, though he reported later that he had been at work on the subject for more than a quarter of a century. Indeed, a noted British criminologist has suggested that if there were a Nobel Prize for criminology, Sutherland would surely merit it for his white-collar crime work.[17] Nonetheless, it is clear that Sutherland had not sufficiently thought through many of the problems attendant upon the concept. The definition of white-collar crime, for instance, has always represented something of an intellectual nightmare. This is probably because Sutherland desired to employ the concept to buttress his theory of "differential association," an aggregation of theorems (of highly unequal power) about human learning attempting to explain not only white-collar crime, but all criminal behavior.[18] Since the same theory can embrace confidence games, rape, car theft, embezzlement, and antitrust violations with equal hospitality, it mattered little whether any of these phenomena—or, indeed, non-criminal activities—were precisely differentiated. In addition, by keeping his definition loose, Sutherland could bring under his microscope a large variety of business behaviors which he found offensive. Indeed, anyone reading the definition of white-collar crime offered by Sutherland in the first footnote in the reprinted article might conclude that he is being subjected to a parody of pedantic obscurantism. Nor did later definitional efforts by Sutherland show much improvement.

In fact, the definitional waters were so muddied by Sutherland that today it sometimes appears wiser to move upstream than to attempt a purification project.[19] The difficulty of such a move lies in the fact that the term "white-collar crime" and the spirit it represents were magnetic enough to draw the concept deeply into criminological and popular thought. The foreign literature nicely illustrates the appeal of Sutherland's formulation, with direct translation of the phrase "white-collar crime" into *crime en col blanc*, *criminalita in colletti bianchi*, *Weisse-Kragen-Kriminalität*, and *el delito de cuello blanco*.[20] In the Netherlands, a recent article sought to find "a good Dutch word" for white-collar crime and suggested that the editors of the journal extend a prize for the best entry.[21]

In addition, Sutherland often provided discrepant and sometimes contradictory statements regarding the seriousness of white-collar crime. In one piece of writing, for example, he declared that "fraud" was the most prevalent crime in the United States;[22] in another, that priority lay with "family neglect."[23] The truth of the matter is that there is no reasonable manner in which to determine the monetary cost of white-collar crime. Other kinds of alleged consequences of white-collar crime, such as lowered social, moral, and interpersonal trust, may be measured, but it is an exceedingly intricate (and perhaps an impossible) task to demonstrate casual relationships between such phenomena and white-collar crime, even presuming agreement might be achieved on an operational meaning of white-collar crime. Thus, statements about the heinousness of white-collar crime most fundamentally represent tactics to call dramatic attention to forms of behavior that the writers believe (but cannot really demonstrate) have serious consequences for important aspects of social life; as, indeed, they may.

The final article in this introductory section provides an overview and some interpretations of the consequences of Sutherland's pioneering work on white-collar crime. In it Donald J. Newman, a professor in the School of Criminal Justice, State University of New York, Albany, discusses matters which have aroused controversy since the introduction of the term. He also provides a sense of the research which has followed in the wake of Sutherland's formulation, and the theoretical implications of such work. It might be noted that while Newman published this piece in 1958, almost a generation ago, his observations remain preeminently accurate and germane today, a commentary on both the quality of thinking that went into the article and the difficulty that scholars in the area of white-collar crime have encountered in trying to break through some of the barriers indicated by Newman. Thus, for instance, Newman observes that "white-collar *crime* rather than white-collar *criminals* has been the basic orientation in research," a condition that still prevails. The article clearly conveys the intellectual excitement that Newman feels in regard to the possibilities of work in this area. "The concept of white-collar crime," he points out in his conclusion, "has forced the theoretician into an analysis of highly complex and very abstract relationships within our social system. No longer is the criminologist a middle-class observer studying a lower-class behavior. He now looks upward at the most powerful and prestigeful strata, and his ingenuity in research and theory will be tested, indeed." Since this article was first published, it seems fair to say, social scientists have largely failed to meet the tasks with which Newman challenges them though today, more than at any other period since the initial appearance of work on white-collar crime, the climate is particularly receptive to the kind of research work and theorizing called for by Newman.

## *Notes*

1. Edwin H. Sutherland, "White-Collar Criminality," *American Sociological Review* 5 (February, 1940), pp. 1–12.

2. Edward A. Ross, Review of Giddings, "Principles of Sociology," *Educational Review*, 12 (June, 1896), p. 92. See also Julius Weinberg, *Edward Alsworth Ross and the Sociology of Progressivism* (Madison: State Historical Society of Wisconsin, 1972).

3. John Reed, *Ten Days That Shook the World* (New York: International Publishers, 1919), p. 1.

4. Edward A. Ross, *Seventy Years of It* (New York: Appleton-Century, 1936), pp. 99–100.

5. *Ibid.*, p. 180.

6. Joyce O. Hertzler, "Edward Alsworth Ross: Sociological Pioneer and Interpreter," *American Sociological Review*, 16 (October, 1951), p. 598. See also John Gillin, "The Personality of Edward Alsworth Ross," *American Journal of Sociology*, 42 (January, 1937), pp. 534–542.

7. Edwin H. Sutherland, *White Collar Crime* (New York: Dryden Press, 1949), p. v.

8. See Soss, *Seventy Years of It, op. cit.*, and regarding Sutherland see Jon Snodgrass, "The Gentle and Devout Iconoclast," in *The American Criminological Tradition: Portraits of Men and Ideology in a Discipline.* Ph.D. dissertation, University of Pennsylvania, 1972, pp. 217–308.

9. See Ferdinand Tonnies, *Community and Society* (1887), trans. Charles P. Loomis (East Lansing: Michigan State University Press, 1957).

10. Snodgrass, *op. cit.*, p. 289.

11. Edwin H. Sutherland, *The Professional Thief* (Chicago: University of Chicago Press, 1937).

12. Edwin H. Sutherland, "Crime of Corporations," in Karl Schuessler, ed., *On Analyzing Crime* (Chicago: University of Chicago Press, 1973), pp. 95–96.

13. Sutherland, *White Collar Crime, op. cit.*, p. 210.

14. New York: Social Science Research Council, 1938.

15. See Schuessler, *op. cit.*, pp. xxv–xxx.

16. Sutherland, *White Collar Crime, op. cit.*, pp. 231–238.

17. Hermann Mannheim, *Comparative Criminology* (Boston: Houghton Mifflin, 1965), p. 470.

18. For a discussion of postulates and criticisms of the "differential association" theory, and of rebuttals to such criticisms, see Edwin H. Sutherland and Donald R. Cressey, *Criminology,* 9th ed., (Philadelphia: Lippincott, 1974), pp. 71–93.

19. A particularly valuable effort to unravel some of the definitional dilemmas surrounding "white-collar crime" is found in Marshall B. Clinard and Richard Quinney, *Criminal Behavior Systems: A Typology,* 2nd ed. (New York: Holt, Rinehart and Winston, 1973), pp. 187–224.

20. See, e.g., Georges Kellens, "Du 'Crime en col blanc' au 'Delit de chevalier,'" *Annales de la faculté de droit de Liège,* 30 (1968), pp. 61–124; Giuseppe G. Loschiavo, "La Mafia della lupara e quella dei 'colletti bianchi,'" *La Giustizia Penale,* 68 (1963), pp. 336–344; Markus Binder, "Weisse-Kragen-Kriminalität," *Kriminalistik,* 16 (June, 1962), pp. 251–255; Edwin H. Sutherland, *El Delito de cuello blanco,* trans. Rosa del Olmo (Caracas: Ediciónes de la Biblioteca Universidad Central de Venezuela, 1969).

21. Jac. van Weringh, "White Collar Crime: Ein Terreinverkenning," *Nederlands Tijdschrift voor Criminologie,* 11 (September, 1969), pp. 133–144.

22. Edwin H. Sutherland, *Principles of Criminology,* 4th ed. (Philadelphia: Lippincott, 1947), p. 38.

23. Edwin H. Sutherland, "Control of Crime," in Schuessler, *op. cit.*, p. 171.

# 1

# THE CRIMINALOID

*Edward Alsworth Ross*

The Edda has it that during Thor's visit to the giants he is challenged to lift a certain gray cat. "Our young men think it nothing but play." Thor puts forth his whole strength, but can at most bend the creature's back and lift one foot. On leaving, however, the mortified hero is told the secret of his failure. "The cat—ah! we were terror-stricken when we saw one paw off the floor; for that is the Midgard serpent which, tail in mouth, girds and keeps up the created world."

How often today the prosecutor who tries to lay by the heels some notorious public enemy is baffled by a mysterious resistance! The thews of Justice become as water; her sword turns to lath. Though the machinery of the law is strained askew, the evildoer remains erect, smiling, unscathed. At the end, the mortified champion of the law may be given to understand that, like Thor, he was contending with the established order, that he had unwittingly laid hold on a pillar of society and was therefore pitting himself against the reigning organization in local finance and politics.

Reprinted from *The Atlantic Monthly*, 99 (January, 1907), pp. 44–50.

The real weakness in the moral position of Americans is not their attitude toward the plain criminal, but their attitude toward the quasi-criminal. The shocking leniency of the public in judging conspicuous persons who have thriven by antisocial practices is not due, as many imagine, to sycophancy. Let a prominent man commit some offense in bad odor and the multitude flings its stones with right goodwill. The social lynching of the self-made magnate who put away his faded, toil-worn wife for the sake of a soubrette proves that the props of the old morality have not rotted through. Sex righteousness continues to be thus stiffly upheld simply because man has not invented *new* ways of wronging woman. So long ago were sex sins recognized and branded that the public, feeling sure of itself, lays on with promptness and emphasis. The slowness of this same public in lashing other kinds of transgression betrays, not sycophancy or unthinking admiration of success, but perplexity. The prosperous evildoers that bask undisturbed in popular favor have been careful to shun—or seem to shun—the familiar types of wickedness. Overlooked in Bible and prayer book, their obliquities lack the brimstone smell. Surpass as their misdeeds may in meanness and cruelty, there has not yet been time enough to store up strong emotion about them; and so the sight of them does not let loose the flood of wrath and abhorrence that rushes down upon the long-attainted sins.

The immunity enjoyed by the perpetrator of new sins has brought into being a class for which we may coin the term "criminaloid." (Like "asteroid," "crystalloid," "anthropoid," the term "criminaloid" is Latin–Greek, to be sure, but so is "sociology.") By this we designate those who prosper by flagitious practices which have not yet come under the effective ban of public opinion. Often, indeed, they are guilty in the eyes of the law; but since they are not culpable in the eyes of the public and in their own eyes, their spiritual attitude is not that of the criminal. The lawmaker may make their misdeeds crimes, but, so long as morality stands stock-still in the old tracks, they escape both punishment and ignominy. Unlike their low-browed cousins, they occupy the cabin rather than the steerage of society. Relentless pursuit hems in the criminals, narrows their range of success, denies them influence. The criminaloids, on the other hand, encounter but feeble opposition, and, since their practices are often more lucrative than the authentic crimes, they distance their more scrupulous rivals in business and politics and reap an uncommon worldly prosperity.

Of greater moment is the fact that the criminaloids lower the tone of the community. The criminal slinks in the shadow, menacing our purses but not our ideals; the criminaloid, however, does not belong to the half-world. Fortified by his connections with "legitimate business," "the regular party organization," perhaps with orthodoxy and the *bon ton*, he may even bestride his community like a Colossus. In his sight and in their own sight the old-style, square-dealing sort are as grasshoppers. Do we not hail him as "a man who does things," make him director of our banks and railroads, trustee of our hospitals and libraries? When Prince Henry visits us, do we not put him on the reception committee? He has far more initial weight in the community than has the arraigning clergyman, editor, or prosecutor. From his example and his excuses spreads a noxious influence that tarnishes the ideals of ingenuous youth on the threshold of active life. To put the soul of this pagan through a Bertillon system and set forth its marks of easy identification is, therefore, a sanitary measure demanded in the interest of public health.

*The key to the criminaloid is not evil impulse, but moral insensibility.* The director who speculates in the securities of his corporation, the banker who lends his depositors' money to himself under divers corporate aliases, the railroad official who grants a secret rebate for his private graft, the builder who hires walking delegates to harass his rivals with causeless strikes, the labor leader who instigates a strike in order to be paid for calling it off, the publisher who bribes his textbooks into the schools, these reveal in their faces nothing of the wolf or vulture. Nature has not foredoomed them to evil by a double dose of lust, cruelty, malice, greed, or jealousy. They are not degenerates tormented by monstrous cravings. They want nothing more than we all want—money, power, consideration —in a word, success; but they are in a hurry and they are not particular as to the means.

The criminaloid prefers to prey on the anonymous public. He is touchy about the individual victim and, if faced down, will even make him reparation out of the plunder gathered at longer range. Too squeamish and too prudent to practice treachery, brutality, and violence himself, he takes care to work through middlemen. Conscious of the antipodal difference between doing wrong and getting it done, he places out his dirty work. With a string of intermediaries between himself and the toughs who slug voters at the polls or the gang of navvies who break other navvies' heads with shovels on behalf of his electric line, he is able to keep his hands sweet and his boots clean. Thus he becomes a consumer of custom-made crime, a client of criminals, oftener a maker of criminals by persuading or requiring his subordinates to break the law. Of course, he must have "responsible" agents as valves to check the return flow of guilt from such proceedings. He shows them the goal, provides the money, insists on "results," but vehemently declines to know the foul methods by which alone his understrappers can get these "results." Not to bribe, but to employ and finance the briber; not to lie, but to admit to your editorial columns "paying matter"; not to commit perjury, but to hire men to homestead and make over to you claims they have sworn were entered in good faith and without collusion; not to cheat, but to promise a "rake-off" to a mysterious go-between in case your just assessment is cut down; not to rob on the highway, but to make the carrier pay you a rebate on your rival's shipments; not to shed innocent blood, but to bribe inspectors to overlook your neglect to install safety appliances—such are the ways of the criminaloid. He is a buyer rather than a practitioner of sin, and his middlemen spare him unpleasant details.

Secure in his quilted armor of lawyer-spun sophistries, the criminaloid promulgates an ethics which the public hails as a disinterested contribution to the philosophy of conduct. He invokes a pseudo-Darwinism to sanction the revival of outlawed and bygone tactics of struggle. Ideals of fellowship and peace are "unscientific." To win the game with the aid of a sleeveful of aces proves one's fitness to survive. A sack of spoils is nature's patent of nobility. A fortune is a personal attribute, as truly creditable as a straight back or a symmetrical face. Poverty, like the misshapen ear of the degenerate, proves inferiority. The wholesale fleecer of trusting, workaday people is a "Napoleon," a "superman." Labor defending its daily bread must, of course, obey the law; but "business," especially the "big proposition," may free itself of such trammels in the name of a "higher law." The censurers of the criminaloid are "pin-headed disturbers" who would imitate him if they had the chance or the brains.

*The criminaloid is not antisocial by nature.*   Nationwide is the zone of devastation of the adulterator, the rebater, the commercial freebooter, the fraud promoter, the humbug healer, the law-defying monopolist. Statewide is the burnt district of the corrupt legislator, the corporation-owned judge, the venal inspector, the bought bank examiner, the mercenary editor. But draw near the sinner and he whitens. If his fellowmen are wronged clear to his doorstep, he is criminal, not criminaloid. For the latter loses his sinister look, even takes on a benign aspect, as you come close. Within his home town, his ward, his circle, he is perhaps a good man, if judged by the simple old-time tests. Very likely he keeps his marriage vows, pays his debts, "mixes" well, stands by his friends, and has a contracted kind of public spirit. He is ready enough to rescue imperiled babies, protect maidens, or help poor widows. He is unevenly moral: oak in the family and clan virtues, but basswood in commercial and civic ethics. In some relations he is more sympathetic and generous than his critics, and he resents with genuine feeling the scorn of men who happen to have specialized in virtues other than those that appeal to him. Perhaps his point of honor is to give bribes, but not to take them; perhaps it is to "stay bought," that is, not to sell out to both sides at once.

This type is exemplified by the St. Louis boodler, who after accepting $25,000 to vote against a certain franchise was offered a larger sum to vote for it. He did so, but returned the first bribe. He was asked on the witness stand why he had returned it. "Because it wasn't mine!" he exclaimed, flushing with anger. "I hadn't earned it."

Seeing that the conventional sins are mostly close-range inflictions, whereas the long-range sins, being recent in type, have not yet been branded, the criminaloid receives from his community the credit for the close-in good he does, but not the shame of the remote evil he works.

Sometimes it is time instead of space that divides him from his victims. It is tomorrow's morrow that will suffer from the patent soothing syrup, the factory toil of infants, the grabbing of public lands, the butchery of forests, and the smuggling-in of coolies. In such a case, the short-sighted many exonerate him; only the far-sighted few mark him for what he is. Or it may be a social interval that leaves him his illusion of innocence. Like Robin Hood, the criminaloid spares his own sort and finds his quarry on another social plane. The labor grafter, the political "striker," and the blackmailing society editor prey upward; the franchise grabber, the fiduciary thief, and the frenzied financier prey downward. In either case, the sinner moves in an atmosphere of friendly approval and can still any smart of conscience with the balm of adulation.

It is above all the political criminaloid who is social. We are assured that the king of the St. Louis boodlers was "a good fellow—by nature, at first, then by profession. . . . Everywhere Big Ed went, there went a smile also and encouragement for your weakness, no matter what it was." The head of the Minneapolis ring was "a good fellow—a genial, generous reprobate . . . the best-loved man in the community . . . especially good to the poor." "Stars-and-Stripes Sam" was the nickname of a notorious looter of Philadelphia, who amassed influence by making "a practice of going to lodges, associations, brotherhoods, Sunday schools, and all sorts of public and private meetings, joining some, but making at all speeches patriotic and sentimental." The corrupt boss of another plundered city is reported to be "a charming character," possessing "goodness of heart and personal charm," and loved for his "genial, hearty kindness." He shrank from robbing anybody, but was equal, however, to robbing everybody. Of this type was Tweed, who had a "good heart," donated $50,000 to the poor of New York, and was sincerely loved by his clan.

It is now clear why hot controversy rages about the unmasked criminaloid. His home town, political clan, or social class insists that he is a good man maligned, that his detractors are purblind or jealous. The criminaloid is really a borderer between the camps of good and evil, and this is why he is so interesting. To run him to earth and brand him, as long ago pirates and traitors were branded, is the crying need of our time. For this Anak among malefactors, working unchecked in the rich field of sinister opportunities opened up by latter-day conditions, is society's most dangerous foe, more redoubtable by far than the plain criminal, because he sports the livery of virtue and operates on a Titanic scale. Every year that sees him pursue in insolent triumph his nefarious career raises up a host of imitators and hurries society toward moral bankruptcy.

*The criminaloid practices a protective mimicry of the good.*   Because so many good men are pious, the criminaloid covets a high seat in the temple as a valuable private asset. Accordingly he is often to be found in the assemblies of the faithful, zealously exhorting and bearing witness. Onward thought he must leave to honest men; his line is strict orthodoxy. The upright may fall slack in devout observances, but he cannot afford to neglect his church connection. He needs it in his business. Such simulation is easier because the godly are slow to drive out the open-handed sinner who eschews the conventional sins. Many deprecate prying into the methods of any brother "having money or goods ostensibly his own or under a title not disapproved by the proper tribunals." They have, indeed, much warrant for insisting that the saving of souls rather than the salvation of society is the true mission of the church.

The old Hebrew prophets, to be sure, were intensely alive to the social effect of sin. They clamor against "making the ephah small and the shekel great," falsifying the balances, "treading upon the poor." "Sensational," almost "demagogic," is their outcry against those who "turn aside the stranger in his right," "take a bribe," "judge not the cause of the fatherless," "oppress the hireling in his wages," "take increase," "withhold the pledge," "turn aside the poor in the gate from their right," "take away the righteousness of the righteous from him." No doubt their stubborn insistence that God wants "mercy and not sacrifice," despises feast days, delights not in burnt offerings, will not hear the melody of viols, but desires judgment to "run down as waters and righteousness as a mighty stream," struck their contemporaries as extreme. Over against their antiquated outlook may be set the larger view that our concern should be for the sinner rather than the sinned against. He is in peril of hell fire whereas the latter risks nothing more serious than loss, misery, and death. After all, sin's overshadowing effect is the pollution of the sinner's soul; and so it may be more Christian not to scourge forth the traffickers from the temple, but to leave them undisturbed where good seed may perchance fall upon their souls.

Likewise, the criminaloid counterfeits the good citizen. He takes care to meet all the conventional tests—flag worship, old-soldier sentiment, observance of all the national holidays, perfervid patriotism, party regularity and support. Full well he knows that giving a fountain or a park or establishing a college chair on the Neolithic drama or the elegiac poetry of the Chaldeans will more than outweigh the dodging of taxes, the grabbing of streets, and the corrupting of city councils. Let him have his way about charters and franchises, and he will zealously support that "good government" which consists in sweeping the streets, holding down the "lid," and keeping taxes low. Nor will he fail in that scrupulous correctness of private and domestic life which confers respectability. In politics, to be sure, it is often necessary to play the "good fellow"; but in business and finance a studious conformity to the *convenances* is of the highest importance. The criminaloid must perforce seem sober and chaste, "a good husband and a kind father." If in this respect he offend, his hour of need will find him without support, and some callow reporter or district attorney will bowl him over like any vulgar criminal.

The criminaloid, therefore, puts on the whole armor of the good. He stands having his loins girt about with religiosity and wearing the breastplate of respectability. His feet are shod with ostentatious philanthropy; his head is encased in the helmet of spread-eagle patriotism. Holding in his left hand the buckler of worldly success and in his right the sword of "influence," he is "able to withstand in the evil day and, having done all, to stand."

*The criminaloid plays the support of his local or special group against the larger society.* The plain criminal can do himself no good by appealing to his "Mollies," "Larrikins," or "Mafiosi," for they have no social standing. The criminaloid, however, identifies himself with some legitimate group, and when arraigned he calls upon his group to protect its own. The politically influential Western land thieves stir up the slumbering local feeling against the "impertinent meddlers" of the forestry service and the land office. Safe behind the judicial dictum that "bribery is merely a conventional crime," the boodlers denounce their indicter as "blackening the fair name" of their state, and cry, "Stand up for the grand, old commonwealth of Nemaha!" The city boss harps artfully on the chord of local spirit and summons his bailiwick to rebuke the upstate reformers who would unhorse him. The law-breaking saloon keeper rallies merchants with the cry that enforcement of the liquor laws "hurts business." The labor grafter represents his exposure as a capitalist plot and calls upon all Truss Riveters to "stand pat" and "vindicate" him with a re-election. When a pious buccaneer is brought to bay, the Reverend Simon Magus thus sounds the denominational bugle: "Brother Barabbas is a loyal Newlight and a generous supporter of the Newlight Church. This vicious attack upon him is, therefore, a covert thrust at the Newlight body and ought to be resented by all the brethren." High finance, springing to the help of self-confessed thieves, meets an avenging public in this wise: "The integrity trust not only seeks with diabolical skill a reputation to blast, but, once blasted, it sinks into it wolfish fangs and gloats over the result of its fiendish act"—and adds, "This is not the true American spirit." Here twangs the ultimate chord! For in criminaloid philosophy it is "un-American" to wrench patronage from the hands of

spoilsmen, un-American to deal federal justice to rascals of state importance, un-American to pry into arrangements between shipper and carrier,
un-American to pry the truth out of reluctant magnates.

The claims of the wider community have no foe so formidable as the
scared criminaloid. He is the champion of the tribal order as opposed to
the civil order. By constantly stirring up on his own behalf some sort of
clannishness—local, sectional, partisan, sectarian, or professional—he re-
kindles dying jealousies and checks the rise of the civic spirit. It is in line
with this clannishness that he wants citizens to act together on a personal
basis. He does not know what it is to rally around a principle. Fellow
partisans are "friends." To scratch or to bolt is to "go back on your
friends." The criminaloid understands sympathy and antipathy as springs
of conduct, but justice strikes him as hardly human. The law is a club
to rescue your friends from and to smite your enemies with, but it has
no claim of its own. He expects his victims to "come back" at him if they
can, but he cannot see why everything may not be "arranged," "settled
out of court." Those inflexible prosecutors who hew to the line and cannot be "squared" impress him as fanatical and unearthly, as monsters who
find their pleasure in making trouble for others. For to his barbarian eyes
society is all a matter of "stand in."

So long as the public conscience is torpid, the criminaloid has no
sense of turpitude. In the dusk and the silence, the magic of clan opinion
converts his misdeeds into something rich and strange. For the clan lexi-
con tells him that a bribe is a "retaining fee," a railroad pass is a "courtesy," probing is "scandal mongering," the investigator is an "officious
busybody," a protest is a "howl," critics are "foul harpies of slander,"
public opinion is "unreasoning clamor," regulation is "meddling," any
inconvenient law is a "blue" law. As rebate giver he is sustained by the
assurance that "in Rome you must do as the Romans do." As disburser
of corruption funds he learns that he is but "asserting the higher law
which great enterprises have the right to command." Blessed phrases
these! What a lint for dressing wounds to self-respect! Often the rem-
iniscent criminaloid, upon comparing his misdeeds with what his clans-
men stood ready to justify him in doing, is fain to exclaim with Lord
Clive, "By God, sir, at this moment I stand amazed at my own moderation!" When the revealing flash comes and the storm breaks, his difficulty
in getting the public's point of view is really pathetic. Indeed, he may
persist to the end in regarding himself as a martyr to "politics" or "yellow
journalism" or the "unctuous rectitude" of personal foes or "class envy"
in the guise of a moral wave.

*The criminaloid flourishes until the growth of morality overtakes the
growth of opportunities to prey.* It is of little use to bring law abreast
of the time if morality lags. In a swiftly changing society the law inevi-

tably tarries behind need, but public opinion tarries behind need even more. Where, as with us, the statute has little force of its own, the backwardness of public opinion nullifies the work of the legislator. Every added relation among men makes new chances for the sons of Belial. Wider interdependencies breed new treacheries. Fresh opportunities for illicit gain are continually appearing, and these are eagerly seized by the unscrupulous. The years between the advent of these new sins and the general recognition of their heinousness are few or many according to the alertness of the social mind. By the time they have been branded, the onward movement of society has created a fresh lot of opportunities, which are, in their turn, exploited with impunity. It is in this gap that the criminaloid disports himself. The narrowing of this gap depends chiefly on the faithfulness of the vedettes that guard the march of humanity. If the editor, writer, educator, clergyman, or public man is zealous to reconnoiter and instant to cry aloud the dangers that present themselves in our tumultuous social advance, a regulative opinion quickly forms and the new sins soon become odious.

Now, it is the concern of the criminaloids to delay this growth of conscience by silencing the alert vedettes. To intimidate the molders of opinion so as to confine the editor to the "news," the preacher to the "simple Gospel," the public man to the "party issues," the judge to his precedents, the teacher to his textbooks, and the writer to the classic themes—such are the tactics of the criminaloids. Let them but have their way, and the prophet's message, the sage's lesson, the scholar's quest, and the poet's dream would be sacrificed to the God of Things As They Were.

# 2

# WHITE-COLLAR CRIMINALITY

*Edwin H. Sutherland*

This paper is concerned with crime in relation to business. The economists are well acquainted with business methods but not accustomed to consider them from the point of view of crime; many sociologists are well acquainted with crime but not accustomed to consider it as expressed in business. This paper is an attempt to integrate these two bodies of knowledge. More accurately stated, it is a comparison of crime in the upper, or white-collar, class, which is composed of respectable, or at least respected, business and professional men; and crime in the lower class, which is composed of persons of low socioeconomic status. This comparison is made for the purpose of developing the theories of criminal behavior, not for the purpose of muckraking or of reforming anything except criminology.

The criminal statistics show unequivocally that crime, *as popularly conceived and officially measured*, has a high incidence in the lower class and a low incidence in the upper class; less than 2 per cent of the persons committed to prisons in a year belong to the upper class. These statistics

Reprinted from *American Sociological Review*, 5 (February, 1940), pp. 1–12, by permission of The American Sociological Association.

refer to criminals handled by the police, the criminal and juvenile courts, and the prisons, and to such crimes as murder, assault, burglary, robbery, larceny, sex offenses, and drunkenness; it does not include traffic violations.

The criminologists have used the case histories and criminal statistics derived from these agencies of criminal justice as their principal data. From them, they have derived general theories of criminal behavior. These theories are that, since crime is concentrated in the lower class, it is caused by poverty or by personal and social characteristics believed to be associated statistically with poverty, including feeblemindedness, psychopathic deviations, slum neighborhoods, and "deteriorated" families. This statement, of course, does not do justice to the qualifications and variations in the conventional theories of criminal behavior, but it presents correctly their central tendency.

The thesis of this paper is that the conception and explanations of crime which have just been described are misleading and incorrect, that crime is, in fact, not closely correlated with poverty or with the psychopathic and sociopathic conditions associated with poverty, and that an adequate explanation of criminal behavior must proceed along quite different lines. The conventional explanations are invalid principally because they are derived from biased samples. The samples are biased in that they have not included vast areas of criminal behavior of persons not in the lower class. One of these neglected areas is the criminal behavior of business and professional men, which will be analyzed in this paper.

The "robber barons" of the last half of the nineteenth century were white-collar criminals, as practically everyone now agrees. Their attitudes are illustrated by these statements: Colonel Vanderbilt asked, "You don't suppose you can run a railroad in accordance with the statutes, do you?" A. B. Stickney, a railroad president, said to sixteen other railroad presidents in the home of J. P. Morgan in 1890, "I have the utmost respect for you gentlemen, individually; but as railroad presidents I wouldn't trust you with my watch out of my sight." Charles Francis Adams said, "The difficulty in railroad management . . . lies in the covetousness, want of good faith, and low moral tone of railway managers, in the complete absence of any high standard of commercial honesty."

The present-day white-collar criminals, who are more suave and deceptive than the "robber barons," are represented by Krueger, Stavisky, Whitney, Mitchell, Foshay, Insull, the Van Sweringens, Musica-Coster, Fall, Sinclair, the many other merchant princes and captains of finance and industry, and by a host of lesser followers. Their criminality has been demonstrated again and again in the investigations of land offices, railways, insurance, munitions, banking, public utilities, stock exchanges, the oil industry, real estate, reorganization committees, receiverships, bankruptcies, and politics. Individual cases of such criminality are reported frequently, and in many periods more important crime news may be found on the financial pages of newspapers than on the front pages. White-collar criminality is found in every occupation, as can be discovered readily in casual conversation with a representative of an occupation by asking him, "What crooked practices are found in your occupation?"

White-collar criminality in business is expressed most frequently in the form of misrepresentation in financial statements of corporations, manipulation in the stock exchange, commercial bribery, bribery of public officials directly or indirectly in order to secure favorable contracts and legislation, misrepresentation in advertising and salesmanship, embezzlement and misapplication of funds, short weights and measures and misgrading of commodities, tax frauds, misapplication of funds in receiverships and bankruptcies. These are what Al Capone called "the legitimate rackets." These and many others are found in abundance in the business world.

In the medical profession, which is here used as an example because it is probably less criminalistic than some other professions, are found illegal sale of alcohol and narcotics, abortion, illegal services to underworld criminals, fraudulent reports and testimony in accident cases, extreme cases of unnecessary treatment, fake specialists, restriction of competition, and fee splitting. Fee splitting is a violation of a specific law in many states and a violation of the conditions of admission to the practice of medicine in all. The physician who participates in fee splitting tends to send his patients to the surgeon who will give him the largest fee rather than to the surgeon who will do the best work. It has been reported that two-thirds of the surgeons in New York City split fees and that more than one-half of the physicians in a central western city who answered a questionnaire on this point favored fee splitting.

These varied types of white-collar crimes in business and the professions consist principally of violation of delegated or implied trust, and many of them can be reduced to two categories: (1) misrepresentation of asset values and (2) duplicity in the manipulation of power. The first is approximately the same as fraud or swindling; the second is similar to the double-cross. The latter is illustrated by the corporation director who, acting on inside information, purchases land which the corporation will need and sells it at a fantastic profit to his corporation. The principle of this duplicity is that the offender holds two antagonistic positions, one of which is a position of trust that is violated, generally by misapplication of funds, in the interest of the other position. A football coach, permitted to referee a game in which his own team is playing, would illustrate this antagonism of positions. Such situations cannot be completely avoided in a complicated business structure, but many concerns make a practice of assuming such antagonistic functions and regularly violating the trust thus delegated to them. When compelled by law to make a separation of their functions, they make a nominal separation and continue by subterfuge to maintain the two positions.

An accurate statistical comparison of the crimes of the two social classes is not available. The most extensive evidence regarding the nature and prevalence of white-collar criminality is found in the reports of the larger investigations to which reference was made. Because of its scattered character, that evidence is assumed rather than summarized here. A few statements will be presented as illustrations rather than as proof of the prevalence of this criminality.

The Federal Trade Commission in 1920 reported that commercial bribery was a prevalent and common practice in many industries. In certain chain stores, the net shortage in weights was sufficient to pay 3.4 per cent on the investment in those commodities. Of the cans of ether sold to the Army in 1923 to 1925, 70 per cent were rejected because of impurities. In Indiana, during the summer of 1934, 40 per cent of the ice-cream samples tested in a routine manner by the Division of Public Health were in violation of law. The Comptroller of the Currency in 1908 reported that violations of law were found in 75 per cent of the banks examined in a three-month period. Lie detector tests of all employees in several Chicago banks, supported in almost all cases by confessions, showed that 20 per cent of them had stolen bank property. A public accountant estimated, in the period prior to the Securities and Exchange Commission, that 80 per cent of the financial statements of corporations were misleading. James M. Beck said, "Diogenes would have been hard put to it to find an honest man in the Wall Street which I knew as a corporation lawyer" (in 1916).

White-collar criminality in politics, which is generally recognized as fairly prevalent, has been used by some as a rough gauge by which to measure white-collar criminality in business. James A. Farley said, "The standards of conduct are as high among officeholders and politicians as they are in commercial life," and Cermak, while mayor of Chicago, said, "There is less graft in politics than in business." John Flynn wrote, "The average politician is the merest amateur in the gentle art of graft compared with his brother in the field of business." And Walter Lippmann wrote, "Poor as they are, the standards of public life are so much more social than those of business that financiers who enter politics regard themselves as philanthropists."

These statements obviously do not give a precise measurement of the relative criminality of the white-collar class, but they are adequate evidence that crime is not so highly concentrated in the lower class as the usual statistics indicate. Also, these statements obviously do not mean that every business and professional man is a criminal, just as the usual theories do not mean that every man in the lower class is a criminal. On the other hand, the preceding statements refer in many cases to the leading corporations in America and are not restricted to the disreputable business and professional men who are called quacks, ambulance chasers, bucket-shop operators, dead-beats, and fly-by-night swindlers.*

The financial cost of white-collar crime is probably several times as great as the financial cost of all the crimes which are customarily regarded as the "crime problem." An officer of a chain grocery store in one year embezzled $600,000, which was six times as much as the annual losses from five hundred burglaries and robberies of the stores in that chain. Public enemies numbered one to six secured $130,000 by burglary and robbery in 1938, while the sum stolen by Krueger is estimated as $250,-000,000, or nearly two thousand times as much. The *New York Times* in 1931 reported four cases of embezzlement in the United States with a loss of more than a million dollars each and a combined loss of $9 million. Although a million-dollar burglar or robber is practically unheard of, these million-dollar embezzlers are small-fry among white-collar criminals. The estimated loss to investors in one investment trust from 1929 to 1935 was $580,000,000, due primarily to the fact that 75 per cent of the values in the portfolio were in securities of affiliated companies, although it advertised the importance of diversification in investments and its expert services in selecting safe securities. In Chicago, the claim was made six years ago that householders had lost $54,000,000 in two years during the administration of a city sealer who granted immunity from inspection to stores which provided Christmas baskets for his constituents.

The financial loss from white-collar crime, great as it is, is less important than the damage to social relations. White-collar crimes violate trust and therefore create distrust, which lowers social morale and produces social disorganization on a large scale. Other crimes produce relatively little effect on social institutions or social organization.

White-collar crime is real crime. It is not ordinarily called crime, and calling it by this name does not make it worse, just as refraining from calling it crime does not make it better than it otherwise would be. It is called crime here in order to bring it within the scope of criminology, which is justified because it is in violation of the criminal law. The crucial question in this analysis is the criterion of violation of the criminal law.

---

* Perhaps it should be repeated that "white-collar" (upper) and "lower" classes merely designate persons of high- and low-socioeconomic status. Income and amount of money involved in the crime are not the sole criteria. Many persons of "low" socio-economic status are "white-collar" criminals in the sense that they are well dressed, well educated, and have high incomes; but "white-collar" as used in this paper means "respected," "socially accepted and approved," "looked up to." Some people in this class may not be well dressed or well educated or have high incomes, although the "upper" classes usually exceed the "lower" classes in these respects, as well as in social status.

Conviction in the criminal court, which is sometimes suggested as the criterion, is not adequate because a large proportion of those who commit crimes are not convicted in criminal courts. This criterion, therefore, needs to be supplemented. When it is supplemented, the criterion of the crimes of one class must be kept consistent in general terms with the criterion of the crimes of the other class. The definition should not be the spirit of the law for white-collar crimes and the letter of the law for other crimes, or in other respects be more liberal for one class than for the other. Since this discussion is concerned with the conventional theories of the criminologists, the criterion of white-collar crime must be justified in terms of the procedures of those criminologists in dealing with other crimes. The criterion of white-collar crimes, as here proposed, supplements convictions in the criminal courts in four respects, in each of which the extension is justified because the criminologists who present the conventional theories of criminal behavior make the same extension in principle.

First, other agencies than the criminal court must be included, for the criminal court is not the only agency which makes official decisions regarding violations of the criminal law. In many states, the juvenile court, dealing largely with offenses of the children of the poor, is not under the criminal jurisdiction. The criminologists have made much use of case histories and statistics of juvenile delinquents in constructing their theories of criminal behavior. This justifies the inclusion of agencies other than the criminal court that deal with white-collar offenses. The most important of these agencies are the administrative boards, bureaus, or commissions; and much of their work, although certainly not all, consists of cases that are in violation of the criminal law. The Federal Trade Commission recently ordered several automobile companies to stop advertising their interest rate on installment purchases as 6 per cent, since it was actually 11½ per cent. Also it filed complaint against *Good Housekeeping*, one of the Hearst publications, charging that its seals led the public to believe that all products bearing those seals had been tested in their laboratories, which was contrary to fact. Each of these involves a charge of dishonesty, which might have been tried in a criminal court as fraud. A large proportion of the cases before these boards should be included in the data of the criminologists. Failure to do so is a principal reason for the bias in their samples and the errors in their generalizations.

Second, for both classes, behavior that would have a reasonable expectancy of conviction if tried in a criminal court or substitute agency should be defined as criminal. In this respect, convictability rather than actual conviction should be the criterion of criminality. The criminologists would not hesitate to accept as data a verified case history of a person who was a criminal but who had never been convicted. Similarly, it is justifiable to include white-collar criminals who have not been convicted, provided reliable evidence is available. Evidence regarding such cases appears in many civil suits, such as stockholders' suits and patent-infringement suits. These cases might have been referred to the criminal court but they were referred to the civil court because the injured party was more interested in securing damages than in seeing punishment inflicted. This also happens in embezzlement cases, regarding which surety companies have much evidence. In a short consecutive series of embezzlements known to a surety company, 90 per cent were not prosecuted because prosecution would interfere with restitution or salvage. The evidence in cases of embezzlement is generally conclusive and would probably have been sufficient to justify conviction in all cases in this series.

Third, behavior should be defined as criminal if conviction is avoided merely because of pressure which is brought to bear on the court or substitute agency. Gangsters and racketeers have been relatively immune in many cities because of their pressure on prospective witnesses and public officials; professional thieves, such as pickpockets and confidence men who do not use strong-arm methods, are even more frequently immune. The conventional criminologists do not hesitate to include the life histories of such criminals as data, because they understand the generic relation of the pressures to the failure to convict. Similarly, white-collar criminals are relatively immune because of the class bias of the courts and the power of their class to influence the implementation and administration of the law. This class bias affects not merely present-day courts, but also, to a much greater degree, affected the earlier courts which established the precedents and rules of procedure of the present-day courts. Consequently, it is justifiable to interpret the actual or potential failures of conviction in the light of known facts regarding the pressures brought to bear on the agencies which deal with offenders.

Fourth, persons who are accessory to a crime should be included among white-collar criminals as they are among other criminals. When the Federal Bureau of Investigation deals with a case of kidnapping, it is not content with catching the offenders who carried away the victim; they may catch and the court may convict twenty-five other persons who assisted by secreting the victim, negotiating the ransom, or putting the ransom money into circulation. On the other hand, the prosecution of white-collar criminals frequently stops with one offender. Political graft almost always involves collusion between politicians and businessmen, but prosecutions are generally limited to the politicians. Judge Manton was found guilty of accepting $664,000 in bribes, but the six or eight important commercial concerns that paid the bribes have not been prosecuted. Pendergast, the late boss of Kansas City, was convicted for failure to report as a part of his income $315,000 received in bribes from insurance companies, but the insurance companies which paid the bribes have not been prosecuted. In an investigation of an embezzlement by the president of a bank, at least a dozen other violations of law which were related to this embezzlement and which involved most of the other officers of the bank and the officers of the clearing house were discovered, but none of the others was prosecuted.

This analysis of the criterion of white-collar criminality results in the conclusion that a description of white-collar criminality in general terms will be also a description of the criminality of the lower class. The respects in which the crimes of the two classes differ are the incidentals rather than the essentials of criminality. They differ principally in the implementation of the criminal laws that apply to them. The crimes of the lower class are handled by policemen, prosecutors, and judges with penal sanctions in the form of fines, imprisonment, and death. The crimes of the upper class either result in no official action at all, or result in suits for damages in civil courts, or are handled by inspectors and by administrative boards or commissions with penal sanctions in the form of warnings, orders to cease and desist, occasionally the loss of a license, and only in extreme cases by fines or prison sentences. Thus, the white-collar criminals are segregated administratively from other criminals and, largely as a consequence of this, are not regarded as real criminals by themselves, the general public, or the criminologists.

This difference in the implementation of the criminal law is due principally to the difference in the social position of the two types of offenders. Judge Woodward, when imposing sentence upon the officials of the H. O. Stone and Company, bankrupt real estate firm in Chicago, who had been convicted in 1933 of the use of the mails to defraud, said to them, "You are men of affairs, of experience, of refinement and culture, of excellent reputation and standing in the business and social world." That statement might be used as a general characterization of white-collar criminals, for they are oriented basically to legitimate and respectable careers. Because of their social status they have a loud voice in determining what goes into the statutes and how the criminal law as it affects themselves is implemented and administered. This may be illustrated from the Pure Food and Drug Law. Between 1879 and 1906, 140 pure food and drug bills were presented in Congress and all failed because of the importance of the persons who would be affected. It took a highly dramatic performance by Dr. Wiley in 1906 to induce Congress to enact the law. That law, however, did not create a new crime, just as the federal Lindbergh kidnapping law did not create a new crime; it merely provided a more efficient implementation of a principle which had been formulated previously in state laws. When an amendment to this law, which would bring within the scope of its agents fraudulent statements made over the radio or in the press, was presented to Congress, publishers and advertisers organized support and sent a lobby to Washington which successfully fought the amendment principally under the slogans of "freedom of the press" and "dangers of bureaucracy." This proposed amendment also would not have created a new crime, for the state laws already prohibited fraudulent statements over the radio or in the press; it would have implemented the law so it could have been enforced. Finally, the administration has not been able to enforce the law as it has desired because of the pressures by the offenders against the law, sometimes brought to bear through the head of the Department of Agriculture, sometimes through congressmen who threaten cuts in the appropriation, and sometimes by others. The statement of Daniel Drew, a pious old fraud, describes the criminal law with some accuracy: "Law is like a cobweb; it's made for flies and the smaller kinds of insects, so to speak, but lets the big bumblebees break through. When technicalities of the law stood in my way, I have always been able to brush them aside easy as anything."

The preceding analysis should be regarded neither as an assertion that all efforts to influence legislation and its administration are reprehensible nor as a particularistic interpretation of the criminal law. It means only that the upper class has greater influence in molding the criminal law and its administration to its own interests than does the lower class. The privileged position of white-collar criminals before the law results to a slight extent from bribery and political pressures, but principally from the respect in which they are held and without special effort on their part. The most powerful group in medieval society secured relative immunity by "benefit of clergy," and now our most powerful groups secure relative immunity by "benefit of business or profession."

In contrast with the power of the white-collar criminals is the weakness of their victims. Consumers, investors, and stockholders are unorganized, lack technical knowledge, and cannot protect themselves. Daniel Drew, after taking a large sum of money by sharp practice from Vanderbilt in the Erie deal, concluded that it was a mistake to take money from a powerful man on the same level as himself and declared that in the future he would confine his efforts to outsiders, scattered all over the country, who wouldn't be able to organize and fight back. White-collar criminality flourishes at points where powerful business and professional men come in contact with persons who are weak. In this respect, it is similar to stealing candy from a baby. Many of the crimes of the lower class, on the other hand, are committed against persons of wealth and power in the form of burglary and robbery. Because of this difference in the comparative power of the victims, the white-collar criminals enjoy relative immunity.

Embezzlement is an interesting exception to white-collar criminality in this respect. Embezzlement is usually theft from an employer by an employee, and the employee is less capable of manipulating social and legal forces in his own interest than is the employer. As might have been expected, the laws regarding embezzlement were formulated long before laws for the protection of investors and consumers.

The theory that criminal behavior in general is due either to poverty or to the psychopathic and sociopathic conditions associated with poverty can now be shown to be invalid for three reasons. First, the generalization is based on a biased sample which omits almost entirely the behavior of white-collar criminals. The criminologists have restricted their data, for reasons of convenience and ignorance rather than of principle, largely to cases dealt with in criminal courts and juvenile courts, and these agencies are used principally for criminals from the lower economic strata. Consequently, their data are grossly biased from the point of view of the economic status of criminals and their generalization that criminality is closely associated with poverty is not justified.

Second, the generalization that criminality is closely associated with poverty obviously does not apply to white-collar criminals. With a small number of exceptions, they are not in poverty, were not reared in slums or badly deteriorated families, and are not feebleminded or psychopathic. They were seldom problem children in their earlier years and did not appear in juvenile courts or child-guidance clinics. The proposition, derived from the data used by the conventional criminologists, that "the criminal of today was the problem child of yesterday" is seldom true of white-collar criminals. The idea that the causes of criminality are to be found almost exclusively in childhood is similarly fallacious. Even if poverty were extended to include the economic stresses which afflict business in a period of depression, it is not closely correlated with white-collar criminality. Probably at no time within the last fifty years have white-collar crimes in the field of investments and of corporate management been so extensive as during the boom period of the twenties.

Third, the conventional theories do not even explain lower-class criminality. The sociopathic and psychopathic factors which have been emphasized doubtless have something to do with crime causation, but these factors have not been related to a general process that is found both in white-collar criminality and lower-class criminality; therefore, they do not explain the criminality of either class. They may explain the manner or method of crime—why lower-class criminals commit burglary or robbery rather than false pretenses.

In view of these defects in the conventional theories, a hypothesis is needed that will explain both white-collar criminality and lower-class criminality. For reasons of economy, simplicity, and logic, the hypothesis should apply to both classes, for this will make possible the analysis of causal factors freed from the encumbrances of the administrative devices which have led criminologists astray. Shaw and McKay and others, working exclusively in the field of lower-class crime, have found the conventional theories inadequate to account for variations within the data of lower-class crime and from that point of view have been working toward an explanation of crime in terms of a more general social process. Such efforts will be greatly aided by the procedure which has been described.

The hypothesis which is here suggested as a substitute for the conventional theories is that white-collar criminality, just as other systematic criminality, is learned; that it is learned in direct or indirect association with those who already practice the behavior; and that those who learn this criminal behavior are segregated from frequent and intimate contacts with law-abiding behavior. Whether a person becomes a criminal or not is determined largely by the comparative frequency and intimacy of his contacts with the two types of behavior. This may be called the "process of differential association." It is a genetic explanation both of white-collar criminals and lower-class criminality. Those who become white-collar criminals generally start their careers in good neighborhoods and good homes, graduate from colleges with some idealism, and, with little selection on their part, get into particular business situations in which criminality is practically a folkway, becoming inducted into that system of behavior just as into any other folkway. The lower-class criminals generally start their careers in deteriorated neighborhoods and families, find delinquents at hand from whom they acquire the attitudes toward, and the techniques of, crime through association with delinquents and through partial segregation from law-abiding people. The essentials of the process are the same for the two classes of criminals. This is not entirely a process of assimilation, for inventions are frequently made, perhaps more frequently in white-collar crime than in lower-class crime. The inventive geniuses for the lower-class criminals are generally professional criminals, while the inventive geniuses for many kinds of white-collar crime are generally lawyers.

A second general process is social disorganization in the community. Differential association culminates in crime because the community is not organized solidly against that behavior. The law is pressing in one direction and other forces are pressing in the opposite direction. In business, the "rules of the game" conflict with the legal rules. A businessman who wants to obey the law is driven by his competitors to adopt their methods. This is well illustrated by the persistence of commercial bribery in spite of the strenuous efforts of business organizations to eliminate it. Groups and individuals are individuated; they are more concerned with their specialized group or individual interests than with the larger welfare. Consequently, it is not possible for the community to present a solid front in opposition to crime. The better business bureaus and crime commissions, composed of businessmen and professional men, attack burglary, robbery, and cheap swindles but overlook the crimes of their own members. The forces which impinge on the lower class are similarly in conflict. Social disorganization affects the two classes in similar ways.

I have presented a brief and general description of white-collar criminality on a framework of argument regarding theories of criminal behavior. That argument, stripped of the description, may be stated in the following propositions:

1. White-collar criminality is real criminality, being in all cases in violation of the criminal law.

2. White-collar criminality differs from lower-class criminality principally in an implementation of the criminal law, which segregates white-collar criminals administratively from other criminals.

3. The theories of the criminologists that crime is due to poverty or to psychopathic and sociopathic conditions statistically associated with poverty are invalid because, first, they are derived from samples which are grossly biased with respect to socioeconomic status; second, they do not apply to the white-collar criminals; and third, they do not even explain the criminality of the lower class, since the factors are not related to a general process characteristic of all criminality.

4. A theory of criminal behavior which will explain both white-collar criminality and lower-class criminality is needed.

5. A hypothesis of this nature is suggested in terms of differential association and social disorganization.

# 3

# WHITE-COLLAR CRIME:
# AN OVERVIEW AND ANALYSIS

*Donald J. Newman*

## I: INTRODUCTION

Possibly the most significant recent development in criminology, especially since World War II, has been the emergence of the concept "white-collar" crime as an area of scientific inquiry and theoretical speculation. It is true, of course, that this crime itself is not wholly new; robber barons have been exposed in the past, and muckrakers have long decried corruption and venality in high places. But the generalization of such phenomena and the incorporation of facts concerning illegal behavior of the higher classes into theories of crime causation is a product of recent effort. The speeches and publications of Edwin Sutherland culminating in his 1949 study[1] not only gave the name "white-collar" to this new area, but stimulated wide-spread research and, not incidentally, caused a furor in criminological circles concerning the appropriateness of this concept as a legitimate focus of research and theory.

Reprinted, with permission, from a symposium on "Crime and Correction" appearing in *Law and Contemporary Problems*, Vol. 23 (Autumn, 1958), No. 4, published by the Duke University School of Law, Durham, North Carolina. Copyright, 1959, by Duke University.

White-collar crime is markedly different both legally and sociologically from more conventional crime, and the controversy over its criminological appropriateness centers around three major issues:

1. Are the law violations in question really crimes?
2. Can the behavior of the offenders involved be equated with conceptual meanings of criminal behavior, particularly since violators neither think of themselves nor are commonly thought of as criminals?
3. What is to be gained, other than confusion and imprecision, by the reformulation of definitions of crime to include behavior customarily "punished" civilly or by administrative action rather than by the conventional, and probably more precise, criminal procedures?

However these questions are answered, no one can deny that every single recent textbook in criminology includes a comprehensive discussion of white-collar crime. Included also, as inevitable as the concept itself, are the arguments, pro and con, about the criminal nature of this form of lawbreaking. The majority opinion of these sociological writers seems to be that white-collar criminality is a legitimate area of criminological research, although it is customarily set apart as a special type or "behavior system" of crime. While many of the criticisms of such inclusion remain essentially unanswered and all writers recognize the theoretical import and research problems of broadening the concept of crime, none can ignore the numerous research studies and monographs which have appeared in recent years. The studies of Sutherland,[2] Clinard,[3] Hartung,[4] Lane,[5] Cressey,[6] and Newman,[7] the cases described by Irey and Slocum,[8] and various papers on the frequency of lawbreaking among "respectable" segments of our population[9] have supported the general thesis of white-collar criminality.

The relative recency of this interest in what Morris calls "upperworld" crime[10] is the result of the convergence of many cultural factors in our time and place. In the first place, contemporary society has necessarily created legislation specifically designed to control economic and political activities and, therefore, particularly aimed at the more powerful social classes. Rapid industrialization, urbanization, the replacement of the entrepreneur by the corporation, and the development of labor unions and cooperatives have all combined to give us a new world requiring new means of social control. We have come to realize that the conventional laws regarding theft and other socially-injurious conduct are inapplicable or ineffective today in many very important relationships. Some cherished common-law principles—e.g., *caveat emptor*, the fellow-servant doctrine, and so on—have been necessarily reversed or revised by the demands of industrial society. From the late nineteenth century to the present day, a major legal trend has been the development of administrative or regulatory laws designed to control commercial dealings and to codify industrial obligations. Deviations from these laws form the basis of white-collar crime.

In addition to this legal trend, the interest in white-collar crime is a result of a maturity, of both theory and method, within the field of sociology. Early criminologists oriented themselves to the "pathologies" of the social system, taking conventional definitions of societal "diseases" and offering conventional "cures." Criminals were "convicts," and cause lay in personal pathologies or individual environmental defects. In this, these writers reflected their own class values and their training, as well as the spirit of the times.[11]

It is probably a truism that the more any type of behavior is studied, the less clear-cut, the less distinct, it becomes. So it is with crime. Criticism of inmate samples, rejection of personal pathology theories, the blending of data from social class and social psychological research all aided, even forced, the criminologist to revise some of his postulates. The conception of "degrees" of "deviation" from legal norms took the place of a criminal, noncriminal dichotomy.[12] A broadening interest was generated, too, by the sociological concern with institutions and the structural-functional theories of social systems. Crime came to be viewed as normative within various contexts. Merton said "certain phases of social structure generate the circumstances in which infringement of social codes constitutes a normal response"[13] and elaborated the thesis of illegality as a "latent" function of political and economic organization.[14] The increase of regulatory laws during the depression of the 'thirties and the war years of the 'forties merged with changing sociological concepts to form the context from which interest in white-collar criminality developed.

## II: THE NATURE OF WHITE-COLLAR CRIME

*White-Collar Crime Defined.* The chief criterion for a crime to be "white-collar" is that it occurs as a part of, or a deviation from, the violator's occupational role. Technically, this is more crucial than the type of law violated or the relative prestige of the violator, although these factors have necessarily come to be major issues in the white-collar controversy, first, because *most* of the laws involved are not part of the traditional criminal code, and second, because *most* of the violators are a cut above the ordinary criminal in social standing. Such crimes as embezzlement, larceny by bailee, certain forgeries, and the like, however, are essentially occupational and thus white-collar crimes, and yet are tried under the penal code. Likewise farmers, repairmen, and others in essentially nonwhite-collar occupations could, through such illegalities as watering milk for public consumption, making unnecessary "repairs" on television sets, and so forth, be classified as white-collar violators. . . .

The vast bulk of white-collar legislation is regulatory rather than penal in philosophy, is administrative in procedure, and by its qualifications is directed chiefly toward the business and professional classes of our society.

This is apparent in the widely accepted definition by Sutherland that a white-collar crime is "a crime committed by a person of respectability and high social status in the course of his occupation."[15] These crimes are usually violations of trust, either "duplicities" or "misrepresentations," placed in the person (or the corporation, for that matter) by virtue of his occupational norms and high position in the society.[16]

Of course, these violations of trust must also be violations of law, and not merely unethical practices or noncriminal deviations from informal conduct norms within a business or profession. And around the legal status of such violations has arisen a theoretical conflict that continues to the present day. Are such trust violations really crimes? Must theories be revised to include these lawbreakers? If these questions are answered affirmatively, then, indeed, the science of criminology must revise its postulates and reformulate many of its theories.

*The Legal Basis of White-Collar Crime*   The majority of laws underlying white-collar crime differ from conventional criminal laws in five ways: (1) in origin, (2) in determination of responsibility, or intent, (3) in philosophy, (4) in enforcement and trial procedure, and (5) in sanctions used to punish violators. In the first place, most white-collar laws have been legislatively created as of a given date, and some of them are in derogation of common-law principles. These, then, are *mala prohibita*, crimes created by legislative bodies, in contrast to most of the conventional criminal code, which is viewed as merely a legislative expression of "natural" crimes, *mala in se*. Secondly, most regulatory laws define their violations as misdemeanors rather than the implicitly more serious felonies of penal law. Furthermore, the question of intent, so prominent in the criminal code, is irrelevant to conviction under many regulatory laws, although intentional violations, if proved, may increase the punishment. In these respects, white-collar violations are legally much more like traffic laws and municipal ordinances than statutes of the criminal code.

The legal distinctiveness of white-collar legislation is seen even more clearly in procedural variations from those more commonly used in conventional criminal cases. Most of the federal regulatory legislation and much of its counterpart on state levels rely for enforcement not on the police and public prosecutors, but on specially-created investigatory and enforcement bodies. Probably the most familiar of these is the Bureau of Internal Revenue, but many similar agencies exist within the framework of other legislation. Of course, in the final analysis, police and the criminal court *can* be used, but in general, the enforcement of such laws is not a common police activity.

In white-collar legislation, the same agency or commission which directs investigation also conducts hearings on cases and administers numerous punishments or sanctions short of prison terms or the other conventional penal sanctions. In a strict sense, these hearings are not trials, and, therefore, the formal criminal procedures are often absent, as, indeed, are the many protections given defendants in criminal proceedings. Of course, the findings of such hearings may be appealed to conventional courts, and here the precise, if more cumbersome, formal procedural rules apply. This administrative process of investigation and hearing parallels more closely the practices in juvenile court than those in its criminal counterpart.

Since laws proscribing *mala prohibita* are remedial in nature, they are liberally construed, so that the goal remains prevention or correction of existing illegalities rather than the repression or punishment of violators. In this respect, various sanctions other than the criminal punishments of imprisonment, probation, and fines are used by the enforcing agencies. Violators of such laws may be subjected to warnings; injunctions; consent decrees; seizure and destruction of products; civil suits for damages, like the treble-damage suits sanctioned in the case of OPA violations during the wartime emergency; license revocation, where applicable; and similar informal or civil processes. Legislation also provides for the use of more traditional sanctions by criminal courts, however, in cases warranting such action. The discretion to press criminal charges rather than civil action is another function of the enforcing agency. Sutherland's survey of the records of seventy large corporations showed a total of 980 adverse decisions against these companies, 158 of which were criminal proceedings, 298 made by civil courts, 129 by equity courts, while the remainder were administrative actions discussed above.[17] ...

The relatively infrequent use of criminal sanctions is undoubtedly a reflection of many factors including the high social status of many violators and the lack of consensus about the "criminal nature" of their behavior, but it is also consistent with the remedial philosophy of the laws in question. Since the purported aim of enforcement is to correct economic wrongs, prevent public injury, and the like, cases are more likely "settled" or wrongs prevented from continuing in contrast to the eye-for-eye philosophy implicit in conventional criminal actions. Certainly, burglars and bank-robbers are not merely "warned" nor issued cease-and-desist orders.

Then, too, the conventional criminal law is based on a theory of individual responsibility and guilt, the *mens rea* nature of intent, that is inconsistent with and difficult to apply in many white-collar cases. Quite often, white-collar violators are corporations, cooperatives, or labor unions, and while legal responsibility may fix to a corporation as it does to a person, the use of the criminal sanctions of imprisonment or probation is virtually impossible in such cases. The diffuse nature of the perpetrator (the corporate body), as well as the diffuse nature of the victim (the public), does not fit many white-collar cases to the usual criminal format. Then, too, the virtual absence of the necessity of intent, of *mens rea*, on the part of violators makes criminal sanctions seem inappropriate.

Of course, in any behavioral definition of crime, the focus is not on behavior *tried*, but on behavior *triable*. Sutherland puts it "An unlawful act is not defined as criminal by the fact that it is punished, but by the fact that it is punishable."[18] This means that while one person may be tried in a criminal court for behavior remarkably similar to that of another which, at the discretion of the investigating agency, results only in a civil suit or a warning, both would be "criminals," since the emphasis is on the behavior in question rather than the formality of legal process. . . .

*Advocates of the Concept of White-Collar Crime.*    Those sociological writers who advocate the inclusion of upperworld violations in criminological context admit the uniqueness of regulatory laws and the class differential between white-collar and ordinary criminals. The differences they see, however, are viewed as differences of degree, not of kind.[19] . . .

Meeting another criticism of inclusion, advocates admit that even though white-collar legislation differs from the conventional criminal code in respect to the importance of wilful intent, the "accidental" violator is rare. Sutherland's study of corporation records indicated the persistent nature of such lawbreaking, 97.1 per cent of his sample being "recidivists" by having two or more adverse convictions or administrative decisions, with an average per corporation of fourteen such decisions.[20] This is hardly accidental. Likewise, Clinard reports not only the deliberate nature of many black market violations, but the high proportion of businessmen who felt that most such violations by their colleagues were, indeed, intentional.[21] . . .

## III: THE SIGNIFICANCE OF WHITE-COLLAR CRIME TO CRIMINOLOGICAL THEORY AND RESEARCH

*Theoretical Implications of White-Collar Crime.*    Regardless of the "persuasive" nature of definitions of white-collar crime, it is apparent that criminology must face up to its inclusion. This is not to say that it must be equated with burglary, so that theories relating to burglars are discarded as inadequate by failing to explain corporate violations. Nevertheless, the research on upper-strata criminality must be viewed as a challenge to those particularistic theories which explain crime in terms of personal inadequacies or essentially lower-class characteristics, such as poverty or poor home life. The challenge is to the generalization of such factors to all criminal behavior, but danger lies in preventing descriptive research on samples of ordinary, lower-strata violators. Low intelligence, poverty, discrimination, personality, deviation, and the like may be crucial variables in some *types* of crime, and their absence among white-collar violators should not completely invalidate their usefulness.

Studies of upperworld crime have taken criminology a step closer to the conceptualization of its subject matter as "deviant," rather than disorganized or pathological, behavior. This is in keeping with the general trend in "problem" areas of sociology. Deviant behavior in this framework is approached through a study of social processes common to *all* behavior, with an emphasis on degrees of variations from norms, role conflicts, status differentials, and so forth. In short, this approach casts the problem of conforming *versus* deviant behavior within a broad sociological analysis of culture and of the interaction of personality and subcultural variants. Obviously, white-collar crime is crucial in such a context. Debates about whether such phenomena are "real" crimes becomes significant in themselves. Aubert comments:

> For purposes of theoretical analysis it is of prime importance to develop and apply concepts which preserve and emphasize the ambiguous nature of white-collar crimes and not to "solve" the problem by classifying them as either "crimes" or "not crimes." Their controversial nature is exactly what makes them so interesting from a sociological point of view and what gives us a clue to important norm conflicts, clashing group interests, and maybe incipient social change.[22]

White-collar legislation represents the major *formal* controls imposed upon the occupational roles of the most powerful members of our society. Whether he likes it or not, the criminologist finds himself involved in an analysis of prestige, power, and differential privilege when he studies upperworld crime. He must be as conversant with data and theories from social stratification as he has been with studies of delinquency and crime within the setting of the urban slum. He must be able to cast his analysis not only in the framework of those who *break* laws, but in the context of those who *make* laws as well. This, of course, necessitates the development of enlarged, if not wholly new, theoretical models. Fortunately, the bibliography of studies of stratification and power is extensive and growing even larger.[23] There remains for the criminologist the task of relating white-collar crime to class differences in interaction, in styles of life, aspirations, child-rearing, mobility patterns, prestige symbols, and the host of other sociological variables important to the understanding of motives and differential behavior patterns in a multiclass society.

*Research Methods in the Study of White-Collar Crime.* Research nal statistics do not ordinarily contain data of corporation illegality, and problems posed by the concept of white-collar crime are manifold. Crimi-prison samples rarely contain white-collar violators. There is no centralized source which tabulates the extent of, and any trends in, white-collar crime similar to the FBI's *Uniform Crime Reports*, which tabulates ordinary crimes known to the police. Many federal agencies publish decisions in cases under their jurisdiction, however, and such official sources formed the basis of Sutherland's analysis. Clinard's *Black Market* grew out of sources available to him in his wartime position as Chief of the Analysis and Reports Branch of the Office of Price Administration.[24] He utilized case records, field reports, interviews, information from congressional hearings, public-opinion surveys dealing with price regulations, and various other channels of data. The extremely careful documentation of his study reflects the excellence of many of these sources. Hartung interviewed businessmen concerning law violations in the wholesale meat industry,[25] while Newman sampled consumer's responses to actual cases of food adulteration.[26] Lane interviewed top management in twenty-five industrial concerns and analyzed decisions of the Federal Trade Commission, the National Labor Relations Board, and some cases within the Department of Labor.[27] . . .

Missing from these research techniques are psychometric data, clinical interviews, extensive life histories, matched samples, and the other procedures more familiar to students of ordinary criminal behavior. Many of these techniques may not be applicable to white-collar crime; others are virtually impossible to apply. White-collar *crime* rather than white-collar *criminals* has been the basic orientation in research. At any rate, efforts in this field have been frugal when compared to conventional crime or delinquency and have been devoted in good part to the demonstration of the criminal nature of, and social damage caused by, upperworld lawbreaking. They have not been primarily etiological, although causes have not been completely ignored. In fact, white-collar phenomena have been fitted into or tested against many theories. The emphasis has been, however, on demonstrating the existence and danger of such behavior. Vold argues that implicit in most studies of white-collar crime is an appeal not only to modify criminological theory, but to reform values so that white-collar violations *become* generally defined as reprehensible. He says:

> The persons who argue in favor of the term "white collar crime" are really asking for a change in the cultural attitudes and conceptions of the community as a whole so that such behavior will be considered criminal, rather than be viewed as a kind of misconduct to be handled by non-criminal procedures. The real plea is for a change in the mores basic to attitudes about what is to be considered right or wrong in business practice.[28]

Some sociologists feel that the inclusion of upperclass lawbreaking in criminological theory is still too narrowing. Since the sociological emphasis is on processes in producing deviant *behavior* rather than on defining crime, criminology should not limit itself to formal laws as the norms from which deviation is measured. Conduct which violates *any* group norm should also be studied.

While such an approach undoubtedly has theoretical merit, practical

considerations of measuring conduct norms, obtaining consensus on unethical practices, and otherwise discovering behavioral standards from
which deviations can be observed pose almost insurmountable problems
within the possibilities of present-day research techniques. Deviation from
conduct norms is not to be ignored, however, and any future research will
surely be welcome, but broadening "crime" to "nonconformity" is at
present beyond all but the most speculative hypotheses.

## IV: THEORIES OF WHITE-COLLAR CRIME

White-collar crime not only challenges particularistic explanations of
lawbreaking, but requires a theoretical explanation in itself. Sutherland
sought the explanation in his theory of differential association. He explains:

> The hypothesis of differential association is that criminal behavior is
> learned in association with those who define such behavior favorably and
> in isolation from those who define it unfavorably, and that a person in an
> appropriate situation engages in such criminal behavior if, and only if,
> the weight of the favorable definitions exceed the weight of the un-
> favorable definition.[29]

Very roughly, this position puts forth the argument that within certain businesses and occupations, lawbreaking is normative. Incumbents
in these occupations, being relatively isolated from possible other association where this criminal activity is not common, learn attitudes, values,
motives, rationalizations, and techniques favorable to this type of crime.
The normative nature of the lawbreaking is a result of various disorganiz-
ing factors within the general culture, such as excessive competition, the
emphasis on success rather than the means of succeeding, the impersonality of urban business practices, and the like. In general, this theory views
white-collar crime as a natural product of conflicting values within our
economic and class structures and the white-collar criminal as an individual
who, through associations with colleagues who define their offenses as
"normal" if not justified, learns to accept and participate in the antilegal
practices of his occupation. The emphasis is on a fundamental learning
process and does not rely on personality deficiencies as the root of such
crime.

Clinard, while agreeing in principle with the differential-association
hypothesis, argues that it fails adequately to account for all cases of lawbreaking, at least where black-market violations were concerned, and does
not sufficiently account for individual differences in legal conformity
within many business enterprises. He feels that more attention should be
paid to certain personality traits of individual violators. He says:

Such a theory does not adequately explain why some individuals who were familiar with the techniques and the rationalizations of black market violations and were frequently associated with persons similarly familiar, did not engage in such practices. . . . [I]t is suggested that *some*, but by no means all, persons tended to accept or reject black market opportunities according to their basic personality make-up. Some of these general personality patterns, which probably were important in accounting, in some instances, for participation, or lack of participation, in the black market, were egocentricity, emotional insecurity or feelings of personal inadequacy, negative attitudes toward other persons in general, the relative importance of status symbols of money as compared with nationalism, and the relative lack of importance of one's personal, family or business reputation.[30]

. . . Robert Lane, answering the question of corporate violation, supports, in general, the differential-association hypothesis by pointing to the consistency of law violations in certain firms, even when management has changed several times. He tentatively states: "It seemed to be the position of the firm, rather than any emotional qualities of its management which led it to violate."[31] He does not reject, however, the possible influence which men with varying tolerations of governmental authority may exert on the behavior of their firms.

Not all theoretical effort has been directed to the explanation of differential lawbreaking. Most criminologists, in fact, have been more concerned with accounting for the very existence of upper-strata crime in our society than with variation in offense rates within a business or profession. Hartung suggests that such crime is a result of "social differentiation" rather this disorganization," and points to subcultural value divergencies within a common set of economic and political ideals as the basis of such violations.[32] Taft stresses the "exploitive" nature of our society and sees white-collar crime as a mere social-class variation of common motives and practices. He puts it this way:

American culture demands that we be individualists, conformers, materialists, and so on, but the ways in which we strive for these culturally determined goals are determined by the ways which are approved in these primary groups. The underprivileged slum dweller joining a gang commits the "no-collar" type of crime. The businessman joining Rotary becomes a noncriminal competitor if possible, but a white-collar criminal if such a course is essential to his prestige. Some fortunate people are able to achieve success without exploitation of their fellows, but these, we hold, are a minority, not a majority, because our system well-nigh compels most of us to be exploitative.[33]

White-collar crime cannot be fully understood without a knowledge of the value conflicts implicit in the governmental regulations of business.

Contrasted with often-stated ideals of "free competition," the "law of supply and demand," and philosophies of individual success (or failure), the state regulation of commerce is viewed by some as an infringement on basic rights, as unjustified, unnecessary, discriminatory or otherwise contrary to the "American way." Every regulatory law has had a stormy legislative history; most, in fact, represent compromise bills to lessen the dissatisfaction of multiple-interest groups. Quite possibly, many white-collar violations reflect ideological conflicts, how individual offenders or corporations feel about governmental "interference," rather than an acceptance of criminal patterns. White-collar offenses, thus, may represent, in part at least, a protest against what is felt to be "bad" law, similar to violations of prohibition. Vold points to the impossibility of gaining legal conformity unless laws are "accepted and respected by most of the important power groups or elements in the organized political state."[34]

The most important theoretical implication of white-collar crime is that it presents a problem almost exclusively sociological, or at least sociolegal, in nature. . . . [T]o comprehend it [adequately], a fundamental knowledge of class structure, values, roles and statuses, and the many other essentially social processes and concepts, is needed. Criminology has frequently been guilt of studying delinquency and crime out of its culture context or of concentrating, microscopically, on the family as the single, most definitive cultural unit. White-collar crime does not lend itself to such an approach. . . . [B]y its very acceptance in criminological circles, white-collar crime will force researchers to explain more thoroughly the relationship of personality to subcultural influences, to make more thoroughgoing explorations of role and role conflicts,[35] and to deal much more comprehensively with social deviation in general.

## V: THE CONTROL OF WHITE-COLLAR CRIME

We have very little success controlling any kind of crime in our society, as attested by increasing crime rates. Our methods of control have been repressive on the one hand and rehabilitative on the other, with some lip-service to prevention. The punishment of individual lawbreakers is an integral part of our religious and political heredity, just as individual readjustment is a tradition of our public welfare, charitable, and correction programs. Perhaps these two approaches are not mutually exclusive; it cannot be debated here. The traditional forms which each of these philosophies take, however—chiefly imprisonment and public stigma in the first instance and case-work, psychotherapy, vocational training and the like in the latter—are, for the most part, inappropriate in white-collar crime, for reasons already discussed.

The legal philosophy basic to regulatory legislation is essentially remedial rather than punitive. The admitted purpose of administrative agencies is to help individuals and businesses under their jurisdiction comply with the law and, thus, to prevent violations from occurring. Many times, educational, inspectional, and corrective programs supersede enforcement activities of administrative personnel. Perhaps this should not be the case. Would white-collar crime decline if warnings, injunctions, consent decrees, and damage suits were abandoned in favor of the exclusive use of fines, probation, and imprisonment? Clinard reports that imprisonment, even for sentences as short as six months, was the punishment most feared by businessmen, according to their own testimony. The other criminal court sanctions of fines and suspended sentences had little effect in insuring compliance with government OPA regulations.[36] He concludes, however, that punishment, either administrative or criminal, does little to control white-collar offenders, except to increase caution and cleverness in the methods of their evasions. He feels that the only effective control rests on "the voluntary compliance with the regulations of society by the vast majority of the citizens."[37]

Newman reported on public opinion of punishment as a means of control. He [demonstrated] that the public—*i.e.*, victims—will punish white-collar violators much more severely than administrative agencies actually do, particularly in cases of food law violations which potentially threaten their own health as well as their pocketbooks.[38] ... A second hypothesis, however, to the effect that respondents would select penalties comparable to those meted in ordinary criminal cases (long prison sentences) had to be abandoned. While about one-fifth of the respondents indicated that they would sentence some violators to prison for more than one year, the majority selected fines, warnings, seizures, and jail terms as their judgments. The conclusion was: "In effect, respondents viewed food adulteration as more comparable to serious traffic violations than to burglary."[39] Fuller, however, stresses the necessity of *convincing* the public that white-collar crimes are more serious than conventional offenses and calls for strict enforcement of the laws.[40]

There has been a general trend away from punishment—at least severe, stigmatizing punishment—as an effective method of dealing with all sorts of social deviation. Instead, a variety of educational and social-readjustment programs have been suggested. Many of these programs, possibly effective with delinquents, alcoholics, and the like, are grossly inappropriate in white-collar crime. Modifications of them, however, have been suggested and, to a limited extent, are used by various enforcing agencies. Lane proposes an educational and experimental program involving the interaction of government and business management personnel. Pointing out the ambiguity of many regulatory laws, he proposes a clarification of provisions, improved communications between business and government, a study of social pressures and community attitudes, with an eye to building respect for the law, and a "dry-run" experimental period whenever a new regulation is introduced. The purpose of this is for "business and government to re-examine their relationship and to attempt to recreate a mutual respect which will facilitate their partnership in a democratic society."[41]

Professions have long prided themselves on their self-policing policies based, in some cases at least, upon rather elaborate codes of ethics. Since recognized professional status carries with it the highest social prestige, there has been a tendency, among diverse kinds of businesses to become "professionalized." Thus, undertakers become "morticians," house salesmen, "realtors," druggists, "pharmacists," publicity becomes "public relations," and so on. Accompanying this trend has been the formalizing of business responsibilities, obligations, and even personal conduct into ethical codes. . . .

If white-collar crime is intrinsic to and normative within the value structure of our society, then no punishment or treatment program will effectively eradicate it. It cannot be "cured" by externally imposed sanctions; major value realignment becomes necessary. Caldwell, however, warns social scientists about stressing such a solution. He reproves the confusion of ethics with science and argues that no special values are, in themselves, superior to others. A sociologist may "show how to reduce social problems by removing one side or the other of a conflict of values but he cannot advocate either side and remain a scientist."[42] The desire to reduce social problems at all, however, is itself a value position, for the implicit purpose in all studies of crime is not only knowledge of lawbreaking, but control, or cure, or prevention. Much more must be known, of course, about the functional relationship of values and roles and deviant behavior. Nevertheless, the theoretical criminologist is increasingly orienting himself to consideration of values and broad social processes as inducive to many types of crime. White-collar crime, along with many other types of law violation, has been related to many essentially urban, industrial characteristics. Impersonality, materialism, intense economic competition, status-striving, and other such "American characteristics" have been labeled the root factors in all crime. If so, what can be done about them?

At this stage of criminological growth, only very speculative judgments about control can be made. In all likelihood, efforts must be directed to the distribution of our societal *rewards*, rather than our usual emphasis on control through the manipulation of *punishments*. This involves the creation of new opportunities for wealth, security, education, prestige, and self-respect by the reduction of discrimination, favoritism, and nepotism in these reward channels. The price of this may be greater than we are willing to pay. Taft asks, "What liberties are we prepared to sacrifice in the interest of crime prevention? ... Can criminogenic political corruption be eliminated and yet democracy be retained?"[43]

This really brings us to a new frontier in criminology. The concept of white-collar crime has forced the theoretician into an analysis of highly complex and very abstract relationships within our social system. No longer is the criminologist a middle-class observer studying lower-class behavior. He now looks upward at the most powerful and prestigeful strata, and his ingenuity in research and theory will be tested, indeed.

## Notes

1. Edwin H. Sutherland, *White Collar Crime* (New York: Dryden Press, 1949).

2. *Ibid.* See also Albert Cohen, Alfred Lindesmith, and Karl Schuessler, eds., *The Sutherland Papers* (Bloomington: Indiana University Press, 1956).

3. Marshall B. Clinard, *The Black Market* (New York: Holt, 1952).

4. Frank E. Hartung, "White-Collar Offenses in the Wholesale Meat Industry in Detroit," *American Journal of Sociology*, 56 (July, 1950), pp. 25–34.

5. Robert E. Lane, "Why Businessmen Violate the Law," *Journal of Criminal Law, Criminology and Police Science*, 44 (July, 1953), pp. 151–165.

6. Donald R. Cressey, *Other People's Money: The Social Psychology of Embezzlement* (New York: Free Press, 1953). Cressey, however, limits his definition of criminality to violation of the penal law. See his "Criminological Research and the Definition of Crimes," *American Journal of Sociology*, 56 (May, 1951), pp. 546–551.

7. Donald J. Newman, "Public Attitudes Toward a Form of White-Collar Crime," *Social Problems*, 4 (January, 1953), pp. 228–232.

8. Elmer L. Irey and William Slocum, *The Tax Dodgers* (New York: Greenberg, 1948).

9. For examples see James S. Wallerstein and Clement J. Wyle, "Our Law-Abiding Law-Breakers," *National Probation*, 25 (March–April, 1947), pp. 107–112; Virgil W. Peterson, "Why Honest People Steal," *Journal of Criminal Law and Criminology*, 38 (July–August, 1947), pp. 94–103.

10. Albert Morris, *Criminology* (New York: Longmans, Green, 1935), pp. 152–158.

11. See, especially C. Wright Mills, "The Professional Ideology of Social Pathologists," *American Journal of Sociology*, 49 (September, 1943), pp. 165–180; George B. Vold, *Theoretical Criminology* (New York: Oxford, 1958).

12. See especially Marshall B. Clinard, *The Sociology of Deviant Behavior* (New York: Rinehart, 1957); and Edwin M. Lemert, *Social Pathology* (New York. McGraw-Hill, 1951), for systematic analyses of this approach.

13. Robert K. Merton, "Social Structure and Anomie," *American Sociological Review*, 3 (October, 1938), pp. 672–682.

14. Robert K. Merton, *Social Theory and Social Structure* (Glencoe, Ill.: Free Press, 1949).

15. Sutherland, *op. cit.*, p. 2.

16. Edwin H. Sutherland, "White-Collar Criminality," *American Sociological Review*, 5 (February, 1940), p. 2.

17. Sutherland, *White Collar Crime, op. cit.*, p. 22.

18. Sutherland, *White Collar Crime, op. cit.*, p. 35.

19. Sutherland, "White-Collar Criminality," *op. cit.*, p. 5.

20. Sutherland, *White-Collar Crime, op. cit.*, p. 20.

21. Clinard, *The Black Market, op. cit.*, pp. 235–236.

22. Vilhelm Aubert, "White-Collar Crime and Social Structure," *American Journal of Sociology*, 58 (November, 1952), p. 264.

23. See, for example, Joseph A. Kahl, *The American Class Structure* (New York: Rinehart, 1957). For a provocative analysis of power structure, see C. Wright Mills, *The Power Elite* (New York: Oxford, 1956), as well as Mills's *The New Men of Power: America's Labor Leaders* (New York: Harcourt, Brace, 1948) and *White Collar* (New York: Oxford, 1951). For an analysis of upper middle-class values, see David Riesman, *The Lonely Crowd* (New Haven: Yale University Press, 1952).

24. Clinard, *The Black Market, op. cit.*, pp. viii–x.

25. Hartung, *op. cit.*

26. Newman, *op. cit.*, pp. 228–229.

27. Lane, *op. cit.*

28. Vold, *op. cit.*, p. 259.

29. Sutherland, *White Collar Crime, op. cit.*, p. 234.

30. Clinard, *The Black Market, op. cit.*, pp. 309–310. Also see Walter C. Reckless, *The Crime Problem*, 2nd. ed. (New York: Appleton-Century-Crofts, 1955), pp. 26–42.

31. Lane, *op. cit.*, p. 163.

32. Frank E. Hartung, *Law and Social Differentiation* (Ann Arbor: University of Michigan Microfilms, 1949).

33. Donald R. Taft, *Criminology*, 3rd ed. (New York: Macmillan, 1956).

34. Vold, *op. cit.*, p. 257.

35. For an example of exploratory research in this problem, although not in the area of white-collar crime, see Neal Gross, Ward S. Mason, and Alexander W. Mc-Eachern, *Explorations in Role Analysis* (New York: Wiley, 1958).

36. Clinard, *The Black Market, op. cit.*, p. 244.

37. *Ibid.*, p. 261.

38. Newman, *op. cit.*, pp. 230–231.

39. *Ibid.*, p. 231.

40. Richard C. Fuller, "Morals and the Criminal Law," *Journal of Criminal Law and Criminology*, 32 (March–April, 1942), pp. 624–630.

41. Lane, *op. cit.*, p. 165.

42. Robert G. Caldwell, *Criminology* (New York: Ronald Press, 1956), pp. 178–179.

43. Taft, *op. cit.*, p. 757.

# III

# CORPORATE AND BUSINESS WHITE-COLLAR CRIME

In 1948, the nation's two hundred largest industrial corporations controlled 48 percent of the manufacturing assets of the United States. Today, these firms control 58 percent, while the top five hundred firms control about 75 percent of these assets.[1] Similarly, 75 percent of all corporate stock in the United States is held by the richest 2 percent of the country's families.[2] "The danger that this superconcentration poses to our economic, political and social structure cannot be overestimated," a recent American attorney general noted.[3] In the same vein, a Canadian political leader called attention to what he labeled "the corporate rip-off," insisting that "the corporations have become the real welfare bums."[4]

Antagonism to business and corporate enterprise has deep roots in Western civilization, particularly within intellectual circles. Such hostility finds expression, for instance, in the views of the British writer C. S. Lewis.

> The greatest evil is not now done in those sordid "dens of crime" that Dickens loved to paint. It is not done even in concentration camps and labor camps. In those we see its final result. But it is conceived and ordered (moved, seconded, carried and minuted) in clean, carpeted, warmed and well-lighted offices, by quiet men with white collars and cut fingernails, and smooth-shaven cheeks who do not need to raise their voices. Hence, naturally enough, my symbol for Hell is something like ... the offices of a thoroughly nasty business concern.[5]

Attempting to interpret the background for such views, Robert Heilbroner, an economist, remarks on the corporation's "insatiable wealth-seeking, its dehumanizing calculus of plus and minus, its careful inculcation of impulses and goals that should at most be tolerated." Heilbroner finds antipathy to the corporate and business world to be rooted particularly in feelings of impotence created in people by forces that manipulate their existence in an impersonal and faceless manner:

> What, then, explains the fury with which we turn on the corporation for despoiling the air and water, and for vending shoddy or dangerous wares? I suspect that the answer lies more in our resentment of the kind of presence the corporation represents than in the particular crime it commits (which, I repeat, I have no wish to condone or minimize). What fuels the public protest against corporate misbehavior . . . is an aspect of a widely shared frustration with respect to all bastions of power that are immense, anonymous and impregnable, and yet inextricably bound up with the industrial society that few of us wish to abandon.[6]

The present surge in consumer advocacy may be traced to some of the attitudes noted above. Also, the business community is more readily stigmatized than other segments of "respectable" society. White-collar crimes by professionals, such as doctors and lawyers, for example, arouse lesser amounts of social concern because the high status of members of these professions immunizes them from the more severe effects of illegal behavior.[7] Moreover, professional groups have special sanctioning bodies to deal with deviants so that they often are able to avoid airing their dirty business in public. These considerations prevail not only in the realm of white-collar crime, but also in regard to the more traditional offenses. A doctor caught using narcotics, for example, is generally punished by having his prescription-writing privileges revoked for a period of time while the underclass addict is apt to do time in prison or a civil commitment facility.

In addition, there are checks upon professions built into ethnical codes which maintain that service is owed clients above and beyond economic considerations. However inadequately such ideals are realized, they present a distinct departure from the acquisitive spirit that underlies business, in which the fundamental rule appears to be to do whatever you can get away with in order to make and keep as much money as possible. As powerful social forces, corporations also often are able to influence legislative action so that the criminal law is not employed against actions which are patently detrimental to consumer interests, in the manner that the automobile industry successfully lobbied to remove criminal penalties from a bill aimed at preventing the knowing marketing of unsafe automobiles.[8]

There are striking pressures that promote white-collar crime in business. The decline of the laissez-faire ethic has imposed contradictory conditions on business operations. On the other hand, there is an espousal of the doctrine of fierce competition while on the other hand, as Michael Conant has noted with regard to antitrust conspiracies in the motion picture industry, they "search for security—for protection against market uncertainty."[9]

For the foregoing reasons, among others, business and corporate white-collar crime have received the greatest amount of attention from social scientists. It is also possible as well that such offenses represent the most serious kind of depredations, deserving of the most intense scrutiny. Certainly, the ready availability of records of administrative agencies and federal regulatory boards undoubtedly conditioned Sutherland's concentration upon corporate violations to epitomize his newly minted concept of white-collar crime. "Crime of Corporations," the first paper in Part III, was read during the spring of 1948 before the Toynbee Club, a group of sociology students and faculty members at DePauw University. In an informal manner, Sutherland spelled out the ingredients that were to be arrayed more formally and formidably in his classic monograph, *White Collar Crime*. The major drawback in the paper remains its failure to differentiate between the corporations and their management personnel. It was the absence of relevant material going to the heart of his concept that forced Sutherland to "humanize" or "anthropomorphize" the corporations and which seems to have led him into taking rather too literally the personifications that he himself had created.

Corporations are, of course, legal entities, and they may be subjected to criminal prosecution, though a corporation obviously cannot be imprisoned. For the purpose of criminological analysis, however, corporations cannot readily be considered persons, except by recourse to the type of extrapolatory fiction that once brought about the judicial punishment of inanimate objects.[10] Sutherland attempted to resolve this dilemma by maintaining, not without some acerbity, that the crimes of corporations are the crimes of their executives and managers, an assertion that contains some truth, some inaccuracy, and a good deal of uncertainty. Nonetheless, Sutherland's prose makes a strong impact— his spare, staccato style and his forceful insistence that acts which cause criminally harmful consequences must be viewed as criminal acts.

Violations of wartime regulations, particularly those within the ken of the Office of Price Administration, provide material for the examination of white-collar crime conducted by Marshall B. Clinard, a professor of sociology. Such violations took place in an atmosphere marked by notable ambivalence. On the one hand, there was an overriding patriotic esprit de corps and commitment to the objectives of World War II. On the other hand, in some commercial enterprises and civilian activities there was virtually ubiquitous flaunting of government regulations designed to serve the war effort.

Clinard's work is noteworthy for its intellectual kinship with Sutherland's earlier contributions, as a deliberate effort is made to address the subject of wartime regulations so that cumulative and complementary material is forthcoming. Clinard, for example, measures his data against Sutherland's theory of differential association, finding "several limitations" in Sutherland's position. For Clinard, "there can be no single explanation of the OPA violations," although he suggests that intensive examination of the "life organizations of the violators" could yield fruitful conclusions; and he recommends, in particular, concentration on the "different integration of the several roles which the individual plays in society."

Clinard's theme reappears in Robert E. Lane's "Why Businessmen Violate the Law." Lane, a professor of political science, concentrates on the structure of a business firm and its industry-wide position as these items relate to white-collar crime, but he also feels compelled, as Clinard did, to call special attention to the "more personal characteristics" of managers of business firms, although he grants that materials regarding such characteristics are "not readily accessible."

In an attempt to interpret management attitudes from an analysis of violation patterns, Lane notes that there was "no evidence of a consistently 'antiregulation' or 'antigovernment' or 'antiauthority' policy on the part of any firm or its management." The contradiction between Lane's conclusions and Sutherland's statement regarding the "professional-thief" nature of corporate crime may stem from the different spheres being described: Sutherland is dealing primarily with the country's largest corporations and Lane with a population of smaller New England manufacturers. It must also be kept in mind that Lane had the benefit of later research and theorizing upon which to base his work, while Sutherland's was a pioneering effort.

Lane's list of ways to reduce corporate violations clearly indicates that, however uncontaminated his research findings, his general predilections are quite dissimilar to Sutherland's. Lane, for instance, notes that "ambiguous laws lead to a higher rate of violation"; Sutherland, it will be remembered, was more inclined to find the laws quite clear-cut and the violations preeminently deliberate. Terms such as "ambiguous" and "explicit" or "clear" are basically value judgments, of course, and the discrepant conclusions of the authors indicate more than anything else the critical eye with which writings on so sensitive a subject as white-collar crime must be read.

The 1961 antitrust violations in the heavy electrical equipment industry are described in detail in the fourth paper in this part, which concentrates on the behavior and views of the perpetrators. These antitrust cases represent the most widely publicized and carefully studied corporate offenses in the history of the United States.[11] The antitrust cases, in fact, are often referred to in other readings in this volume to buttress or to rebut points regarding white-collar crime, though several authors take pains to point out that the 1961 price-fixing schemes should not be taken to represent the wider range of more subtle and more complex forms of corporate white-collar crime.

The reading on violations by General Electric, Westinghouse, and other manufacturers attempts to abstract from congressional hearings, interviews, and other reports those items most directly related to prior studies of white-collar crime. Its review of Sutherland's ideas in terms of the 1961 cases finds many of the classical views on white-collar crime strikingly on target, while others are said to be notably awry, though both the unique nature of the particular case and the passage of time since Sutherland first wrote must be noted. The conclusion of the article asks for more work of a similar nature before it will venture very far theoretically; in essence, its author takes his stand with Huntington Cairns that "the history of social theory is too largely a record of generalizations wrung from insufficient facts."[12]

The heavy electrical equipment antitrust violations point out the atmosphere within which the offenses were committed, and the kinds of rationalizations the violators employed to justify their behavior even after apprehension. Probably most white-collar offenses employ devices whereby normative boundaries can be "neutralized."[13] And, given the lack of severity of the judicial response to these offenses, the unorganized nature of the public's reaction, and the general "invisibility" of the offenses—which makes them difficult to detect and, subsequently, to condem—businessmen have not had a difficult time excusing their behavior and maintaining a self-conception as "honest" people.

Since corporate and business crimes are committed within a context of organizational and economic transactions, it is to be expected that features of these transactions and relationships will influence both the occasion for crime and the nature of the specific offenses. In the last paper in this part, William N. Leonard and Marvin G. Weber analyze violations by automobile dealers within the context of pressures applied by the manufacturers. Such pressures are seen as part of the normal market conditions of the industry.

Leonard and Weber make it clear that violations may arise from sources outside the immediate control of the offenders since certain clear limits are placed on their degree of business freedom. On the other hand, despite the forcefulness of their position, one of their own illustrations—that of the repair mechanic who refuses to go along with an exorbitant charge of a customer for a minor amount of work—indicates that the pressures, however intense, are not totally inexorable. The article, nonetheless, moves our attention to larger forces and conditions which bear upon the process of white-collar criminalization. Corporations, like nations, often act in response to others and within an intricate framework of interaction. To view corporate and business white-collar crimes as simply the behavior of greedy people in a greedy world is to stereotype much too simply a highly complex social process.

## Notes

1. Joseph Goulden, *The Superlawyers* (New York: Dell, 1973), p. 11.
2. Robert Heilbroner, *In the Name of Profit* (New York: Warner, 1973), p. 205.
3. Goulden, *op. cit.*
4. *New York Times*, November 3, 1972.
5. C. S. Lewis, *The Screwtape Letters and Screwtape Purposes* (New York: Macmillan, 1961), p. xxv.
6. Heilbroner, *op. cit.*, p. 200.
7. Richard D. Schwartz and Jerome H. Skolnick, "Two Studies of Legal Stigma," in Howard S. Becker, ed., *The Other Side: Perspectives on Deviance* (New York: Free Press, 1964), pp. 103–117.

8. Charles McGarry, *Citizen Nader* (New York: Saturday Review Press, 1972), p. 85.

9. Michael Conant, *Antitrust in the Motion Picture Industry* (Berkeley: University of California Press, 1972), p. 1.

10. E. P. Evans, *The Criminal Prosecution and Capital Punishment of Animals* (London: Heinemann, 1906).

11. See further: Charles A. Bane, *The Electrical Equipment Conspiracies* (New York: Federal Legal Publications, 1973); Fred J. Cook, "The Great Electrical Conspiracy," in *The Corrupted Land* (New York: Macmillan, 1966), pp. 32–72; John G. Fuller, *The Gentlemen Conspirators* (New York: Grove Press, 1962); Walter Goodman, "Business: A Way of Life," in *All Honorable Men* (Boston: Little, Brown, 1963), pp. 7–99; John Herling, *The Great Price Conspiracy* (Washington, D.C.: Luce, 1962); Richard A. Smith, "General Electric: A Crisis of Antitrust," in *Corporations in Crisis* (Garden City, N.Y.: Doubleday, 1963), pp. 97–138; Clarence C. Walton and Frederick W. Cleveland, Jr., *Corporations on Trial: The Electric Cases* (Belmont, Calif.: Wadsworth, 1964).

12. Huntington Cairns, *Law and the Social Sciences* (New York: Harcourt, Brace, 1935).

13. Gresham M. Sykes and David Matza, "Techniques of Neutralization: A Theory of Delinquency," *American Sociological Review*, 22 (December, 1957), pp. 664–670.

# 4

# CRIME OF CORPORATIONS

*Edwin H. Sutherland*

About twenty years ago I began to study violations of law by businessmen and have continued the study intermittently to the present day. This study was begun for the purpose of improving the general explanations of criminal behavior. The theories of crime which were then current and which are still current emphasized social and personal pathologies as the causes of crime. The social pathologies included, especially, poverty and the social conditions related to poverty, such as poor housing, lack of organized recreational facilities, the ignorance of parents, and family disorganization. The personal pathology emphasized in the earlier period was feeble-mindedness; the early theory asserted that feeblemindedness is inherited and is the cause of both poverty and crime. At about the time I started the study of business crimes, the personal pathology which was used to explain crime was shifting from defective intelligence to defective emotions, as represented by such concepts as frustration, the inferiority complex, and the Oedipus complex.

These theories that crime is due to social and personal pathologies had considerable support from the fact that a very large proportion of the

Reprinted from Albert Cohen, Alfred Lindesmith, and Karl Schuessler (eds.), *The Sutherland Papers* (Bloomington: Indiana University Press, 1956), pp. 78–96.

persons arrested, convicted, and committed to prisons belong to the lower economic class.

In contrast to those theories, my theory was that criminal behavior is learned just as any other behavior is learned and that personal and social pathologies play no essential part in the causation of crime. I believed that this thesis could be substantiated by a study of the violation of law by businessmen. Businessmen are generally not poor, are not feebleminded, do not lack organized recreational facilities, and do not suffer from the other social and personal pathologies. If it can be shown that businessmen, without these pathologies, commit many crimes, then such pathologies cannot be used as the explanation of the crimes of other classes. The criminologists who have stated the theories of crimes get their data from personal interviews with criminals in the criminal courts, jails, and prisons, or from criminal statistics based on the facts regarding such criminals. But when businessmen commit crimes, their cases go generally before courts under equity or civil jurisdictions or before quasi-judicial commissions, seldom before the criminal courts. Consequently, the criminologists do not come into contact with these businessmen and have not included their violations of law within general theories of criminal behavior.

I have used the term "white-collar criminal" to refer to a person in the upper socioeconomic class who violates the laws designed to regulate his occupation. The term "white collar" is used in the sense in which it was used by President Sloan of General Motors, who wrote a book entitled *The Autobiography of a White Collar Worker.** The term is used more generally to refer to the wage-earning class that wears good clothes at work, such as clerks in stores.

I wish to report specifically on a part of my study of white-collar crimes. I selected the seventy largest industrial and commercial corporations in the United States, not including public utilities and petroleum corporations. I have attempted to collect all the records of violations of law by each of these corporations, so far as these violations have been decided officially by courts and commissions. I have included the laws regarding restraint of trade; misrepresentation in advertising; infringement of patents, copyrights, and trademarks; rebates; unfair labor practices, as prohibited by the National Labor Relations Law; financial fraud; violations of war regulations; and a small miscellaneous group of other laws. The records include the life careers of the corporations, which average about forty-five years, and the subsidiaries as well as the main corporations. In this search, I have been limited by the available records found in a university library, and this is far from complete. I am sure that the number of crimes I shall report on is far smaller than the number actually decided by courts and commissions against these corporations.

* Editor's Note: Though he was a meticulous scholar, Sutherland missed the title of the source of his definition, which was A. P. Sloan's *Adventures of a White-Collar Man* (New York: Doubleday, 1941).

This tabulation of the crimes of the seventy largest corporations in the United States gives a total of 980 adverse decisions. Every one of the seventy corporations has a decision against it, and the average number of decisions is 14.0. Of these seventy corporations, 98 per cent are recidivists; that is, they have two or more adverse decisions. Several states have enacted habitual criminal laws, which define an habitual criminal as a person who has been convicted four times of felonies. If we use this number and do not limit the convictions to felonies, 90 per cent of the seventy largest corporations in the United States are habitual criminals. Sixty of the corporations have decisions against them for restraint of trade, fifty-four for infringements, forty-four for unfair labor practices, twenty-seven for misrepresentation in advertising, twenty-six for rebates, and forty-three for miscellaneous offenses.

These decisions have been concentrated in the period since 1932. Approximately 60 per cent of them were made in the ten-year period subsequent to 1932, and only 40 per cent in the forty-year period prior to 1932. One possible explanation of this concentration is that the large corporations are committing more crimes than they did previously. My own belief is that the prosecution of large corporations has been more vigorous during the later period and that the corporations have not appreciably increased in criminality.

Of the seventy large corporations, thirty were either illegal in their origin or began illegal activities immediately after their origin, and 8 additional corporations should probably be added to this thirty. Thus, approximately half of the seventy corporations were either illegitimate in birth, or were infant and juvenile delinquents, as well as adult criminals.

All of the 980 adverse decisions were decisions that these corporations violated laws. Only 159 of these 980 decisions were made by criminal courts, whereas 425 were made by courts under civil or equity jurisdiction and 361 by commissions. The most important question regarding white-collar crime is whether it is really crime. That is a difficult and somewhat technical question, and I shall not attempt to deal with it here since I have published another paper on that question. The general conclusion stated in that paper is that the violations of law which were attested by decisions of equity and civil courts and by administrative commissions are, with very few exceptions, crimes.

The statistics which I have presented are rather dry and may not mean much to the average student who is not a specialist in this field, but the prevalence of white-collar crimes by large corporations can be illustrated more concretely. If you consider the life of a person, you find that from the cradle to the grave he has been using articles which were sold or distributed in violation of the law. The professional criminals use the word "hot" to refer to an article which has been recently stolen. For the purpose of simplicity of statement, I wish to use this word to refer to articles manufactured by corporations, but I shall expand the meaning to include any official record without restricting it to recent times and shall refer to a class of articles rather than articles manufactured by a particular concern. Using the word in this sense, we can say that a baby is assisted into this world with the aid of "hot" surgical instruments, rubbed with "hot" olive oil, wrapped in a "hot" blanket, weighed on "hot" scales. The father, hearing the good news, runs a "hot" flag up on his flag pole, goes to the golf course and knocks a "hot" golf ball around the course. The baby grows up surrounded by such articles and is finally laid to rest in a "hot" casket under a "hot" tombstone.

I now wish to describe in more detail violations of some of the specific laws and shall take first misrepresentation in advertising. Although the Pure Food and Drug Law contains a provision prohibiting misrepresentation on the labels of foods and drugs, the administrators of that law have not published regular reports including the names of the corporations that have been found to be in violation of the law. I shall therefore restrict the discussion to the misrepresentations in advertisements which have been decided on by the Federal Trade Commission.

This is one of the less important white-collar crimes in comparison with the others. Decisions have been made in ninety-seven cases against twenty-six of seventy corporations. No decisions were made against forty-four of the seventy large corporations under this law. Of these forty-four corporations against which no decisions were made, twenty-seven may be classed as nonadvertising corporations. That is, they do not advertise for purposes of their sales, although they may advertise for general goodwill or for the goodwill of the newspapers and journals. They sell their products to expert buyers, who cannot be influenced by advertising. It would be a waste of money for U.S. Steel to distribute pamphlets among the expert buyers of its products, claiming that its products were made from the finest ores or with Bessemer steel imported from England or to show a picture of a movie star in a Pullman saying, "I always select railroads which use rails made by U.S. Steel, because they are better rails" or a picture of a baseball manager saying, "I feel that my players are safer if they ride the trains on rails made by U.S. Steel, because these rails are safer." If these large corporations which do not advertise for sales purposes are eliminated, approximately 60 per cent of the large corporations which do advertise for sales purposes have decisions against them for misrepresentation in advertising.

These misrepresentations in advertising are not, in most cases, mere technical violations. The Federal Trade Commission each year makes a survey of several hundred thousand advertisements in periodicals and over the radios. From these they select about 50,000 which are questionable, and from these they pick out about 1,500 as patently false, making adverse decisions against about 1,000 of these each year. Also, in their selection, they tend to concentrate on certain products in one year and other products in other years. About 1941, they concentrated on false advertisements of vitamins and issued desist orders against about twenty-five firms on this one product. The advertisements of vitamins at that time claimed with practically no qualifications that vitamins would restore vigor, aid digestion, eliminate sterility, prevent miscarriage, increase sex vigor, decrease blood pressure, reduce neuritis, reduce insomnia, stop falling hair, cure hay fever and asthma, cure alcoholism, prevent tooth decay, eliminate pimples, make chickens lay more eggs, and keep the dog in good health.

   Misrepresentations fall into three principal classes: First, some advertisements are designed to sell products which are physically dangerous, with the dangers denied, minimized, or unmentioned. Most of these advertisements are in the drug and cosmetic businesses. Only two of the seventy large corporations have decisions against them for advertisements of this nature.

   Second, some advertisements exaggerate the values of the products, and this is equivalent to giving short weights. An extreme case of advertisements of this nature was a case decided against two hoodlums in Chicago about 1930. They sold a bottle of medicine at a price of $10 to a blind man with the claim that this would cure his blindness. When analyzed, the medicine was found to consist of two aspirins dissolved in Lake Michigan water. The hoodlums were convicted and sentenced to six months' imprisonment. The advertisements by large corporations are frequently of this class, except that they are not so extreme and are not followed by convictions in criminal courts and imprisonment. Garments advertised and sold as silk or wool are almost entirely cotton. Alligator shoes not made from alligator hides, walnut furniture not made from walnut lumber, turtle-oil facial cream not made from turtle-oil, Oriental rugs not made in the Orient, Hudson seal furs not made from the skins of seals are further instances of such misrepresentation. Caskets advertised as rustproof are not rustproof, garments as mothproof when they are not mothproof, garden hose as three-ply when it is only two-ply, and radios as "all-wave reception" that do not receive all waves. Electric pads are advertised with switches for high, medium, and low heat, when in fact they have only two degrees of heat. Storage eggs are sold as fresh eggs, old and reconditioned stoves as new stoves, and worn and reconditioned hats as new hats. Facial creams sold as skin foods, corrective of wrinkles, do not feed the skin or correct wrinkles. Some corporations advertise that their tea is made from tender leaves, especially picked for these corporations, when in fact their tea is purchased from lots brought in by importers who sell the same tea to other firms. Cigarettes are advertised as having been made from the finest tobacco, for which the company pays 25 per cent more, but other cigarettes are also made from the "finest tobacco" for which the manufacturers pay 25 per cent more than they do for chewing tobacco.

The third class of misrepresentation overlaps the two preceding and is separated from them principally because certain advertisements do special injury to the competitors rather than to consumers. One mail-order company advertised its furnaces as containing features which no other furnaces contained, when in fact the furnaces of competitors contained the same features. Consumers Research Service, which claimed to make impartial and unbiased appraisals of automobiles, was found to be receiving payments from an automobile company for reporting that their cars were superior.

I wish to describe a few of the important cases of misrepresentation in advertising. A prominent automobile manufacturer originated the 6 per cent installment purchase plan in 1935. This plan as advertised stated that the interest rate on unpaid balances on cars purchased on the installment plan was only 6 per cent. The Federal Trade Commission, after an investigation, reported that the interest rate was actually in excess of 11 per cent and that the exaggeration in the interest rate was nearly 100 per cent. Before the commission had ordered the pioneer firm to desist from this misrepresentation, practically all the other large automobile companies adopted the same method of taking money under false pretenses. Again, in 1936, all the important automobile companies were ordered on two counts to desist from misrepresentation in advertising their cars. First, they quoted a price which did not include necessary parts and accessories, the price for the car as actually equipped being 10 per cent higher than the advertised price. In addition, they added handling charges independent of transportation costs, which further increased the price required. Second, they advertised a picture of a car which was not the model actually named and priced. Again, in 1941, three of the four principal manufacturers of automobile tires were ordered to desist from misrepresentation in their advertisements of special sales prices on the Fourth of July and on Labor Day. These companies advertised prices which were reductions of 20 to 50 per cent from the regular prices. When the Federal Trade Commission investigated, it found that the 20 per cent reduction was actually only an 8 per cent reduction and the 50 per cent reduction only an 18 per cent reduction. In addition, one tire company was found to have engaged in misrepresentation in two respects. First, it advertised that with its tires a car would stop 25 per cent quicker. It did not say 25 per cent quicker than what, but the implication was 25 per cent quicker than with tires of other manufacturers; this was not true. Second, it made claims for the greater safety of its tires on the basis of the fact that these tires were used in the Indianapolis Speedway races, whereas in fact the Speedway tires had been especially constructed, so that there was no assurance that the company's tires for regular passenger cars were safer than other tires.

When the Federal Bureau of Investigation hunts kidnappers, it tries to find everyone who is in any way accessory to the kidnapping. The Federal Trade Commission, similarly, has attempted to some degree to bring into the picture those who are accessory to misrepresentation in advertising. They have, for instance, issued desist orders to many of the advertising agencies that prepare the advertising campaigns for the manufacturers. Though these desist orders have included many small and unimportant advertising agencies, they have included also the largest and most prominent agencies.

Also, practically all the newspapers and popular journals have participated in dissemination of false advertisements. These include publications which range from the Gannett publications at one extreme to the *Journal of the American Medical Association* at the other. Although the *Journal of the American Medical Association* claims that it does not carry advertisements which have not been checked and found to be true, it has for years carried advertisements of Philip Morris cigarettes. In earlier years, the Philip Morris Company had claimed that these cigarettes cured irritated throats and in later years claimed that they produced less irritation in the throat than other cigarettes. As proof of their truth, these advertisements cited the opinions and experiments of physicians many, if not all, of whom had received payment for their statements. Competing tobacco companies employed other physicians, who performed experiments and gave testimony which conflicted with the testimony in the *Journal of the American Medical Association*. The Philip Morris Company made a grant of $10,000 to St. Louis University to test these propositions. The medical school insisted on complete freedom in its methods of testing and in making its report. The report was that no accurate method of testing throat irritation or of testing the effect of the substances in question had been devised and that conflicting claims of experimenters were all bunk. The Philip Morris Company gave no publicity to that report, but their advertisements continued to appear in the *Journal of the American Medical Association*.

I do not want to take the time to go into similar detail in regard to other types of violations of law, but I shall describe a few incidents involving violations of the National Labor Relations Law. This law was enacted first in 1933 and in more developed form in 1935. It stated that collective bargaining had proved to be a desirable policy and prohibited employers from interfering with the efforts of employees to organize unions for purposes of collective bargaining. A violation of this law was declared to be an unfair labor practice. Decisions have been made against forty-three of the seventy large corporations, or 60 per cent, with a total of 149 decisions. Of these forty-three corporations, 72 per cent are recidivists, or repeaters; thirty-nine used interference, restraint, and coercion; thirty-three discriminated against union members; thirty-four organized company unions; thirteen used labor spies; and five used violence. Violence has been confined largely to the steel and automobile industries. One steel corporation from 1933 to 1937 purchased 143 gas guns, while the police department of Chicago purchased in the same years only thirteen; the steel corporation also purchased 6,714 gas shells and grenades, while the Chicago police department purchased only 757. The corporations customarily argue that they purchase this military equipment merely to protect themselves against the violence of the unions. Doubtless the equipment is used for protective purposes, but it is also used on some occasions for aggression. I wish to report one decision of the National Labor Relations Board concerning the Ford Motor Company. Henry Ford is reported to have said in 1937, "We'll never recognize the United Automobile Workers Union or any other union." The Ford Corporation organized a service department, under the supervision of Harry Bennett, an expugilist, and staffed it with 600 members equipped with guns and blackjacks. Frank Murphy, at the time Governor of Michigan and previously mayor of Detroit, said, regarding this service department, "Henry Ford employs some of the worst gangsters in our city."

In 1937 the United Automobile Workers Union was attempting to organize the employees in the River Rouge plant of the Ford Motor Company. A public announcement was made that the organizers would distribute literature at this plant at a specified time. Reporters and others gathered in advance. When a reporter asked a guard what they were going to do when the organizers arrived, the guard replied, "We are going to throw them to hell out of here." The organizers arrived, went with their literature up onto an overhead pass into one of the entrances. There they were informed that they were trespassing on private property. According to many witnesses they turned quietly and started away. As they were leaving, they were attacked by the service staff. They were beaten, knocked down, and kicked. Witnesses described this as a "terrific beating" and as "unbelievably brutal." The beating not only occurred on the overhead pass but was continued into the public highway. One man's back was broken and another's skull fractured. The cameras of reporters, who were taking pictures of the affray, were seized by the guards and the films destroyed. A reporter who was taking a picture from the highway was observed by a guard, who shouted, "Smash that camera!" The reporter jumped into the automobile of another reporter, and they were chased by the guards at a speed of 80 miles an hour through the streets of Detroit until they could secure refuge in a police station. According to prearranged plans, women organizers arrived later to distribute literature. As they alighted from the streetcar at the entrance to the plant, they were attacked by the guards and pushed back into the cars. One woman was knocked down and kicked. While these assaults were being committed, city policemen were present but did not interfere; the director of the service department was also present.

I wish next to give a few illustrations of embezzlement and violation of trust by officers of corporations. Seiberling organized the Goodyear Rubber Company and was its manager for many years. Because of financial difficulties in the corporation, he lost control of it in 1921. His successors found that Seiberling was short nearly $4,000,000 in his account with the company; that is, he had embezzled that amount from the company. The suits which were brought resulted in a settlement by which Seiberling agreed to reimburse the company. He not only did this but also secured credit from Ohio financiers and started the Seiberling Rubber Company, which has been quite successful.

President Sloan, Mr. Raskob, and other officers of General Motors developed a plan to pay bonuses to the officers and directors of General Motors. Under this plan, President Sloan secured a total payment from the corporation of $20,000,000 between 1923 and 1928. When suits were started in later years, these excessive payments prior to 1930 were not included in the suits because of the statute of limitations. The court held, however, that these officers had appropriated by fraudulent methods of calculating their bonuses approximately $4,000,000 and ordered them to repay this amount to the corporation.

George Washington Hill and other officers of the American Tobacco Company were criticized and sued for appropriating corporate funds for their enormous salaries and bonuses. One of these suits was to be tried before Judge Manton in the federal court in New York City. Shortly before the trial, Judge Manton suggested to the attorney for the American Tobacco Company that he needed to borrow $250,000. The attorney mentioned this to the assistant to the president of the American Tobacco Company, who mentioned it to Lord and Thomas, the advertising firm for the company, and Lord and Thomas lent Judge Manton the $250,000. Judge Manton decided the case in favor of the American Tobacco Company. Probably his decision was correct, but he was convicted of receiving a bribe, the attorney for the company was disbarred from practice in federal courts, and the assistant to the president, who made the arrangements, was promoted immediately after the decision to the position of vice president, where he was entitled to a bonus. In another suit, the American Tobacco Company paid from its own treasury $260,000 to the complainant, $320,000 to its law firm, and made other payments to bring the total for fixing this case to approximately a million dollars. A court later ordered the officers, against whom the suit was brought, to reimburse the corporation for these payments.

Finally, I wish to discuss the violation of the antitrust laws. Restraint of trade was prohibited by the Sherman Antitrust Act of 1890 and by several subsequent laws, as well as by the laws of most of the states. Decisions that such laws were violated have been made against sixty of the seventy large corporations in 307 cases. Three motion-picture corporations stand at the top of the list for restraint of trade with twenty-two, twenty-one, and twenty-one decisions, respectively. Thus, 86 per cent of the seventy corporations have decisions against them for restraint of trade, and 73 per cent of the corporations with such decisions are recidivists. Although no decisions have been made against the other ten corporations, other evidence indicates that probably every one of them has, in fact, violated these laws. These decisions tend to corroborate the statement made by Walter Lippmann: "Competition has survived only where men have been unable to abolish it." Not law but expediency and practicability have determined the limits of restraint of trade. Big Business does not like competition, and it makes careful arrangements to reduce it and even eliminate it. In certain industries, the negotiations among large corporations to avoid competition are very similar to international diplomacy, except that they are more successful.

For competition these businessmen have substituted private collectivism. They meet together and determine what the prices shall be and how much shall be produced; they also regulate other aspects of the economic process. This is best illustrated by the trade associations, although it is not limited to them. These trade associations not only fix prices and limit production, but also they have set up systems of courts with penalties for violation of their regulations. Their system of justice applies both to their own members, in which case they have a semblance of democracy, and also to nonmembers, in which case they resemble dictatorship and racketeering. Among ninety-two trade associations investigated in 1935 to 1939, twenty-eight had facilities for investigating or snooping on their members, eleven had provisions for fining those who violated regulations, and eighteen had provisions for boycotting the offenders.

Although businessmen often complain that the antitrust law is so vague that they cannot determine whether they are violating the law or not, a very large proportion of the decisions against these seventy corporations are for making agreements to have uniform prices; that is, not to compete as to prices. This practice is clearly in violation of the antitrust law, and no one at all acquainted with its provisions and with the decisions made under it could have the least doubt that such behavior is illegal. Also, many of the agreements limit production. Businessmen have insisted for at least seventy-five years on limiting production in order to keep prices from falling. Though many people have regarded as ridiculous the agricultural policy of killing little pigs, it is in principle the policy which industrial corporations have been using for many generations, long before it was ever applied in agriculture.

What significance do these violations of the antitrust law have? The economic system, as described by the classical economists, was a system of free competition and *laissez faire*, or free enterprise, as we call it today. Free competition was the regulator of the economic system. The laws of supply and demand, operating under free competition, determined prices, profits, the flow of capital, the distribution of labor, and other economic phenomena. When profits in an industry were high, other businessmen rushed into that industry in the hope of securing similar profits. This resulted in an increase in the supply of commodities, which produced a reduction in prices, and this in turn reduced profits. Thus, the excessive profits were eliminated, the prices were reduced, and the public had a larger supply of the commodity. Through this regulation by free competition, according to the classical economists, Divine Providence produced the greatest welfare of the entire society. Free competition was, to be sure, a harsh regulator. Cut-throat practices were general, and in the achievement of the welfare of the total society weaker establishments were often ruined.

Because free competition regulated the economic system, governmental regulation was unnecessary. The economic system of the classical economists developed primarily because business revolted against the governmental regulations of the feudal period, which were not adapted to the changing conditions of the eighteenth century. Government kept out of business after this system was established, except as it enforced contracts, protected the public against larceny and fraud, and enforced the principles of free competition by the common-law prohibition of restraint of trade.

During the last century this economic and political system has changed. The changes have resulted principally from the efforts of businessmen. If the word "subversive" refers to efforts to make fundamental changes in a social system, the business leaders are the most subversive influence in the United States. These business leaders have acted as individuals or in small groups, seeking preferential advantages for themselves. The primary loyalty of the businessman has been to profits, and he has willingly sacrificed the general and abstract principles of free competition and free enterprise in circumstances that promised a pecuniary advantage. Moreover, he has been in a position of power and has been able to secure these preferential advantages. Although businessmen had no intention of modifying the economic and political system, they have produced this result. The restriction of the principle of free competition has been demonstrated by the practically universal policy of restraint of trade among large corporations.

The restriction of free enterprise has also come principally from businessmen. Free enterprise means, of course, freedom from governmental regulation and governmental interference. Although businessmen have been vociferous as to the virtues of free enterprise and have, in general, insisted that government keep its hands out of and off business, businessmen above all others have put pressure on the government to interfere in business. They have not done this *en masse*, but as individuals or as small groups endeavoring to secure advantages for themselves. These efforts of businessmen to expand the governmental regulations of business are numerous and have a wide range. One of the best illustrations is the early and continued pressure of business concerns to secure tariffs to protect them from foreign competition. Many statutes have been enacted as the result of pressure from particular business interests to protect one industry against competition from another, as illustrated by the tax on oleomargarine. Another illustration is the fair trade laws of the federal and state governments, which prohibit retail dealers from cutting prices on trademarked articles. The federal fair trade law was enacted in 1937. The bill was presented by Senator Tydings, as a rider to a District of Columbia appropriations bill, where it could not be discussed on its merits. The bill was prepared by the law partner of the Senator, and this law partner was the attorney for the National Association of Retail Druggists. The bill was supported by many national associations of manufacturers and dealers, who were opposed to the competitive principle and to free enterprise. The bill was opposed by the Department of Justice and the Federal Trade Commission, which have been attempting to preserve the principle of free competition and free enterprise.

In fact, the interests of businessmen have changed, to a considerable extent, from efficiency in production to efficiency in public manipulation, including manipulation of the government for the attainment of preferential advantages. This attention to governmental favors has tended to produce two results: First, it has tended to pauperize business in the sense in which charity tends to pauperize poor people; second, it has tended to corrupt government. But the most significant result of the violations of the antitrust laws by large business concerns is that these have made our system of free competition and free enterprise unworkable. We no longer have competition as a regulator of economic processes; we have not substituted efficient governmental regulation. We cannot go back to competition. We must go forward to some new system—perhaps communism, perhaps cooperativism, perhaps much more complete governmental regulation than we now have. I don't know what lies ahead of us and am not particularly concerned, but I do know that what was a fairly efficient system has been destroyed by the illegal behavior of big business.

Furthermore, the businessmen have practically destroyed our system of patents by the same procedures. The system of patents was authorized in our Constitution to promote the development of science and the arts. The patent system has become one of the principal methods of promoting monopoly. Not one patent in a hundred pays even the costs of registration. Patents are important for business establishments primarily because they can be used to eliminate or regulate competitors. This is illustrated by the variation in the extent to which corporations apply for patents and bring suits for infringement of patents. In industries such as steel, very few patents are secured and very few patent-infringement suits initiated, because establishments in this country are protected from competition by the heavy capital investment. On the other hand, in industries such as the chemical industry and the manufacture of electrical equipment, new competitors can start with a very small investment. The large companies protect themselves against competition by taking out patents on every possible modification of procedure, bringing suits on every possible pretext, and granting licenses to use patents only with a highly regimented and bureaucratic control. The patent is important principally because it is a weapon for fighting competitors. This can be seen in the practice of some of the small concerns, where widespread monopoly is not threatened. The Miniature Golf Corporation secured a patent on its vacant-lot recreation and filed scores of suits against anyone who used this method without a paid license from them. The Good Humor Corporation engaged in patent litigation for more than a decade with the Popsicle Company and other manufacturers of ice-cream bars to determine which firm had invented this contribution to science and the arts. Similarly, the Maiden-form Brassiere Company and the Snug-Fit Foundations, Inc., were before the courts for many years regarding their patented designs, each charging the other with infringement.

The general conclusion from this study of the seventy large corporations is that the ideal businessman and the large corporation *are* very much like the professional thief:

First, their violations of law are frequent and continued. As stated previously, 97 per cent of the large corporations are recidivists.

Second, illegal behavior by the corporations is much more prevalent than the prosecutions indicate. In other words, only a fraction of the violations of law by a particular corporation result in prosecution, and only a fraction of the corporations which violate the law are prosecuted. In general, a few corporations are prosecuted for behavior which is industry-wide.

Third, the businessman who violates laws regulating business does not lose status among his business associates. . . . Leonor F. Loree, chairman, of the Kansas City Southern, knowing that his company was about to purchase stock of another railway, went into the market privately and secretly purchased shares of this stock in advance of his corporation, and then, when the price of the stock increased, sold it at the higher price, making a profit of $150,000. This profit, of course, was made at the expense of the corporation of which he was chairman, and he could make the profit because as an officer he knew the plans of the corporation. The courts, however, determined that this profit was fraudulent and ordered Mr. Loree to reimburse the corporation for the violation of his trust. Shortly after this decision became generally known, Mr. Loree was elected president of the New York Chamber of Commerce, perhaps in admiration of his cleverness.

Fourth, businessmen feel and express contempt for legislators, bureaucrats, courts, "snoopers," and other governmental officials and for the law, as such. In this respect, also, they are akin to the professional thieves, who feel and express contempt for police, prosecutors, and judges. Both professional thieves and corporations feel contempt for government because government interferes with their behavior.

Businessmen, being like professional thieves in these four respects, are participants in organized crime. Their violations of law are not identical and haphazard, but they have definite policies of restraint of trade, of unfair labor practices, of fraud and misrepresentation.

Businessmen differ from professional thieves principally in their greater interest in status and respectability. They think of themselves as honest men, not as criminals, whereas professional thieves, when they speak honestly, admit they are thieves. The businessman does regard himself as a lawbreaker, but he thinks the laws are wrong or at least that they should not restrict him, although they may well restrict others. He does not think of himself as a criminal, because he does not conform to the popular stereotype of the criminal. This popular stereotype is always taken from the lower socioeconomic class.

I have attempted to demonstrate that businessmen violate the law with great frequency, using what may be called the methods of organized crime. I have attempted in another place to demonstrate that these violations of law are really crimes. If these conclusions are correct, it is very clear that the criminal behavior of businessmen cannot be explained by poverty, in the usual sense, or by bad housing or lack of recreational facilities or feeblemindedness or emotional instability. Business leaders are capable, emotionally balanced, and in no sense pathological. We have no reason to think that General Motors has an inferiority complex or that the Aluminum Company of America has a frustration-aggression complex or that U.S. Steel has an Oedipus complex or that the Armour Company has a death wish or that the DuPonts desire to return to the womb. The assumption that an offender must have some such pathological distortion of the intellect or the emotions seems to me absurd, and if it is absurd regarding the crimes of businessmen, it is equally absurd regarding the crimes of persons in the lower economic class.

# 5

# CRIMINOLOGICAL THEORIES OF VIOLATIONS
# OF WARTIME REGULATIONS

*Marshall B. Clinard*

Within recent years there have been a number of papers which have attempted to reformulate criminological theory so as to include not only violations of the customary criminal law but violations of the white-collar type, where the measures taken are generally either civil or administrative in character.[1] White-collar crime has not been integrated into criminological theory in part because its scientific implications have not as yet been fully recognized. This is indicated by the fact that practically no research is now being done in this field. There is also an element of doubt upon the part of some as to whether such behavior actually is criminal. Moreover, there is possibly some hesitancy of otherwise scientific writers to examine the behavior of business concerns since this involves certain values of the economic system which are partially in the mores of our day and should not be questioned.

This paper is a description of violations of the price and rationing regulations issued by the Office of Price Administration.[2] The interest is primarily in the violations by wholesaler and manufacturing concerns and

Reprinted from *American Sociological Review*, 11 (June, 1946), pp. 258–270, by permission of The American Sociological Association.

retailers, not those by consumers, or persons stealing or counterfeiting ration currency.

Since the establishment of the OPA in February, 1942, nearly 600 price and rent regulations and almost twenty ration orders have been issued. The prices of over 8,000,000 articles are regulated by this agency. Many of these regulations and orders act as controls over the behavior of almost every consumer in the United States, and almost every person engaged in business activity is governed by one or more of the specific trade regulations. This means that the regulations exercised control over 130,000,000 people, including the owners of several million rental dwellings and 2,000,000 business establishments, of which 380,000 are preretail establishments (wholesale and manufacturing), and the balance retail, including 600,000 food stores and 250,000 gas stations.

These new controls over business were the most drastic ever issued in this country, even though businessmen have long been under some regulation and have been subject to government reports. Moreover, in a nation which has long been characterized by widespread disrespect for law, one had to contend with such factors as previous business practices which were legal before the enactment of the OPA, a shortage of supplies and poor distribution, a bitter attack on the OPA by special interests, hostility of businessmen toward wartime regulations which they often tended to regard as New Deal measures, and discussions among themselves and in trade journals which might tend to reinforce this hostility. One also had to contend with the reluctance of certain legislative groups to give sufficient financial support to the agency for enforcement.

The public has overwhelmingly supported these controls, as shown by all surveys that have been made, the proportion favoring price control ranging from 80 to 97 per cent.[3] Other evidence that public opinion has been in favor of the OPA is the fact that the courts in 1944, for example, decided 96 per cent of all litigation, both civil and criminal, in favor of the OPA. Further indication of public support is indicated by the active assistance of volunteer price panel members and assistants who at a single time have numbered as many as 200,000. Even businessmen support the government price-control program, as was indicated in a 1945 survey of 434 wholesalers in fifteen cities where only one out of four thought the government was doing a poor job in controlling prices in general, and one out of three thought that it was doing a poor job in their own type of business.

The majority of these regulations and controls have been in effect for over three years and during this time have received extensive explanation, wide publicity, and wide newspaper coverage of prosecutions. Appeals have been made for the price-control program based not only on the intellectual reasons for the existence of the regulations as inflationary controls, but also frequent appeals to patriotism as a basis for compliance, which ordinarily cannot be used to enforce law in peacetime. Members of most concerns involved had a member of the immediate family in the armed service. Studies of profits of concerns and their own statements on opinion surveys indicate the majority of them made either equal profits or actually greater profits than they made before the war and that many of the concerns involved in OPA violations were in excellent financial condition. On one national opinion survey, approximately one-half of the food wholesalers reported they were making satisfactory profits. Examining the push and pull of these two sets of factors, however, one would anticipate that the positive-factors might sufficiently counterbalance the negative factors so that one might not have expected quite the extensive violations of these wartime laws as actually occurred.

There has been much discussion as to whether these violations actually constitute crimes, since in only a small number of cases is the issue of willfulness raised and in even fewer cases is a criminal sanction sought. Sutherland has correctly indicated that the essential nature of a crime is not willfulness or even that a penalty has been imposed, but rather that the unlawful act is punishable.[4] The crucial issue is the existence of a violation which may be followed by some sort of penalty. Hall, similarly, has advanced the thesis that the distinction between crimes and torts, and between the customary use of the term "penal" as opposed to "non-penal," is artificial and not logical theoretically.[5]

Following this reasoning, for criminological purposes, nearly all violations of OPA regulations constitute criminal acts. Violations of the Emergency Price Control Act are defined by Congress as socially injurious and a violation of law. If, in the administrator's judgment, there is unlawful behavior he may institute court action or settle the claim. Whether the violation is handled by civil or criminal measures is the agency's decision. The only specific limitation is that the criminal sanction can be employed only in cases where the violation was willful. There is, moreover, no implication that the criminal sanction will be employed in all willful cases, thus leaving the use of alternative measures entirely to the agency. In Canada, on the other hand, where formal action is deemed necessary in the event of a price or rationing violation, all offenses are dealt with by criminal prosecution rather than by civil action, with the exception of a few cases where the license was canceled. Moreover, five states and some seventy-five municipalities in the United States have enacted black-market statutes and ordinances making violations of the OPA's law a misdemeanor punishable by fine or imprisonment.

An examination of cases, including rationing cases under the Second War Powers Act, would show that in thousands of cases involving almost identical violations sometimes administrative measures have been used, at other times civil, and occasionally criminal prosecution. Cases involving evasive violation where there is definite willfulness, such as falsification of records and inventories in rationing cases, are handled sometimes with an injunction suit, with a suspension order proceeding, and at other times with criminal prosecution. In certain cases, it is felt that the purposes of enforcement would be better accomplished if an injunction were used, even if the violators' actions were willful. Experience has shown that it would be impossible to use the criminal sanction in all cases where it might be used, since criminal cases require considerable preparation, and the capacity of the Justice Department and the federal courts to handle a large number of cases is limited.

A study of rationing-suspension order cases under the Second War Powers Act, which are entirely administrative in character, would show that many of these cases, largely gasoline, involved violations which were both extensive and evasive. All rationing-suspension order proceedings involve wrongful diversion of strategic supplies. It is not necessary for the OPA to prove willfulness, but proof of willfulness may affect the length of the suspension order. Of particular interest in this connection is the Supreme Court decision in the *Steuart Oil Company* case which upheld the validity of the suspension order.[6] The company maintained that it was a penalty and that the OPA did not have authority to use such penal action. It was the contention of the OPA that it was not a penalty, but withdrawal of an allocation. The Supreme Court said that the suspension order was remedial but conceded that it was an injury to the person suspended. From the point of view of criminology, however, it seems that the suspension of a business for periods ranging up to the duration of the war is a penalty regardless of the legal interpretation.

Another OPA sanction—the injunction—is used in cases where there has been a violation or to prevent future violations. It has been the major sanction, and many of the most serious cases have been handled with an injunction simply because it is quickly and more easily obtained. It is particularly useful where there is a failure to keep records, which is in many instances a way of avoiding the detection of such violations as side payments. In fact, several courts have objected to the use of injunctions to hide willful violations that might be punished by other measures. It is also of interest that characteristically both a treble damage and an injunction suit for past violations are used, the treble damage suit being definitely penal in nature.[7] The court has held that an injunction does not follow in all cases where a violation is shown. Thus, in the *Hecht* decision,[8] where the defendant had made every effort to comply with every regulation even though there were extensive violations, the Supreme Court stated that the court did not have to grant an injunction as it would not accomplish any further purpose. Injunctions have been and continue to be granted, however, in cases where willfulness is not raised.

Two other sanctions that the OPA has available for price violations are the license suspension and treble damage suits. The former is considered suitable for serious cases and is used only after at least two violations have occurred over a period of time. A formal license warning notice must be issued after the first violation and there must be another violation before this sanction can be instituted. The treble damage actions are of three types: the administrator's own, for violations in the course of trade or business; the administrator's consumer suit, where the administrator sues to recover for a violation at the retail level; and the suit where the consumer himself sues for treble damages. The first two suits are considered penalties, whereas the latter suit is considered largely as a remedial action, particularly if the recovery is only for the single amount of the overcharge. The penal nature of the treble damage action is recognized by the fact that no money paid to the United States Treasury as the result of a treble damage settlement or suit brought by the OPA can be deducted as a business expense under the Internal Revenue statutes. In the case of all treble damage suits, Congress has differentiated between violations which were not willful and negligent and those which were willful or negligent. If the defendant is able to establish the former contention only the single amount of the overcharge can be awarded. The defendants have not been very successful in establishing this so-called "Chandler defense," since the courts usually do not consider it if the OPA later shows that there were side payments, falsification of records, tie-in sales, and other violations demonstrating willfulness, or if there was an absence of proper records, failure to instruct employees, and other similar violations.

While it has already been indicated that the question of willfulness is not essential in order to judge violations of price and rationing regulations as crimes, it might be well to point out the extent to which violations are intentional. Since most regulations have been in existence for several years and have been accompanied by wide publicity both in newspapers and trade journals, it appears unlikely that many businessmen, after the initial period of price control, could be ignorant of the provisions of the regulations. Estimates by a group of wholesalers in 1945 show that one-third believe most violations to be deliberate. More specifically, 10 per cent felt that everyone violates deliberately, 14 per cent estimated over three-fourths, and another 11 per cent felt that more than half of all violations were deliberate. Perhaps an even more empiric index is the extent of evasive violations such as falsification of records, including those in connection with side payments. When a violation is evasive, there can be no question but that it was intentional and that the person was familiar with the provisions of the regulation, as well as the nature of the investigations, at least enough to try to cover it up. Of the group of food wholesalers interviewed in 1945, more than one out of five thought this to be a frequent practice. Moreover, 57 per cent of the wholesalers interviewed in this same survey stated that enforcement efforts are effective in securing compliance, which would indicate awareness that many of the actions described here are intentional violations of the law.

Even when violations of government regulations are intentional, many businessmen, while they may regard themselves as law violators, do not consider that they have committed crimes and, therefore, could not possibly be treated as criminals.[9] Some representative statements of this view are the following by food wholesalers.

> "I sure wouldn't think any man should go to jail for a price violation." (*Grocery dealer in St. Louis*)

> "I don't think jail is good. That's for hoodlums and gangsters." (*Grocery dealer in Chicago*)

> "It would be a terrible thing to go to jail, pretty hard for a man's family, too. Jail is for racketeers. That is just another day for them but very different for a legitimate businessman." (*Fruit and vegetable dealer in Los Angeles*)

While this attitude was by no means unanimous among businessmen, as shall be indicated shortly, this view is general enough to make it obvious that among many of the business group the mores are not involved in such violations. Such laws are *malum in prohibita,* and the force of public opinion has as yet not been sufficiently developed to make such laws *malum in se.* In fact, the great extension of modern criminal law has come in those fields where there is no unanimity that such behavior is criminal either on the part of the general public or the important classes or groups involved.[10] Actually, the injury to society is far greater in many of these crimes, which may involve several hundred thousand dollars, and the example of disobedience of law is far more flagrant than in the case of most ordinary crimes. Perhaps, as Fuller has suggested, enforcement of the law and education as to its purpose will bring about greater consensus in society that crimes committed by businessmen are as much crimes as those of the lower socioeconomic class.[11]

In connection with the criminal prosecution of business violators, against whom the OPA probably brought more cases than other agencies, the attitude of the courts is most important. While the opinions of the courts are undoubtedly the reflection, in part, of public opinion in general or the opinion of certain social classes, at the same time the attitude of the community toward certain laws, particularly new laws, is influenced by the attitudes of its judges.

Most OPA criminal cases were generally well selected before being turned over to the Department of Justice for prosecution, as is indicated by the fact that convictions were secured in over 94 per cent of the cases in 1944. Yet the sentences imposed on OPA violators after conviction were in general extremely mild. For example, during the year

1944, of 3,486 persons who were convicted of violations of the price and rationing regulations, only 27 per cent received imprisonment or imprisonment and fine. Of the total convicted, 46 per cent received only a fine, and 28 per cent were placed on probation. During the fiscal year ending June 30, 1944, only 470 persons were received in federal prisons for price and rationing violations. Of the total group, ninety-seven received a sentence of a year and a day or more. Only eighty, or 17 per cent, were sentenced for price violations, of whom one-fourth received sentences of a year and a day or more. One reason for the light sentences was the attitude toward offenses of this type, but still another reason was the fact that the offenders seldom had a criminal past or other circumstances which would warrant a severe sentence. As the judges on occasion stated from the bench, they "would not make criminals of reputable businessmen."

The length of some of the sentences imposed on businessmen who had willfully violated the OPA regulations and in so doing made large sums of money were almost trivial compared with the sentences given offenders who violated ordinary criminal laws pertaining to property offenses. Of course, because of their reputation, a short sentence may be as effective with businessmen as a long sentence with lower-class criminals. Likewise, a large fine may be more difficult for an ordinary criminal to pay than for a businessman, and the former might conceivably prefer a short imprisonment to such a large fine.

While this method of dealing lightly with violators who had no previous record may be in line with advanced criminological theory, it raises certain questions, also from the view of society in general, that the penalty of imprisonment which was the most feared by businessmen according to their own statements was so seldom invoked as a deterrent for others. A survey of wholesalers' opinions revealed that they considered imprisonment a far more effective penalty than any other OPA action, including fines.[12] In fact, some 65 per cent made this statement. Some of the comments are illustrative of this view. About jail sentences they had this to say:

> "Jail is the only way: nobody wants to go to jail."

> "Everybody gets panicky at the thought of a jail sentence."

> "A jail sentence is dishonorable, it jeopardizes the reputation."

> "It [jail] spoils the offender's reputation and frightens the other fellow."

With regard to fines and other money penalties businessmen[13] had this to say:

> "They don't hurt anybody."

"They're never missed."

"People are making enough money nowadays to pay a fine easily. It just comes out of the profits like a tax."

"The violators violate again, so they must not care about paying a fine."

Total violations of OPA regulations by business concerns, both retail and preretail, have undoubtedly been a large figure. Violations of this type uncovered during 1944 alone numbered 338,029. This figure represents violations by approximately 11 per cent of the business firms of the United States.[14] The number of food dealers found in violation was 197,799, including 62,382 meat and dairy dealers. Apparel concerns found in violation were 17,848.

The estimates of about one out of ten business concerns in violation is undoubtedly too low because not all concerns were investigated. Of those investigated, approximately 57 per cent were found in violation, which, if applied to the total concerns, would be approximately 1,100,000 violations. On the other hand, this figure may be too high because the fields of business selected for investigation by the OPA are likely to be those in which there is more evidence of violations than in the case of other business fields[15] and there may also be some duplication of business concerns in the above figures.

During 1944 there were actions in 322,131 cases of violation. Warnings or other informal adjustments, including dismissals, were issued in 271,874 cases, or 84 per cent of the total cases. In the remaining 16 per cent of the cases, administrative action was used in 26,763, and court proceedings were instituted in 28,902 cases. Of these 55,666 cases, representing some 3 per cent of all business establishments, there were 10,504 (or 19 per cent) settlements and 2,745 (or 5 per cent) suits in treble damage cases against manufacturers and wholesalers; 6,171 (or 11 per cent) settlements and 1,373 (or 2 per cent) suits in treble damage cases against retailers; 10,088 (or 18 per cent) rationing-suspension order proceedings; 13,074 (or 23 per cent) injunction suits; and 145 (or 0.3 per cent) license-suspension suits for price violation. There were 2,223 (or 4 per cent) suits brought by the OPA under local legislation, and criminal prosecution was begun by the Department of Justice against 3,934 defendants, or 7 per cent. In 1914, $21,000,000 was collected in treble damages and fines.

The extensive volume of these cases can well be illustrated by comparing the number of enforcement cases of the OPA with those of other federal agencies. Without doubt, the OPA has brought more actions, including more court actions, against violations by businessmen than all other federal regulatory agencies, with exception of the Bureau of Internal Revenue, in the past ten years.[16] In fact, approximately one-half of all civil cases in the federal courts during 1945 were for violations of the price, rationing, and rent regulations, and nearly one-sixth of all criminal cases were for such violations. The Securities and Exchange Commission during the ten-year period 1934 to 1944 annually brought court action in only an average of eighty-five cases, fifty-one being civil actions and thirty-four (232 defendants) being criminal prosecutions by the Department of Justice. The Federal Trade Commission in 1944 dealt with about 900 violations of which less than 5 per cent involved court proceedings. The Food and Drug Administration annually brings action against some 3,500 concerns, filing injunctions in about thirty-five cases and using criminal prosecution in 380 cases, 91 per cent of the convictions resulting in fines only. In view of the limited enforcement staffs of these agencies, these figures probably do not show the extent of the actual violations. The OPA has a much larger enforcement staff, consisting of over 3,000 investigators and 600 attorneys in addition to volunteer assistance; and while inadequate to investigate several million business concerns, it has had a staff much larger than any agency other than the Bureau of Internal Revenue. The large number of court actions brought by the OPA was also a reflection of a stronger policy in dealing with business violators, a policy that was in part made possible by the fact that it was a wartime measure.

Analysis of several thousand price violations indicates that they may be classified into a number of different types[17] in much the same fashion as violations of the customary criminal law can be classified. Because of the extent of these wartime controls there is latitude for considerable variation in types of violation. The absence of previous experience with wartime regulatory measures restricting the economic life of the entire population indicates that patterns of violation have developed in a relatively short period of time. The majority of violations of price regulations are by the seller rather than the buyer. This is so because under the provisions of the Price Act a buyer for ultimate consumption may not ordinarily be a violator and from the further fact that the initiation of a price violation ordinarily originates with the seller. Violations by a seller fall into three main types: (1) direct violations in the form of straight overceiling charges, including overceiling purchases in the course of trade or business when such practices are forbidden; (2) indirect overceiling sales, involving the use of evasive practices to cover up the violation and to hamper detection of a violation; and (3) violations of record keeping and reporting requirements. Price violations by the buyer, in those regulations where such behavior is prohibited, are derivative in the sense that the seller ordinarily initiates the transaction. Even assuming the purchaser to be a willing buyer, if he pays a price above ceiling he must pass on the overcharge, provided he is not the ultimate consumer and does not wish to sell at a loss.

It is unnecessary here to give examples of the first type of price violation. Examples of the second, or evasive, type of price violation are numerous. One practice is to secure cash payments in addition to those which appear to have been made in the regular transaction at ceiling price. These "cash-on-the-side" payments are not recorded or reported and are oftentimes difficult to ascertain unless the buyer "talks." The invoice is made out at the correct ceiling price and from all that appears on the buyer's records no price violation took place. Often charges are made for goods which are not actually delivered. Often side payments are treated as a loan, which the seller in fact never repays to the buyer. In other instances it has been disclosed that side payments are received and covered up by the seller's placing one of his employees on the payroll of the buyer to draw a salary for services which are actually not rendered. There have also been instances wherein sellers have refused to supply certain commodities to purchasers unless they agree to buy stock in corporations in which the sellers are interested. The stock, of course, is worth only a small fraction of the price paid. Those buyers who become stockholders are plentifully supplied with wanted commodities at what appear to be ceiling prices. Still other side payments are in the form of patronage dividends. Extra charges also consist of gifts, tips, bets, bribes, kickbacks, and fictitious quantity estimates. Occasionally, charges are made for delivery or other services not formerly performed or previously performed free, charges made for fictitious legal or brokerage services, and pyramiding of mark-ups through dummy jobbing concerns.

A further evasive method devised to violate price ceilings is through the use of "tying" agreements. This practice consists of making the purchase of an unwanted commodity the condition of purchasing a desired commodity. The seller will refuse to deliver the desired commodity unless a purchase is made of a product for which there is little or no demand or upon which his margin of profit is high. Tie-in sales may be direct in their nature in that the purchaser is specifically given to understand that he cannot purchase the wanted commodity without purchasing the less desirable product, or they may be indirect in those instances where word is passed out to the purchasers that it is desirable that they order and purchase products other than those wanted.

Still another type of evasive practice is that involving quantity or quality violations. In such cases, there may be a short weight of the commodity. Other cases may involve grading violations, such as upgrading, failure to grade, or improper labeling of the commodity. In some instances there is reduction in size or inferior composition or construction, such as the use of substitute materials of inferior grade, blending with less expensive grades of materials, reduction in amount of materials used, and decrease in length of guarantee periods.

The third type of price violation, record keeping and reporting violations, does not in and of itself directly affect prices charged or received and is, therefore, classified as nonsubstantive. This type may be further broken down into those which involve failure to comply with records and reports requirements and those where there is neglect or intentional refusal to comply in order to cover up substantive violations. The purpose of these requirements is to aid the public and the OPA in enforcing price ceilings. Violations of these requirements permit the seller to evade detection of his substantive violations and hamper the public and the OPA in their enforcement activity, since it is often difficult, if not impossible, to tell what the seller's maximum prices are unless proper records are kept. Investigations indicated that the records of many businessmen have not been adequately kept even in peacetime. It was largely for this reason, as well as because of the prevalence of evasive violations, that base period pricing methods such as the General Maximum Price Regulation (GMPR) were very difficult to enforce.

There are indications from both studies[18] as well as reports in trade journals that nearly all types of these violations were frequent, although there were considerable variations from industry to industry. A national survey of wholesalers' opinions in 1945 as to the frequency of various types of violations indicates that the most frequent violation, in their opinions, involves tie-in sales; second in importance was selling above ceiling; third was falsification of records, including side payments; and fourth was quality deterioration. The frequency of tie-in sales, exceeding even selling above ceiling, is probably indicative of enforcement activities which drove under cover the more open violations. Evasive violations are more difficult to detect. Of the wholesalers interviewed, 38 per cent contended that tie-in sales were frequent, 27 per cent thought that selling above the ceiling and quality deterioration were frequent, and 22 per cent felt that falsification of records, including side payments, was frequent. Many wholesalers, however, contended that tie-in sales and quality deterioration were more or less accepted practices in the trade during peacetime.

Actually, a large proportion of OPA violations are various types of fraud, as they constitute devices for obtaining money fraudulently by misrepresentation. Certainly the delivery of goods in which the quantity or quality is not the same as the invoice specifies is fraud. Even if the OPA statute were not in existence, in many cases where lack of good faith in the contract action could be shown, there would be the right of recovery under existing state and federal laws.

This wide-scale violation of law requires some systematic explanation. If this behavior is called criminal, as we have contended it is, such an assumption discounts traditional ways of explaining crime on the basis of such factors as heredity, feeblemindedness, poverty, race, immigrant background, and probably psychopathology.[19] Moreover, studies which show that offenders are generally youthful are invalidated by the fact that offenders of this type are generally middle-aged. In fact, it may be assumed that such offenders are likely to be more highly educated and usually married, so that neither the fact of education nor marital status would appear to be important in connection with such criminal behavior.

Assuming that such behavior does require explanation, several theories may be advanced. It is not the intention of this paper to make definitive answers, but rather to suggest several lines along which further research can be carried out. The most obvious approach is situational. The assumption may be made that businessmen are alike as to personality and what makes one individual violate rather than another is the pressure of profits and supplies.[20] Fortunately, there is one study which suggests tentative answers to this question.[21] As the result of interviews with several hundred producers and distributors of consumer goods, it was concluded that sales and profits were not related to price violations. On the other hand, an acute shortage of supplies, irrespective of sales, contributed to price increases.

Another situational approach is the contention that large firms comply with the regulations and small ones do not. It has been suggested that large firms consider their reputations, are aware of their social responsibility, employ so many persons that violations could not be kept secret, are more frequently and thoroughly investigated by the OPA, and have large staffs to become familiar with and explain all regulations. Small firms, on the other hand, are thought to have little reputation to lose, do not keep adequate records and, therefore, could make frequent cash transactions which might involve violations, and are not as frequently investigated by the OPA. However, a survey which sought an answer to this particular problem among Chicago business concerns, while inconclusive, suggests that size of the firm alone does not appear to be an important factor in violation.[22]

A second type of explanation is one which may be termed "differential association." This explanation implies that the person has acquired certain antisocial norms through association with other persons which predispose him to violate the law. Such differential association may be of three types. It may involve persons who have had a previous criminal record or those who have been associated with persons previously engaged in criminal behavior. Other differential association may rather have been confined to acquiring knowledge and experience with unethical or illegal practices of the business world. Sutherland has suggested[23] this as a general explanation of white-collar crime and, more specifically with reference to OPA violations, has stated his opinion that

> In general, this seems to me to be fairly well in accord with the theory of differential association; not that the local grocer or the customers of

that grocer violate these regulations by associating with gangsters, but that they violate the regulations (1) because they had, prior to enactment of the law, contact with such patterns of behavior and a whole organized set of customs and attitudes in connections with them, and these continue to operate after the law declares the practices to be illegal; (2) because specific stimulations and techniques are acquired from others who are violating the law.[24]

A third type, closely related to the previous one, is the development of sufficient negative attitudes toward the OPA and government regulations which are so reinforced by similar beliefs of other businessmen that the regulations are not considered legal.

The first type of explanation, which traces price and rationing violations to association with previous criminal norms, is rather widely held, particularly among the general public. The idea became widespread due primarily to an unfortunate publicity policy in the early days of the OPA which was intended to awaken the public to the dangers of price and rationing violations. Statements were issued that organized racketeers were engaging in black-market activities and there were a large number of articles in magazines and newspapers, as well as motion-picture shorts, which described such cases. The term "black market" itself became almost synonymous with organized criminal behavior, whereas actually it should be used more correctly to describe any price or rationing violation, whether in legitimate channels such as ordinary business or otherwise. Even businessmen appear to have been influenced by such stories, for in interviews they will occasionally refer to a mysterious black market. Actually, with the exception of one type of activity, there appears to be little evidence of any organized criminal underworld engaging in price and rationing violations. The one exception has been the theft and counterfeiting of ration currency, which has been largely a field of professional criminal activities. Contrary to popular impression, a relatively small percentage of offenders have any previous criminal record, exclusive of traffic violations, although it is possible that many businessmen may have engaged in white-collar criminality for which they were never prosecuted. If we consider price and rationing cases involving criminal prosecution, which probably represents a sample of more flagrant OPA cases, we find that only about one out of ten are reported to have had a criminal record. Of those imprisoned, which may or may not represent the more serious cases, although they are more likely to have been more serious than those who were fined or placed on probation, only about one-third have criminal records. Those prosecuted criminally are chiefly violators of the rationing orders, including dealers who violated the rationing provisions, as well as those who stole or counterfeited the currency. A relatively few persons have been prosecuted for price violations, and the proportion who have a criminal record is even smaller. It is likely that one reason why such a small number of persons have been prosecuted for price violations is the fact that few persons of this type have previous records of criminal behavior and this makes the possibility of conviction difficult.

The fact that businessmen have been associated with others who have engaged in customary business practices of a quasi-legal character appears to have some partial validity in explaining violations. In some businesses, such as gasoline and apparel, it appears to be more important than in others. Such an etiology appears to be typical of certain marginal operators who have come into the business to make a quick fortune.

While it is likely that many cases of violations of price and rationing regulations, where there has been continuous and intimate association with differential norms, can be satisfactorily explained by a theory of differential association, there are several limitations in such a general theory. Without going into great detail, a few major objections may be briefly stated. Such a theory does not adequately explain why some individuals who are familiar with the techniques of violation, as well as frequently associating with persons similarly familiar, do not engage in such practices. It is doubtful whether any businessman can participate in a given line of business for any length of time without acquiring a rather complete knowledge of practices in his trade. Certainly besides talking with competitors and customers, he has ample opportunity to read of techniques of violations in newspapers and trade journals. It is difficult to explain, therefore, the fact that thousands of business concerns, even in those commodities where one expects less group ethics, appear to comply fully with the regulations.

A second criticism of differential association is that the behavior is accounted for in terms of a single role that the person is playing, which in this case is the role of a businessman. The same individual may play a variety of roles, and behavior such as that involved in violating a law may well involve an integration of several different roles. In the case of offenders of the lower socioeconomic classes, there is likely to be more similarity in the behavior of different roles in which the person is engaged. When we are considering offenders of the white-collar class, there is probably less similarity in the several roles. Still another difficulty in differential association as an explanation of behavior is that the theory tends to overemphasize the more recent developments in the individual's personality rather than the importance of early behavior patterns in the formation of personality. These early behavior patterns may well be important enough to counterbalance later association with criminal or antisocial conduct.

Finally, the theory of differential association does not allow sufficiently either for independent invention of a complex technique or the need for acquiring any technique for violations which are extraordinarily simple. The validity of this particular statement should, of course, be ascertained by further detailed study of a number of cases. Certainly many OPA violations involving similar techniques have appeared in isolated areas. In many violations only a single person appears to have been involved. There appears, for example, to be ample evidence that rather complex evasive violations of rent regulations have appeared in relatively isolated areas, and they appear to have been independently devised, since there is ordinarily little association among landlords.

Some suggest the explanation that compliance is determined by whether attitudes of businessmen are in favor of, intermediate, or hostile to price control, the origin of which may be sought in their attitudes toward past profit trends, profit expectations, price expectations, long-range considerations, fairness of the regulations, and certain misconceptions which they may have had about the purposes of price control. A survey of Chicago manufacturers and distributors shows that when attitudes toward price control are cooperative there are less violations, and when they are hostile there are likely to be more violations.[25] The results, however, indicate that attitudes do not appear to be the cause of violations, but rather only one element of a larger situation.

It appears that there can be no single explanation of OPA violations. They are not the result entirely of either supply and demand, profits, or types of businesses. Likewise, violations do not appear to arise to any degree out of contacts with criminal conduct norms or result from negative attitudes toward the OPA. Differential association with deviant norms of the business world explains some cases, but not all; nor does it explain why some engage in such activity, while others do not although they have had extensive differential association. These cases of white-collar crime offer an excellent opportunity for examining the life organization of violators to ascertain what set of factors make up for conformist and nonconformist behavior. Why is it that some businessmen who have been presented with numerous opportunities to violate do not do so, while others with only limited opportunity have readily violated?

Solution of this problem appears to be in the individual's personality pattern. There may be psychogenic characteristics, general reaction patterns, such as disregard for the rights of society in general, or basic attitudes, such as attitudes toward law and the importance of reputation which were developed in the early years of life. These may be a result of the different integration of the several roles which each individual plays in society. As Sellin states, "An important function of etiological research is, therefore, the formulation of generalizations which permit us to differentiate the violator from the conformist, in terms of personality structure or growth process."[26] Besides Sellin, Sutherland[27] and Dunham and Lindesmith[28] have suggested that this is one of the most crucial issues in criminological research. Perhaps before finding an answer to this question, criminology will have to await further understanding of the nature of personality differences. The life histories of violators of wartime regulations offer us an opportunity for some preliminary conclusions as to why persons do not conform to law.

# Notes

1. See Edwin H. Sutherland, "White-Collar Criminality," *American Sociological Review*, 5 (February, 1940), pp. 1–12; "Is 'White Collar Crime' Crime?" *American Sociological Review*, 10 (April, 1945), pp. 132–139; and "Crime and Business," *Annals of the American Academy of Political and Social Science*, 217 (September, 1940), pp. 112–118; see also articles by Jerome Hall: "Interrelationships of Criminal Law and Torts," *Columbia Law Review*, 43 (September, 1943), pp. 753–779, 967–1001; "Prolegomena to a Science of Criminal Law," *University of Pennsylvania Law Review*, 89 (March, 1941), pp. 549–580; and "Criminal Attempts—A Study of Foundations of Criminal Liability," *Yale Law Journal*, 49 (March, 1940), pp. 789–840.

2. See further Marshall B. Clinard, *The Black Market: A Study of White Collar Crime* (New York: Holt, 1952).

3. See *Public Opinion on Control of Prices, Wages, Salaries during War and Reconversion* (Chicago: National Opinion Research Center, 1947).

4. Sutherland, "Is 'White Collar Crime' Crime?" *op. cit.*

5. Hall, "Interrelationships of Criminal Law and Torts," *op. cit.*, pp. 999–1000.

6. *Steuart & Brother, Inc.* v. *Bowles*, 322 U.S. 398 (1944).

7. An injunction without treble damage action to recover the amount of the overcharge is analogous to serving a hypothetical injunction on a bank robber as he comes out of a bank with his loot, to cease and desist from further violations but allowing him to retain the stolen money. Many injunctions, which prevent the possibility of future violations, are similar in nature to serving an injunction on a bank robber as he goes into a bank to rob it.

8. *The Hecht Company* v. *Bowles*, 321 U.S. 321 (1944).

9. To reason that because some businessmen do not approve of the law and, therefore, see no reason for obeying it seems little more valid, from the standpoint of protection of society in general, than to state that because some criminals of the lower socioeconomic class do not approve of some criminal laws they can violate them.

10. Richard C. Fuller, "Morals and the Criminal Law," *Journal of Criminal Law and Criminology*, 32 (March–April, 1942), pp. 624–630.

11. *Ibid.*, pp. 629–630.

12. This opinion is further supported by a survey of OPA district enforcement attorneys who reported that where sentences were generally adequate observance of regulations was best, and a converse situation existed where sentences were inadequate.

13. In 1945, approximately 2,500 housewives were asked what the government should do with retailers who intentionally violated price regulations. Slightly over one-third thought they should be fined, 8 per cent would give them a jail sentence, 21 per cent would make them close their stores for a while, and 12 per cent would make them pay up to three times the amount of the overcharge (Office of Price Administration, *Opinion Briefs*, No. 7, April 12, 1945).

14. This includes only cases of the OPA Enforcement Department. Many cases were investigated by price panel volunteers of the Price Department who took actions without referring cases to the Enforcement Department. Rent cases, and practically all consumer cases, are not included in any of the figures. Also not included are the large number of private treble damage suits brought by consumers against dealers nor the majority of prosecutions under local legislation of which there are no accurate records. In New York City alone in 1944 there were 18,875 prosecutions of retailers by the New York Department of Markets, and the sheriff's office in the three-month period during January 15, 1945, prosecuted over 4,000 wholesale dealers.

15. For other estimates of the extent of violations of OPA regulations, see George Katona, *Price Control and Business* (Bloomington, Ind.: Principia Press, 1945), pp. 47–48, 57–58.

16. The estimated annual grand total of all OPA violations, including consumer, rent, retail and preretail, which is approximately 900,000, is equal to the total crimes known to the police, which is also approximately 900,000 (*Uniform Crime Reports*, vol. 15, no. 1).

17. For other classifications of white-collar crime, see Sutherland, "White Collar Criminality," *op. cit.*, p. 2; *Tenth Annual Report of the Securities and Exchange Commission*, pp. 143–146; and *1944 Report of the Federal Trade Commission*, pp. 38–44, 57–59.

18. For example, see Katona, *op. cit.*, and various studies of the Bureau of Labor Statistics.

19. See Sutherland, "White Collar Criminality," *op. cit.*

20. In this regard, a comment by a nonprocessing meat slaughter is interesting: "When I sold to black markets I couldn't sleep at night; since I comply [summer, 1943] I can't sleep at night because I am losing money" (Katona, *op. cit.*, p. 47).

21. Katona, *op. cit.*, p. 141.

22. *Ibid.*, p. 129.

23. Sutherland, "Crime and Business," *op. cit.*, p. 116.

24. Extract from letter to author, August 6, 1943. Reviewing Harry Lever and Joseph Young, *Wartime Racketeers*, Sutherland has suggested that if enforcement of new regulations could be started promptly, the development of many new patterns of violation could be prevented (*American Sociological Review*, 10 [December, 1945], pp. 817–818).

25. Katona, *op. cit.*, p. 170.

26. Thorsten Sellin, *Culture Conflict and Crime* (New York: Social Science Research Council, 1938), p. 40.

27. Edwin H. Sutherland, "The Relation between Personal Traits and Associational Patterns," in Walter Reckless, ed., *The Etiology of Delinquent and Criminal Behavior* (New York: Social Science Research Council, 1943), pp. 131–138.

28. Alfred R. Lindesmith and H. Warren Dunham, "Some Principles of Criminal Typology," *Social Forces*, 19 (March, 1941), pp. 307–314.

# 6

# WHY BUSINESSMEN VIOLATE THE LAW

*Robert E. Lane*

Recent interest in the problem of illegality in the business community focuses attention on the considerable scope of this phenomenon. Thus, in 1951, the National Labor Relations Board formally ordered 115 firms to cease certain illegal practices and informally adjusted another 796 cases. In the same year, the Federal Trade Commission investigated 869 cases of deceptive practices and found business management guilty of illegal practices in 107; the Wage and Hour and Public Contracts Divisions of the Department of Labor inspected 33,479 establishments and found 56 per cent of them guilty of violations of the law. Of course, these represent only a fraction of the cases of violation, but they insistently raise the question: Why do some businessmen violate these laws while others do not? This paper is an attempt to contribute to the growing evidence and doctrine in this field. It is based upon the following sources of information: (1) interviews with top management in twenty-five New England industrial firms; (2) interviews with seven leaders of govern-

Reprinted by special permission of the *Journal of Criminal Law, Criminology and Police Science*, Copyright © 1953 by Northwestern University School of Law, Vol. 44, No. 2.

mental regulatory agencies; (3) analysis of the cases reported in Federal Trade Commission Decisions, Decisions and Orders of the National Labor Board, court cases arising from these decisions, and court cases arising from the action of the Wage and Hour and Public Contracts Divisions of the Department of Labor; and (4) a statistical study of the violations of trade practice and labor regulation in the New England shoe industry.

## THE ECONOMICS OF VIOLATION

Most businessmen and most responsible government officers, at least from the sample interviewed, believe that businessmen run afoul of the law for economic reasons—they want to "make a fast buck."[1] They are led to transgress because, to be specific, if they adopt an advertising campaign which overstates the facts or if they reclassify their personnel into "management" positions (and so avoid the overtime provisions of the Fair Labor Standards Act) or if they get rid of the union (and the union demands), their profit positions will reflect these acts in a favorable manner. Thus, the manufacturers of bottling crowns may agree, illegally, to fix a scale of prices and standardize their products,[2] a jewelry manufacturer illegally fixes his discount rates so as to attract chain retail outlets without regard to savings in costs to himself,[3] a Southern textile manufacturer fires two employees seeking to establish a union and therefore a union wage scale.[4]

But there are two difficulties with this simple economic explanation. In the first place, it probably doesn't cover some of the cases where management-union relations are involved. Thus, an important life insurance company finds itself involved with the National Labor Relations Board because one of its supervisors fired a man who had testified previously before the board—Why? Not because of economic reasons, but because he had made the supervisor "look silly" in public.[5] The other objection to the economic motivation argument is that it really doesn't explain much. Two films with similar opportunities for breaking the law may show different records: One violates the law, another does not. Why? The simple explanation based on economic motivation does not tell us.

Pushing the economic argument further, however, perhaps "need" rather than "opportunity for gain" is the criterion, perhaps if one firm is in a more desperate situation than the other it will be more likely to violate the law. Or it may be that a firm which will abide by the law when it is prosperous, will violate the law when it is necessitous.[6]

To support this point of view, take the case of a small tool-making organization in Chicago in the immediate postwar period. In 1947, when this firm employed twenty-five men and enjoyed relative prosperity, the

International Association of Machinists organized the firm and, in an election, won the contractual right to represent the employees in collective bargaining. By 1949, however, the number of employees had fallen to twelve and the firm was in a serious position. It was at this point that the president of the firm decided to terminate his relationship with the union and, illegally, refused to bargain collectively with them. Although he later explained that this was because he doubted whether the union really represented the men, his letter to the union explaining his position gave other reasons. The union wage scale, he said, is "responsible for placing our industry in a noncompetitive and embarrassing position. . . . During the period of the time in question, our company sustained very substantial losses. . . . It is for these reasons that we were obliged to terminate our contract and withdrew recognition from the union."[7]

### Table 1. Growth and Decline of Labor Relations and Trade Practices Violators and Nonviolators in the Shoe Industry over a 10- to 15-Year Period (1936–1950)*

|  | Declined | No change | Grew |
|---|---|---|---|
| Labor relations violators | 26% | 31% | 42% |
| Misrepresentation cases | 50 | 38 | 12 |
| Nonviolators | 31 | 31 | 38 |

*Only those for whom there are data over a 10-year period are here recorded.

Is a weak or declining financial position a common cause for violation? In order to find out the relationships between the fortunes of a firm and violation of the law, a study of the 275 shoe-manufacturing firms in New England was made and the records of violators of labor relations laws and trade practices laws analyzed. Since data on the financial position of these firms were difficult to obtain, reported number of employees was used to indicate growth and decline. The record is as indicated in Tables 1 and 2.[8]

By concentrating on the time period immediately before and after the violation a more precise analysis is possible:

### Table 2. Relation of Growth and Decline of Firms to Violation of Labor Relations and Trade Practices (Misrepresentation) Laws

|  | Year of violation and preceding year | | | Year subsequent to violation and following year | | |
|---|---|---|---|---|---|---|
|  | De-clined | No change | In-creased | De-clined | No change | In-creased |
| Labor relations violators | 7% | 73% | 20% | 25% | 50% | 25% |
| Misrepresentation cases | 25 | 75 | 0 | 33 | 67 | 0 |

These data reveal several new aspects of the problem. For one thing, it seems apparent that violation of the trade practices laws is more closely associated with economic decline than is violation of the labor relations laws. Violation of these trade practices laws is associated with decline before the event, thus suggesting a causal relationship, and declines after the violation, thus suggesting that apprehension and conviction are in some way punishing to a firm. On the other hand, the complex of events which caused the Chicago tool firm to break the law seems not to have been prevalent in the New England shoe industry; here economic condition was more or less irrelevant to the question of lawbreaking.

Comparing the figures for trade practice violation and labor relations violation suggests that the two laws do not appear in the same light to industrialists busy in the processes of making the nation's goods. For one thing, the labor relations laws are more recent than the trade practice laws and most of the violations (63 per cent) occurred during the first three and a half years of the National Labor Relations Act. Thus, it might be said that violation of recent laws is less related to the prosperity of the firms than violation of the older established (and accepted) laws of the land. But there is another factor. The trade practices acts prohibit false advertising, misleading statements, price fixing, illegal discounts, and related activities. These activities, however, seem closer to the normally accepted ideas of "immoral" or "criminal" behavior and their prohibition corresponds more to the businessman's concept of right and wrong. Therefore, in addition to the recentness of the law, there is a question of the closeness of the law to the moral judgments of the businessmen who must live within it.

There are other pieces of evidence which tend to support the idea that the more profitable firms do not violate some laws as easily and quickly as the less profitable firms. An analysis of the incidence of violation of the Fair Labor Standards Act (1938) shows that there is a higher proportion of violations in those industries suffering relative hard times. This seems also to be true of price-control legislation, for during the war "compliance with price-control regulations seemed to be more satisfactory among firms with rising profits than among those with declining profits."[9]

## AMBIGUITY, IGNORANCE, AND DIFFICULTY OF COMPLIANCE

In one sense, it is quite unfair to management to consider a large number of the recorded cases as willful violations of the law. In all those instances culminating in "leading cases," no one knows the law until the court has spoken. While these cases may indicate a propensity to probe the law's farthest limits, this is quite different from deliberate infraction of a known law. Following this line of reasoning, the officers of the Cement Institute can hardly be thought guilty of illegal motives when they administered their basing-point system, since the system had a history of several decades during which it was regarded as legal.[10] Nor can the management of the Mt. Clemens Pottery Company be considered guilty of illegal design for not paying overtime on the basis of portal to portal rates, since, until the court spoke, their employees were not thought to be on the job until they were, in fact, working for the company.[11]

But setting aside questions of ambiguous law (and all laws are ambiguous at their margins), may there not be many cases where management runs afoul of the law simply because they are not aware of its stated provisions? Can management be expected to keep posted on the variety of national and state laws affecting their operations? Some businessmen interviewed thought that this was a serious matter, and among the executives of the smaller companies a few expressed regret over the amount of time necessary to preserve a law-abiding record. The agencies themselves show a recognition of this problem of unintentional violation, the Federal Trade Commission stating:

> It is manifestly difficult to draft a statement of policy on a broad base which does not afford an evasive device to the willful violator while seeking to avoid unduly harsh treatment of the unintentional or casual violator.[12]

Even more specific is the Wages and Hours and Public Contracts Divisions statement:

> The divisions knew that violators generally may be placed in three groups—those who willfully violate; those who are in violation because of ignorance of the law; and those who inadvertently misapply provisions of the law, thus committing technical violations.[13]

On the other hand, most of the businessmen interviewed felt that, with the help of their lawyers and the loose-leaf services, they were unlikely to be caught off-guard by unfamiliar legislation. Speaking of violators of the price-control laws during the war, one observer says, "It appears unlikely that, after the initial period, many businessmen are ignorant of the provisions" of the law.[14] There are no data on this question of "knowledge of the law among violators," but we will attempt to get at it indirectly.

The hypothesis that ignorance and improper technical advice is a primary cause of violation is often supported by the belief that the smaller firms violate the law out of proportion to their numbers in the business population, partly, at least, because of poor legal counsel. A majority of the administrators polled expressed this point of view, and it is common among businessmen. But, if we examine the data of the 275 shoe manu-facturers in New England (Table 3), this does not seem to be true, at least in this instance.

Table 3. *Per Cent of Violations of Labor Relations and Trade Practices Legislation in New England Shoe Industry by Size (1933-1949)*

| Size groups (no. of employees) | Per cent of size group who violated NLRA and LMRA | Per cent of size group who violated trade practice laws (misrepresentation) |
|---|---|---|
| Under 100 | 10.9 | 0 |
| 101 – 500 | 14.0 | 5.9 |
| 501 –1,000 | 30.0 | 15.0 |
| Over 1,000 | 11.1 | 33.3 |

Since there can be little doubt that large companies hire more and better counsel and are better informed on the law, these data should go far toward supporting those managers who claimed that "ignorance" of the law was not a legitimate excuse.[15]

Could one, then, reverse the principle—larger companies with superior legal resources violate more, proportionately, than smaller companies? No, this is not possible either, as Table 4 and Figure 1, showing the relation-ship of size to wage and hour violations, will quickly prove.
There is, in fact, no clear relationship between size (and therefore legal services) and violation; each industry and each regulatory measure has a pattern of its own.[16]
If, as seems likely, management only very rarely violates the law be-cause of ignorance of the relevant provisions, perhaps it is possible that management sometimes finds it genuinely difficult to comply with the known law. Does the law require the impossible? Of the twenty-five man-ufacturers consulted, none believed that he was handicapped by inade-quate records, personnel, or facilities in complying with labor relations

Table 4. *Per Cent of Inspected Establishments in Three Industries in Substantial Violation of Fair Labor Standards Act and Public Contracts Act by Size of Establishment (1948)*

| Number of employees | Per cent of inspected establishments in substantial violation | | |
|---|---|---|---|
| | Textile and related products | Leather and leather goods | Metals and metal products |
| 4– 7 | 42 | 42 | 52 |
| 8– 19 | 31 | 38 | 43 |
| 20– 49 | 34 | 32 | 37 |
| 50– 99 | 25 | 34 | 33 |
| 100–199 | 28 | 38 | 29 |
| 200–499 | 26 | 42 | 27 |
| 500 or more | 35 | 30 | 22 |

legislation. These laws were opposed on other grounds. One, the smallest (thirty-five employees) felt that he was handicapped in obeying the wages and hours laws because he did not have the necessary records. None of the others felt that this was a burden. Although a number felt that trade practices regulation created hazards for them, only two felt that they were handicapped in complying because of lack of data or cost records. Of course, it is expensive to maintain such records, but often, as it turns out, these records have multiple uses and are only partly chargeable to government regulation.

On the basis of the above considerations, we may say that although ambiguous provisions of the law and factually contested situations often lead to "violation" (in a technical sense) ignorance of the law and incapacity to respond seem, in most cases, to be relatively unimportant causes of violation.

*Figure 1. Relation of Rate of Violation of Wage and Hour Laws (1948)
to Size of Establishment in Metal, Shoe, and Textile Industries*

*Per cent of inspected establishments in substantial violation of wages and hours laws
1948*

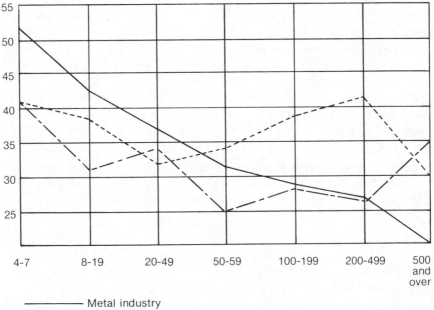

——————— Metal industry
- - - - - - - Leather (shoe) industry
- — - — - Textile industry

VIOLATORS AND THEIR ASSOCIATES

Edwin H. Sutherland, a few years prior to his death, reformulated his theory of criminal behavior in order to explain violations of the law by business management. Central among his ideas is the doctrine of "differential association,"[17] a doctrine which holds that men who associate with those who favor violation (or at least are indifferent to it) more than with those who oppose any violation of law, are more likely themselves to be violators. It is based on the common view that men pick up most of their opinions and orientations from their associates, and it has much evidence to support it in the criminological literature. Note, however, that there are two parts to the doctrine: (1) positive association with men contemptuous of the law and (2) isolation from those who uphold legality, even if the laws in question are distasteful.

But what kind of evidence of business friendship groups and their opinions on legality is available? Not much; the evidence must be circumstantial.

One approach might be to examine the policies of different firms in the same "interest groups," on the grounds that common association of directors and ranking officers might create a common pattern.[18] One clue to the rate of violation of the labor relations laws is given by the proportions between representation cases and unfair labor practice cases, the fewer unfair labor practice cases per representation case, the more law-abiding the management. An analysis of the violation rates in the Mellon interest group, the du Pont interest group, the Cleveland interest group, and two firms associated with the Avery family (U.S. Gypsum and Montgomery Ward) shows that there is little common policy among the firms in each group. It doesn't appear that any common association (or even control) has an influence on attitudes toward the law. Incidentally, however, it is notable that the incidence of violation in the firms of these big business interests is markedly lower than the general rates for all business.

An analysis of the rates of violation of labor relations laws in the shoe industry gives some support to the differential association hypothesis. This may be found in the fact that in some shoe-manufacturing communities none of the shoe firms violates, whereas in other shoe-manufacturing communities almost half of the firms get into trouble with the law. There may be several reasons for this, but it seems fairly conclusive that one of the reasons is the difference in attitude toward the law, the government, and the morality of illegality. Table 5 shows how these rates of violation vary in eight New England communities. It would be interesting, in this respect, to examine in more detail the special ideological environment of a businessman operating in the "rugged individualist" city of Auburn,

Maine. It seems probable that a manager who lunched and played golf with other business managers of Auburn, Maine, would feel differently and behave differently from the manager who was surrounded by the businessmen of Brockton, Massachusetts. This point of view was supported indirectly by the managers interviewed, who generally agreed that they followed community patterns of behavior, in terms of wage scales, vacations, union recognition, and so forth.

Table 5. Per Cent of Firms Violating Labor Relations Laws
in Selected Communities

| Place | Number of shoe firms | Number of violating firms | Per cent of violating |
|---|---|---|---|
| Haverhill, Mass. | 28 | 2 | 7.0 |
| Lynn, Mass. | 27 | 1 | 3.7 |
| Brockton, Mass. | 17 | 0 | 0.0 |
| Boston, Mass. | 16 | 0 | 0.0 |
| Manchester, N.H. | 10 | 3 | 30.0 |
| Auburn, Me. | 9 | 4 | 44.4 |
| Lowell, Mass. | 8 | 3 | 37.5 |
| Cambridge, Mass. | 5 | 2 | 40.0 |

But the idea of differential association has two parts to it: association with men whose attitudes encourage violation and isolation from men whose attitudes discourage violation. Is there any evidence of such isolation? How could this be proved?

There is evidence of such isolation and, although it is not conclusive, it is worth looking at. In the first place, there is the question of reading matter, which ranges in attitude from temperate periodicals, such as *The Harvard Business Review* and *Fortune,* to some trade journals that serve to keep alive government-business hostility beyond the point of usefulness. It is possible for men to immerse themselves in a section of the press so hostile to government that violation of the law must seem most appropriate. By the same token, they may isolate themselves from journals which preserve a balance between criticism and neutral reporting. These choices, furthermore, extend to selection of luncheon clubs, radio programs, daily papers, and other vehicles for attitudes and ideas.

The problem of isolation from divergent points of views is much more serious in small towns than in large cities with their cosmopolitan press, diversified social life, and greater tolerance for heterodoxy. Big-city business management does, as a matter of fact, seem to accept restrictions of the law somewhat more readily than small-town management. This is not only a commonsense proposition, borne out by impressionistic observation of management in the twenty-five interviews, but it is also supported by our study of the shoe industry, as indicated by Table 6. Again, it must be true that there are many factors at work, but on the whole the results seem to confirm the differential association hypothesis.

## THE PERSONAL EXPERIENCES AND
## PERSONALITY OF VIOLATORS

Even when we have accounted for the financial needs of a firm and for the ambiguity or difficult requirements of the law, possible management ignorance with respect to the law, and social pressures, there still remains the personality and personal experiences of the individual managers. It is impossible and wrong to make of this matter a wholly fatalistic process whereby the situation of the firm, the incidence of the law, and the degree of social pressure combine to eliminate the power of decision among the firm's managers. We must include these more personal characteristics too, even though they are not readily accessible.

One of the defects of the fatalistic interpretation of business violation is that it impersonalizes business leadership. While in the larger corporations there may be a tendency toward impersonalization through frequent group consultation, the use of legal counsel, guidance of cost accountants, reliance on market reports, and so forth, the marginal figures of Ford, Girdler, Rand, Avery, Weir, and others suggest that, within the margin and without benefit of publicity, temperament and psychic factors are still important determinants of business policy. Among smaller firms this is even more certainly true.

Among the variety of personal characteristics and experiences two may be considered here as representative of the wide range of factors of this kind: (1) previous experience with regulation and (2) personal attitudes toward authority as expressed in the law. To take first the matter of previous experience with regulation, how may this affect business responses to new and additional measures?

One approach is to find out whether the experience of violation and conviction leads to further violation or leads to a more law-abiding pattern of behavior. Unlike the crime records, the records of business violation show that recidivism is infrequent; violation and apprehension is not the preface to future violation, it is likely to be the end of the matter.

### Table 6. Violators of Labor Relations and Fair Trade Laws by Size of Town

| Size town | Number of shoe firms | Number of violators (labor relations) | Per cent of violators (labor relations) | Number of violators (trade practice) | Per cent of violators (trade practice) |
|---|---|---|---|---|---|
| Under    5,000 | 20 | 0 | 0 | 2 | 10.0 |
| 5,000– 10,000 | 34 | 8 | 23.6 | 3 | 8.5 |
| 10,000– 25,000 | 46 | 9 | 26.5 | 2 | 4.3 |
| 25,000–100,000 | 87 | 10 | 11.5 | 2 | 2.3 |
| Over    100,000 | 76 | 8 | 10.4 | 2 | 2.6 |

Thus, out of 200 violators of the National Labor Relations Act between December, 1935, and August 21, 1947, only thirteen, or 6.5 per cent, were repeaters.[19] This pattern is also true of violators of the trade practice laws: There were 188 orders and stipulations in 1948 to 1949, but only four punitive orders indicating serious second offenders.[20]

Another method of showing the effect of previous regulation on the rate of violation is to examine the effect of some of the newer regulatory measures in industries that have always been under close public supervision. If it is true that experience of regulation teaches management how to keep within the law, what to expect, what kind of legal counsel to hire, and, perhaps, what to do to minimize the impact of the regulation, we should expect these regulated industries to have lower rates of violation under the newer measures. In fact, this does seem to be the situation, at least with respect to the wages and hours laws. While 7 per cent of all inspected establishments were in "serious" violation of the Fair Labor Standards Act in the fiscal year 1948, the averages of certain industries accustomed to other forms of government regulation were: alcoholic beverages, 2 per cent; heat, light, power, water, 2 per cent; drugs and medicines, 3 per cent.[21]

But men do not react solely on the basis of what they "know" from such experiences to be true. They also respond to their inward feelings, which sometimes transcend and override their knowledge. Among these feelings, the emotional responses to authority have been singled out for much discussion by psychologists and their associates, so that it begins to appear that this is a central feature of individual adjustment to society. At least for the discussion of men's responses to governmental regulation, attitudes toward authority might seem to be among the most important of all phases of emotional life.

For obvious reasons, this line of analysis cannot be pursued in any detail—it would require psychoanalytic case studies for satisfactory study —but a few fragments of information will suggest caution before we go out on this particular limb. One such piece of evidence comes from a study made of the violation pattern of seventy large corporations, where it was found that there was great consistency of behavior toward specific laws over long periods of time when the managing personnel changed several times over. It seemed to be the position of the firm, rather than any emotional qualities of its management, which led it to violate. The obverse of this situation was shown in the fact that there was no tendency to react against a wide range of laws, no evident general antiregulation animus, at any one time.[22]

This is evidently a general pattern. In our sample of 275 New England shoe manufacturers, there were forty-five violations of the labor laws, involving thirty-five firms, and twenty violations of the trade practice laws, involving fourteen firms. In addition, there were two firms engaged in court cases under the wages and hours laws. In no instance did a firm violate more than one law. There was no evidence of a consistently "anti-regulation" or "antigovernment" or "antiauthority" policy on the part of any firm or its management.

But caution along these lines does not mean rejection of the thesis. We know that men tolerate restrictive governmental authority in different degrees and express this difference in their decisions and behavior. When, for example, the National Labor Relations Board says of a firm, "the respondent, under the active personal leadership of its president, . . . frustrated its employees' organizational efforts by a campaign of willful unfair labor practices"[23] we infer that this firm is guided by a man who has invested much emotional energy into a joint attack upon unions and the law. Something other than economic forces and social pressure is here at work.

## REDUCING THE RATE OF VIOLATION

It is one thing to suggest the causes of violation; it is something else again to discover the cures. Nevertheless, it is curious, considering the talent and resources available both to the business community and the national government, that so little has been done to discover and promote such cures. Compared to the attention given to industrial relations, business-government relations have almost been ignored. This state of affairs is reflected in the limited nature of suggestions for reducing the rate of violation and minimizing business-government friction offered by businessmen and administrators.

When questioned on the most appropriate means of reducing friction and violation of the law, twenty-five managers interviewed on this problem suggested, in order of frequency, the following policies:

1. Stop the drift to socialism and the restriction of freedom.
2. Economize, cut the government payroll, balance the budget.
3. Increase governmental efficiency, pass Hoover recommendations, eliminate waste.
4. Increase government familiarity with business processes.
5. Cut controls to absolute minimum (allowing trade practice, or sweatshop, or antitrust controls only—or none).
6. Reduce uncertainty by stabilizing rules and regulations.
7. Recruit a better grade of government personnel and reduce turnover.
8. Increase morality and honesty in government-business relations.

Regrettably, these suggestions were rarely supported with specific data or an indication of how they might have reduced the rate of violations in the business community had they been applied earlier.

The seven highly placed administrators consulted on this general problem naturally turned toward other kinds of solutions. The principal suggestions might be summarized as follows:

1. The development of a more sympathetic attitude toward business problems on the part of administrators.

2. Enlargement of the educational program of government, attempting to convey information not only on the provisions of the law, but the reasons it was enacted and the goals it seeks to establish.

3. Establishment of greater consultative relationships with business, particularly with the key men in each industrial area.

4. Critical re-examination of administrative procedures to reduce duplication and unnecessary paper work.

5. Sympathetic liaison with the professions allied to business management—law, public relations, personnel, etc.

Both of these sets of "solutions" offer a useful agenda for consideration and discussion, but much remains to be done. In connection with this agenda, the preceding analysis of the causes of violation seems to indicate a more particular focus on certain kinds of situations and circumstances. These may be briefly outlined as follows:

1. While it is generally (but not universally) true that "economic" gain is necessary for violation to take place, marginal and declining firms are more likely to violate the law than prosperous firms. Any help the government can extend to these firms will, therefore, probably reduce the rate of violation.

2. Ambiguous laws lead to a higher rate of violation. In spite of occasional business opposition, therefore, it is desirable for responsible administrators to have authority to issue legally binding interpretations of the laws they administer, providing these are subject to adequate court review. Furthermore, administrators should weigh more heavily the effects of uncertainty in calculating whether or not to "stick their necks out."

3. Although it is rare that businessmen violate a law because they do not know of its provisions, the government could do much to improve the channels of information between management and the regulatory agencies. There is no reason that these should be monopolized by third parties or by the legal profession.

4. Since violation is a product, in part, of social pressure and community attitudes, government and business should jointly seek to build respect for law—even distasteful law enforced by a repugnant administration. Government cannot do this alone; business cannot do this without

a record of fair dealing by the government. It is a task for both elements of society. Further study would quickly reveal the communities where this is most urgent.

5. Government should approach each manager as a unique individual with a unique set of experiences, a personality different from all others, confronted by a problem which looms large, even though he be one of thousands in an official's lifetime. Only thus can the personal and individual nature of business decisions be understood and personal inclinations to violate be met and headed off by responsible government.

More could be said of a specific nature: Better business bureaus and local chambers of commerce could do much to stop violation at its source; governmental cease-and-desist orders could often be recast so as to give more attention to what is proscribed and less to proving guilt; trade journals could reconsider the effects of hostile expressions which may build circulation, but create a trade sentiment which breeds friction and violation; the impact of new laws could be lessened by a "dry-run" period of education and experimentation; and so forth. But, these suggestions, like those of the business community and those of the administrators, need further study and research.

What is clear from all this, however, is the need for both business and government to re-examine their relationship and to attempt to re-create a mutual respect which will facilitate their partnership in a democratic society.

## Notes

1. An exceptionally good statement of this position was contained in a letter to the author from Corwin Edwards, director of the Bureau of Industrial Economics of the Federal Trade Commission: "I think the economic explanation of violations of law is the principal one. Inadequate enforcement certainly carries a heavy responsibility, but by decreasing the risk it strengthens the economic incentive to violate. Though there are some cases where the law is difficult to obey, these seem to me to be relatively few as compared to those in which it is merely more profitable not to obey."

2. *Crown Manufacturers Assn. of America*, 45 F.T.C. 89 (1948).

3. *Kreisler Mnfg. Corp.*, 45 F.T.C. 136 (1948).

4. *Sellers Mnfg. Co. & Textile Workers Union of America, C.I.O.*, 92 NLRB 279 (1950).

5. *John Hancock Mutual Life Insur. Co. & Samuel Kohen*, 92 NLRB 122 (1950).

6. Violations of price control and rationing seems to be less related to financial need than to the opportunity to make more than "ordinary" profits. See Marshall B. Clinard, *The Black Market: A Study of White Collar Crime* (New York: Holt, 1952), pp. 313–326.

7. *Toolcraft Corp. & Die & Toolmakers Lodge 113, Intl. Assn. of Machinists*, 92 NLRB 655 (1950).

8. The data on growth and decline of shoe firms are taken from the roughly annual *Directory of New England Manufacturers* (Boston: George D. Hall Co., 1936–

1950). Data included information on (1) twenty-four violators of labor relations regulations; (2) ten violators of misrepresentation provisions of the trade practices laws; and (3) a control group of eighteen firms, selected at random, which violated neither law.

Since the National Labor Relations Act was most likely to be violated where there were union men in the shop, inquiry was made to ascertain the extent of unionism in the New England shoe industry. There were forty-seven nonviolating firms petitioning for elections during this period (1935–1950) and most other firms included a few union men. Thus the presence of union men was not a highly selective factors.

9. George Katona, *Prince Control and Business* (Bloomington, Ind.: Principia Press, 1946), p. 241.

10. See *F.T.C.* v. *Cement Institute*, 333 U.S. 683 (1948).

11. See *Anderson* v. *Mt. Clemens Pottery Co.*, 328 U.S. 680 (1946).

12. *Annual Report*, 1948, p. 116.

13. *Ibid.*, pp. 28–29.

14. Marshall B. Clinard, "Criminological Theories of Wartime Regulations," *American Sociological Review*, 11 (June, 1946), p. 262.

15. In interpreting these data, one caution should be considered. The large firm with more foremen is exposed to more opportunities for discriminatory firing under the labor relations law, misclassification under the wages and hours law, or other violations of labor laws. Similarly, if a firm has many products it is exposed to more possibilities for violating the fair competition laws. The force of this consideration is weakened, however, by (1) violations under some laws in some industries apparently decrease with size, and (2) analysis of the actual cases shows that they are relatively rarely the product of low-level decisions.

16. See Katona, *op. cit.*, p. 165; Clinard, *The Black Market, op. cit.*, p. 325. This discussion of ignorance, size, and violation, although inconclusive, opens up a wide and fertile field for inquiry. What organization of information is necessary to keep a firm within the law? What size firm can best support such technical advice and counsel? What can government do for the small businessman and how effective is the present effort? Do the trade associations perform valuable services in this area or, as some managers informed the author, do they merely repeat each other and the special looseleaf services (Prentice-Hall, Commerce Clearing House, etc.)? Information along these lines might assist enforcement procedures in a manner that policing could not approach.

17. Edwin H. Sutherland, *White Collar Crime* (New York: Dryden Press, 1949), p. 234.

18. The sources of information on "interest groups" were Temporary National Economic Committee, *The Distribution of Ownership in the 200 Largest Non-Financial Corporations* (Washington, D.C.: Government Printing Office, 1940), pp. 1514ff; and National Resources Committee, *The Structure of the American Economy, Part I, Basic Characteristics* (Washington, D.C.: Government Printing Office, 1939), p. 158.

19. Calculated from a random sample taken from National Labor Relations Board, *Table of Cases Decided*, vol. 1–74 (December 7, 1939, through August 21, 1947).

20. *Federal Trade Commission Decisions*, vol. 45 (July 1, 1948, to June 30, 1949).

21. Wage and Hour and Public Contracts Divisions, *Annual Report*, 1948, Table E, pp. 162–165.

22. Sutherland, *op. cit.*, p. 264.

23. *Salant & Salant, Inc. and Amalgamated Clothing Workers of America, CIO*, 92 NLRB 345 (1950).

# 7

# THE HEAVY ELECTRICAL EQUIPMENT
# ANTITRUST CASES OF 1961

*Gilbert Geis*

An inadvertent bit of humor by a defense attorney provided one of the major criminological motifs for "the most serious violations of the anti-trust laws since the time of their passage at the turn of the century."[1] The defendants, including several vice presidents of the General Electric Corporation and the Westinghouse Electric Corporation—the two largest companies in the heavy electrical equipment industry—stood somberly in a federal courtroom in Philadelphia on February 6, 1961. They were aptly described by a newspaper reporter as "middle-class men in Ivy League suits—typical businessmen in appearance, men who would never be taken for lawbreakers." Several were deacons or vestrymen of their churches. One was president of his local chamber of commerce; another, a hospital board member; another, chief fund raiser for the Community Chest; another, a bank director; another, director of the taxpayer's association; another, organizer of the local Little League.

The attorney for a General Electric executive attacked the government's demand for a jail sentence for his client, calling it "cold-blooded."

Reprinted from Marshall Clinard and Richard Quinney (eds.), *Criminal Behavior Systems* (New York: Holt, Rinehart and Winston, 1967), pp. 139–150. Copyright © 1967 by Holt, Rinehart and Winston, Inc. Reprinted by permission of Holt, Rinehart and Winston, Inc.

The lawyer insisted that government prosecutors did not understand what it would do to his client, "this fine man," to be put "behind bars" with "common criminals who have been convicted of embezzlement and other serious crimes."[2]

The difficulty of defense counsel in considering antitrust violations "serious crimes," crimes at least equivalent to embezzling, indicates in part why the 1961 prosecutions provide such fascinating material for criminological study. Edwin H. Sutherland, who originated the term "white-collar crime" to categorize offenders such as antitrust violators, had lamented that his pioneering work was handicapped by the absence of adequate case histories of corporate offenders. "No first-hand research from this point of view has ever been reported."[3] Sutherland noted, and, lacking such data, he proceeded to employ prosaic stories of derelictions by rather unimportant persons in small enterprises upon which to build an interpretative and theoretical structure for white-collar crime.

To explain corporate offenses and offenders, Sutherland had to rely primarily upon the criminal biographies of various large companies, as these were disclosed in the annals of trial courts and administrative agencies. In the absence of information about human offenders, the legal fiction of corporate humanity, a kind of economic anthropomorphism, found its way into criminological literature. Factual gaps were filled by shrewd guesses, definitional and semantic strategies, and a good deal of extrapolation. It was as if an attempt were being made to explain murder by reference only to the listed rap sheet offenses of a murderer and the life stories and identification data of several lesser offenders.[4]

Sutherland was writing, of course, before the antitrust violations in the heavy electrical equipment industry became part of the public record. Though much of the data regarding them is tantalizingly incomplete and unresponsive to fine points of criminological concern, the antitrust offenses nonetheless represent extraordinary case studies of white-collar crime, that designation which, according to Sutherland, applies to behavior by "a person of high socioeconomic status who violates the laws designed to regulate his occupational activities"[5] and "principally refers to business managers and executives."[6] In particular, the antitrust cases provide the researcher with a mass of raw data against which to test and to refine earlier hunches and hypotheses regarding white-collar crime.

## FACTS OF THE ANTITRUST VIOLATIONS

The most notable characteristic of the 1961 antitrust conspiracy was its willful and blatant nature. These were not complex acts only doubtfully in violation of a highly complicated statute. They were flagrant, criminal offenses, patently in contradiction to the letter and the spirit of the Sherman Antitrust Act of 1890, which forbade price-fixing arrangements as restraints upon free trade.[7]

The details of the conspiracy must be drawn together from diverse second-hand sources, because grand jury hearings upon which the criminal indictments were based were not made public. The decision to keep the records closed was reached on the ground that the traditional secrecy of grand jury proceedings took precedence over public interest in obtaining information about the conspiracy and over the interest of different purchasers in acquiring background data upon which to base civil suits against the offending corporations for allegedly fraudulent sales.[8]

The federal government had initiated the grand jury probes in mid-1959, apparently after receiving complaints from officials of the Tennessee Valley Authority concerning identical bids they were getting from manufacturers of highly technical electrical equipment, even though the bids were submitted in sealed envelopes.[9] Four grand juries were ultimately convened and subpoenaed 196 persons, some of whom obviously revealed the intimate details of the price-fixing procedures. A package of twenty indictments was handed down, involving forty-five individual defendants and twenty-nine corporations. Almost all of the corporate defendants pleaded guilty; the company officials tended to enter pleas of *nolo contendere* (no contest) which, in this case, might reasonably be taken to indicate that they did not see much likelihood of escaping conviction.

The pleas negated the necessity for a public trial and for public knowledge of the precise machinations involved in the offenses. At the sentencing hearing, fines amounting to $1,924,500 were levied against the defendants, $1,787,000 falling upon the corporations and $137,000 upon different individuals. The major fines were set against General Electric ($437,500) and Westinghouse ($372,500). Much more eye-catching were the jail terms of thirty days imposed upon seven defendants, four of whom were vice presidents; two, division managers; and one, a sales manager.

The defendants sentenced to jail were handled essentially the same as other offenders with similar dispositions. They were handcuffed in pairs in the back seat of an automobile on their way to the Montgomery County Jail in Norristown, Pennsylvania, fingerprinted on entry, and dressed in the standard blue denim uniforms. During their stay, they were described as "model prisoners," and several were transferred to the prison farm. The remainder, working an eight-hour day for 30 cents, earned recognition from the warden as "the most intelligent prisoners" he had had during the year on a project concerned with organizing prison records. None of the seven men had visitors during the Wednesday and Saturday periods reserved for visiting; all indicated a desire not to be seen by their families or friends.

Good behavior earned the men a five-day reduction in their sentence.

Toward the end of the year, the remaining defendants, who had been placed on probation, were released from that status, despite the strong protests of government officials. The judge, the same man who had imposed the original sentences, explained his action by noting that he "didn't think that this was the type of offense that probation lent itself readily to or was designed for." Supervision was seen as meaningless for men with such clean past records and such little likelihood of recidivism, particularly since the probation office was already "clogged to the gunwales"[10] with cases.

The major economic consequences to the corporations arose from civil suits for treble damages filed against them as provided in the antitrust laws. The original fines were, of course, negligible: For General Electric, a half-million dollar loss was no more unsettling than a $3 parking fine would be to a man with an income of $175,000 a year. Throughout the early stages of negotiations over the damage suits, General Electric maintained that it would resist such actions on grounds which are noteworthy as an indication of the source and the content of the rationale that underlay the self-justification of individual participants in the price-fixing conspiracy:

> We believe that the purchasers of electrical apparatus have received fair value by any reasonable standard. The prices which they have paid during the past years were appropriate to value received and reasonable as compared with the general trends of prices in the economy, the price trends for materials, salaries, and wages. The foresight of the electrical utilities and the design and manufacturing skills of companies such as General Electric have kept electricity one of today's greatest bargains.[11]

By 1962, General Electric was granting that settlements totaling between $45 and $50 million would have to be arranged to satisfy claimants. Municipalities and other purchasers of heavy electrical equipment were taking the period of lowest prices, when they assumed the price-rigging was least effective, using these prices as "legitimate," and calculating higher payments as products of the price conspiracy. The initial General Electric estimate soon proved untenable. A mid-1964 calculation showed that 90 per cent of some 1,800 claims had been settled for a total of $160 million, but General Electric could derive some solace from the fact that most of these payments would be tax-deductible.

## TECHNIQUES OF THE CONSPIRACY

The modus operandi for the antitrust violators shows clearly the awareness of the participants that their behavior was such that it had better be carried on as secretly as possible. Some comparison might be made between the antitrust offenses and other forms of fraud occurring in lower economic classes. It was one of Sutherland's most telling contentions that neither the method by which a crime is committed nor the manner in which it is handled by public agencies alters the essential criminal nature of the act and the criminal status of the perpetrator.[12] Selling faucet water on a street corner to a blind man who is led to believe that the product is specially prepared to relieve his ailment is seen as no different from selling a $50 million turbine to a city which is laboring under the misapprehension that it is purchasing the product at the best price possible from closed competitive bidding. The same may be said in regard to methods of treatment. Tuberculosis, for example, remains tuberculosis and its victim a tubercular whether the condition is treated in a sanitarium or whether it is ignored, overlooked, or even condoned by public authorities. So too with crime. As Miss Stein might have said: A crime is a crime is a crime.

Like most reasonably adept and optimistic criminals, the antitrust violators had hoped to escape apprehension. "I didn't expect to get caught and I went to great lengths to conceal my activities so that I wouldn't get caught," one of them said.[13] Another went into some detail concerning the techniques of concealment:

> It was considered discreet to not be too obvious and to minimize telephone calls, to use plain envelopes if mailing material to each other, not to be seen together on traveling, and so forth . . . not leave wastepaper, of which there was a lot, strewn around a room when leaving.

The plans themselves, while there were some slight variations over time and in terms of different participants, were essentially similar. The offenders hid behind a camouflage of fictitious names and conspiratorial codes. The attendance roster for the meetings was known as the "Christmas card list" and the gatherings, interestingly enough, as "choir practice."[14] The offenders used public telephones for much of their communication, and they either met at trade association conventions, where their relationship would appear reasonable, or at sites selected for their anonymity. It is quite noteworthy, in this respect, that while some of the men filed false travel claims, so as to mislead their superiors regarding the city they had visited, they never asked for expense money to places more distant than those they had actually gone to—on the theory, apparently, that whatever else was occurring, it would not do to cheat the company.

At the meetings, negotiations centered about the establishment of a "reasonable" division of the market for the various products. Generally, participating companies were allocated essentially that part of the market which they had previously garnered. If Company A, for instance, had under competitive conditions secured 20 per cent of the available business, then agreement might be reached that it would be given the opportunity to submit the lowest bid on 20 per cent of the new contracts. A low price would be established, and the remainder of the companies would bid at approximately equivalent, though higher, levels. It sometimes happened, however, that because of things such as company reputation or available servicing arrangements, the final contract was awarded to a firm which had not submitted the lowest bid. For this, among other reasons, debate among the conspirators was often acrimonious about the proper division of spoils, about alleged failures to observe previous agreements, and about other intramural matters. Sometimes, depending upon the contract, the conspirators would draw lots to determine who would submit the lowest bid; at other times, the appropriate arrangement would be determined under a rotating system that was conspiratorially referred to as the "phase of the moon."

## EXPLANATIONS OF THE CONSPIRACY

Attempts to understand the reasons for and the general significance of the price-fixing conspiracy have been numerous. They include re-examination of the antitrust laws,[15] as well as denunciations of the corporate ethos and the general pattern of American life and American values.[16] A not inconsiderable number of the defendants took the line that their behavior, while technically criminal, had really served a worthwhile purpose by "stabilizing prices" (a much-favored phrase of the conspirators). This altruistic interpretation almost invariably was combined with an attempted distinction among illegal, criminal, and immoral acts, with the offender's expressing the view that what he had done might have been designated by the statutes as criminal, but either he was unaware of such a designation or he thought it unreasonable that acts with admirable consequences should be considered criminal. The testimony of a Westinghouse executive during hearings by the Senate Subcommittee on Antitrust and Monopoly clearly illustrates this point of view:

> *Committee attorney*: Did you know that these meetings with competitors were illegal?
>
> *Witness*: Illegal? Yes, but not criminal. I didn't find that out until I read the indictment. . . . I assumed that criminal action meant damaging someone, and we did not do that. . . . I thought that we were more or less working on a survival basis in order to try to make enough to keep our plant and our employees.

This theme was repeated in essentially similar language by a number of witnesses. "It is against the law," an official of the Ingersoll-Rand

Corporation granted, but he added: "I do not know that it is against public welfare because I am not certain that the consumer was actually injured by this operation." A Carrier Corporation executive testified that he was "reasonably in doubt" that the price-fixing meetings violated the antitrust law. "Certainly, we were in a gray area. I think the degree of violation, if you can speak of it that way, is what was in doubt." Some of these views are gathered together in a statement by a former sales manager of the I-T-E Circuit Breaker Company:

> One faces a decision, I guess, at such times, about how far to go with company instructions, and since the spirit of such meetings only appeared to be correcting a horrible price level situation, that there was not an attempt to actually damage customers, charge excessive prices, there was no personal gain in it for me, the company did not seem actually to be defrauding, corporate statements can evidence the fact that there have been poor profits during all these years. . . . So I guess morally it did not seem quite so bad as might be inferred by the definition of the activity itself.

For the most part, personal explanations for the acts were sought in the structure of corporate pressures rather than in the avarice or lack of law-abiding character of the men involved. The defendants almost invariably testified that they came new to a job, found price fixing an established way of life, and simply entered into it as they did into other aspects of their job. This explanatory scheme fit into a pattern that Senator Philip A. Hart of Michigan, during the subcommittee hearings, labeled "imbued fraud."[17]

There was considerable agreement concerning the manner in which the men initially became involved in price fixing. "My first actual experience was back in the 1930s," a General Electric official said. "I was taken there by my boss . . . to sit down and price a job." An Ingersoll-Rand executive said, "[My superior] took me to a meeting to introduce me to some of our competitors . . . and at that meeting pricing of condensers was discussed with the competitors." Essentially the same comment is repeated by witness after witness. A General Electric officer said, "Every direct supervisor that I had directed me to meet with competition. . . . It had become so common and gone on for so many years that I think we lost sight of the fact that it was illegal." Price fixing, whether or not recognized as illegal by the offenders, was clearly an integral part of their jobs. "Meeting with competitors was just one of the many facets of responsibility that was delegated to me," one witness testified. . . .

What might have happened to the men if, for reasons of conscience or perhaps through a fear of the possible consequences, they had objected to the "duty" to participate in price-fixing schemes? This point was raised only by the General Electric employees, perhaps because they alone had some actual evidence upon which to base their speculations. In 1946, General Electric had first issued a directive, number 20.5, which spelled out the company's policy against price fixing in terms stronger than those found in the antitrust laws. A considerable number of the executives believed, in the words of one, that the directive was only for "public consumption," and not to be taken seriously. One man, however, refused to engage in price fixing after he had initialed the document forbidding it. A witness explained to the Senate subcommittee what followed:

> [My superior] told me, "This fellow is a fine fellow, he is capable in every respect except he was not broad enough for his job, that he was so religious that he thought, in spite of what his superiors said, he thought having signed that, that he should not do any of this and he is getting us in trouble with competition.

The man who succeeded the troublesome official, one of the defendants in the Philadelphia hearing, said that he had been told that he "would be expected to do otherwise" and that this "was why I was offered that promotion to Philadelphia because this man would not do it." At the same time, however, the General Electric witnesses specified clearly that it was not their job with the company that would be in jeopardy if they failed to price-fix, but rather the particular assignment they had. "If I didn't do it, I felt that somebody else would," said one, with an obvious note of self-justification. "I would be removed and somebody else would do it."

Westinghouse and General Electric differed considerably in their reactions to the exposure of the offenses, with Westinghouse electing to retain in its employ persons involved in the conspiracy, and General Electric deciding to dismiss the employees who had been before the court. The reasoning of the companies throws light both on the case and on the relationship between antitrust offenses and the more traditionally viewed forms of criminal behavior.

Westinghouse put forward four justifications for its retention decision. First, it declared, the men involved had not sought personal aggrandizement—"While their actions cannot in any way be condoned, these men did not act for personal gain, but in the belief, misguided though it may have been, that they were furthering the company's interest"; second, "the punishment incurred by them already was harsh" and "no further penalties would serve any useful purpose"; third, "each of these individuals is in every sense a reputable citizen, a respected and valuable member of the community and of high moral character"; and fourth, there was virtually no likelihood that the individuals would repeat their offense.[18]

General Electric's punitive line toward its employees was justified on the ground that the men had violated not only federal law but also a basic company policy and that they therefore deserved severe punishment. The company's action met with something less than whole-hearted acclaim; rather, it was often interpreted as an attempt to scapegoat particular individuals for what was essentially the responsibility of the corporate enterprise and its top executives. "I do not understand the holier-than-thou attitude in GE when your directions came from very high at the top," Senator Kefauver said during his committee's hearings; while Senator John A. Carroll of Colorado expressed his view through a leading question: "Do you think you were thrown to the wolves to ease the public relations situation . . . that has developed since these indictments?" he asked a discharged General Electric employee. The witness thought that he had.

Perhaps most striking is the fact that though many offenders quite clearly stressed the likely consequences for them if they failed to conform to price-fixing expectations, not one hinted at the benefits he might expect, the personal and professional rewards, from participation in the criminal conspiracy. It remained for the sentencing judge and two top General Electric executives to deliver the harshest denunciations of the personal motives and qualities of the conspirators to be put forth during the case.

The statement of Judge J. Cullen Ganey, read prior to imposing sentence, received widespread attention. In it, he sharply criticized the corporations as the major culprits, but he also pictured the defendants in a light other than that they chose to shed upon themselves:

> They were torn between conscience and an approved corporate policy, with the rewarding objective of promotion, comfortable security, and large salaries. They were the organization, or company, man; the conformist who goes along with his superiors and finds balm for his conscience in additional comforts and security of his place in the corporate set-up.[19]

The repeated emphasis on "comfort" and "security" constitutes the basic element of Ganey's view of the motivations of the offenders. Stress on passive acquiescence occurs in remarks by two General Electric executives viewing the derelictions of their subordinates. Robert Paxton, the retired company president, called antitrust agreements "monkey business" and denounced in vitriolic terms one of his former superiors who, when Paxton first joined General Electric, had put him to work attempting to secure a bid on a contract that had already been prearranged by a price-fixing agreement. Ralph Cordiner, the president and board chairman of General Electric, thought that the antitrust offenses were motivated by drives for easily acquired power. Cordiner's statement is noteworthy for its dismissal of the explanations of the offenders as "rationalizations":

One reason for the offenses was a desire to be "Mr. Transformer" or "Mr.

Switchgear"* . . . and to have influence over a larger segment of the industry. . . . The second was that it was an indolent, lazy way to do business. When you get all through with the rationalizations, you have to come back to one or the other of these conclusions.

There were other explanations as well. One truculent offender, the sixty-eight-year-old president of a smaller company who had been spared a jail sentence only because of his age and the illness of his wife, categorically denied the illegality of his behavior. "We did not fix prices," he said. "I can't agree with you. I am telling you that all we did was recover costs." Some persons blamed the system of decentralization in the larger companies, which, they said, placed a heavy burden to produce profit on each of the relatively autonomous divisions, particularly when bonuses— "incentive compensation"—were at stake; others maintained that the "dog-eat-dog" business conditions in the heavy electrical equipment industry were responsible for the violations. Perhaps the simplest explanation came from a General Electric executive. "I think," he said, "the boys could resist everything but temptation."

## PORTRAIT OF AN OFFENDER

The highest-paid executive to be given a jail sentence was a General Electric vice president, earning $135,000 a year—about $2,600 every week. The details of his career and his participation in the conspiracy provide additional insight into the operations of white-collar crime and white-collar criminals.

The General Electric vice president was one of the disproportionate number of Southerners involved in the antitrust violations. He had been born in Atlanta and was forty-six years old at the time he was sentenced to jail. He had graduated with a degree in electrical engineering from Georgia Tech and received an honorary doctorate degree from Siena College in 1958; he was married and the father of three children. He had served in the Navy during World War II, rising to the rank of lieutenant commander; he was a director of the Schenectady Boy's Club, on the board of trustees of Miss Hall's School, and, not without some irony, he was a member of Governor Rockefeller's Temporary State Committee on Economic Expansion.

Almost immediately after his sentencing, he issued a statement to the press, noting that he was to serve a jail term "for conduct which has been interpreted as being in conflict with the complex antitrust laws." He

---

* Earlier, a witness had quoted his superior as saying: "I have the industry under my thumb. They will do just about as I ask them." This man, the witness said, "was known as Mr. Switchgear in the industry."

commented that "General Electric, Schenectady, and its people have undergone many ordeals together and we have not only survived them, but have come out stronger, more vigorous, more alive than ever. We shall again." Then he voiced his appreciation for "the letters and calls from people all over the country, the community, the shops, and the offices . . . expressing confidence and support."[20]

The vice president was neither so sentimental about his company nor so certain about the complexity of the antitrust regulations when he appeared before the Kefauver committee five months later. "I don't get mad, Senator," he said at one point, referring to his behavior during a meeting with competitors; but he took another line when he attempted to explain why he was no longer associated with General Electric:

> When I got out of being a guest of the government for thirty days. I had found out that we were not to be paid while we were there [A matter of some $11,000 for the jail term], and I got, frankly, madder than hell.

Previously, he had been mentioned as a possible president of General Electric, described by the then president, as "an exceptionally eager and promising individual." Employed by the company shortly after graduation from college, he had risen dramatically through the managerial ranks, and passed that point, described by a higher executive, "where the man, if his work has been sufficiently promising, has an opportunity to step across the barrier out of his function into the field of general management." In 1946, he had his first contact with price fixing, being introduced to competitors by his superior and told that he "should be the one to contact them as far as power transformers were concerned in the future."

The meetings that he attended ran a rather erratic course, with numerous squabbles between the participants. Continual efforts had to be made to keep knowledge of the meetings from "the manufacturing people, the engineers, and especially the lawyers," but this was achieved, the witness tried to convince the Kefauver committee, because commercial transactions remained unquestioned by managerial personnel so long as they showed a reasonable profit. The price-fixing meetings continued from 1946 until 1949. At that time, a federal investigation of licensing and cross-patent activities in the transformer industry sent the conspirators scurrying. "The iron curtain was completely down" for a year, and sales people at General Electric were forbidden to attend gatherings of the National Electrical Manufacturers' Association, where they had traditionally connived with competitors.

Meetings resumed, however, when the witness' superior, described by him as "a great communicator, a great philosopher, and, frankly, a great believer in stabilities of prices," decided that "the market was getting in chaotic condition" and that they "had better go out and see what could be done about it." He was told to keep knowledge of the meetings from Robert Paxton, "an Adam Smith advocate" and then the plant works manager, because Paxton "don't understand these things."

Promoted to general manager in 1954, the witness was called to New York by the president of General Electric and told specifically, possibly in part because he had a reputation of being "a bad boy," to comply with the company policy and with the antitrust laws and to see that his subordinates did so too. This instruction lasted as long as it took him to get from New York back to Massachusetts, where his superior there told him, "Now, keep on doing the way that you have been doing but just . . . be sensible about it and use your head on the subject." The price-fixing meetings therefore continued unabated, particularly as market conditions were aggravated by overproduction which had taken place during the Korean War. In the late 1950s, foreign competition entered the picture, and lower bids from abroad often forced the American firms to give up on particular price-fixing attempts.

In 1957, the witness was promoted to vice president, and again brought to New York for a lecture from the company president on the evils of price fixing. This time, his "air cover gone"—he now had to report directly to top management—he decided to abandon altogether his involvement in price fixing. He returned to his plant and issued stringent orders to his subordinates that they were no longer to attend meetings with competitors. Not surprisingly, since he himself had rarely obeyed such injunctions, neither did the sales persons in his division.

The witness was interrogated closely about his moral feelings regarding criminal behavior. He fumbled most of the questions, avoiding answering them directly, but ultimately coming to the point of saying that the consequences visited upon him represented the major reason for a re-evaluation of his actions. He would not behave in the same manner again because of what "I have been through and what I have done to my family." He was also vexed with the treatment he had received from the newspapers: "They have never laid off a second. They have used some terms which I don't think are necessarily—they don't use the term 'price fixing.' It is always 'price rigging' or trying to make it as sensational as possible."[21] The taint of a jail sentence, he said, had the effect of making people "start looking at the moral values a little bit." Senator Hart drew the following conclusions from the witness's comments:

> *Hart*: This was what I was wondering about, whether absent the introduction of this element of fear, there would have been any re-examination of the moral implications.
>
> *Witness*: I wonder, Senator. That is a pretty tough one to answer.
>
> *Hart*: If I understand you correctly, you have already answered it. . . . After the fear, there came the moral re-evaluation.

All things said, the former General Electric vice president viewed his situation philosophically. Regarding his resignation from the company, it was "the way the ball has bounced." He hoped that he would have "the opportunity to continue in American industry and do a job," and he wished some of the other men who had been dismissed a lot of good luck. "I want to leave the company with no bitterness and to go out and see if I can't start a new venture along the right lines." Eight days later, he accepted a job as assistant to the president in charge of product research in a large corporation located outside of Philadelphia. Slightly more than a month after that, he was named president of the company, at a salary reported to be somewhat less than the $74,000 yearly received by his predecessor.


## A SUMMING-UP

The antitrust violations in the heavy electrical industry permit a re-evaluation of many of the earlier speculations about white-collar crime. The price-fixing behavior, flagrant in nature, was clearly in violation of the criminal provisions of the Sherman Antitrust Act of 1890 which had been aimed at furthering "industrial liberty." Rather, the price-fixing arrangements represented attempts at "corporate socialism," and in the words of Senator Kefauver to a subcommittee witness:

> It makes a complete mockery not only of how we have always lived and what we have believed in and have laws to protect, but what you were doing was to make a complete mockery of the carefully worded laws of the government of the United States, ordinances of the cities, rules of the REA's [Rural Electrification Administration], with reference to sealed secret bids in order to get competition.

The facts of the antitrust conspiracy would seem clearly to resolve in the affirmative any debate concerning the criminal nature and the relevance for criminological study of such forms of white-collar behavior,[22] though warnings regarding an indefinite and unwarranted extension of the designation "crime" to all acts abhorrent to academic criminologists must remain in force. Many of Sutherland's ideas concerning the behavior of corporate offenders also receive substantiation. His stress on learning and associational patterns as important elements in the genesis of the violations receives strong support;[23] so too does his emphasis on national trade conventions as the sites of corporate criminal conspiracies.[24]

Others of Sutherland's views appear to require overhaul. His belief, for example, that "those who are responsible for the system of criminal justice are afraid to antagonize businessmen"[25] seems less than totally true in terms of the electrical industry prosecutions. Sutherland's thesis that "the customary pleas of the executives of the corporation . . . that they were ignorant of and not responsible for the action of the special department . . . is akin to the alibi of the ordinary criminal and need not be taken seriously"[26] also seems to be a rather injudicious blanket condemnation. The accuracy of the statement for the antitrust conspiracy must remain moot, but it would seem important that traditional safeguards concerning guilty knowledge as a basic ingredient in criminal responsibility be accorded great respect. Nor, in terms of antitrust data, does Sutherland appear altogether correct in his view that "the public agencies of communication, which continually define ordinary violations of the criminal code in a very critical manner, do not make similar definitions of white-collar crime."[27]

Various analytical schemes and theoretical statements in criminology and related fields provide some insight into elements of the price-fixing conspiracy. Galbraith's caustic observation regarding the traditional academic view of corporate price-fixing arrangements represents a worthwhile point of departure:

> Restraints on competition and the free movement of prices, the principal source of uncertainty to business firms, have been principally deplored by university professors on lifelong appointments. Such security of tenure is deemed essential for fruitful and unremitting thought.[28]

It seems apparent, looking at the antitrust offenses in this light, that the attractiveness of a secure market arrangement represented a major ingredient drawing corporate officers to the price-fixing violations. The elimination of competition meant the avoidance of uncertainty, the formalization and predictability of outcome, the minimization of risks. It is, of course, this incentive which accounts for much of human activity, be it deviant or "normal," and this tendency that Weber found pronounced in bureaucracies in their move from vital but erratic beginnings to more staid and more comfortable middle and old age.[29]

For the conspirators there had necessarily to be a conjunction of factors before they could participate in the violations. First, of course, they had to perceive that there would be gains accruing from their behavior. Such gains might be personal and professional, in terms of corporate advancement toward prestige and power; they might be vocational, in terms of a more expedient and secure method of carrying out assigned tasks. The offenders also apparently had to be able to neutralize or rationalize their behavior in a manner keeping with their image of themselves as law-abiding, decent, and respectable persons.[30] The ebb and flow of the price-fixing conspiracy also clearly indicates the relationship, often overlooked in explanations of criminal behavior, between extrinsic conditions and illegal acts. When the market behaved in a manner the executives thought satisfactory or when enforcement agencies seemed particularly threatening, the conspiracy desisted. When market conditions deteriorated, while corporate pressures for achieving attractive profit-and-loss statements remained constant, and enforcement activity abated, the price-fixing agreements flourished.

More than anything else, however, a plunge into the elaborate documentation of the antitrust cases of 1961 and an attempt to relate them to other segments of criminological work points up the considerable need for more and better monographic field studies of law violators and of systems of criminal behavior, followed by attempts to establish theoretical guidelines and to review and refine current interpretative viewpoints. There have probably been no more than a dozen, if that many, full-length studies of types of criminal (not delinquent) behavior in the past decade. The need for such work seems overriding, and the 1961 antitrust cases represent but one of a number of instances, whether in the field of white-collar crime, organized crime, sex offenses, personal or property crimes, or similar areas of concern, where we are still faced with a less than adequate supply of basic and comparative material upon which to base valid and useful theoretical statements.

# Notes

1. Judge J. Cullen Ganey, in *Application of the State of California*, 195 F. Supp. 39 (E.D. Pa. 1961).

2. *The New York Times* (February 7, 1961).

3. Edwin H. Sutherland, *White Collar Crime* (New York: Dryden Press, 1949), p. 240. Note: "Private enterprise remains extraordinarily private. . . . We know more about the motives, habits, and most intimate arcana of primitive peoples in New Guinea . . . than we do of the denizens of executive suites in Unilever House, Citroen, or General Electric (at least until a recent Congressional investigation)." Roy Lewis and Rosemary Stewart, *The Managers* (New York: New American Library, 1961), pp. 111–112.

4. For an elaboration of this point, see Gilbert Geis, "Toward a Delineation of White-Collar Offenses," *Sociological Inquiry*, 32 (Spring, 1962), 160–171.

5. Edwin H. Sutherland in Vernon C. Branham and Samuel B. Kutash, *Encyclopedia of Criminology* (New York: Philosophical Library, 1949), p. 511.

6. Sutherland, *White Collar Crime, op. cit.*, p. 9, fn. 7.

7. *United States Statutes*, 26 (1890), p. 209; *United States Code*, 15 (1958), 1, 2. See also William L. Letwin, "Congress and the Sherman Antitrust Law, 1887–1890," *University of Chicago Law Review*, 23 (Winter, 1956), pp. 221–258; and Paul E. Hadlick, *Criminal Prosecutions under the Sherman Anti-Trust Act* (Washington, D.C.: Ransdell, 1939).

8. Note, "Release of the Grand Jury Minutes in the National Deposition Program of the Electrical Equipment Cases," *University of Pennsylvania Law Review*, 112 (June, 1964), pp. 1133–1145.

9. John Herling, *The Great Price Conspiracy* (Washington, D.C.: Robert B. Luce, 1962), pp. 1–12; John G. Fuller, *The Gentleman Conspirators* (New York: Grove Press, 1962), pp. 7–11. See also Myron W. Watkins, "Electrical Equipment Antitrust Cases—Their Implications for Government and Business," *University of Chicago Law Review*, 29 (August, 1961), pp. 97–110.

10. Telephone interview with Judge Ganey, Philadelphia, August 31, 1964; *The New York Times* (December 20, 1961).

11. *The New York Times* (February 7, 1961).

12. Edwin H. Sutherland, "White-Collar Criminality," *American Sociological Review*, 5 (February, 1940), pp. 1–12.

13. U.S. Senate, Subcommittee on Antitrust and Monopoly, Committee on the Judiciary, 87th Cong., 2d Sess. 1961, "Administered Prices," *Hearings*, pts. 27 and 28. Unless otherwise indicated, subsequent data and quotations are taken from these documents. Space considerations dictate omission of citation to precise pages.

14. The quotation is from an excellent article by Richard Austin Smith, "The Incredible Electrical Conspiracy," *Fortune*, 63 (April, 1961), pp. 132–137, and 63 (May, 1961), pp. 161–164ff.

15. See Leland Hazard, "Are Big Businessmen Crooks?" *The Atlantic*, 208 (November, 1961), pp. 57–61.

16. See Anthony Lewis, *The New York Times* (February 12, 1961).

17. *Hearings*, pt. 27, p. 16773. Analysis of the relationship between occupational norms and legal violations could represent a fruitful line of inquiry. See Earl R. Quinney, "The Study of White Collar Crime: Toward a Reorientation in Theory and Research," *Journal of Criminal Law, Criminology, and Police Science*, 55 (June, 1964), pp. 208–214.

18. Sharon, Pa., *Herald* (February 6, 1961).

19. *The New York Times* (February 7, 1961).

20. Schenectady, N.Y., *Union-Star* (February 10, 1961).

21. *Hearings*, pt. 27, p. 17076. A contrary view is expressed in Alan J. Dershowitz, "Increasing Community Control over Corporate Crime—A Problem in the Law of Sanctions," *Yale Law Journal*, 71 (December, 1961), footnoted material pp. 287–289. It has been pointed out that *Time* (February 17, 1961, pp. 64ff) reported the conspiracy in its business section, whereas it normally presents crime news under a special heading of its own. Donald R. Taft and Ralph W. England, Jr., *Criminology*, 4th ed. (New York: Macmillan, 1964), p. 203.

22. See Edwin H. Sutherland, "Is 'White Collar Crime' Crime?" *American Sociological Review*, 10 (April, 1945), pp. 132–139. Note: "It may be hoped that the Philadelphia electric cases have helped to dispel this misapprehension. . . . It should now be clear that a deliberate or conscious violation of the antitrust laws . . . is a serious offense against society which is as criminal as any other act that injures many in order to profit a few. Conspiracy to violate the antitrust laws is economic racketeering. Those who are apprehended in such acts are, and will be treated as, criminals." Lee Loevinger, "Recent Developments in Antitrust Enforcement," *Antitrust Section, American Bar Association*, 18 (1961), p. 102.

23. Sutherland, *White Collar Crime, op. cit.*, pp. 234–257.

24. *Ibid.*, p. 70.

25. *Ibid.*, p. 10.

26. *Ibid.*, p. 54.

27. *Ibid.*, p. 247.

28. John Kenneth Galbraith, *The Affluent Society* (Boston: Houghton Mifflin, 1958), p. 84. See also Richard Hofstadter, "Antitrust in America," *Commentary*, 38 (August, 1964), pp. 47–53.

29. Max Weber, *The Theory of Social and Economic Organization*, trans. by A. M. Henderson and Talcott Parsons (New York: Oxford University Press, 1947), pp. 367–373.

30. See Donald R. Cressey, *Other People's Money: The Social Psychology of Embezzlement* (New York: The Free Press, 1953); Gresham M. Sykes and David Matza, "Techniques of Neutralization: A Theory of Delinquency," *American Sociological Review*, 22 (December, 1957), pp. 664–670.

# 8

# AUTOMAKERS AND DEALERS:
# A STUDY OF CRIMINOGENIC MARKET FORCES

*William N. Leonard and Marvin Glenn Weber*

That the American culture contains criminogenic elements leading to blue-collar crime, white-collar crime and noncriminal exploitation has been recognized by sociologists. Sutherland defined a white-collar crime as one "committed by a person of respectability and high social status in the course of his legitimate occupation."[1] White-collar crime included such acts as false and deceptive advertising, mislabeling of goods, price fixing, selling adulterated goods, violating weights and measures statutes, performing illegal operations (by doctors), fee-splitting (by lawyers), and others. Thus crime could no longer be defined solely as the illegal activity of blue-collar, low-class and pathological persons, but extended to all classes, with the prestige group at the top setting a pattern of lawlessness reflected and emulated by subgroups.

Reprinted by permission from the *Law & Society Review* (official publication of The Law and Society Association), Vol. 4, No. 3 (February, 1970), pp. 407–424. Copyright by The Law and Society Association.

## THE THEORY OF OCCUPATIONAL CRIME

Other sociologists have advocated use of the term "occupational crime" to refer to illegal business activities. Newman noted that "farmers, repairmen, and others in essentially non-white-collar occupations, could through such illegalities as watering milk for public consumption, making unnecessary 'repairs' on television sets and so forth, be classified as white-collar violators."[2] In his study of wartime black market operations, Clinard listed gasoline station operators as white-collar criminals.[3] Following these studies, Quinney proposed an expansion of the concept of white-collar crime to include all violations which occur in the performance of occupational duties regardless of the social status of the offender. The essential point of the act, whether classed as white-collar crime or occupational crime, was that it occurred in a legitimate occupation but violated the legal and commercial codes established by statute.[4]

A further refinement in occupational crime has been suggested by Bloch and Geis—the separation of such crime on the basis of the nature of the occupation. They recognize three categories of occupational crime: (1) those committed by independent individuals and professionals, such as doctors and lawyers; (2) those of employees against corporations (or government) such as embezzlements by bank employees (or welfare workers); and (3) those committed by policy-making officers of corporations.[5] The latter class includes conspiracies to fix prices, misrepresentation of merchandise, labor exploitation, and other illegal activities.

## FAILURE TO ANALYZE MARKET STRUCTURE

Insufficient attention has been focused by sociologists on the extent to which market structure—that is, the economic power available to certain corporations in concentrated industries—may generate criminal conduct. In the studies of the electrical industry conspiracy, for example, sociologists concentrated on the noncriminal backgrounds and the prestigious positions of the corporate officials who had engaged in the slippery conspiracy to violate the anti-trust laws. Other sociologists concerned themselves with the problems of individual versus corporate guilt, and the extent to which the officials involved were aware of the illegal character of their price-fixing activities. Geis and others have pointed out that "to meet with competition [had become] common and [had] gone on for so many years" that some individuals in the electrical corporations had lost sight of its illegality.[6] Nonetheless, the gentlemen conspirators went to great lengths to avoid detection, using blank stationery, adopting assumed names, meeting secretly in motels to rig bids according to the phase of the moon, and using other cloak and dagger tactics.

What Geis and other commentators failed to recognize is that price fixing of an effective character (whereby an increase in industry price yields higher revenues and profits) could not succeed unless two economic conditions existed:

1. The industry was concentrated with the bulk of output in the hands of a few producers who could easily get together; and
2. Demand for the product or products was price inelastic, that is, the buyers of heavy electrical equipment (in this case utilities) would not reduce purchases if prices were increased.

These economic conditions made it possible for officers of a few electrical equipment manufacturers to conspire to fix industry price on a wide range of heavy electrical items and insured the effectiveness of their actions.[7] The name of the game is profits, and unless illegal activity actually generates profits, it will not become accepted practice in any industry. Geis correctly noted that the price-fixing agreements flourished when market conditions deteriorated and antitrust enforcement abated, yet pressures for profits from each company division remained insistent.[8]

Market structure can also illuminate the three classes of crime cited by Bloch and Geis, particularly since it delimits the freedom of action of the individuals concerned and the impact of their crime on others. Policy-making officers of corporations have a wide range of discretionary action, and their decisions affect thousands of persons. Large corporations can increase profits not merely by fixing prices (illegal) or raising prices in concentrated industries (legal), but by such steps as improving products, shifting investments, increasing advertising and sales promotion, merging, branching, or better cost control. A second Bloch-Geis class, the independent individual, may possess considerable freedom of action if he is a professional—doctor, lawyer, certified public accountant, and the like—but if he operates a filling station or dealership as the agent of a large company, or is a small businessman competing against large firms, his range of discretion is severely restricted, and the impact of his behavior circumscribed. Last, those employees who commit crimes against corporations or government—e.g., embezzlement—have the least freedom of action and criminal impact. Nonetheless, the laws determining the legality of employee behavior are the most definitive. Laws or codes which seek to define the ethics of the professional person, small businessman, or big businessman are vague, or if statutory (like the antitrust laws) can often be circumvented.[9] In general, the standards of ethics of the professional appear more likely to govern his behavior than the laws against deceptive practices or discriminatory pricing seem to affect the actions of businessmen, large or small. In the market place, it is still *caveat emptor*. One of the large problems of society is that policy-making businessmen who have a wide scope of discretion and whose choices affect millions of persons have the least clearly defined standards of conduct. A competitive market system supposedly limits their opportunity for consumer deception, fraud, shoddy merchandise and poor service. In the absence of competition, no such limitations exist.

As a result of the failure to introduce analysis of market structure into sociological studies of occupational predatory crime, criticism is directed largely and excessively against the corporate ways of life and the profit system, while corrective action is sought (short of revolution) in public vigilance to detect and prosecute price fixing, discrimination, trying contracts, and other proscribed practices which means more personnel and resources for antitrust. Characteristically, the "more policemen" solution indicates a failure of social science to deal adequately with the basic causes of crime. With respect to occupational crime, the lack of analysis of market structure can easily mean that the criminal roots will never be touched, although the limbs continue to be cut. The need is for a market structure in each industry to allow competitive forces rather than government to do the regulating.[10] Such analysis, it is argued, can throw considerable light on the conditions which produce both white- and blue-collar crime, and lead to practical proposals for correction.

Concentrated market structure generates excessive power in the hands of a few corporations which can use it against suppliers, distributors, and customers and create conditions conducive to corporate profits which may, however, induce those with whom the corporations deal directly—e.g., distributors—to engage in unethical activity against the public. Rather than curb such actions, corporations wink at them.

## MARKET STRUCTURE OF THE AUTOMOBILE INDUSTRY

In economic literature market structure involves these aspects: (1) seller concentration, or market share of the leading producers; (2) buyer concentration, or market share of principal buyers; (3) product differentiation, or extent to which the product can be distinguished in the customer's mind through refinements, advertising, and so forth; (4) entry barriers—e.g., costs of capital, patents, economics of scale, advertising expenses; (5) price elasticity of demand; and (6) growth rate of demand. (Most important are 1, 3, and 4.) The automobile industry stands out both as to seller concentration, and in the height of entry barriers to the industry. Use of the assembly line techniques make it imperative to have a high sales volume (250,000 cars per year at a minimum) in order to attain scale economies. Emphasis on styling (the annual model change, a plethora of models, colors, gimmicks, and so forth) and extensive advertising make it difficult for small companies to compete. Many small manufacturers have gone out of business since 1921 when there were 81 car makers, and there has not been a successful entrant since Chrysler in 1925. The failure of Henry Kaiser, who entered the industry by merger with Fraser in 1947, and the chronic deficits of American Motors, which has three percent of the car output total, documents the difficulty of a new or small company in competing with the "Big Three." Thus the high concentration in the industry, plus entry barriers erected by capital costs, scale economies, and product differentiation, make the automobile industry one of the most solidly entrenched oligopolies among United States industries. This combination of factors also gives the Big Three abnormally high profit rates,[11] and great market power. The very large volume of sales associated with this industry and the concentration of sales in three companies afford the Big Three a market power without parallel in industry. That power can be exercised on suppliers, e.g., the rubber and steel industries from which the carmakers purchase tires and metal at extremely low cost, or against dealers and distributors. The manufacturer-dealer relation in the marketing of automobiles illustrates how the superior market power of the manufacturer can be exercised to coerce dealers and cause criminal behavior on their part.

## MANUFACTURER-DEALER RELATIONS

While only four domestic manufacturers of cars remain, their products are distributed through 30,000 dealers with facilities scattered throughout the United States. Technically, the dealer is an independent businessman. Rarely, however, does he have the capital to acquire more than a fraction of the value of property involved in the dealership. The rest is supplied by the manufacturer, and although the dealer may increase his ownership, rising costs of real estate, equipment and facilities, plus expansion of the dealership, may keep him dependent on the manufacturer for a long time. Further, he operates under restrictive agreement, terms of which are set by the manufacturer.

In the franchise agreement, often referred to as the selling agreement, a dealer contracts to sell and service the products of his manufacturer. The dealer does not receive an exclusive franchise for a given territory, but obtains a location for the sale and servicing of the products, often largely owned by the manufacturer. The dealer promises to display and advertise the manufacturer's cars and trucks. The dealer must also agree to stock parts, provide service to customers and make numerous reports on all phases of the business to the manufacturer. He promises to meet the minimum sales responsibility, or quota of sales established by the manufacturer and if he does not, his franchise is subject to cancellation. No franchise extends for more than five years, and many provide for cancellation within thirty to ninety days. Since the manufacturer's chief concern is the sales of the original product (ninety percent of his income is derived from new car sales and only ten percent from the sale of parts in connection with service to the product), he often cancels dealers for failure to meet sales quotas. However, manufacturers reported to the Federal Trade Commission that they had never cancelled a dealer for failure to have adequate service facilities or for poor service performance.[12]

Dealers are therefore pressured to be sales-oriented and to adopt the manufacturer's position that service is "a necessary evil." The manufacturer normally selects as dealer—(note that dealers cannot choose their successors in the business)—a person who is a salesman, has some capital to invest, and a good reputation in the community. He soon learns that new car sales represent his bread and butter. The manufacturer's sales representatives place unremitting pressure on the dealer to increase sales, and all sorts of contests are initiated to induce higher sales. While the manufacturer has service representatives in the area, they have a status inferior to that of the sales people. The dealer and his sales people may receive bonuses for superior sales performance, but there are no financial rewards for good service. What use is a good reputation for service to a dealer whose franchise is terminated because of a poor sales record? In such a case, the manufacturer, as required by law, pays the dealer a sum equal to his investment in the establishment—the unlucky franchise-holder receives nothing for good will in the community. The direction in which the incentives operate is clear: enhance sales and downgrade service.

One may ask why dealers choose to burden themselves with such franchises. The answer is that if a man wishes to sell and service cars, he has only four domestic manufacturers who can provide this opportunity, and they offer similar franchises. On the other hand, there appear to be numerous persons in the factory and in the field from the ranks of whom the manufacturer may select a dealer. If the prospect lacks sufficient capital, this will be supplied by the manufacturer, but on the latter's terms. Consequently, the manufacturer enjoys a superior bargaining position which is reflected in the franchise.

Between 1954 and 1968 the numbers of franchised dealers of domestic manufacturers declined 35%, from 43,000 to 27,800. Even though the average size of establishment increased and service sales per dealer doubled, the dealer's share of the automobile service market dropped from 43 to 32%. This trend (controlled by the manufacturer) has enabled the manufacturer to concentrate sales in fewer dealerships and to improve supervision over dealers, but has reduced the number of dealer outlets available to those seeking service on their motor vehicles. With the rapid increase in cars on the road over this period, dealers have been hard-pressed to afford service to customers and have lost business to other outlets, principally independent shops and garages, also to service stations and to individuals who prefer to buy parts and make their own repairs. A general shortage of mechanics has plagued the industry, a shortage which has grown steadily worse. In the 1950s, there was one mechanic for every eighty cars on the road, but by 1968 the ratio had risen to one for every one hundred thirty cars. During this period cars have become more complicated, with a large proportion of new cars having power steering, power brakes, air conditioning, push-button windows, and other mechanisms. The heavy pressure of repair work, arising from the growing number of car registrations, the increased complexity of cars and the demand of the public for quick repair service, combined with the shortage of automobile mechanics, produced a situation in which sharp and deceptive practices developed and flourished. The average car operator understands little about the functioning of an automobile, and the multiplication of car mechanisms and parts has increased his ignorance. He is fair game to be plucked by the unscrupulous repair outlets, and evidence exists that plucking is widespread.[13] It is not confined to dealers and their mechanics, although sociological analysis here presented relates primarily to the automobile service performed by dealers.

## EVIDENCE OF CRIMINAL BEHAVIOR

Several years ago, Dr. George Gallup made a nationwide survey to determine the public image for seven occupational groups: new car dealers, bankers, druggists, supermarket managers, undertakers, service station managers, and plumbers. Gallup's interviewers asked respondents: "Rank these businessmen in terms of how honest and trustworthy you think they are." New car dealers trailed every other occupation; only 3% of the public surveyed considered new car dealers "most honest and trustworthy." Plumbers outscored the dealers three to one, undertakers five to one and druggists nearly twenty to one.[14] When the question was turned around and those surveyed were asked whom they considered "least honest and trustworthy," 57% picked the dealer. Undertakers and plumbers were tied for second place, with 29% of the vote.

In a second survey, David Ogilvy found that 54% of the public preferred to take their car to the dealer for service (only 29% preferred to go to the service station), giving as reasons that the dealers specialized in that make of car, had well-trained mechanics, and a good stock of parts. However, a majority of those surveyed went elsewhere for service. Only 38% patronized the dealer; they considered his prices high, they had to wait for service, and they did not trust him. Ogilvy told the dealers that their general reputation was "awful."[15]

Specific instances of unethical and illegal conduct by dealers and their mechanics may be found in a number of places. In 1966, two authors ... reported dozens of cases involving fraud in sales of new cars, accessories not ordered but "forced" on buyers, used cars sold for new, engines switched in cars, excessive finance charges, automotive repair overcharges, "fake" repair diagnoses, and many other abusive practices.· In the vast majority of these cases, dealers and their mechanics were involved.[16]

Since 1965, thousands of letters of complaint concerning automobile warranties and automobile repairs have poured into the Federal Trade Commission and now constitute the thickest consumer file in the commission's 55-year history. Nearly all the letters cite new cars delivered in defective condition, dealers who failed to perform under the warranty, and improper repairs. A report on automobile warranties prepared by the commission's staff late in 1968 [that] sought to find reasons for the failure of motorists to receive proper service from dealers under the warranty ... strongly emphasized the role of manufacturer–dealer relations, particularly the superior market power exercised by the manufacturer vis-à-vis the dealer.

In December 1968, the Subcommittee on Antitrust and Monopoly of the United States Senate opened a series of hearings on automobile repairs; the series received national newspaper and television coverage. Witnesses who spoke on the high cost of automobile repairs cited as a reason the deterioration in automobile service of dealers brought about by the excessive concern of manufacturers for car sales and the treatment of car repairs as a necessary evil. One witness listed a series of "rackets" which characterized some dealerships, specifically:

1. *Forcing accessories.* For example, new cars arrive with accessories which the buyer did not order but must pay for in order to get delivery.

2. *Used car markups.* Since dealers make only $150–$200 per unit on new car sales, they endeavor to compensate for this by large mark-ups on used cars (dealers often make $400 on a $2,000 used car, compared to $150 on a $3,200 new car).

3. *Service gouging.* Dealers also make up for their low returns in the sale of new cars by overcharging for service. This can be managed in many ways: by putting down more labor time than that actually consumed in repairs, by charging for repairs not actually made (or charging for a major tune-up when a minor tune-up is performed), by finding things wrong with the car that do not actually need repair, by replacing parts unnecessarily, and so on.

4. *High finance.* Dealers will often finance cars themselves, borrowing money from a bank or credit agency and lending at a higher rate of interest. Sometimes the dealer will recommend a poor credit risk to a loan shark and receive a commission in return.

5. *Parts pushing.* This involves overcharging for parts, or use of a rebuilt part while charging for a new one. Sometimes the dealer and his mechanics will use a new part when the old one could be repaired at less expense to the customer, or will find a part defective which is not actually so.

6. *Other practices.* Dealers also will sell cars used by fleets for six months or a year as "executive" cars, will turn odometers back to make cars appear less used and engage in other practices which deceive customers.[17]

The witness made it clear that he did not attribute such practices to the majority of dealers and cited Better Business Bureau data indicating other repair outlets engaged in the same or similar practices. . . .

## MARKET STRUCTURE AND CRIMINAL BEHAVIOR IN AUTOMOBILE REPAIRS

It is argued here that what appears to the public as unethical or criminal behavior on the part of dealers and mechanics represents "conditioned" crime, or crime stimulated by conditions over which the dealer or mechanic has but little control. Perhaps a better phrase would be "coerced" crime, since it results from the coercion of strong corporations whose officers can utilize the concentrated market power of their companies to bend dealer and mechanic to serve company objectives. Following Donald Taft, we can term automobile manufacturers "socially dangerous people" since they function as "causers of the causes" of crime. Taft defines "socially dangerous people" as those "who, not technically criminal themselves, nevertheless create conditions which result in crime."[18] Dealers and mechanics operate within systems controlled by outsiders, specifically by a few large automobile manufacturers.

Some description has been given of the franchise system under which the dealer sells and services cars. Terms are set by the manufacturer, and if the dealer does not sell up to quota, he incurs the risk of cancellation. In 1939, a study by the Federal Trade Commission . . . described the Big Three manufacturers as ruthless in pressing their dealers for volume.[19] Since that time, little improvement in the situation has occurred. Complaints by dealers and public hearings led to passage in 1956 of the Automobile Dealers Franchise Act, which required the manufacturer to act in good faith in terminating the dealer. However, the dealer must prove that the manufacturer did not act in good faith in the cancellation, and this is rarely possible. Consequently, the franchise still conveys excessive power to the manufacturer and makes the dealer not an independent businessman, but an agent or pawn of his manufacturer.[20]

In recent years, the pressure on dealers to sell new cars, always intense, has been heightened by the establishment of "factory stores." These are dealerships, located in urban areas, entirely or almost entirely owned by the manufacturer, where the dealer in charge is a compliant captive of the factory. These outlets retail cars below the prices offered by other dealers in the area, which means the markup runs considerably below $200 per car. Though they lose money on new cars, these outlets win substantial cash prizes at the end of the year for sales leadership, and the manufacturer can point to such outlets in talking over sales with other dealers, and ask, "Why can't you sell like Mr. Giveaway?"[21] The major impact of the factory store is to push sales in the area, particularly by stimulating regular dealers to shave prices and profits in order to match sales quotas. Chrysler and Ford, always trying to stay in the competition with General Motors, have backed the factory store as a means of spurring sales.

What is the impact of the system of forcing new car sales upon dealers' service operations? Simply this. If the dealer loses money in new car sales, he will endeavor to make it up somewhere else, and this often means charging excessive prices for service. Lanzilotti puts the case this way:

> The dealer finds himself in the uncomfortable position between the powerful manufacturer on the one hand, and a demanding and not too understanding public on the other. The public appears to gain from automobile forcing through lower prices more closely related to the dealer's actual cost, but may lose as much from parts and accessory forcing and from high repair charges dealers use to offset margins on new car sales.[22]

But the dealer's reaction to high sales pressure and low margins on new cars does not stop with overcharging on repairs or wide margins on used cars. It induces him to perform phony repairs, to charge for new parts when used parts were employed, and to engage in other illicit repair practices. For these, he is not hold accountable by the manufacturer, who, in fact, condones this illicit behavior and never terminates a dealer for poor service.

As for the mechanic, if he is employed by a dealership where abusive practices exist, he becomes part of the system whereby the customer is cheated. He can adapt himself to the unethical climate by learning and practicing the tricks by which customers are parted from their money, or he may rebel and leave the dealership, as one mechanic reported in a newspaper article:

> An Amarillo, Texas man drove his car into a shop for a small repair. The mechanic turned in a ticket for 80 cents, with no charge for labor. Next day the mechanic spied the car still in the shop and found that his original ticket had been replaced by one for $60. When he asked why, the shop

foreman told him that the shop could not make money on 80-cent items, that the owner had been called and "expected" to pay for the service to his car, and that was the reason for keeping the car an extra day and for padding the repair bill. The mechanic phoned the man, told him the true story and quit his job.[23]

Some observers may consider this story unusual, for it would appear more likely that a mechanic under these circumstances would keep his silence and his share of the loot. A further probability is that, having learned how to charge for repairs—and for no repairs—an enterprising mechanic could then establish his own repair shop and select his customers—or victims— for himself. In fact, many do just this. Certainly, unethical repair practices are not the monopoly of dealerships.

But another system operates to induce improper repairs and repair charges by mechanics, no matter where they may be employed. This is the prevailing flat-rate system. Designed as an incentive system for mechanics, it consists of standard times set by automobile manufacturers for repair jobs performed by dealers which, when multiplied by the dealer's flat rate —usually about twice the mechanic's wages in order to cover overhead and profit—indicates what the customer should be charged for a particular operation. For example, if changing a fuel pump is timed at one-half hour, and the labor rate is $8 an hour, the mechanic receives $2 for his labor, the dealer gets $2, and the customer pays $4 for the labor, plus the cost of a new fuel pump. If the mechanic does the job in 15 minutes, he gets paid the same amount, but he can go on to a new job that much more quickly. Of course, he can exceed the time also, but he receives the same sum. The system induces the mechanic to try to beat the time, and this often means a quick and superficial repair. It can also mean the use of a new part rather than fixing an old part which might still be usable but would take more time to repair. Since very little time is allowed by the manufacturer for diagnosis—and rattles, short circuits, and other problems often require considerable time to locate—cursory diagnosis of an automotive problem often results. Also, the mechanic will ordinarily not fake the time to test-drive the car when this ought to be done to check a particular repair. As a result, the flat-rate system encourages rapid and often inadequate repair work. Mechanics in independent garages, service stations, and other repair outlets use *Chilton's Motors* and other manuals which follow closely the times set by manufacturers, and the system operates in these outlets in similar fashion to that found in dealerships. Over the years, the times set for many jobs in these manuals have declined, requiring mechanics to strive even harder to beat the time by whatever method of skill or subtlety they can employ. With a nationwide shortage of skilled mechanics and a rising tide of demand for service, it is no wonder that both technically and ethically improper repairs have increased in frequency.[24]

## THE WARRANTY SHAM

In recent years, motorists by the thousands have complained about the failure of dealers to honor new car warranties. Here again, the responsibility for the wholesale disregard of warranties appears to lie with manufacturers.

At one time, the warranty ran from manufacturer to dealer, and from dealer to car owner. Today the warranty runs directly from manufacturer to owner, and warrants him against defects in material or workmanship for a stated period of time or distance traveled. However, it is the dealer's responsibility to service the car and to be reimbursed by the factory—under terms set unilaterally by the manufacturer.

The trouble began late in 1962 when Chrysler extended the warranty —which covered defects for twelve months or 12,000 miles, whichever came first—to five years or 50,000 miles on the power train—i.e., engine, transmission, steering, suspension and wheels—and all the car makers moved up to a two-year/24,000 mile warranty on the rest of the car.

For Chrysler, whose share of car output had dropped to ten percent, the extended warranty was chiefly a sales gimmick. A company official admitted as much to service managers gathered in Detroit in 1964, adding:

> When you think of it, selling cars is not only the reason for 5/50 and Certified Car Care . . . it's also the one prime reason for any dealership's existence! The other dealership activities—including our service department—are all planned to support our new-car sales operation. So, in a very real sense, we're all involved in selling new cars. [Federal Trade Commission, 1968: 35]

Rarely have so many cats been let out of the bag at one time. Chrysler advertised the warranty liberally as proof of engineering leadership, doubled its sales in a few years, and the other manufacturers all adopted the extended warranty.

But the extended warranty, instead of affording more protection and value to the motorist, actually conveyed less. An increasing number of buyers began to complain of cars delivered new with defects, and many could not get their cars serviced. Apparently Detroit found it expedient to rush the cars off the assembly line and rely on dealers for predelivery inspection to catch flaws, but dealers felt that the allowance provided for inspection was inadequate, and did little more than a carwash. The Federal Trade Commission's investigation of automobile warranties disclosed:

> There is inadequate inspection and quality control at the factory. This overburdens the dealer's predelivery inspection and service facilities and substantially increases the dealer's costs without compensation, other than an allowance in the retail price suggested by the manufacturer. Con-

sequently, the consumer often is delivered a car in unsatisfactory condition.[25]

Further, the manufacturer's labor rate set for dealer's warranty work failed to reimburse them for warranty work (they were paid by Detroit at about two-thirds the rate charged to regular customers), on top of which dealers had to tag, store, and return to the factory parts replaced under the warranty.[26] Making out warranty repair claims involved a great deal of paper work, and frequently these were denied by the factory after the dealer had performed the work.

In view of the cumbersome procedures established for its operation and the extra costs and burden of paperwork with which the dealer was saddled, it is no wonder that car owners, encountered difficulty in obtaining warranty repairs. Dealers could—and had to—earn more in servicing cash customers and tried to avoid warranty work. Typical ploys included telling owners that a repair falling under the warranty was not covered by it, that they could not schedule the car in the shop for a week or more, or that the owner would have to leave it for several days. And often, after the owner had brought the car in, it was not serviced at all.

Despite all the problems, many dealers tried to give good service under the warranty. Yet Consumers Union reported that one-fifth of all new car owners who attempted to have their cars repaired under the warranty found service unsatisfactory. In view of the conditions established by manufacturers for the performance of dealers under the warranty, it is amazing that the proportion of car owners encountering poor service was not several times as large.[27]

But the manufacturers played still one more game with dealers and car buyers. At least one of the Big Three introduced a system of competition among its regions on the basis of which it could award promotions, bonuses, and prizes, part of the competition being to determine which region could underspend its warranty budget (set at so many dollars per car over a given period) by the largest possible percentage. To win out, a region had to hold down its warranty costs by every means possible, including the denial of borderline claims, refusing service, and various tactics. Obviously such a system vitiated the spirit of the warranty and established an additional incentive for unethical behavior on the part of dealers.

## SUMMARY

Coerced occupational crime, whether performed by white- or blue-collar personnel, can be better understood when the conditions affecting the performance of occupational duties are known. In many industries and trades, criminal behavior in an occupation is conditioned by the concentrated market power of producers capable of establishing terms of employment and rewards for the occupation. The analysis of market power also has utility in assessing the corporate and individual responsibility of person who violate the antitrust laws by fixing prices, as in the conspiracy involving manufacturers of heavy electrical equipment successfully prosecuted in 1961. Unless the industry is highly concentrated, a few producers cannot effectively conspire to fix prices and boost profits.

This market power concept as used in regard to the car dealers tends to support three of Taft's explanations that the general culture can be a cause of crime.

1. Our society involves the relative tolerance, acceptance, and even the approval of exploitative behavior either of the white-collar crime type or that of the noncriminal exploiter.[28]

2. Organized businessmen are not inclined to be specific in defining the right ways to conduct business. How truthful should advertisers and sellers feel obligated to be in telling of the merits of their goods, and should they tell the whole truth about their products?[29]

3. Socially dangerous people (causers of the causes)—these dangerous people are those who, not necessarily technically criminal themselves, nevertheless create conditions which result in crime or serve as examples consciously or unconsciously imitated by the potential criminal.[30]

Taft feels that the social system compels the business institution to be exploitative. It is our opinion that additional economic factors must be taken into account. In automobile retailing and repairs, the franchise system controlled by the factory sets the terms of daily operation for dealers. It enables the manufacturer to place pressure on the dealer to sell cars and demotes service to the status of a "necessary evil." The manufacturers' motivation is twofold: (1) he makes nearly ten times as much in selling new cars as in selling parts involved in repairs; and (2) if repair service deteriorates in quality, and/or increases in cost, motorists will be more likely to buy new cars rather than keep the old ones in repair. . . .

Because of the intense emphasis on sales, heightened in recent years by manufacturers' development of factory stores which stimulate sales in an area by aggressive methods, dealers often sell cars for low margins, then endeavor to recoup by higher margins on used cars and by overcharging for repairs. Another consequence of this effort by the dealer to earn a living under conditions controlled from outside is the tolerance of repair practices which deceive and defraud the motorist. Mechanics working both in and outside of dealerships also become involved as defrauders. Most mechanics operate within a flat rate system controlled from Detroit which induces quick and superficial repairs by encouraging the mechanic to "beat the time" set by the factory (or other) manual for particular repair jobs. Inadequate diagnosis, rapid repairs, spurious repairs, and insubstantial testing of repairs made, all result from this system.

In recent years, thousands of complaints have been received from new car buyers who found their cars delivered in defective condition and could not obtain service under the warranty. On examination, the warranty turned out to be a "sales gimmick" of the manufacturer, not an assurance of mechanical reliability. Manufacturers used the warranty to limit their liability under the law and further limited the effectiveness of the warranty by establishing cumbersome paperwork and procedures for dealers and by compensating the dealers in labor and parts below the levels charged for regular repairs. As a result, dealers tended to avoid warranty work, or provided poor service to new car owners. Dealers made motorists wait for service, often failed to work on cars brought into the shop or told owners they could not fix them, sometimes "discovered" additional repairs which could be charged, and padded bills. The improper behavior of dealers encountered by motorists who sought to have the warranties honored reflects the market power of manufacturers, who unilaterally drafted the warranties and made the representation to car buyers—but then undermined warranty service by creating conditions which induced dealers to operate unethically in providing repairs.

In sum, the frequent unethical actions of dealears and mechanics in furnishing repair service to the public must largely be regarded as coerced occupational crime resulting from a market structure in the automotive industry which provides the auto-maker with potential, and applied, criminogenic power.

## Notes

1. Edwin H. Sutherland, *White Collar Crime* (New York: Dryden Press, 1949), p. 9.

2. Donald J. Newman, "White-Collar Crime," *Law and Contemporary Problems*, 23 (Autumn, 1958), pp. 735–753.

3. Marshall B. Clinard, *The Black Market* (New York: Holt, Rinehart and Winston, 1952).

4. Earl R. Quinney, "The Study of White Collar Crime: Toward a Reorientation in Theory and Research," *Journal of Criminal Law, Criminology and Police Science*, 55 (June, 1964), pp. 208–214.

5. Herbert A. Bloch and Gilbert Geis, *Man, Crime and Society* (New York: Random House, 1967), p. 402.

6. Gilbert Geis, "White-Collar Crime: The Heavy Electrical Equipment Antitrust Cases of 1961," in Marshall B. Clinard and Richard Quinney, eds., *Criminal Behavior Systems: A Typology* (New York: Holt, Rinehart and Winston, 1967), p. 145.

7. Marvin Wolfgang, Leonard Savitz, and Norman Johnston, eds., *The Sociology of Crime and Delinquency* (New York: Wiley, 1962), p. 361.

8. Geis, *op. cit.*, p. 151.

9. Wolfgang, Savitz and Johnston, *op. cit.*, pp. 20–24.

10. Chief Justice Warren has stated: "An industry that does not have a competitive structure will not have competitive behavior." See *U.S. v. DuPont De Nemours and Company*, 351 U.S. 397 (1956).

11. From 1960 to 1967, General Motors earned 20.5 percent return on investments; Ford obtained 14.3 percent; and Chrysler 11.8 percent. All industries averaged about 8–9 percent in this period; see Federal Trade Commission, *Staff Report on Automobile Warrantees* (Washington, D.C.: U.S. Government Printing Office, 1968), p. 159.

12. *Ibid.*, pp. 118–119.

13. *Ibid.*, p. 109.

14. Respondents ranked as honest trustworthy: bankers—74 percent; druggists— 56 percent; supermarket managers—14 percent; undertakers—16 percent; service station managers—14 percent; plumbers—8 percent; and new car dealers—3 percent. See David Ogilvy, "What's Wrong with Your Image—And What You Can Do About It," speech to annual convention of National Automobile Dealers Association, in Las Vegas, Nevada, February 3, 1965.

15. *Ibid.*, pp. 4–6.

16. San Crowther and Irwin Winehouse, *Highway Robbery* (New York: Stein and Day, 1966).

17. William M. Leonard, *Statement Before the Senate Subcommittee on Antitrust and Monopoly*, Washington, D.C., December 3, 1968.

18. Donald R. Taft, "Influence of the General Culture on Crime," *Federal Probation* 30 (September, 1966), pp. 15–23.

19. Federal Trade Commission, *Report on the Motor Vehicle Industry* (Washington D.C.: U.S. Government Printing Office, 1939), p. 1076.

20. A district court in New Jersey recently termed "unfair" Chrysler's system of sales quotas which would allow the corporation to terminate half of its dealers at any given time. See *Schwartz Motors v. Chrysler* (New Jersey Court, District, Civil Action, March 11, 1969), pp. 1230–68.

21. William M. Leonard, *op. cit.*, p. 18.

22. Robert F. Lanzilotti, "The Automobile Industry," in Walter Adams, ed., *The Structure of American Industry* (New York: Macmillan, 1961), pp. 350–351.

23. William M. Leonard, "The Auto-Repair Jungle," *Newsday*, January 11, 1969, p. 6.

24. See statements of Harold Halfpenny, *Independent Garage Owners of America* (U.S. Senate, 1969), p. 309; and James W. Hall, *Independent Garage Owners of America* (U.S. Senate, 1969), p. 334.

25. Federal Trade Commission, *op. cit.*, p. 35.

26. *Ibid.*, p. 93.

27. Manufacturers were obviously suspicious that their dealers might cheat them by authorizing repairs not covered under the warranty and set up this system of checks.

28. Donald R. Taft and Ralph W. England, *Criminology*, 3rd ed. (New York: Macmillan, 1964), p. 276.

29. *Ibid.*, pp. 38–39.

30. Taft, *op. cit.*, p. 17.

# IV

# COMMERCIAL AND PROFESSIONAL WHITE-COLLAR CRIME

Black-market dealings in meat, illegal dispensing of prescriptions by pharmacists, income-tax evasion, violation of rent-control ceilings, and imposition of extralegal working conditions on household help are the white-collar offenses dealt with in this section. A major characteristic these behaviors share is that their perpetrators rarely regard themselves as criminals or, indeed, as deserving of censure or punitive treatment.

The contrast in this regard between traditional and white-collar offenders is often striking. Take, for instance, the response of a professional thief who is asked: "If you were to describe yourself in one word, would the description invariably be 'criminal'?" The thief answers: "Yes, definitely. That's what I am. I never think of myself in any other way."[1] Quite different is the act of a criminal who had violated the Sherman Antitrust Act and issued the following view of his behavior: "Next Monday, I will start serving a thirty-day jail term, along with six other *businessmen*, for conduct which has been *interpreted* as being in conflict with the *complex* antitrust laws"[2] (italics added). The same kind of reasoning is seen in the response of a senior partner of the banking firm of J. P. Morgan to questions from a congressional committee investigating the crimes of Richard Whitney, former president of the New York Stock Exchange:

> Sure, but you use the word stealing. It never occurred to me that Richard Whitney was a thief. What occurred to me was that he had gotten into a terrible jam, and had made improper and unlawful use of securities; that his brother was proposing to try and make good his default. . . . It made me ill almost that all the time he could have been deceiving his wife and community. Well, it was just—inconceivable.[3]

Perhaps the point is best made by noting that in 1955 two members of the Attorney General's National Committee to Study the Antitrust Laws supported their opposition of criminal penalties for antitrust conspiracies with the following reasoning:

> Of all the great industries that contributed most to the winning of the war there is hardly one that has not been branded either by indictment or injunction suit as violators of this criminal statute.
>
> Our enemies do not fail to take advantage of that strange anomaly, in their never-ending charge that we are a nation of criminal monopolists.[4]

Imagine, if you will, anyone suggesting that we no longer regard armed robbery or burglary as crimes in view of the fact that the prosecution of individuals for these acts was giving the United States a bad reputation abroad.

Illustrations of the flattering self-image of white-collar criminals abound, but no one has traced the source of these self-images or systematically investigated the consequences of reinforcement or impairment of the offenders' view of themselves. It can be argued that strong self-images as fundamentally law-abiding and decent citizens allow the white-collar offenders to suffer through assaults on that viewpoint and to emerge ready to perform comfortably in roles that the defining elements of the society wish for them. Certainly, most of the thrust toward keeping traditional kinds of offenders and delinquents out of prison is geared to such a goal. It can also be argued, of course, that failure to penetrate the caul of self-righteousness of the white-collar offenders permits them to continue their criminal career and others like them to do the same things they had done, unhampered by the possible mediating influences of guilt and anxiety.

It is the issue of self-definition and social definition regarding white-collar offenders that triggers the notable exchange of views between Frank E. Hartung, a professor of sociology at Wayne State University, and Ernest W. Burgess (1886–1966), a professor of sociology at the University of Chicago at the time this exchange took place. Hartung had studied violations of wartime regulations imposed upon the wholesale meat industry in Detroit. Burgess finds such an enterprise pejorative and argues that a crucial distinction must be drawn between offenses which arouse strong public disapproval and those kinds of acts which are regarded with only mild disfavor—if, indeed, they are viewed with any moral disapprobation at all. It is worth observing that Burgess uses Edward A. Ross's article (reprinted as the first reading in this volume) to buttress a position quite at odds with that of Ross, who was concerned with jolting people into taking a more severe stand against white-collar offenders. Ignoring the direction of the Ross polemic, Burgess relies upon the material in Ross's article to support his observation that white-collar offenses do not arouse strong public indignation.

At the time of his exchange with Hartung, Burgess was one of the most preeminent members of the sociological establishment, with a reputation founded primarily on his work in predicting the success and failure of marriages (Burgess himself, ironically, was a lifelong bachelor).[5]

Hartung's rebuttals to Burgess are often telling, though he allows himself to be led into quibbling over peripheral factual matters, such as whether or not half the adults in the United States participated in the black market. The jousting should be recognized for the semantic bout that it is. Hartung cares to call criminals those persons who violate the criminal law; Burgess prefers to restrict the term to persons who regard themselves as criminals. Both writers are trapped in a definitional labyrinth of Sutherland's creation, in which a major concern becomes whether or not an act really is criminal. The truth of the matter is that the statutory nature of the act as well as the public interpretations and the offenders' views of themselves all constitute elements of the behavior, and it is important to study both in order to understanding the phenomenon thoroughly.

On pragmatic grounds (or, perhaps more accurately, in terms of the biases of the editors of this volume), Hartung's position seems considerably more reasonable than Burgess's because it tends to point toward equality under law and to make more definitional "sense." Burgess, for instance, would appear to be in a vulnerable position were he to extrapolate his position to maintain that murderers who do not regard themselves as criminals (as, for instance, Raskolnikov in Dostoevsky's *Crime and Punishment*) ought not to be included in studies of homicide.

The exchange of views between Hartung and Burgess provides a background for the remaining four readings in this section. Vilhelm Aubert, a professor at the University of Oslo, expands upon the necessity to ask the right questions rather than to debate about white-collar crime definitions. He wants to know why it is that certain acts are proscribed by a legislative body while other acts, seeming of equivalent social consequence, go unattended. Aubert also argues that "the terminology one accepts in the present controversy (about the proper definition of white-collar crime) will depend upon how much one wants to get rid of these white-collar activities," a viewpoint that is not altogether persuasive. While the degree of reformist zeal may, of course, condition acceptance or rejection of various definitions of a subject matter, other elements (such as logic and analytical utility) appear equally apt to play into definitional preference. It is, in fact, noteworthy that the writers in the present volume so often feel obliged, in disputing Sutherland's usage of the term "white-collar crime," to stress that they nonetheless are strongly dedicated to the eradication of the practices embraced within Sutherland's definition.

Rationalizations and matters of self-image are related to the broader question of occupational orientation in the article by sociologist Richard Quinney, as he examines prescription violations among retail pharmacists. Deviant behavior, Quinney maintains, is a function of social structure, and he demonstrates that pharmacists attuned to the "business" role are wont to violate regulations to a much greater extent than those oriented to a "professional" role. Quinney's work does not, of course, unravel the threads of the causal situation. Do the same set of prior circumstances lead a person to regard pharmacy work as a business and also to violate the law, or is there a chain of causal linkages, first leading to the adoption of the business stress and then pushing toward the violations once that business orientation comes into play? Only longitudinal studies could untangle such basic issues: studies that began examining a cohort of pharmacy students as they entered into the business-profession, and then followed them through their careers, separating out the violators from the nonviolators and comparing them in regard to the material gathered as the study proceeded. The absence of such intensive work, as well as work in regard to other professionals, such as doctors—in terms of billing, fee-splitting, ghost surgery, Medicaid and similar crimes—is one of the clear lacunae in the corpus of material on white-collar crime.

In his study of rent-control violations in Honolulu, Harry V. Ball, presently a member of the sociology department at the University of Hawaii, offers support for the view that deprivation suffered as a consequence of a legal enactment influences violation; as the author reports, "the tendency to perceive one's treatment under the law to be unfair and thus be tempted to violate the law appeared directly related to the law's severity." In his conclusion, Ball pays editorial tribute to the large majority of conforming landlords in Honolulu; by indirection, he may lead readers to wonder why it was that these law-abiding persons did not come to define the statute in the same manner as their violating compatriots.[6] The issue is, of course, beyond the purview of Ball's study, but it is one that in its generic form has persistently challenged students of criminal behavior.

The final reading in the section represents an attempt to obtain data on the extent of a certain form of income-tax violation. Harold Groves, a professor of economics, employs an array of rather meticulous techniques to determine the amount of underreporting of rental income by landlords in a Wisconsin city. About one in twelve of these landlords, he discovers, did not indicate any rental receipts on their tax returns, while another one in four did not even file tax returns, though it is very likely that they were liable for taxes. No statement is offered regarding the possible criminal implications of these behaviors: in tax prosecutions, it must be proved that failure to pay was a knowing act and that it involved a certain percentage more than what was paid (25 percent for federal taxes). Other tax studies have shown that failure to pay may be related to the tightness of enforcement procedures; thus, there was a phenomenally sharp increase in bank interest reported by taxpayers after the Internal Revenue Service required banks to forward to it statements on the amount of interest, above a certain figure, paid to persons with savings accounts. Groves does not attempt to provide an explanation for the differences between those who honestly report their rental incomes and those who do not, though he advances some tentative structural interpretations, relating to the nature of their property and similar economic factors.

## Notes

1. Tony Parker and Robert Allerton, *The Courage of His Convictions* (New York: Norton, 1962), p. 65.

2. Quoted in *New York Times*, February 25, 1961.

3. John Brooks, *Once in Golconda* (New York: Harper Colophon, 1970), p. 285.

4. Attorney General's National Committee to Study the Antitrust Laws, *Report* (Washington, D.C.: Government Printing Office, 1955), p. 353.

5. Information relating to Burgess' professional and personal life can be found in Robert E. L. Faris, *Chicago Sociology, 1920–1932* (Chicago: University of Chicago Press, 1970).

6. This is the perspective adopted by "control" theorists in their approach to deviance and crime. See, for example, Travis Hirschi, *Causes of Delinquency* (Berkeley: University of California Press, 1969), especially pp. 10–11 and 16–34.

# 9

# WHITE-COLLAR OFFENSES IN THE WHOLESALE MEAT INDUSTRY IN DETROIT

*Frank E. Hartung*

This article is a tentative and partial statement of some of the theoretical considerations presented by a study of white-collar crime. It deals with violations of Office of Price Administration regulations in the Detroit wholesale meat industry and is part of a larger study of law and social differentiation. The points briefly to be considered are (1) the objective basis on which white-collar offenses are to be considered as criminal, (2) whether an act committed without deliberate intention is to be regarded as criminal, (3) the significance of white-collar offenses for current criminological theories, and (4) a characteristic of these offenses which distinguishes them from usual crimes and which has special significance for the community.

A white-collar offense is defined as a violation of law regulating business, which is committed for a firm by the firm or its agents in the conduct of its business.[1] Thus, the $60-a-week clerk who embezzled about one

Reprinted from *American Journal of Sociology*, 56 (July, 1950), pp. 25–34, by permission of The University of Chicago Press. Copyright 1950 by The University of Chicago Press.

million dollars from the Mergenthaler Linotype Company for his personal use is not a white-collar criminal as here defined. But Richard Whitney, who embezzled a like amount from a children's trust fund in order to carry out certain operations for his Wall Street firm, does meet the terms of the definition.

A question about this type of offense is whether it is "really" criminal. The problem is that of the application of criteria to behavior. There is a widely held view that white-collar offenses are criminal. In this view two criteria are stipulated for a criminal act: (1) An act must have been proscribed (or in some cases prescribed) by a duly constituted legislative body and (2) the legislative body must have declared such an act to be punishable, with the sanctions specified. In jurisprudence the "pure-theory-of-law" school and some other writers have explicitly accepted these criteria.[2] In criminology, Sutherland and Clinard have shown that white-collar offenses meet these two criteria and are therefore to be considered as criminal.[3] . . .

Specifically, the Emergency Price Control Act of 1942, as amended, and the Second War Powers Act, as amended, stated it to be the purpose of the acts in the interest of national security to stabilize prices; to prevent abnormal increases in prices; to prevent profiteering, manipulation, or other disruptive practices resulting from abnormal market conditions or scarcity caused by, or contributing to, the national emergency; to protect persons with relatively fixed incomes against undue impairment of their standard of living; to prevent hardships to business, schools, and universities; to prevent a postwar collapse of values; and to permit certain voluntary practices by the government and business to accomplish these purposes. Certain agencies were specifically stated to have the duty of working for these objectives. The penalties that were established involved damages, fines, imprisonment, and partial or complete suspension of the right to do business.

These two statutes which regulated business meet the test of the criteria of formally defined proscribed and prescribed acts and of punishability. The agencies charged with the enforcement and administration of this type of regulatory law need not, of course, be concerned primarily with the application of allowable criminal sanctions. Indeed, with hardly any exception, save that of the pre-Taft–Hartley National Labor Relations Board, federal agencies appear to have been more concerned with obtaining compliance with the law than with punishing violations. For whatever reasons, these agencies have not defined themselves as being white-collar police departments charged with law enforcement. The various OPA administrators, charged with the responsibility of discharging the provisions of the laws creating OPA, perhaps fortunately did not have a criminological viewpoint in their work. It was also evident to this writer, from extended discussions with OPA enforcement attorneys over more than a year, that most of these attorneys defined their positions as administrative, law enforcement in any police sense of the term being secondary in their eyes. Nevertheless, violations of the two laws named above and of the regulations to which they give rise, since they had the full force and effect of law, can legally, logically, and technically be classified as criminal acts. They are so regarded in this paper. And, just as in the case of other statutes and other offenses, the repeal, abrogation, or expiration of these laws and regulations removed what were formerly violations of them from the classification of criminal. They may be just as irritating, immoral, or abominable today as they were in June, 1946, but they are no longer criminal. We cannot properly be concerned in criminology with what *should* be criminal, but only with what *is* criminal.

The formal definition of crime implies that the distinction between civil and criminal sanctions does not, in fact, distinguish between two different types of sanctions. The distinction between civil and criminal sanctions seems to be less meaningful, at least in the case of the laws here considered, than that between misdemeanor and felony. A brief consideration of "willfulness" in reference to OPA sanctions and of the indecision of Congress as to which violations should or should not be criminal will serve to make this lack of distinction a little more evident.

It is beyond the limitations of this paper to consider the congressional debates, hearings, and bills which resulted in the creation of OPA. It may be noted, however, that Congress was in grave doubt as to the distinction that should be made between "civil" and "criminal." The Emergency Price Control Act as passed in the House in 1942 provided criminal penalties for the violation of *any* of the provisions of the prohibitory section (sec. 4) and also for making statements or entries which were false in any material respect in any document or report required under the record-keeping sections (secs. 2 and 202). It was not until the act came out of the conference committee that criminal prosecutions were limited to "willful" violations, with prosecutions subject to the control and supervision of the United States Attorney General. This is, it seems, an indication of the artificial distinction between "civil" and "criminal."

It is generally believed that willfulness, or criminal intent, is necessary to the commission of a criminal act. This is, however, by no means a universal criterion.[4] In enforcement of the OPA statutes and regulations, it was not always necessary to establish willfulness in the so-called "civil" sanctions. An interesting innovation came with the "Chandler defense" amendment in 1944 to the treble damage sanction. If a defendant in such action could show both that his overceiling violation was not willful and that he took reasonable precautions to avoid violation, he was subject to the payment of damages of only $25.00 or the amount of the overcharge, whichever was the greater. This is in contrast to the situation prior to the amendment, when the damages were $50.00 or three times the amount of the overcharge, whichever was the larger. The effect of this amendment was to make the amount of damages dependent upon willfulness, whereas, previous to this, no such requirement was necessary for a valid civil liability.[5] If this is the beginning of a "criminal" test in a civil action, it indicates a point at which the distinction between these two allegedly different types of rules disappears.

It was recognized both in the law and in the enforcement policy of OPA that the unintentional violations were just as inflationary in effect as the willful ones. Effective enforcement required that nonwillful violations had to be curbed just as much as willful ones, a recognition of the principle that the social consequences of behavior are largely independent of the individual's motivation. Enforcement action in the case of unintentional and open violations of OPA regulations relied largely upon the use of the injunction. The purpose of the injunction was simply to prevent violations of "any rule, regulation, order, or subpoena" issued upon authority of the two above laws.

The most common use of the injunction without the use of other sanctions in the preretail meat industry in Detroit was in connection with the open violation of the general provisions of Maximum Price Regulation 574. This regulation established overriding ceiling prices for live cattle and calves purchased for slaughter. It also established maximum amounts which slaughterers could pay for all cattle slaughtered during an accounting period. In addition, it allowed the administrator to establish the maximum percentage of "choice" and "good" cattle which a slaughterer could slaughter or deliver for meat during an accounting period. This regulation was important as a measure to control the price which the ultimate consumer paid for his beef; to prevent a disproportionate disappearance of the lower grades of beef through upgrading of the lower to the higher grades; and to prevent the smaller slaughterers from being driven out of business by the integrated large packers, who also process their kill. The small slaughterers account for only about 15 per cent of wholesale cattle slaughter, but are extremely important in local operations. OPA believed that enforcement of MPR 574 was largely successful in accomplishing these objectives.

About twenty-five instances of violation of MPR 574 were proceeded against in the Detroit district OPA office. All save one were open violations, in that the record-keeping and report-filing requirements were met. The source of the cattle, the prices paid, and the descriptions required were all properly recorded. The exceptional case, an attempt at evasive violation of MPR 574 through the hidden ownership of a farm and the clandestine slaughter of uninspected cattle thereon, was proceeded against criminally, all defendants being found guilty after a jury trial and sentenced to fines and prison terms.

One may question whether an open violation, unintentional in motivation, which could readily be discerned by an inspection of purchase invoices should be considered criminal. In answer to this, the declared purposes of the Second War Powers Act should be recalled. The object of MPR 574 was to implement this law so far as the price of beef and the distribution of beef were concerned. Since these violations resulted in a serious and substantial diversion of rationed meats, their effect upon the rationing program resulted in as much harm to the public welfare and to civilian food planning and were as damaging to the war effort as if they had been intentional. Indeed, in ration-suspension proceedings, which involved a much more serious sanction than the injunction, it was held that a failure to observe the rules relating to food processing, rationing, and distribution was demonstrative of incapacity to serve as a trustee of scarce, rationed commodities, since the trust involved heavy community responsibilities. In addition, these violators obtained through their illegal acts a distinct competitive advantage over those slaughterers who observed the law.

It is concluded, on the basis of the above discussion, that those acts in which there is an absence of intention to violate are nevertheless criminal acts if they meet the tests of formally defined social injury and of the possibility of legal sanctions.

The Emergency Price Control Act and the Second War Powers Act provided a variety of sanctions in the case of violations. Specifically, they are: License Warning Notice, injunction, criminal contempt, monetary damages, suspension of dealing in rationed commodities, suspension of license to deal in controlled commodities, fine or imprisonment, and both fine and imprisonment.

The types of violations were: open overceiling sales or purchases, evasive overceiling sales or purchases, and violations in reporting or recording. The last type was not a substantive violation but was often indicative of evasive violations and was usually so considered in investigations. Table 1 is a summary of the violations committed and formal sanctions imposed in the Detroit wholesale meat industry for the period December, 1942, through June 30, 1946, as indicated by an exhaustive search of OPA records. It includes only those cases in which a formal sanction was applied. Consequently, it excludes a number of serious cases still in litigation at the time this study was completed, as well as those which were dropped or dismissed.

Several interesting facts are revealed in Table 1 and the data on which the table is based. For one thing, these offenses tend to resemble more usual criminal offenses in several ways: They range from systematic to technical violations; there are both single offenders and repeated offenders. Table 1 shows that eighty-three different firms and 132 personal (not corporate) defendants had 122 cases charged against them in which they committed 195 offenses, for which 233 sanctions were imposed by the courts and by OPA. The 122 cases do not by any means tell the whole story of offenses committed. This is because one case usually included a number of separate offenses. In court proceedings, the number of counts was as high as nineteen, each count representing one violation. If all these counts had been totaled, the number of offenses would have been in excess of 1,000. The category "Violations: total," therefore, is only the total of three types of offenses—open, evasive, and record keeping. It can be stated without qualification that all evasive violations were willful, in that the perpetrators of them knew that they were offending and took pains to avoid detection. It cannot be said that all open violations were inad-

*Table 1. Summary of Violations and Sanctions in the Detroit Wholesale Meat Industry (December, 1942, through June 30, 1946)*

| | |
|---|---|
| Number of cases | 122 |
| Number of concerns | 83 |
| Number of personal defendants | 132 |
| Persons having previous criminal records[a] | 2 |
| | |
| Violations | |
|   (1)  Open overceiling | 65 |
|   (2)  Evasive overceiling | 58 |
|   (3)  Record keeping | 72 |
|     Total[b] | 195 |
| | |
| Damages paid: total | $132,811.71 |
| Range of damages[c] | $40.00–$6,000.00 |
| Fines paid: total | $97,500.00 |
| Range of fines[c] | $100.00–$15,000.00 |
| | |
| Sanctions imposed | |
|   (1)  License warning notice | 45 |
|   (2)  Injunction | 63 |
|   (3)  Damages | 58 |
|   (4)  Prison only | 3 |
|   (5)  Prison and fine | 12 |
|   (6)  Fine only | 22 |
|   (7)  Suspended sentence | 6 |
|   (8)  Probation | 8 |
|   (9)  Suspension order[d] | 16 |
|     Total | 233 |
| | |
| Prison terms: total months | 105–177 |
| Range of prison terms[c] | 3 mo.–1 yr. |

[a] As indicated by a check of Detroit police department and Federal Bureau of Investigation records.
[b] Not the actual number of offenses but the total of the three types of violations, tallying one complaint for an injunction or one criminal information as one case, regardless of the number of counts alleged.
[c] Exact limits not given, so as to avoid possible identification.
[d] Estimated total days of partial or total suspension of business: 2,129.

vertent, because there is good evidence to show that a number of them were as studied and deliberate as were the evasive ones. Open violations did not result in criminal prosecution. In sixteen cases of suspension-order proceedings, however, violations led to the imposition of this serious sanction. Suspension of the right to deal in certain commodities, for a stipulated period, was often at least as serious as a fine.

On the other hand, open violations and violations in record keeping were sometimes wholly inadvertent and technical. Violations in record keeping were always diligently investigated because they might have been indicative of evasive violations.

A second significant item in Table 1 is that only two of the 132 personal defendants had a previous criminal record. Neither of these two men, however, could in any way have been regarded as a gangster or a racketeer; neither of the convictions was for activities related to the meat industry, and both had been committed outside Michigan some years previously. The violations in the Detroit wholesale meat industry were committed by persons more or less well established in the different levels of the industry, from slaughterers to processors to wholesalers and to peddlers. It is this fact which, to a greater extent than any other, leads to the conclusion that the established businessman or firm was the black marketeer. The importance of this for a general theory of criminality is great. Without going into a detailed discussion, the following may be indicated. There is the problem of accounting for the commission of offenses by persons who have not previously offended, so far as is known.[6] If these cases are criminal and typical of OPA violations—and it is the position of this writer that they are—it becomes necessary to incorporate the description and analysis of these offenses and offenders into the field of criminology. From this it follows that a perhaps drastic modification of now accepted criminological generalizations and theories becomes necessary. This is indicated because the current generalizations are based upon a biased sample of offenders. There is no available information on white-collar offenders as far as the usual "factors" are concerned: broken home, childhood experiences, race, nativity or nationality background, amount of formal education, occupational training and experience, physical characteristics à la Hooton and Sheldon, and the like. Imagine what a cry of outraged ego would have electrified Congress if, upon establishing an evasive overcharge, the OPA had inquired into the businessman's love life to ascertain if he were frustrated or had investigated at what grade he had quit school or had measured his cephalic index and his mesomorphy or had tried to obtain any of the usual items that comprise the subject matter of current empirical studies of offenders. To restate Sutherland, the study of white-collar crime will not so much reform the criminal as it will the criminologists. It should be stated specifically that current criminological theory fails to account for the offenders whose acts have been studied in this paper. "Factors" in crime, such as broken home, race and nativity, amount of formal education, and the like, seem to be practically meaningless as far as these offenders are concerned. Shaw's approach, excellent as it is so far as institutionalized crime is concerned, is of little use here. Perhaps the two approaches of most promise are those of Sutherland and Taft.[7] The violations studied in this paper are systematic in Sutherland's meaning of that term. It is not clear, however, just how adequately "differential association" plus "opportunity" will account for them. In regarding crime as a product of American culture, Taft's approach faces the problem of accounting for the fact not only that a high proportion of businessmen and firms did not violate OPA regulations, but also that many deliberately refused to do so when they thought it was safe. At any rate, the approaches of Sutherland and Taft are infinitely to be preferred to the psychoanalytic. The latter viewpoint is of no help here, at least as it is expounded by Aichhorn, Alexander, Abrahamsen, Healy, and Lindner, because it insists that antisocial behavior—whatever that may be!—is the criterion of crime. (One would like to see the concept of infantile sexuality applied to the company which falsified its records.)

We may now consider another point, namely, a special characteristic of OPA violations which is not found in the usual criminal offenses and which makes them of peculiar significance both to the community at large and to a theory of criminality in particular. Summarily stated, an OPA violation in its very nature not merely involved one offense (by one individual or concern in the conduct of its business affairs) but began a progressive chain of offenses which did not stop until the ultimate consumer paid the amount involved in all the offenses of the given chain.

Table 2 illustrates this feature of white-collar offenses. This table is a partial census made by this writer, through a search of Detroit district office OPA records, of the sources of supply of a firm we shall call "Company 219." This firm was involved in three OPA cases, with the following total of sanctions imposed on it: two injunctions, $12,000 in fines, twenty-four months' imprisonment and nine years' probation. Table 2 refers to only one of three cases of Company 219. We were able to establish, through a search of Detroit OPA records, that at least four Detroit retail outlets were involved in OPA actions as a consequence of selling at over-ceiling prices the poultry which they had bought from Company 219 at prices in excess of their legal purchase prices. This poultry had been purchased by the company in the deals listed in Table 2. This table shows the following in round numbers where the data were obtainable from OPA records: the weight of live pounds of poultry purchased, the amount of the ceiling price, the amount of the illegal side-money paid by the company and received by the sources, and the action taken against the sources by OPA. These actions are summarized in the right-hand column.

It may be stated almost categorically that any preretail or wholesale firm engaged in price-ceiling violations set into operation a series or chain of price violations which eventually resulted in the ultimate consumer's paying more for his goods than he should have had to under the law. If, at any stage in the process of putting goods into the possession of the ultimate consumer, a price violation occurred, this violation was passed on to the succeeding stages. If the violation were committed by the primary wholesaler or processor, all the succeeding secondary wholesalers and the retail outlet were progressively involved. If the violation were by a secondary wholesaler, all the stages after him were involved. One may make an analogy here with a pebble dropped into a pond, which sets

Table 2. *Summary of Violations Committed by, and Sanctions Imposed on, Sources of Supply of One Criminal Violator*

| Sources | Pounds of Poultry | Ceiling price | Illegal side-money | Action taken by OPA |
|---|---|---|---|---|
| 1 | 41,000 | $14,000.00 | $2,200.00 | Charged as co-conspirator, but not co-defendant |
| 2 | 20,000 | 7,000.00 | 700.00 | ? |
| 3 | 33,000 | ? | 1,700.00 | Treble damages of $5,100.00; License Warning Notice |
| 4 | 52,000 | ? | 3,600.00 | One year and one day in prison; $3,000.00 fine; six months in prison; $150.00 fine (two defendants) |
| 5 | 25,000 | ? | 1,100.00 | Treble damages of $3,300.00; License Warning Notice |
| 6 | 22,000 | ? | 500.00 | Double damages of $1,000.00; License Warning Notice |
| 7 | 10,000 | ? | 300.00 | Treble damages of $900.00; injunction |
| 8 | 3,200 | ? | 300.00 | Double damages of $600.00; License Warning Notice |
| 9 | ? | 20,000.00 | 2,000.00 | Charged as co-conspirator but not co-defendant |
| 10 | ? | ? | ? | ? |
| 11 | ? | ? | ? | ? |
| 12 | ? | ? | ? | ? |
| 13 | 11,500 | ? | 300.00 | Statute of limitations |
| 14 | 12,500 | ? | 300.00 | Statute of limitations |
| 15 | 2,000 | ? | 50.00 | Statute of limitations (apparently non-willful) |
| 16 | 23,000 | ? | 750.00 | Treble damages of $2,250.00; License Warning Notice |
| 17* | 70,000 | ? | 2,100.00 | Treble damage suit; judgment of $6,300.00 collected |
| Total | 325,200 | | 15,900.00 | $22,600.00 damages and fines; 2 prison terms, 1 injunction, 5 License Warning notices, 2 charges of conspiracy |

* Does not include seven other larger shipments of source 17.

up a series of successive waves. No wholesaler could commit a violation "by himself," so to speak, but must inevitably have directly involved other firms in his violation. The retailers who paid above the ceiling legally allowed them in the course of trade or business were thereby violating OPA regulations. Let it not be assumed that they all absorbed this excess price and sold to the ultimate consumer at their legal ceiling price— thereby breaking even or perhaps losing money. The chain of violations was completed by their overcharges to their customers. As a matter of fact, in its enforcement program, the OPA often "worked" this chain of violations from the middle to both ends and from one end to the other. The retail customers of a violating wholesaler were investigated. The wholesale suppliers of violating retailers were investigated. It was possible to establish the existence of these chains by following through OPA investigations, as we did in the case of Company 219.

This chain effect was by no means unique to the wholesale meat industry in Detroit. Not only the meat industry nationally, but also the entire business community subject to OPA control in which there are two or more steps in the handling of goods before the ultimate purchaser obtained them would show this characteristic. We found this to be the case not only in wholesale meat but also in fish, poultry, eggs and dairy products, produce, groceries, and sugar. The investigation of all these categories, save meat, has been partial but still intensive enough to establish an empirical basis for the above generalization. It may be remarked, incidentally, that each industry, apparently spontaneously, developed techniques, particularly in evasive violations, which were peculiar to it and designed for its "needs." In addition, it may be indicated that the necessary involvement of others and the setting into operation of a chain of violations are not unique to OPA violations. This would be true of certain other laws regulating business. OPA violations, in their chain effect, are similar to the bribing of policemen and the operation of organized vice, in that neither of these types of activities can be carried through by the initiator of the illegal deeds but must necessarily involve other persons. This writer is not presently attempting a theory of either criminality in general or of white-collar crime in particular but is merely throwing the problem open for discussion, so to speak. Perhaps part of the answer is to be found in a typological approach to offenses and offenders.[8]

In summary, we may make the following points: (1) Violations of OPA regulations in the preretail meat industry are criminal acts, in that they meet the criteria of formally defined, proscribed and prescribed acts and of punishability. (2) The distinction between civil and criminal sanctions is held not to distinguish between two different types of sanctions. (3) Willfulness or deliberate intent to violate is not essential to making a white-collar offense a criminal act. (4) At least in the industry considered in this paper, the commission of an offense almost always necessarily involved the commission of another similar offense by a different party.

# COMMENT

*Ernest W. Burgess*

The theory of white-collar crime implicit in this paper is that little or no distinction should be made between different violations or violators of all laws or regulations which have the sanction of a penalty. It is a legalistic and not a sociological position to regard these as one and the same.

Many years ago Edward A. Ross made a distinction between crimes recognized by law for generations and disapproved by the mores and what he called "criminaloids," which are new offenses as the result of recent legislation or of regulations by governmental agencies, carrying with them a penalty for violation. If all persons violating traffic regulations, health ordinances, etc., are to be considered criminals, then the numbers of criminals in the population undoubtedly greatly outnumber those who have never committed an act that is against the law or the regulations of some governmental agencies.

The point, then, is not to consider all violators of statutes, ordinances, and regulations as a homogeneous group. The differences are far greater than the resemblances between the automobilist who exceeds the speed limit, the OPA violator, and the burglar. Legally, they all violate a law or a regulation and are subject to a penalty. Sociologically, they are different, and it is the differences that are significant. OPA violations in the Detroit wholesale meat industry are unsatisfactory evidence of crime in any but the technical, legal sense of the word. The following are outstanding differences between these violations and offenses generally recognized as criminal by the community.

1. There is no evidence presented that OPA violators conceived themselves as criminal or were so considered by the public. In fact, for only two out of 122 is a previous criminal record reported.

2. The Emergency Price Control Act and the Second War Powers Act were suddenly imposed upon businessmen, defining many business transactions as offenses which had previously been legal.

3. No concerted organized effective attempt was made by civic leaders, churches, schools, the press, and governmental agencies to apply social condemnation to violations by businessmen and to purchases by consumers. Consequently, these acts were not stigmatized by the public as falling in the same category as murder, burglary, robbery, forgery, and rape.

4. Large sections of the population, comprising perhaps over half the adults, participated in black-market purchases during the war.

5. Few cases of violation (only 6.4 per cent) drew prison sentences,

and these were very light as compared with non-white-collar "crimes," averaging only from three months to one year.

The attempt to make little or no distinction between white-collar crime and other offenses promises confusion rather than clarification in criminology. It is important to distinguish between offenses which carry with them strong public disapproval and those violations of regulations (or recently enacted statutes) in which large sections of the public are willing accomplices.

# REJOINDER

## *Frank E. Hartung*

The opponents of the concept of white-collar crime are in disagreement as to why it should be opposed. Paul W. Tappan is opposed to the concept because, he says, its proponents are sociological and not legalistic. Professor Burgess objects because "it is a legalistic and not a sociological position."

Professor Burgess makes the point that all violators of all statutes carrying a penalty are not a homogeneous group. With this I agree, particularly as in a footnote to the reading I specifically referred to a typological approach to offenses and offenders. However, why should not traffic-ordinance violators be considered as criminal, since upon conviction, they are subject to fine or imprisonment or perhaps both? In its "Offense Classifications" *Uniform Crime Reports* has four classifications for traffic offenses. More important, though, and quite fundamental is Professor Burgess' rejection of the proposition that all who are found guilty of violating criminal laws are to be considered criminals. He says that the violations referred to in the reading are "unsatisfactory evidence of crime in any but the technical legal sense of the word." On what other but a "technical legal" basis should one be adjudged criminal? Professor Burgess argues as if violations of the mores should be considered criminal; presumably this is why he alleges that the present article is not sociological. It is anomalous that today a sociologist should defend an informal definition of crime. The ludicrous position taken by the psychoanalysts on "infant criminality" is an example of where the informal definition leads one. In psychoanalysis the newly born infant is said to be criminal because of his antisocial conduct: Antisocial behavior is criminal; the infant defecates in public and has no respect whatever for the rights and wishes of others; this is antisocial, and, therefore, the infant is criminal!

It is high time for sociologists—for everyone—to discard the "antisocial" and "mores" approach to crime. Anyway, it is against the mores to violate the law.

Let me now briefly consider Professor Burgess' numbered comments.

1. Although it is not included in the present article, I have considerable evidence that OPA violators and the public both considered OPA violations to be criminal. I hope to publish some of this material soon, based upon extensive interviews with both violating and nonviolating meat wholesalers and an areal sample of more than 600 Detroit adults.[9]

2. Not all OPA "controls" were so sudden as many people suppose. The two statutes and the regulations discussed in this article incorporated numerous laws which had been enacted as long ago as 1906 and which were supported by the vast majority of the packing industry. The law against selling uninspected meat is an old one; so, too, is the local law against selling contaminated meat. The new and sudden provisions in OPA were rationing and ceiling prices.

3. A number of public opinion studies made during and just after the war showed that the public defined OPA violations as being criminal.

4. To assert that "perhaps over half the adults participated in black-market purchases" is simply romanticism.

5. Many people will doubtless find it reasonable to believe that an "outstanding difference" between white-collar and non-white-collar crimes is that the former result in fewer and lighter prison terms. (Is not Professor Burgess saying here that white-collar crimes are *really* crimes?) However, because of the complete absence of any comparative studies I myself will be very wary of accepting this assertion as true. It is estimated that only about 3 per cent of the major crimes committed in this country result in prison terms. And, of course, not all these sentences are for the legally allowable maximum term.

If the proposition is true that the concept of white-collar crime promises confusion in criminology, as Professor Burgess claims, it is only because it calls into question the doubtful generalizations based upon the older and biased samples of the criminal population. In my opinion, Sutherland's analysis of white-collar crime is the most significant advance in criminology since Goring's *The English Convict* and Healy's *The Individual Delinquent*. It has definite implications for sociological theory in general and for urban sociology in particular.

# CONCLUDING COMMENT

*Ernest W. Burgess*

A criminal is a person who regards himself as a criminal and is so regarded by society. He is the product of the criminal-making process. Professor Hartung gives no evidence that the so-called "white-collar" criminal that he studied could be included under this definition. Under his definition of criminals the great majority of adults are criminals. But that is only because he employs a legalistic and not a sociological definition of the criminal. My point that half the adult population participated in black-market transactions is one not of "romanticism" but of fact.

## Notes

1. See Edwin H. Sutherland, *White Collar Crime* (New York: Dryden Press, 1949), p. 9.

2. See, for example, Hans Kelsen, *General Theory of Law and State* (Cambridge: Harvard University Press, 1945); William Ebenstein, *The Pure Theory of Law* (Madison, Wis.: University of Wisconsin Press, 1945); Jerome Hall, "Prolegomena to a Science of Criminal Law," *University of Pennsylvania Law Review*, 89 (March, 1941), pp. 549–580.

3. Sutherland, *op. cit.*; Marshall B. Clinard, "Criminological Theories of Violation of Wartime Regulations," *American Sociological Review*, 11 (June, 1946), pp. 258–270.

4. See Livingston Hall, "Statutory Law of Crimes, 1887–1936," *Harvard Law Review*, 50 (February, 1937), pp. 616–657. Hall shows that in many states one may be committed to prison without the protection of either or both of the rules of criminal intent and the presumption of innocence, for a number of offenses.

5. *Bowles v. Rack*, 55 F. Supp. 865 (1944).

6. Violations of local ordinances and state laws are not included in this study. These cases number in the hundreds over a period of a few years. One large packer, for example, has been found guilty about thirty times in three years of violating Michigan pure-food laws!

7. Edwin H. Sutherland, "A Theory of Criminology," *Principles of Criminology*, 4th ed. (Philadelphia: Lippincott 1939), chap. 1; Donald R. Taft, "Crime as a Product of American Culture," in *Criminology* (New York: Macmillan, 1942), chap. 15.

8. See Alfred R. Lindesmith and H. Warren Dunham, "Some Principles of Criminal Typology," *Social Forces*, 19 (March, 1941), pp. 307–314.

9. See Frank E. Hartung, *Law and Social Differentiation* (Ann Arbor, Mich.: University of Michigan Microfilms, 1949), chap. 6.

# 10

# WHITE-COLLAR CRIME AND SOCIAL STRUCTURE

*Vilhelm Aubert*

One sign of maturity in a research field is the constant and conscious utilization of specific empirical findings to throw light on general theoretical problems. As long as this takes place only as a caprice of occasional deviants, a science has not reached the stage where research becomes genuinely cumulative. The study of crime is in this respect a pertinent example of missed opportunities. The numerous studies in the etiology of criminal and delinquent behavior have, by and large, constituted an applied field, where research might instead also have been oriented toward basic social theory or at least toward theories of the middle range.

One main obstacle to the development of a fruitful theoretical orientation is to be found in the tendency to treat criminal behavior, on the one hand, and the system of legal sanctions, on the other, as two separate problems. In our opinion, crime and punishment are most fruitfully handled as two aspects of a group process or two links in a specific type of social interaction.

It is frequently impossible to discover the sociopsychological origins

Reprinted from *American Journal of Sociology*, 58 (November, 1952), pp. 263–271, by permission of The University of Chicago Press. Copyright 1952 by The University of Chicago Press.

and functions of criminal behavior without insight into the social processes behind the enactment of the corresponding parts of the criminal legislation. The social norms and mores that gave impetus to the enactment and the groups that uphold these norms are important to know for purposes, also, of tracing the criminal recruitment mechanisms. The nature of the norms thus legally sanctioned may, for instance, to some extent determine whether the criminals tend to be rebels, psychopaths, or rational profit seekers.

The interdependence of the origin and function of social norms and the origin of deviations is seen very clearly in societies which make political activities criminal. Unless we know fairly well the location and scope of the groups supporting the legislation, the function it serves in those groups, and the social norms it is based upon, we shall not succeed in explaining and predicting offenses. As we shall see later, this type of interdependence is apparent in the study of white-collar crimes. In the study of more "orthodox" or "classical" crimes it has, however, been largely ignored, in spite of occasional programmatic pleas for an interaction approach.[1]

There are some fairly obvious reasons why the origin and functions of deviant behavior—criminal or not—have been the main focus of scientific attention, to the neglect of the complementary phenomenon of norm-conformity and pressure to conform. It seems somehow to be "natural" to ask why the deviants become deviants and not why the conforming majority conform and support definitions of specific types of behavior and attitudes as deviations and prosecute them as such. Merton made the parallel observation concerning the sociology of knowledge that it seems more "natural" to search for a causal explanation of scientific and other intellectual "errors" than to inquire into the whys and wherefores of "truth." But, he proceeds, the "Copernican revolution" in the sociology of knowledge came when the scientists began to ask for explanations not only of the mistakes, but also of the true, plausible, or valid knowledge.[2] A similar revolution is much needed in the study of criminology and criminal law.

It is, by the way, likely that its close relationship to law explains why criminology in this respect has remained a more obedient servant of society's conventions than many other fields of social science. There is an understandable resistance on the part of lawmakers, judges, and lawyers to become the object of scientific studies, as the criminals are. And this resistance becomes effective by virtue of the close association between them and the criminologists.

There are other factors which may help us to understand the strong scientific attraction inherent in deviant behavior. In contrast to conformity, deviant behavior is dramatic and often highly entertaining. In Gestalt terminology, deviation is the "figure" against the "ground" of conformity. There can be little doubt that much scientific effort in sociology has been drawn to the outstanding and dramatic—although theoretically isolated—events, at the expense of the dull trivialities which frequently may provide us with better keys to the understanding of general problems.

The recent concern among social scientists with white-collar crime tends to bring long-neglected relationships between criminal behavior, criminal law, penal sanctions, and social structure into focus. The unexpected and somehow deviant nature of many recent laws defining white-collar crimes has made it natural to ask for an explanation of the norms themselves and not only of their infringements. As soon as this happens, new theoretical vistas are immediately opened.

Although white-collar crime today in itself is a very important practical problem, its research importance does not lie within the specific field itself. What is theoretically important is that white-collar crime seems to be one of those phenomena which are particularly sensitive to—and therefore highly symptomatic of—more pervasive and generalizable features of the social structure. That is why the field merits even more attention than it is given today.

Although the selection of white-collar crime as a field of research is a real achievement, the discussion has had an unfortunate slant. Not the least responsible for this is the pioneer in the study of white-collar crime, the late E. H. Sutherland. His formulation of the problem, "Is white-collar crime a crime?"[3] has given rise to futile terminological disputes, which are apt to become clouded by class identifications and ideological convictions.

The discussion some years ago between Hartung and Burgess demonstrates some dangers inherent in this way of phrasing the problem.[4] Hartung seemed to interpret the question of whether white-collar crimes are crimes or not as a research problem and gave an affirmative answer as if it were a significant result of his studies. Although the material presented by Hartung is of considerable interest, the conclusion seems less significant, since the problem mentioned is largely a matter of definition. Burgess on the other hand rejects Hartung's (and Sutherland's) answer on the basis of a theory about differences in causation, the implication being that there exists a specific "criminal-making process" common to all traditional crimes but not white-collar crimes, providing these former crimes with a uniform explanation. In view of the evidence, this seems hardly less dogmatic than the opposite view.

When Burgess suggests that "a criminal is a person who regards himself as a criminal and is so regarded by society," he is suggesting a subtle and in some ways significant criterion. It has the disadvantage, however, that only very careful attitude studies can reveal if it applies or not in a concrete case. For this end, a unifying concept of those who fulfill the criterion is much needed. But if it were to be taken for granted without further research that all traditional crimes fulfill the criterion while none of the white-collar crimes do, it is merely a way to dispose of a complicated empirical problem in the guise of mere conceptual clarification and definition.

Sutherland defined white-collar crime as "a crime committed by a person of respectability and high social status in the course of his occupation."[5] As a prototype of white-collar crimes, he focused special attention on crimes committed by businessmen in the course of their business activities. Hartung uses a somewhat narrower definition: "A white-collar offense is defined as a violation of law regulating business, which is committed for a firm by the firm or its agents in the conduct of its business." Cressey seems implicitly to be using a wider concept—in accordance with Sutherland's explicit definition—a concept broad enough to include also embezzlement.[6] In the following, we shall primarily have in mind white-collar crimes in the more narrow sense, those crimes which all the cited writers would accept as such.

The following characteristics of white-collar crimes are claimed to be established by the research done on these problems, primarily Sutherland's.

As far as the "law in books" is concerned, white-collar crimes have much in common with most "traditional" crimes. Statutes define a penal sanction against them. According to Norwegian law, these may be quite severe; for price violation they may amount to as much as three years' imprisonment. It is maintained that the situation is similar according to American law, although the evidence is not equally clear.

The "law in action" is, however, in this field characterized by slow, inefficient, and highly differential implementation. And, it is maintained, more so than in other areas of the criminal law. Sometimes the lack of efficient implementation is foreshadowed already in the "law in books" by the setting up of special types of enforcement machinery or the failing to solve obvious enforcement problems. Frequently, however, there is a real gap between the two levels of the law.

White-collar crimes are numerous and, as it follows from the definition, committed by people of high social status, which usually also means high income.

A trivial conclusion to be drawn from this is that low socioeconomic status and associated factors cannot be considered crucial in the explanation of crime in general; that is, if white-collar crimes were to be considered crimes. It is, moreover, possible that the acknowledged existence of white-collar crimes may tend to draw some of the attention away from these factors in other areas of criminal behavior also. The same may happen to theories that explain crimes in terms of personality disorganization, low intelligence, physical type, or the like, although such theories are not meant to cover white-collar crime.

There is usually no clear-cut opposition between the white-collar criminals and the general public, who are themselves often violating the same laws on a modest scale. The public has customarily a condoning, indifferent, or ambivalent attitude. It must be admitted that this conclusion is based to a large extent upon impressionistic observation rather than systematic surveys, although some surveys exist.

It has been established in some studies that the white-collar criminal finds support for his behavior in group norms, thus tending to break down further the view that violations of laws are rooted in man's raw nature, in his unrestrained biological impulses. We must agree with Merton's statement that "certain phases of social structure generate the circumstances in which infringement of social codes constitutes a 'normal response.' "[7] It is nothing new in criminology that crimes are frequently committed by persons who give each other social (and other) support in groups in pursuance of criminal careers.[8] But what distinguishes the white-collar criminal in this respect is that his group often has an elaborate and widely accepted ideological rationalization for the offenses and is a group of great social significance outside the sphere of criminal activity—usually a group with considerable economic and political power.

This brief survey does not give a definite answer to the question: "Is white-collar crime a crime?" The definition of an activity as "crime" is always, apart from its scientific merits, a "persuasive definition."[9] It contains an element of propaganda. The terminology one accepts in the present controversy will depend upon how much one wants to get rid of these white-collar activities. Disregarding that, for the moment, we have seen that white-collar crimes have at least one characteristic in common with all the conventional crimes: They are forbidden by law, and the law stipulates a penal sanction against infringements. But with respect to the other characteristics mentioned (respectively, differential and inefficient implementation; status of violators; tolerance of public; and social support of offenders), they seem to differ somewhat from many other types of law violations. It should be noted, however, that some of these differences are only differences in degree and emphasis. Furthermore, the crimes which fall outside the white-collar category are not as homogeneous as some writers seem to believe, which makes comparisons even more difficult.

For purposes of theoretical analysis, it is of prime importance to develop and apply concepts which preserve and emphasize the ambiguous nature of the white-collar crimes and not to "solve" the problem by classifying them as either "crimes" or "not crimes." Their controversial nature is exactly what makes them so interesting from a sociological point of view and what gives us a clue to important norm conflicts, clashing group interests, and maybe incipient social change. One main benefit to be derived from the study of white-collar crimes springs from the opportunity which the ambivalence in the citizen, in the businessman, and among lawyers, judges, and even criminologists offers as a barometer of structural conflicts and change-potential in the larger social system of which they and the white-collar crimes are parts.

The laws against white-collar crime are usually not in obvious and apparent harmony with the mores. They are largely an outcome of the increased complexity of modern industrial society, a complexity which requires legal control of activities with long-range and often very indirectly damaging effects. Price regulation, intending to curb inflation, is a pertinent example. An illegal price will frequently create no immediate reaction and invoke no sanctions from the mores in the community. A tie-in with the mores can only be established through public acceptance of relatively complicated means-end hypotheses from modern economic science. As long as these hypotheses have not become integrated parts of the individual's moral system, there will be a gap between the letter of the law and the requirements of the informal norms of the daily interaction between the members of society.

There can be small doubt that this gap exists in many modern societies. And in some areas, in relation to some groups, there is not only a gap but a conflict between the laws and the mores or ideologies which one traditionally accepted. In such cases, ambivalence may arise in the attitudes toward white-collar crimes, originating in a loyalty divided between the laws and the traditional beliefs. These ambivalent attitudes, their detailed structures and functions, are the most fruitful stating point for empirical research on white-collar crime in its relation to social structure.

With detailed surveys of these attitudes in hand, research should be further oriented toward the actual external cross pressures that operate in this area of opinion formation. What is, more specifically, the content of the partly conflicting group norms? How can we locate the opinion leaders ("norm speakers") and followers ("norm receivers") within the relevant groups? How can we give an adequate description of an individual's position as a member of more than one group, as illustrated by his conflicting roles as a law-abiding member of the nation and as a loyal member of the business community? How does group membership affect the perception of specific white-collar crimes and of sanctions against them? Under what conditions of group membership, previous norms, personal interests, etc., do the threat of penal sanctions exert pressure (and how strong a pressure) toward conformity with the legal norms? What are the sanctions that exert pressure toward conformity with conflicting norms?[10]

All these problems, selected at random, have fairly obvious empirical implications. Answers would be highly relevant to current social theory. One basic methodological problem will, of course, be to develop precise and psychologically meaningful criteria of group membership.

Our approach does not lead to any extensive search for the idiosyncratic motivation of individual deviations from legal norms. It is assumed as a working hypothesis that the white-collar criminal is usually no "genuine deviant." He is only apparently so, as long as his group and its norms are unknown. Festinger has recently pointed out the fallacy of attributing deviant behavior or opinions to an individual when his group affiliations are not adequately understood.[11] Here lies a field of the utmost theoretical importance, requiring the most subtle research techniques.

We assume that white-collar crimes are determined by social norms, accepted and enforced by groups and individuals with whom the individual identifies, groups which tend to give social support to the illegal activity. On the other hand, the legal rules and their enforcement are also determined by social norms, accepted and enforced by other kinds of social groups with which the legislators and enforcement agencies identify themselves and with which even the violators often have some measure of identification. The problems of the etiology of crime and of punishment seem then to relate to the same set of basic theoretical concepts. Moreover, it must be assumed that there is a constant process of interaction between the groups involved and some interdependence of the conflicting social norms. The individual's behavior and attitudes, under cross pressure from both, can no more be understood on the basis of the one alone than on the basis of the other alone.

In the light of the preceding, I shall present a few aspects of two studies that have recently been carried out in Oslo. Both of them are concerned with types of behavior which fulfill, or nearly so, Sutherland's definition of white-collar crimes.

In the first study, we made a survey of the attitudes of certain types of businessmen toward the rationing of goods and price regulation and toward their violation. It was already known that the number of such violations was great, as shown by the criminal statistics for postwar years. The general impression of the survey confirmed the statistics, although we made no systematic attempt to discover violations within our probability sample from a few business branches in Oslo. The survey concentrated on perceptions and attitudes only.[12]

The roles and attitudes of our subjects seem to be analyzable in terms of Stouffer's concepts, "universalistic" and "particularistic obligations."[13] The businessman has conflicting roles as a law-abiding citizen and as a member of the business community. The felt universalistic obligation is to obey the law, an obligation which finds some support in the "general sense of justice," but which is not fortified by very strong or efficient sanctions against breach. The felt particularistic obligation implies avoidance only of certain blatant offenses and, on the other hand, resistance to these laws in general. This is an obligation to business colleagues, supported by their ideology and frequently also by profit motives. In general, it seems that the particularistic obligation takes precedence over the universalistic obligation. Subjects do, however, vary considerably in this respect. Our data do not, unfortunately, permit us to explain these variations.

The attitude toward the legal regulations was negative in general. But, on a more specific level, it was frequently admitted that parts of the legal structure were necessary. This ambivalence was even more marked in the attitudes toward violations and violators of the laws. On the one hand, on a general level, these were frequently condemned in principle. Most often, however, the respondents defended and tried to justify many types of specific violation. It was apparent that they perceived at least two general types of violators: "the good established firms" and "the outsiders" (including new firms, small firms, disreputable firms, etc.). Violations by the former category were considered much more harmless than those committed by the "outsiders." It seems that the businessmen in this case have developed norms of their own, more tolerant and therefore partly contrasting with the legal norms.

Here lies a problem of more general importance. Burgess and others pointed out that legal definitions of crimes are inadequate in the study of causation, because the types of behavior legally classified together need not show any uniformity in terms of etiology. The perception of an act as criminal on the part of violators and public is presented as a more suitable criterion. We have found that on the basis of such a criterion it will be necessary to classify some violations of a specific law as criminal and others as not. Detailed studies of attitudes toward specific laws would therefore be necessary in order to make any kind of statement about criminal behavior, if Burgess's criterion were to be accepted.

There was a tendency on the part of our respondents to structure their attitudes in a way which did not correspond to legal definitions. Irrespective of the terminology one accepts, we shall expect different motivation on the part of those who violate the regulations in an "acceptable" way and those who do it with less decorum, as, for example, a free-lance black marketeer. We notice furthermore that some of those who violate the laws in nonacceptable ways engage in behavior which does not possess all the characteristics ascribed to white-collar crimes by Sutherland, in spite of the fact that they meet his explicit definition of white-collar crime.

The results indicate that the concept "white-collar crime" may not be of such general usefulness in building up hypotheses about crime causation as some have believed. Most likely, the main merit of the concept has been to draw attention to new and important data useful in showing the one-sidedness of many previous generalizations about criminal behavior. The concept does, furthermore, take on increased significance if we look at the phenomena discussed from the other side; that is, if we focus on the etiology of criminal law and law enforcement.

Most of the laws and a very significant part of the enforcement machinery that make up the legal background of economic regulation in Norway aim specifically at the business group, which contains at least a large segment of people with high socioeconomic status. It seems justified to interpret the growing number of legally defined crimes in this area as a symptom of a slow change in Norwegian social structure, where two partly competing social hierarchies, each with its own marks of distinction, are existing peacefully side by side. Of these, the labor movement and the government agencies it controls represent the ascendant hierarchy, while the business group and its fringes represent the descendant hierarchy. It seems that the definition of new legal crimes of the white-collar brand has served an important social function by giving the ascendant group a feeling of possessing the economic power corresponding to its political supremacy. We do, on the other hand, find traces of resistance to implementation in the social structure in general and in the enforcement machinery. The result is slowness and inefficiency, which create a feeling of harmlessness among the violators. This may then serve the function of pacifying the businessmen and in that way insure the social peace which Norway has enjoyed after the war.[14]

If the preceding speculations prove to have some basis in reality, it appears that causes and functions of white-collar crime legislation differ significantly in some respects from other types of criminal legislation.

The second study[15] referred to dealt with a type of behavior which can only be characterized as white-collar crime according to a fairly wide interpretation of Sutherland's definition. We investigated a new piece of social legislation, regulating the working conditions of domestic help. Violations of this law are committed by housewives, frequently citizens of relatively high socioeconomic status, in the course of their occupation. Violations are punishable, although a penal sanction presupposes persistence in violation in spite of warnings. It must be admitted that both the position of the violators and the nature of the sanction make this behavior marginal to current discussions about white-collar crimes. Nevertheless, it raises so many of the same problems that it merits some attention in the present context.

Viewed as a study of criminal—or "criminaloid"—behavior and of crime causation, the survey had some peculiar features. It was, in the first place, not based upon any prison population or population identifiable through police or court records. It was entirely a study of "hidden criminality" and it revealed close to 100 per cent "criminality" in the probability sample which was studied. The identification of violations was based upon a fairly intricate interview, eliciting factual information about the respondent's own behavior and (in interviews with housemaids) their employer's behavior. The respondent was usually ignorant of the laws pertaining to her behavior. A procedure like the one we applied seems to be the logical consequence of a strictly legal definition of criminal behavior.

It did, however, give a rather frightening demonstration of the technical problems involved in the mapping of criminal behavior in this sense.

As for the correlates, or possible causes, they differed considerably from those which usually predominate in criminological theory. It turned out that the age of the victim was associated with the incidence of violation. The insight into the content of the legal norms on the part of the potential violators was another factor of some importance. The size of the family also seemed to have something to do with violations. The factor, however, which seemed most significantly (negatively) associated with violation was the clarity and scope of the contract upon which the work relationship was based.

The aforementioned factors differentiated our respondents. If we want to understand why there are so many "crimes" in the whole group, the newness of the law is significant and its reformative nature likewise. The relative isolation of the victims and the uncontrollability of the illegal behavior probably also have a great deal to do with the high incidence of violations.

If those variables that are mentioned here are significant causally, it goes once more to show that specific types of law violations need specific types of explanations.[16] Using the legal definition of "crime," there is probably little in common between all the phenomena covered by the concept. And the same seems to be true of white-collar crime. This type can also differ very much in its nature and may need quite different causal explanations. We disregard then such global and rather empty principles as the one that "all criminal behavior is learned."

In the present study, we made an attempt to examine rather carefully the conditions determining the form and content of the criminal clause in the new law. This revealed a striking ambivalence on the part of the legislators to the behavior in question. Most likely this ambivalence reflects the existence of two groups in the legislature, groups which are frequently divided on issues of social legislation. This division corresponds roughly to the one described previously, that is, between the left and the right. The legislators expressed a serious wish to put teeth into the new law by supporting it with penal sanctions. On the other hand, however, it was emphasized that the aim of the law was already achieved and sanctions were therefore unnecessary. Furthermore, it would be impossible to enforce the law through inspection in the homes. The resulting criminal clause was a hybrid. It did stipulate a penal sanction, but at the same time, it was made practically unenforceable.[17]

The function of this social legislation as it was finally formulated seems again to be the avoidance of a serious split on the issue between contrasting ideological factions in the legislature and corresponding groups in the population. Perhaps the mere existence of a criminal clause goes some way to satisfy those who on ideological grounds demand action against employers who misuse their housemaids. Its lack of enforcement, on the other hand, protects the opposite interest group against any immediate serious bother. It looks as if, in the kind of social structure one finds in Norway today, this sort of purely formal criminalization serves primarily to preserve "the groupness of the group," according to Llewellyn the basic "law-job."[18]

Let us now summarize some of the experiences from the two Norwegian studies, in so far as they pertain to the discussion of white-collar crime.

The public's and the violators' perceptions of crimes in general are frequently not congruent with legal definitions, the implication being that we may find important differences in motivation and other causal mechanisms within even very specific legal categories. Consequently, we find differences to an even higher degree within broader concepts such as white-collar crime.

According to the definition that "a criminal is a person who regards himself as a criminal and is so regarded by society" some white-collar offenses are crimes while others are not.

But it looks as if at least the large bulk of laws stipulating penalties for white-collar offenses have something in common sociologically. This needs much further study, however. The major variables which account for the defining of such acts as crimes seem to be connected with the concept of multiple social hierarchies or diverse status systems.

Legal definitions of white-collar crime imply a need for the study of hidden criminality, which constitutes the vast majority of these offenses. Out of this arise methodological problems of vast scope, severely limiting the possibility of answering the problem of causation.

In the area of research discussed in this paper, it seems that the most fruitful orientation in the research is a study of the interaction between the legal stimulus and the response of violators and the public. This requires careful study of the legislative process and the machinery of enforcement, as well as the study of individual motives, attitudes, and social situation of offenders.

Finally, the basic concepts involved in such a study should not be of a specifically criminological or legal nature, but belong in a general theory of social psychology.

# Notes

1. Thorsten Sellin, *Culture Conflict and Crime* (New York: Social Science Research Council, 1938), chap. 2.

2. Robert K. Merton, "The Sociology of Knowledge," in Robert K. Merton, *Social Theory and Social Structure* (New York: The Free Press, 1950), p. 222.

3. Edwin H. Sutherland, "Is 'White-Collar Crime' Crime?" *American Sociological Review*, 10 (April, 1945), 132–139.

4. Frank E. Hartung, "White-Collar Offenses in the Wholesale Meat Industry in Detroit," *American Journal of Sociology*, 56 (July, 1950), pp. 25–30, and Ernest W. Burgess' comment which follows (pp. 31–34).

5. Edwin H. Sutherland, *White Collar Crime* (New York: Dryden Press, 1949), p. 9.

6. Donald R. Cressey, "The Criminal Violation of Financial Trust," *American Sociological Review*, 15 (December, 1950), p. 741.

7. Robert K. Merton, "Social Structure and Anomie," *American Sociological Review*, 3 (October, 1938), p. 672.

8. See Muzafer Sherif and Hadley Cantril, *The Psychology of Ego-Involvements* (New York: Wiley, 1947), chap. 10.

9. See Charles L. Stevenson, *Ethics and Language* (New Haven, Conn.: Yale University Press, 1948), pp. 210ff.

10. A theoretical outline of many of the concepts involved in such studies is to be found in Torgny T. Segerstedt, *Social Control as a Sociological Concept* (Uppsala: Lundequistska Bokhandeln, 1948).

11. Leon Festinger, "Informal Communication in Small Groups," in Harold Guetzkow, ed., *Groups, Leadership, and Men* (Pittsburgh, Pa.: Carnegie Press, 1951), p. 32.

12. Full report in Vilhelm Aubert, *Priskontroll og Rasjonering* (Oslo: Institute for Social Research, 1950).

13. Samuel A. Stouffer and Jackson Toby, "Role Conflict and Personality," *American Journal of Sociology*, 56 (March, 1951), pp. 395–406.

14. It will be seen that our interpretation has borrowed something from Thurman Arnold, *The Folklore of Capitalism* and *Symbols of Government* (New Haven, Conn.: Yale University Press, 1937 and 1935, respectively).

15. Full report in Vilhelm Aubert, Torstein Eckhoff, and Knut Sveri, *En Lov i Søkelyset* (Oslo: Institute for Social Research, 1952).

16. For additional evidence from another "unorthodox" kind of crime, see Arnold M. Rose, "The Social Psychology of Desertion from Combat," *American Sociological Review*, 16 (October, 1951), pp. 614–629.

17. The social functions of such statutes have previously been analyzed by Thurman Arnold, *op. cit.*, and Jerome Frank, *Courts on Trial* (Princeton, N.J.: Princeton University Press, 1949).

18. Karl N. Llewellyn, "Law and the Social Sciences, Especially Sociology," *American Sociological Review*, 14 (August, 1949), p. 454.

# 11

# SOCIAL STRUCTURE AND
# RENT-CONTROL VIOLATIONS

*Harry V. Ball*

This study is focused upon the legal controls of residential rents, their differential impressions of fairness upon the landlords, and the relationships between these and violations of rent ceilings in Honolulu in 1952.

Beginning prior to the establishment of Hawaii as a Territory of the United States, the rental housing business in Honolulu operated under what Friedrich has called "the normal law of landlord and tenant."

> Dwellings are let according to the rules of property and contract. The landlord as owner of the dwelling can fix the rent of his property at whatever figure he chooses. If a tenant does not pay his rent, the landlord has such remedies as distress and eviction. Upon the expiration of the lease, the landlord can take possession of the property, refusing to renew the lease for any or no reason. The competition between landlords is supposed to protect the tenant against the charge of extortionate rents.[1]

When the United States became involved in World War II, statutory rent control was introduced in Honolulu by local city-county ordinance under the emergency powers granted that government unit by the legis-

Reprinted from *American Journal of Sociology*, 65 (May, 1960), pp. 598–604, by permission of The University of Chicago Press. Copyright 1960 by The University of Chicago Press.

lature of Hawaii earlier that year, 1941. The stated intent of this ordinance was to prevent speculative and manipulative practices by landlords, while allowing the landlords a fair return on the value of their property. For the period of wartime martial law in Hawaii, 1942 to 1945, the ordinance was in effect by command of the military governor, after which it continued under its original civil jurisdiction. (At no time between 1941 and 1952 did Honolulu operate directly under the rent control authorized by the federal Congress and established through the Office of Price Administration and its successor agencies.)

When direct control of consumer prices was generally abolished in 1947, modified control of residential rent was retained by the federal Congress. Landlords at that time were thus differentiated from most other kinds of businessmen in the regulation of their businesses. However, the independence of the Honolulu controls permitted variations to be introduced between them and the controls operating in the rest of the nation. Whereas most newly constructed rental housing units were exempted by post-1947 legislation from regulation by statutory-administrative law of the federal government, *all* privately owned housing in Honolulu continued under statutory control even after 1947. As a result, the landlords of all the private rental housing units in the city were under the general legal rule not to charge more than the legally established maximum rent. Any person who willfully violated this rule was subject, upon conviction, to penal sanctions consisting of a fine up to $1,000 or imprisonment up to a period of one year.

The inclusiveness of the Honolulu ordinance did *not* mean, however, that the legal maximum rent of every unit in 1952 had been determined by a single standard, by the application of a single criterion or set of criteria. When the ordinance was initiated in December, 1941, it specified May 27, 1941, as the "freeze" or "fair-rent" date: for all units rented on May 27, 1941, the rent and services in effect on that date were declared to constitute the "maximum-rent" and "minimum-service" standards for each unit, regardless of subsequent changes in ownership, tenancy, or landlord-tenant agreements. For units which had not been rented on the fair-rent date but which had been rented sometime between May 27, 1940, and May 26, 1941, inclusive, the ordinance specified that the ceiling and service standards were to be those which had last existed during that specified year. Thus, the statute embodied the principle that "fair rents" are those rents generally prevailing in a "normal market" and, in effect, it defined the state of the housing market of May 27, 1941, as "normal."

Another provision applied to all units not rented between May 27, 1940, and May 27, 1941, but rented subsequently. The ceilings of this class of rental accommodations were to be determined by the Rent Control Commission upon the basis of the rent and services "generally prevailing for comparable housing accommodations" on the fair-rent date. The power to decide matters of "comparability" was vested entirely in the commission.

The ordinance did provide for raising the legal maximum rent of particular units under these ceilings to compensate for "substantial" increases in taxes or other operating and maintenance costs or "substantial capital improvements or alterations." But there could be no raising of the ceiling on grounds of increased market value, even if the housing accommodation had been sold to a new landlord at a cost much greater than the owner's original investment on the fair-rent date. In short, for housing rented between May 27, 1940, and May 27, 1941, or existing then but only subsequently rented there was no provision in the ordinance for explicit specific application of the concept of a "fair return upon investment" to individual accommodations.

In 1945, the Board of Supervisors intervened in a dispute between the local Rent Control Commission and the Federal Housing Administration and amended the ordinance, directing the commission to accept the rent ceilings on new construction provided by the FHA or other authorized federal agencies. According to the rent-control administrator, these FHA ceilings provided the landlord a gross return of about 16 per cent on the cost of construction and land and were considerably higher than the ceilings then being established by the commission upon the basis of comparability. When, in 1947, the federal Congress exempted most new construction from federal rent control, the board again amended this section to authorize the commission to employ its discretion in accepting or rejecting the bases of the ceilings set by federal agencies.

In this situation, the commission did not attempt to "roll back" the ceilings on new construction which had been established between 1945 and 1947 by the FHA. Rather, it adopted (or retained) as the major determinant of the ceilings on subsequent new construction the federal agency's concept of 1947 of a net return of 6.5 per cent of the total of the original cost of construction plus the assessed value of the land.

In the light of the permanence of this special treatment for newly constructed housing, the rent-control administrator and his investigators tended to give comparable considerations to older housing entering the rental market for the first time since May 27, 1940. It became a prevalent practice to establish ceilings on these older units also upon the basis of a 6.5 per cent net return. However, the net return in this instance was based upon an estimate of the original cost of construction rather than the current or replacement cost. Thus, it did not constitute the clear-cut "return on investment" for the current landlord that the net-return formula represented for landlords of newly constructed accommodations. Rather, it constituted a third class of determinations of legal maximum rent.

Thus, while the general rule that no landlord may charge a rent in excess of the legally established maximum applied to all landlords, a number of subclasses of landlords existed by 1952 on the basis of the methods of determining ceilings. The ordinance, the "law in books," had established two substatuses initially, and then it shifted to one mandatory and one optional status. The operations of the commission and its staff, the "law in action," had established three substatuses. Three classes of landlords were created by the three ceilings, and one individual, of course, could belong in more than one class simultaneously:

1. Landlords with fair-rent–date ceilings. The landlord of a unit constructed prior to 1945 which had been given an initial ceiling prior to 1947 according to the last rent charged between May 27, 1940, and May 27, 1941, or the rent levels generally prevailing for comparable housing accommodations on May 27, 1941.

2. Landlords with fair-return ceilings. The landlord of a unit constructed prior to 1945 which had received its initial ceiling in 1947 or later. The ceiling determination provided for roughly a 6.5 per cent return on the estimated original cost of construction plus the assessed value of the land.

3. Landlords with new-construction ceilings. The landlord of a unit constructed in 1945 or later. For the most part, these ceilings were established to provide a 6.5 per cent return on the cost of construction plus the assessed value of the land. This approximated a net return upon investment formula.

The original expressed intent of the rent-control ordinance was to produce rents which would be fair to both landlords and tenants. But in 1952, new-construction ceilings took considerable account of the general postwar inflation, fair-return ceilings in many instances took some account of this inflation, and fair-rent–date ceilings took account of the inflation only with respect to substantial increases in direct operating costs. Thus, the evidence was substantial that these differential treatments would endow the general norm not to violate ceilings with a different meaning for each subclass of landlords.

Let us turn now to a consideration of the other side of this institutional arrangement—the landlords and that part of their conduct which the legal rules regulated. The best estimates are that in Honolulu in 1952 there were about 36,000 private rental units and about 10,000 landlords. The vast majority of the landlords were small investors, described by Grebler as follows:

> He sometimes originated rental housing; more often, rental housing of certain types was built by contractors or operative builders for the purposes of immediate sale to the small investor. The structures have usually

been two to four family dwellings, one of which is typically occupied by the owner, who also frequently performs the simple management functions. The motivation of this kind of investor often is to have the net rental income carry his own housing costs. Small, nonprofessional investors have also entered the field of rental housing without this motivation, attracted by the social distinction of real estate ownership and expectations of above average net returns on invested capital or of capital appreciation.[2]

In Honolulu these small investors very frequently held only one or two units for rent.

The large long-run investors among landlords in Honolulu usually tended to be relatively small by Mainland standards and to be more interested in above-average returns than some large Mainland institutions. It was very rare to find a landlord who held more than fifty units, and the large operators often controlled only one apartment building or one collection of single-family units.[3] The large estates in Hawaii had specialized in land leases rather than in housing operations.

A few speculative sponsors had emerged in postwar Honolulu. Most of their operations centered around large apartment houses in the vicinity of Waikiki; many picked up some windfall profits, and virtually all their units had new-construction ceilings. The operative house builder was not yet significant in the rental market of Honolulu in 1952.

Thus, as a group, the individuals who had entered the rental housing business had usually done so for one or more of the following reasons: the social distinctions attached to landlordism, which were particularly significant in Honolulu; expectations of above-average net returns on investment or of above-average capital appreciation; or a belief that it was a safe, inflation-proof provision for retirement and a business which could be operated by relatively inexperienced survivors. Against these expectations, landlords found themselves singled out for price regulation in 1952, restricted to prices which in most instances took little or no account of inflation, and operating far more complicated businesses than anticipated.

Forty-two landlords of units with fair-rent–date ceilings and eight landlords with new-construction ceilings were interviewed to ascertain what factors they believed should be taken into account in establishing "fair rents." The landlords with the new-construction ceilings, especially the speculative sponsors, gave greatest prominence in their replies to the idea of providing a proper margin of profit, although they were consistently vague about the precise meaning of "proper."

On the other hand, the landlords with fair-rent–date ceilings, who were much more typical of Honolulu landlords, viewed the problem as a personal, complex, and relative matter. What stood out in their replies were: (1) the rents other landlords were believed to be getting for "comparable units" (with considerable variation in the criteria for "comparable"); (2) the amount by which the landlord believed other prices and incomes had generally risen or fallen since the rent in question was established; (3) the original expectations of the landlord in terms of purchasing power—what he had specifically hoped to accomplish with his rent income; and (4) the difficulty in renting a unit at a given price. It was in terms of the last three generally, but especially (2) and (3), that these landlords often volunteered information about the unfairness, as they saw it, of rent control.

It could be concluded that this examination of landlordism, with respect to its special motivation as an occupation and the techniques of determining "fair rent," corroborated the findings produced by the analysis of the legal structure. The multiple modes of legal maximum-rent determination did seem to constitute a gradation of restrictions upon the opportunities of landlords to establish what they considered to be "fair rents."

But were these apparent consequences actually demonstrable for individual landlords? Were individual landlords with fair-rent–date ceilings more likely to feel restricted or deprived than individual landlords with new-construction ceilings? The hypothesis was formed that the proportion of landlords who believed their legal maximum rent to be unfair would be greatest for those with fair-rent–date ceilings, intermediate for those with fair-return ceilings, and least for those with new-construction ceilings.

This hypothesis was tested against data collected from a 5 per cent sample of all rental units within the city of Honolulu which were then registered with the Rent Control Commission. A questionnaire had been mailed to the landlords of each of the 1,522 rental accommodations (in the original sample) which had been established by means of a tenant interview as still in the rental market. A total of 1,068 questionnaires, about 70 per cent, were available for this analysis.[4] One item in the questionnaire asked each landlord to state precisely what rent he believed would provide him a fair return. The responses to this question were classified according to (1) the kind of ceiling determination of the unit in question and (2) whether the landlord's own estimate of a fair rent was above or below the legal maximum rent, as indicated by the record for that unit in the commission's files.

The legal maximum rent was evaluated as unfair in 70.4 per cent of the responses under fair-rent–date ceilings, in 53.6 per cent of the responses under fair-return ceilings, and in 40.3 per cent of the responses under new-construction ceilings—differences statistically significant at the .01 level by the chi-square test. The null hypothesis that they had been produced by chance was rejected. The evaluations by the individual landlords of the unfairness of their ceiling rents did vary consistently with the hypothesized relative deprivations involved in the modes of determining maximum rent.

Since the differential treatments under the law did tend to provide the affected individuals with different meanings for the general norm against violating ceilings, did they also tend to produce differing rates of violation of this general norm? Inkeles has pointed out that "the need for a theory of personality is perhaps most evident in the study of those 'rates' which represent the summary or end-product of thousands or millions of individual decisions and acts, yet which are of distinctive size for different societies or cultures. To illustrate . . . suicide and delinquency rates."[5] Our problem here is analogous to his, but one major qualification should be introduced. This is that different dimensions or components of personality, even different theories of personality, have varying relevance to different sets of institutional arrangements and the actions they are intended to induce or inhibit.

Now one may assume that, insofar as a landlord has a concept of a fair rent which exceeded the legal maximum for some accommodation, he is persistently motivated to seek to reduce the discrepancy. Perhaps this is not sufficient in itself to induce a landlord to violate his ceiling. But it would certainly enter the mind of any landlord who, for whatever reasons, "needs" more money, or serve as reason enough for any landlord who simply "wants" his "fair return" or whatever he originally anticipated from his rental business.

There are thus two problems: first, what the relationship was between the individual violations of ceilings and the individual evaluations of their fairness or unfairness; and, second, what the final relationship was between the legal structure, as expressed in the three methods of determining ceilings and the fact of control itself, and the rates of violations of the ceilings.

To answer these questions, data on the violations among the 1,522 units in the housing sample were required. As indicated previously, the legal maximum-rent and minimum-service standards for each of these units had been obtained from the files of the commission. At the same time, at least one adult tenant of each rental unit was interviewed to determine the rent actually paid and the services actually provided. These two sets of data were compared for each accommodation, and each was accordingly categorized as a "violation" or "nonviolation."

Table 1 presents these categories of violation and nonviolation cross-tabulated by the landlords' evaluations of the fairness or unfairness of their ceilings for their 1,050 responses. The differences were statistically significant at the .01 level. The most striking finding was that not one fair response was located in the violation category. This is strong evidence for the hypothesis that having a concept of a fair rent in excess of one's legal maximum rent was a prominent component in motivating the landlord to violate his ceiling. And it was previously shown that the frequency of occurrence of this was related to the kind of determination of the ceiling involved. On the other hand, 54.6 per cent of the nonviolations also involved an evaluation of an unfair ceiling. Thus, in 67.5 per cent of the instances of declared unfairness, this, while important, was not sufficient to induce an act of violation.

With respect to the second question, the results of the cross-tabulation of violations by mode of ceiling determination were as expected. The proportion of violations was 29.2 per cent for fair-rent–date ceilings, 14.9 per cent for fair-return ceilings, and only 7.3 per cent for new-construction ceilings. The differences were statistically significant at the .01 level. The legal structure did appear to exert more pressure on some persons than on others to engage in nonconformist rather than conformist behavior.[6] And a substantial contribution to the understanding of the "how" was made by the intervening analyses of the differential perceptions and concomitant motivation.

It has been suggested that the real differences with regard to violations lay in opposition to rent control and that the evaluation of unfairness by many violators may have been merely a postviolation rationalization. In other words, opposition to rent control might indicate the extent to which the violations represented an "acting-out" by individuals strongly hostile to authority in general.

Two analyses were made which tested the significance of opposition to rent control and which may be considered at least a partial test of this idea. In the questionnaire each landlord was asked, "Do you believe rent control is necessary in Honolulu at the present time?" He was asked to indicate his answer: "Yes," "Yes, but with changes in the ordinance (law)," or "No." A few respondents wrote "Don't know," or refused to answer at all.

The violation rate for those landlords who indicated rent control was not necessary was 23.2 per cent; for all others, it was 21.2 per cent. The *t*-test did not indicate statistical significance, and neither did a chi-square test with four degrees of freedom performed on the entire array of responses respecting the necessity of rent control.

Finally, this hypothesis was tested: If a landlord defined his ceiling

*Table 1. Percentage Distributions of Ceiling Violations and Nonviolations by Landlord Evaluations*

| Evaluation of ceiling | Violations | Non-violations | Total |
|---|---|---|---|
| Fair | — | 34.0 | 26.4 |
| Don't Know | — | 4.2 | 3.3 |
| Unfair | 92.5 | 54.6 | 63.0 |
| No Response | 7.5 | 7.2 | 7.3 |
| Total | 100.0 | 100.0 | 100.0 |
| No. | 232 | 818 | 1,050 |

to be unfair and was opposed to rent control, he violated his ceiling. For reasons of sample size, this test was limited to units with fair-rent–date ceilings whose landlords had defined the ceilings to be unfair. Of the 179 violation cases in this class, 54.2 per cent of the landlord responses indicated that rent control was not necessary. Of the 321 nonviolation cases, 55.1 per cent so indicated. The difference was not statistically significant, and the null hypothesis was accepted.

In short, opposition to legal rent control, as such, did not appear to play any systematic role in the act of ceiling violation by landlords in Honolulu in 1952. On the other hand, the legal restrictions placed upon previously legitimate methods for achieving still legitimate aspirations, especially that for more money, seems to have been of considerable importance. The persistent anticipation that rent control would soon be eliminated prevented any major movement from rental to other business. And the tendency to perceive one's treatment under the law to be unfair and thus to be tempted to violate the law appeared directly related to the law's severity. It only remains to stress that 77 per cent of the rental units in the city in 1952 were operated in compliance with these legal rules, in spite of widespread opposition to rent control and an overwhelming belief among landlords generally that they were being treated unfairly.

## Notes

1. A. A. Friedrich, "Rent Regulation," in *Encyclopedia of the Social Sciences*, vol. 13 (New York: Macmillan, 1933), p. 293.

2. Leo Grebler, *Production of Housing* (New York: Social Science Research Council, 1950), p. 120.

3. For a detailed discussion of the social history of rent control in Honolulu see Harry V. Ball, "A Sociological Study of Rent Control and Rent Control Violations," Ph.D. Dissertation, University of Minnesota, 1956, pp. 534–837.

4. About 66 per cent of the questionnaires were returned by mail. A 10 per cent sample of the nonrespondents was interviewed. Between respondents and nonrespondents few differences were found, and those which were statistically significant were small in magnitude. For detailed comparisons see Ball, *op. cit.*, pp. 70–77.

5. Alex Inkeles, "Personality and Social Structure," in Robert K. Merton, Leonard Broom, and Leonard S. Cottrell, Jr., eds., *Sociology Today: Problems and Prospects* (New York: Basic Books, 1959), p. 251. I have taken, as a matter of strategy, the position that one should not employ a broader theory or number of ideas about personality than is required by the immediate task at hand.

6. Robert K. Merton, *Social Theory and Social Structure* (New York: The Free Press, 1949), pp. 125–126.

# 12

# OCCUPATIONAL STRUCTURE AND CRIMINAL BEHAVIOR: PRESCRIPTION VIOLATIONS BY RETAIL PHARMACISTS

*Richard Quinney*

An increasing number of sociologists have become interested in the study of occupations, noticeably neglecting at the same time the criminal behavior which occurs within occupations.[1] On the other hand, sociologists concerned with the study of white-collar crime have not made any systematic attempts to consider the social structure of occupations in their explanations of white-collar crime. The purpose of this study is to demonstrate that an analysis of the occupation should be considered in the attempt to explain violations of laws and regulations which control occupational activities and that such an approach makes it possible to learn more about both the structure of the occupation and the criminal behavior which occurs within the occupation. More specifically, the principal problem of the study is to offer an explanation for a type of criminal behavior which occurs in retail pharmacy in terms of an analysis of the occupation.

Reprinted from *Social Problems*, 11 (Fall, 1963), pp. 179–185.

## RESEARCH PROCEDURE

For a study of occupational violation among pharmacists employed in retail establishments—retail pharmacists—it was first necessary to limit the violation to a type that might form a homogeneous unit of behavior and be subject to a common explanation.[2] While violations of the many state and federal statutes and administrative regulations pertaining to retail pharmacy are all regarded legally as misdemeanors and are subject to particular punishments, the behaviors involved are by no means homogeneous. In the attempt to delineate a specific type of behavior that could be explained by a single theory, the various laws and regulations were subjected to a content analysis in terms of basic occupational activity. The laws and regulations (and their accompanying violations) can be classified into three types: regulation of licensure, regulation of the drugstore, and regulation of prescriptions. Although any one type appeared to represent homogeneous behaviors, the most important type of violation in terms of both public welfare and frequency of occurrence is the violation of laws and regulations that control the compounding and dispensing of prescriptions. Prescription violation was therefore selected as the type of behavior for which an explanation would be sought and thus became the dependent variable of the study.

One of the primary aims of the research design was to provide a comparison of prescription violators and nonviolators. These two groups of retail pharmacists were drawn from the population of retail pharmacists within the city limits of Albany, New York. Through the cooperation of the New York State Board of Pharmacy, the names and addresses of the pharmacists, as well as their violation records over a five-year period, were secured. The twenty prescription violators who had been officially detected by state and federal investigators as violating a prescription law or regulation made up the group of prescription violators. The nonviolator group consisted of sixty pharmacists randomly selected from the remaining retail pharmacists who had been investigated but had never been found to violate a prescription law or regulation. The final study group, then, consisted of eighty retail pharmacists, twenty prescription violators and sixty nonviolators.

Data were collected through structured interviews with the retail pharmacists. The interview schedule, designed also for a broader range of problems, obtained information about the pharmacist's background, career in pharmacy, experiences in pharmacy, and attitudes about the occupation.[3] The respondents were not informed that their violation record was known to the researcher, and any idea that the study was partly concerned with violation could not have occurred until the last few minutes of the interview, after the major information had been secured. In addition to the formal interviews, throughout the study there were informal discussions with persons related in various ways to retail pharmacy, including members of the State Board of Pharmacy, instructors in pharmacy, pharmacy, students, physicians, and customers.

## OCCUPATIONAL ROLES IN RETAIL PHARMACY

Most of the sociological studies of occupations have either assumed or demonstrated that occupations are characterized by patterned expectations internalized by the incumbents and reflected in their occupational behavior. On the three occasions that retail pharmacy has received sociological attention, it has been observed that the occupation incorporates two different roles, professional and business.[4] ... These observations were given support in the present research when it was found that 94 per cent of the pharmacists replied in the affirmative to the question, "Do you find that the public expects the pharmacist to be *both* a business man and a professional man?"

From what was known about retail pharmacy, then, it appeared that various aspects of the social and cultural structure of the occupation would have implications for the study of prescription violation, particularly the status of retail pharmacy as both a profession and a business.[5] Thus, the research was guided by the general hypothesis that social strains in the form of divergent occupational role expectations are structured in the occupation of retail pharmacy and that prescription violation may result, depending upon the individual mode of adaptation. Such a conception that crime (or deviant behavior in general) is structured finds supports in Sutherland's idea of "differential social organization," which proposes that in a heterogeneous type of structure alternative and possibly inconsistent standards of conduct are held by the various segments.[6] A similar idea is found in the sociological tradition of functionalism.[7] Both approaches attempt to account for variations in rates of crime between or within social structures. The strategy taken in the present study was to account for variations in rates of criminal behavior within an occupation.

## STRUCTURAL STRAIN AND ADAPTATION

To the retail pharmacist, the existence of two different occupational roles can present a personal dilemma in terms of appropriate occupational behavior. The retail pharmacist is faced with the task of performing his occupational activities with definitions that are not always clear, consistent, and compatible. Structural strain is built into retail pharmacy. The pharmacist must, therefore, make some sort of personal adjustment to the situation.[8]

It was hypothesized that retail pharmacists resolve the dilemma of choosing between different occupational roles—professional and business—by adapting to an *occupational role organization*. Occupational role organization refers to the relative orientation of the retail pharmacist to both the professional and business roles.[9]

The degree to which pharmacists were oriented to the business and professional roles was then measured. By asking the respondents to indicate how important they regard certain activities and goals in pharmacy, it was possible to determine the relative orientation of pharmacists to the two roles. The results suggest that pharmacists orient themselves in different ways to the available roles.[10] It was thus possible to construct a typology of occupational role organizations based on these differences in orientation. Some pharmacists are oriented more to the professional role than to the business role (professional pharmacists—16 per cent of the sample), while others are oriented more to the business role (business pharmacists—20 per cent). Other pharmacists are oriented to both roles (professional-business Pharmacists 45 per cent), while a few appear not to be oriented to either of the roles (indifferent pharmacists—19 per cent).[11] Therefore . . . there appears to be a patterned response in orientation to the two different roles. Retail pharmacists resolve the dilemma of choosing between different occupational roles (or, more generally, adjust to role strain) by adapting to an occupational role organization.[12]

## PRESCRIPTION VIOLATION

The foregoing analysis provides a point of departure for an investigation of the possible behavioral consequences of structural strain. . . . It was hypothesized that prescription violation occurs with greatest frequency among business pharmacists and least among professional pharmacists, with professional-business pharmacists and indifferent pharmacists being intermediate in the frequency of prescription violation.

The hypothesis was tested by cross-tabulating the prescription-violation records and the occupational role organizations of the retail pharmacists. As shown in Table 1, there is a significant association between prescription violation and occupational role organization in the direction predicted. Prescription violation occurred with greatest frequency among the business pharmacists—75 per cent of these pharmacists were violators—and occurred least among professional pharmacists. None of the professional pharmacists was a violator. The professional-business pharmacists and indifferent pharmacists were intermediate in violation: 14 per cent of the professional-business pharmacists and 20 per cent of the indifferent pharmacists were prescription violators. Therefore, in verification of the hypothesis, it was concluded that prescription violation varies according to the types of occupational role organizations in retail pharmacy.

*Table 1.   Relationship between Prescription Violation and*
*Occupational Role Organization*

*Occupational role organizations*

| Prescription violation | Professional N | % | Professional-Business N | % | Indifferent N | % | Business N | % |
|---|---|---|---|---|---|---|---|---|
| Violators | 0 | 0 | 5 | 14 | 3 | 20 | 12 | 75 |
| Nonviolators | 13 | 100 | 31 | 86 | 12 | 80 | 4 | 25 |
| | 13 | 100 | 36 | 100 | 15 | 100 | 16 | 100 |

$x^2 = 28.6$    df $= 3$    P $< .001$

The research findings suggest that location within the structure of the occupation determines the effectiveness of the controls on the individual pharmacist. Pharmacists with an occupational role organization that includes an orientation to the professional role are bound by a system of occupational controls which includes guides for the compounding and dispensing of prescriptions. Pharmacists who lack the professional orientation and are oriented to the business role are less bound by the occupational controls. They stress the merchandising aspects of pharmacy and are primarily interested in monetary gains. The formal controls (particularly legal controls) are made effective by the operation of informal controls (in terms of role expectations) which come mainly from within the occupation.[13] . . .

From a social-psychological position, then, prescription violation is a matter of *differential orientation*. That is, for each pharmacist, orientation to a particular role more than to another provides a perspective in which violation may seem appropriate.[14] Prescription violation is thus explained in terms of the existence of structural strain in the occupation, because of the existence of divergent occupational roles, and in terms of differential orientation of the pharmacists to the roles in the form of adaptations to occupational role organizations.

CONCLUSION

A theory of prescription violation by retail pharmacists was formulated and verified in this study. There are two divergent occupational role expectations in retail pharmacy—professional and business. Pharmacists adjust to this situation of structural strain by orienting themselves in varying degree to the roles, by adopting an occupational role organization. The types of occupational role organizations in turn differ in the extent to which they generate tendencies toward prescription violation. The occupational role organizations which include the professional role orientation restrain the pharmacist from violating, while the occupational role organizations which do not include the professional role orientation do not exercise this restraint on the pharmacist. Therefore, prescription violation occurs with greatest frequency among business pharmacists and least among professional pharmacists, with professional-business pharmacists and indifferent pharmacists being intermediate in frequency of prescription violation. It was thus concluded that prescription violation is related to the structure of the occupation and the differential orientation of retail pharmacists.

In an attempt to explain a homogeneous unit of behavior, this study was limited to only prescription violation by retail pharmacists. It is possible, however, that the theory as developed has implications both for other types of violation in retail pharmacy and for violations which occur in other occupations.

Occupational role strain is a common phenomenon in modern society, due in part to the frequency and rapidity with which changes in occupational role definitions occur and new occupational roles appear.[15] Particularly, it seems evident that the occupational roles of business and profession are by no means unique to retail pharmacy. Numerous observations show that some businesses are in the process of becoming professions, some professions are taking on some of the characteristics of business, and other occupations (similar to retail pharmacy) have already firmly incorporated the business and professional roles. For example, such occupations as dentistry, optometry, chiropody, osteopathy, and even independent general medicine are similar to retail pharmacy in that they possess the characteristics of both a profession and a business. Such occupational careers as real estate agent, accountant, and electrician, while traditionally business-oriented, are now taking on some professional characteristics. Similarly, some of our traditionally professional careers—such as that of the psychologist—are taking on business characteristics as members become private consultants and counselors.

Also, by way of relating occupational role strain to occupational violation, many of these occupations are subject to laws and regulations similar to those of retail pharmacy. The violation of these laws and regulations is similar to prescription violation in that illegal behavior occurs in the course of serving the customer, as in the failure to retain a dental prescription by the dentist, alteration of a prescription for lenses by an optometrist, and the use of a secret method or procedure of treatment in the case of both osteopathy and medicine. It appears likely that the theoretical orientation employed in this study and the research findings of the study are applicable to other occupations and violations.

Finally, the study of prescription violation adds credence to the increasingly popular conception that deviant behavior is a reflection of social structure. . . . If white-collar crime is illegal behavior in the course of occupational activity, then it is reasonable to assume that the occupation itself must become the object of study as well as the illegal behavior which occurs within the occupation. White-collar crime reflects the particular structure of the occupation and is a normal response to one's particular location within the occupation. Criminologists might consider the importance of understanding the occupation in the process of formulating theories of criminal behavior; and, on the other hand, sociologists who study occupations might give some attention to understanding the occupation by an investigation of the criminal behavior in the occupation. Both the structure of the occupation and criminal behavior within the occupation can be better understood if they are considered together.

# Notes

1. Approaches to the sociological study of occupations are presented in Sigmund Nosow and William H. Form, eds., *Man, Work and Society: A Reader in the Sociology of Occupations* (New York: Basic Books, 1962).

2. The importance of delineating homogeneous units of criminal behavior for the purpose of explanation is discussed, among other places, in Marshall B. Clinard, *Sociology of Deviant Behavior* (New York: Holt, 1963), pp. 204–216; Donald R. Cressey, "Criminological Research and the Definition of Crimes," *American Journal of Sociology*, 56 (May, 1951), pp. 546–551; and Alfred R. Lindesmith and H. Warren Dunham, "Some Principles of Criminal Typology," *Social Forces*, 19 (March, 1951), pp. 307–314. For application of this approach see Marshall B. Clinard and Andrew L. Wade, "Toward the Delineation of Vandalism as a Subtype of Juvenile Delinquency," *Journal of Criminal Law, Criminology, and Police Science*, 48 (January–February, 1958), pp. 493–499; and Donald R. Cressey, *Other People's Money: The Social Psychology of Embezzlement* (New York: The Free Press, 1953). The suggestion that homogeneous units be delimited within white collar crime has been made in Vilhelm Aubert, "White Collar Crime and Social Structure," *American Journal of Sociology*, 58 (November, 1952), pp. 263–271; and Gilbert Geis, "Toward a Delineation of White-Collar Offenses," *Sociological Inquiry*, 32 (Spring, 1962), pp. 160–171.

3. For the larger study see the writer's *Retail Pharmacy as a Marginal Occupation: A Study of Prescription Violation*, Ph.D. Dissertation, University of Wisconsin, 1962.

4. Anthony Weinlein, *Pharmacy as a Profession with Special Reference to the State of Wisconsin*, MA Thesis, University of Chicago, 1943; Isador Thorner, "Pharmacy: The Functional Significance of an Institutional Pattern," *Social Forces*, 20 (March, 1942), pp. 321–328; Thelma H. McCormack, "The Druggists' Dilemma: Problems of a Marginal Occupation," *American Journal of Sociology*, 61 (January, 1956), pp. 308–315.

5. Discussions of profession and business as two separate occupational institutions are found in Talcott Parsons, "The Professions and Social Structure" and "The Motivation of Economic Activities," in Talcott Parsons, *Essays in Sociological Theory* (New York: The Free Press, 1949), pp. 185–217; and Theodore Caplow, *The Sociology of Work* (Minneapolis: University of Minnesota Press, 1954), pp. 100–123. Accounts of the historical development of retail pharmacy which document the existence of both professional and business roles may be found in Richard A. Deno, Thomas D. Rowe, and Donald C. Brodie, *The Profession of Pharmacy* (Philadelphia: Lippincott, 1959);

and Edward Kremers and George Urdang, *History of Pharmacy* (Philadelphia: Lippincott, 1951).

6. Sutherland discussed "differential social organization" or "differential group organization" in "Development of the Theory," in Albert K. Cohen, Alfred R. Lindesmith, and Karl F. Schuessler, eds., *The Sutherland Papers* (Bloomington, Ind.: Indiana University Press, 1956), pp. 13–29; and Edwin H. Sutherland and Donald R. Cressey, *Principles of Criminology*, 6th ed. (Philadelphia: Lippincott, 1960), pp. 79–80. This aspect of Sutherland's theory has been pointed out by Donald R. Cressey in "Epidemiology and Individual Conduct: A Case from Criminology," *Pacific Sociological Review*, 3 (Fall, 1960), pp. 38–58.

7. Robert K. Merton, "Social Structure and Anomie," *American Sociological Review*, 3 (October, 1938), pp. 672–682; and Talcott Parsons, *The Social System* (New York: The Free Press, 1951), pp. 249–325.

8. The idea of structural strain is found in Parsons, *The Social System, ibid.* The concept has been recently employed in Neil J. Smelser, *Theory of Collective Behavior* (New York: The Free Press, 1963). Discussions of adjustment to structure role strain (and role conflict) are found in Leonard S. Cottrell, Jr., "The Adjustment of the Individual to His Age and Sex Roles," *American Sociological Review*, 7 (October, 1942), pp. 617–630; J. W. Getzels and E. G. Guba, "Role, Role Conflict, and Effectiveness: An Empirical Study," *American Sociological Review*, 19 (February, 1954), pp. 164–175; William J. Goode, "A Theory of Role Strain," *American Sociological Review*, 25 (August, 1960), pp. 483–496; Neal Gross, Ward S. Mason, and Alexander W. McEachern, *Explorations in Role Analysis* (New York: Wiley, 1958), chaps. 16–17; Samuel A. Stouffer, "An Analysis of Conflicting Social Norms," *American Sociological Review*, 14 (December, 1949), pp. 707–717; Jackson Toby, "Some Variables in Role Conflict," *Social Forces*, 30 (March, 1952), pp. 323–327; Walter I. Wardwell, "The Reduction of Strain in a Marginal Social Role," *American Journal of Sociology*, 61 (July, 1955), pp. 16–25; and Donald M. Wolfe and J. Diedrick Snoek, "A Study of Tensions and Adjustment under Role Conflict," *Journal of Social Issues*, 18 (July, 1962), pp. 102–121.

9. See Ronald G. Corwin, "The Professional Employee: A Study of Conflict in Nursing Roles," *American Journal of Sociology*, 66 (May, 1961), pp. 605–615.

10. After pertinent materials in the sociology of occupations and retail pharmacy were studied, several items were selected through their construct validity to measure professional and business role orientation.

11. It should be noted that this distribution is skewed slightly in the direction of business pharmacists. The reasons for this are that the number of prescription violators in the study sample overrepresents the proportion of violators in the population of retail pharmacists; and, as it will be shown, the group of prescription violators contains a disproportionate number of business pharmacists. Thus, an entirely random sample of retail pharmacists would contain a few more professionally oriented pharmacists.

12. An occupational role organization may be regarded as the integration of the individual's total occupational role system. See Goode, *op. cit.*, pp. 485–487. Each type of occupational role organization represents a particular method for "ego's manipulation of his role structure" in an attempt to reduce role strain.

13. This interpretation finds support in Howard S. Becker and James W. Carper, "The Elements of Identification with an Occupation," *American Sociological Review*, 21 (June, 1956), pp. 341–348; Caplow, *op. cit.*, pp. 113–121; Edward Gross, *Work and Society* (New York: Crowell, 1958), pp. 134–139; Oswald Hall, "The Informal Organization of the Medical Profession," *Canadian Journal of Economic and Political Science*, 12 (February, 1946), pp. 30–44; Louis Kriesberg, "Occupational Controls among Steel Distributors," *American Journal of Sociology*, 61 (November, 1955), pp. 203–212; and Tamotsu Shibutani, *Society and Personality* (Englewood Cliffs, N.J.: Prentice-Hall, 1961), esp. pp. 60, 91–94, 276–278.

14. This is essentially the same as Glaser's concept of "differential identification" (Daniel Glaser, "Criminality Theories and Behavioral Images," *American Journal of Sociology*, 61 [March, 1956], pp. 433–445).

15. See Walter I. Wardwell, "A Marginal Professional Role: The Chiropractor," *Social Forces*, 30 (March, 1952), pp. 339–348.

# 13

# AN EMPIRICAL STUDY OF
# INCOME-TAX COMPLIANCE

*Harold M. Groves*

## INTRODUCTION

Studies of tax compliance in the United States have been aggregate studies proceeding either by intensive audit of a sample of the universe of federal income-tax returns[1] or by a comparison of income estimates with income reported for tax purposes.[2] These studies were pioneering ventures that provided illuminating and highly important information. But they had certain inherent limitations and the full detail uncovered by the audit study was never disclosed to the public. It seemed to us desirable therefore to attempt some research that would start at the other end of the stick so to speak; that is, a project that would make an intensive study of a particular area. Such a study would have the limitation that it would not afford results that could be generalized nationally; however, it might have the advantage that it would disclose the anatomy of noncompliance in greater detail than other approaches and that it might suggest a methodology that could, with suitable resources and a more general access to income-tax returns, be used by others to give definitive answers as to the degree of noncompliance and its breakdown....

Reprinted by permission from the *National Tax Journal*, 11 (December, 1958), pp. 241–301.

More specifically the proposal was to ascertain unreported income and failure to comply with tax obligations by a territorial and sector-of-income approach, hunting with a shotgun, so to speak, where an auditor hunts with a rifle. We would ascertain income by source for a small block of the income-tax universe and use every means available to do so—interviews (especially with the *payers of income*); estimates of expense backed by intensive study of the area; and many other items of supplementary information differing with each source studied. Results obtained would be checked against the returns rendered and nonreporting of income would, where possible, be translated into noncompliance with tax obligations.

A Wisconsin study was indicated both by the fact that returns are uniquely available in that state and because the Wisconsin Tax Department pledged its full cooperation. The pledge was fully honored; without this assistance the study would have been impossible. Income-tax compliance in Wisconsin should be a case of compliance at its best, because here relatively good overlapping federal and state administrations re-enforce each other. Checking Wisconsin returns would not be conclusive as to federal reporting, but it would be highly indicative; cooperation between administrators has developed to the point where little difference in product is expected.

Whether any of these studies was successful in accomplishing its objectives we leave to the reader. Certainly many more difficulties were encountered than had been expected. Studies of interest, dividends, rent, and farm income were attempted. Attention will be given the rent study because we regard it as the most definitive.

The study of rent here reported[3] was confined to residential rent in one Wisconsin city. Our study excluded commercial rent and residential rent received by corporations. It is not unlikely that compliance scores in the case of these types of rent would prove higher than for the type studied. Excluded also were structures characterized by rental transiency—hotels and motels and other structures not amenable to our type of investigations, such as hospitals, dormitories, army barracks, fraternities, and so forth.

First task involved the selection of a sample that would give each landlord of rented residential property a designated, equal probability of being selected in a sample of landlords. We cannot attempt to describe the process in detail here and shall have to impose upon the reader's credulity to share our confidence that it was performed with ample care and advice.[4] By using a building structure as the unit of sampling, it was possible to interview all of the renters of a particular structure, or at least all the renters necessary to establish with some certainty the amount of gross rent arising from the building. In turn, this full accounting of rental payments could then be related to comparable data from the income-tax returns of the landlords. Our sample included 335 landlords[5] which was 6.2 per cent of the estimated number of residential rented structures.

Precautions were taken to do a proper job of interviewing: personnel were carefully chosen and instructed, a preliminary questionnaire was pretested, and so forth. While the purpose of the interview was not fully revealed to the parties interviewed, precaution was taken at every stage to guarantee the confidential character of data pertaining to particular individuals.

Our research team was confronted with this dilemma: in the interest of honesty and public relations we would have much preferred to have made a clean breast of "what we were up to"; in the interest of obtaining all the information we needed, the consensus was that this might prove fatal. We resolved on the basis of what we considered the public interest in favor of an honest but limited disclosure. This leaves us open to the charge of obtaining information on false, or at any rate not fully disclosed, pretenses. And it raises questions as to how frequently such research could be repeated. One might suppose that the American people would voluntarily cooperate in providing information that might disclose tax delinquency for other people . . . but it is at least doubtful that such is the case. It was apparent from the outset that a research objective and an enforcement purpose could not be combined.

Out of an original total of 1129 structures, 625 units were found to be owner-occupied; there were 86 instances of "non-response" in which it was not possible (3 calls) to make contact with persons living in the selected buildings; an additional 65 cases proved to be unusable for a variety of reasons, such as a vacancy or ambiguous information. There were 26 cases in which persons living in the selected buildings refused to be interviewed. A few other cases were eliminated because of ambiguities on tax returns: the reporting of several properties in an aggregate account, reporting of only gross or net data, and the like.

Classified by type of facility our sample included 205 cases of multiple units (apartments and flats); 63 cases of rooms; 48 cases of single-unit structures; 8 of garages, and 11 of subletting. The multiple-unit cases varied in character from so-called "flats," usually with 3 or less units including the unit occupied by the owner, to large apartment houses ranging to over 100 apartments. Rooming facilities included both "incidental rooming" and "operating a rooming house."

It seemed advisable to make a distinction in our data according to the responses of tenants. Cases were classified depending on whether the estimate of gross rent was considered to be "good," "average," or "poor"; approximately 32 per cent, 54 per cent, and 13 per cent of the cases fell into these categories, respectively. The first two classes we considered substantially reliable and the third less dependable but not useless; clearly ambiguous and incomplete cases were deleted from the sample.

In the class of multiple units we found 182 cases and $304,865 of estimated gross rent available for comparisons with tax returns. The comparison yielded the following results: there were 8 cases, totaling $11,261 in estimated rent, in which landlords filed an income-tax return but did not declare rental income; there were 23 cases totaling $25,686 in estimated rent where no income-tax return was filed; in the remaining 151 cases, totaling $257,917 in estimated rent, landlords filed income-tax returns and declared rental income: here a direct comparison between estimated and reported rent was possible.

The eight cases in which landlords reported no rental income when filing their income-tax returns represent the clearest instance of noncompliance. It amounts to nearly 4 per cent of total estimated gross rent. Only two of the eight cases represent sizeable amounts, one for $3,961 and the other for $3,810. The 23 cases for which no income-tax returns were filed represent a persuasive but not altogether certain case of noncompliance. Care was first taken to ensure that there was no ambiguity with regard to ownership. Both property-tax data and the records of the Register of Deeds were checked. Then in each of the 23 cases, city directories and telephone books were examined to confirm that landlords had a filing liability in the city during the relevant year. The main apparent technical chance of error is the misfiling of income-tax returns, but this happens very infrequently.[6] Seven out of the 23 cases had an estimated gross rent of less than $600 (Wisconsin's filing limit), and if these rental incomes were the only source of taxable income to the landlords, the latter would have no filing liability. Calculations were made both on the assumption that these cases involved a filing liability and that they did not. On the first assumption, that all 23 cases involved a filing liability, the noncompliance on the part of non-filers represents 8 per cent of the total estimated gross rent of this class of landlords.

The remaining 151 cases reporting rent reported generally quite faithfully; the understatement of gross rent amounted to only $8,236 or nearly 3 per cent of the total estimated gross rent from all multiple-unit cases.

The total score in the reporting of estimated gross rent for multiple-unit structures was determined within a range of 85.18 per cent to 86.18 per cent, depending on the assumptions regarding non-filers explained above. Further detail was computed to show a breakdown by flats and apartments, but concerning this we can only record here that the latter showed a considerably better score.

Space does not permit a similar analysis of other types of facilities where similar but not identical problems were encountered and were similarly treated. Table 1 presents a summary of gross-rent noncompliance by types of units and indicates a composite score of 80 per cent to 81 per cent for all types combined. It will be noted that renter subletting and garages show a very low level of compliance, but they are also relatively unimportant in the total picture and our sample in these cases is too small to be reliable. A further datum may be added, namely that of those who filed and reported rent in the overall picture the figures reported were 96 per cent of the estimates.

Landlords may evade net rental income on tax returns in two ways, either through the under-reporting of gross income or through the exaggeration of expenses. In moving from gross to net rentals in our estimates it was not possible to follow the procedures used in developing the estimates for gross rentals. Tenants were found to be very vague concerning such items of expense as repairs and maintenance. They would recall that a plumber had been on the premises, for example, but they did not know whether he changed a washer or undertook a major repair. And, of course, renters usually have no knowledge at all concerning such expense items as depreciation, interest, and utilities. Interviewing landlords in order to obtain reliable information also proved to be unsatisfactory.

Decision was made to derive significant ratios through interviewing a sample of property-management experts. The ratios of interest were the average net return that may be expected on capital invested in rental housing and the ratio of expense to gross income (or alternatively of net to gross income) that may be expected with each of several types of rented property. Interviews were consummated with 17 different real-estate firms in the selected city. There was a marked consensus of opinion among the persons interviewed. Invariably the interviewee stated, for example, that the net return on capital invested in flats was within a range of 8 to 10 per cent, while single units earned a net return of 4 or 5 per cent. The percentages we accepted were an arithmetic average of all these estimates. The consensus was that expenses run to about 50 per cent of gross regardless of the type of structure.

As an alternative, we also employed the technique of reconstructing expense items for each individual property. A number of expense items like property taxes, water expense, interest, and depreciation could be and were checked specifically for each property. Certain other items, such as repairs and maintenance and heating expense, could be approximated by "rules of thumb." Illustrative is the belief among real-estate men that repairs and maintenance require on the average one month's gross rental. Some landlords will spend more than this amount for repairs and maintenance while others will spend less. Average costs of heating were computed by engineering consultants who are familiar with the relative costs and efficiencies of various fuels and the proportionate variation in costs associated with different sizes and types of structures. Average consumption costs of gas and electricity were supplied by the local utility company. And so on. There were a few miscellaneous items, such as fire insurance and advertising, for which we found no basis for approximation, but their importance in the total picture was small and we accepted in these cases the amounts claimed on returns.

Table 1.   Summary of Gross Rent Noncompliance for All Types of Units

| Type of unit | Number of cases | Estimated rent | Reported rent | Noncompliance | Ratio of nonreported gross rent to estimated | Ratio of reported gross rent to estimated |
|---|---|---|---|---|---|---|
| Multiple units | 182 | $304,865 | $259,681 | $42,220 to $45,184 | 13.84 to 14.82 | 85.84 to 86.16 |
| Rooms | 62 | 52,739 | 35,459 | 16,747 to 17,280 | 31.76 to 32.77 | 67.23 to 68.24 |
| Single units | 47 | 41,342 | 26,776 | 13,876 to 14,567 | 33.54 to 35.24 | 64.76 to 66.46 |
| Renter subletting | 10 | 4,484 | 1,006 | 2,872 to 3,478 | 63.95 to 77.46 | 22.44 to 36.05 |
| Garages | 8 | 495 | 193 | 302 | 61.01 | 38.99 |
| Total | 309 | $403,925 | $323,113 | $76,008 to $80,811 | 18.62 to 20.01 | 79.99 to 81.18 |

On the basis of the above approaches, three independent estimates with some exceptions were made of expenses by types of units and types of expense. In some cases the ratio methods proved unfeasible. This was particularly true in the special case of incidental renting of rooms in the room-rent category. In this area quite a few cases were found too where landlords neglected to deduct all of the expenses to which they were entitled. An allowance for calculated expense was added in these cases. Where the three methods were used the estimates showed very little variation in results. Ultimate answers (ratios of reported to estimated net rent) differed in no case by more than 5 per cent. In our final calculations we averaged these results.

It may be noted at this point that any relative understatement of gross rent is magnified substantially in percentage terms when it is related to net income. Assume a hypothetical business with a gross income of $100 and a ratio of expense to gross income of 50 per cent. Assume further that all expenses are properly reported and that accordingly the true net income is $50. Assume now that gross is under-reported by 20 per cent; this gives us the following data:

| | |
|---|---|
| Gross income | $100 |
| Reported gross | 80 |
| Expenses | 50 |
| Reported net | 30 |
| True net | 50 |
| Ratio of reported to true net income | 60 |

If now we also assume that expenses are over-reported to the extent of 10 per cent, that is, in the above illustration at $55, we get reported net income of $25 and a 50 per cent compliance ratio. It will be observed from our tables that this is approximately what appears to have happened in our sample of landlords.

Table 2 shows the detail of the ultimate findings. It shows a ratio of aggregate reported to aggregate estimated net rent of nearly 51 per cent.

*Table 2.   Summary of Gross and Net Rent Compliance*

| Type of unit | Number of cases | Ratio of reported gross rent to estimated gross rent | Ratio of reported net rent to estimated net rent |
|---|---|---|---|
| Multiple units | 182 | 86.16 | 56.10 |
| Rooms | 62 | 68.24 | 25.39 |
| Single units | 47 | 66.46 | 48.06 |
| Renter subletting | 10 | 36.05 | 16.58 |
| Garages | 8 | 38.99 | 78.14 |
| Total  All cases | 309 | 81.18 | 50.74 |

Two supplementary phases of the study may be noted briefly. A special analysis of expense items showed that errors in reporting these items are not general or uniform. The ratio of claimed to estimated expenses is relatively high for repairs and maintenance, furniture depreciation, equipment depreciation, and telephone expense. Several of the other items are modestly over-reported while two items, taxes and water, have estimated expenses (and in this case they are actual) larger than claimed expenses. Two expense items, repairs and maintenance, and depreciation, account for approximately 75 per cent of all the overreporting of expenses and the item "repairs and maintenance" alone represents about 50 per cent of over-reporting. Landlords often depreciate both land and buildings and sometimes even adjoining lots.

An effort was also made to determine the tax-liability noncompliance in relation to proper tax compliance. For the major traffic (those reporting net income and rent) this was done in the aggregate; that is, the average reported taxable income was determined along with the marginal rate at which incremental additions to that average income should be taxed. The average non-reported rental income was also determined along with the additional tax that would have been collected had this income been reported. To get a tax-compliance ratio one prorates the present tax between rental income and other income; also the proper tax between ascertained rental and other income (assuming the latter to be correct as stated). He then compares his two answers.[7] The tax-compliance record was found to be 47 per cent as compared with the net-rental-income-compliance ratio of nearly 51 per cent.

The above explanation omits the special treatment necessary for two types of taxpayers—the non-filers and filers not now liable to tax. The filers without tax liability were not numerous and were treated individually. The non-filers posed a problem and projection of a tax liability for them proved to be more a matter of speculation than precise measurement. Nothing is finitely known about the income or exemption status of these landlords. The arbitrary assumptions were made that the net rental income for each case was equal to the sum of all other income received and that each landlord is entitled to two exemptions. The total effect of these assumptions is not crucial to the main conclusion.

One should beware of indicting all income-tax administration on the basis of any evidence here produced. Our study covers only one part of one kind of income in one area. Calculations based on national data indicate that personal-rent income in 1954 was less than 2.5 per cent of total personal income. Residential rent is one of the more difficult areas that income-tax administration is expected to police. However, it should not be too difficult to check rented properties, income from which goes entirely unreported. These could be ascertained from property-tax records. Some approximation of gross income could be calculated by inquiries as to unit-rent payments. Net rent would be much more difficult; here an inquiry or audit might be indicated if returns depart radically from well-established norms.

*Notes*

1. U.S. Treasury Department, *The Audit Control Program*, May, 1951.
2. Selma F. Goldsmith, "Appraisal of Basic Data Available for Constructing Income Size Distributions," *Conference on Research in Income and Wealth*, 13 (New York: National Bureau of Economic Research, 1951), pp. 267–377; Daniel M. Holland and C. Harry Kahn, "Comparison of Personal and Taxable Income," *Federal Tax Policy for Economic Growth and Stability*, Joint Committee on the Economic Report, 84th Congress, 1st session, 1955, pp. 313–338.
3. Most of the work on this study was done by Milton Taylor, then a member of our staff and now professor of economics at Michigan State University.
4. The procedure involved the development of a probability model. The sample unit selected was the "structure," which was used either in whole or in part for residential purposes. A two-stage sampling procedure was used with a between-block interval of three and a within-block interval of six. Blocks with more than the average numbers of renters and structures were so handled as to double their probability of falling in the sample. The size of the sample, we should concede, was determined more by resources of time and staff than by technical criteria of adequacy. The adequacy factor could not be tested; we are confident that the results as a whole are representative for the particular city studied; they are not adequate for all of the detailed breakdown as later identified; and, of course, their representativeness for other cities or the country as a whole are matters we have not studied.
5. Three hundred twenty-five structures plus eleven cases of subletting.
6. A test of filing accuracy was attempted. The only factor of accuracy that could be examined was that of faithfulness in following the alphabet. Six hundred twenty folders were examined, out of which eleven were misplaced. However, in almost all of these cases the out-of-place folder was within a few folders of the proper place and could be found easily.
7. Thus if A has an income of $2,000 and reported rental income of $1,000 and a tax of $10, the tax on his or her rent is $5. If this person should have reported $1,000 more in rent, his or her income should have been $3,000 and the tax perhaps $24. The hypothetical tax on this person's rent would be $16 and the compliance score five out of sixteen or about 30 percent.

# V

# POLITICAL WHITE-COLLAR CRIME

Political white-collar crime differs from other forms of white-collar crime primarily in the occupational setting in which the offense takes place. A person who gains an elective or appointive office acquires with it considerable power to confer favors and to use public resources for personal gain. The officeholder also obtains control of persons and agencies which can be used to engage in illegal activities and to prevent their detection. Political white-collar crime, therefore, offers structural opportunities for violation that differs from those involved in other forms of white-collar crime.

There are, as well, additional variations which would appear to justify delineation of political white-collar crime as a separable entity. Among the more notable of these are that political office is regarded as a public trust, and that the political incumbent has a specific duty to enforce the laws. Thus, one of the ugliest aspects of the Watergate affair was the contrast between the behavior of the participants and the public pronouncements of the leading members of the Nixon administration, with their demands for draconian measures against traditional offenders.

Political behavior, at least in contrast to most occupational activity, especially that in the corporate world, is also apt to be highly visible. By necessity, politicians are public figures, and the mass media, at least in cities with agressive coverage, define it as their business to pry into the professional and, often, the personal behavior of officeholders.

The public trust role-definition of political office may help explain results of studies designed to ascertain the perceived severity of white-collar crimes.

Nonpolitical white-collar offenses were generally found to arouse hardly more, if any more, public concern than traditional offenses[1] while political white-collar crimes, according to a recent survey, engendered considerable moral outrage.[2] Though the Watergate and Agnew scandals may have influenced these findings in terms of the amount of publicity they received, they none-theless appear to capture a fundamental feeling in America, one mirrored in a newspaper interview with a man in a small New England town:

> You believe there's a little larceny in all of us, don't you, and so do I—but I'm damned if the politicians don't have a stomach full of it. It's like a thyroid problem with them. They just can't control it. The greed keeps on growing.[3]

Indeed, after its study of the United States Senate and the House of Representatives, the Ralph Nader investigative group offered the observation that "it could probably be shown by facts and figures that there is no distinctly American criminal class except Congress."[4] In some jurisdictions, in fact, terms of political office are limited to two years and cannot be filled by incumbents, on the assumption that boundaries need to be set on the amount of graft one individual can acquire; or, as rougher critics might put it, "other pigs ought to have their turn at the trough." This condition offers insight into one reason for what some persons regard as almost endemic corruption in American politi-cal life. Officeholders enjoy relatively brief periods of tenure before their jobs become potentially forfeit to the whim of the electorate. To remain in power requires substantial financial backing, and such support is rarely offered for altruistic reasons, but rather is exchanged for partisan favors, many of which undoubtedly are unethical or illegal.

Numerous ideas have been advanced, particularly in the wake of the Watergate scandals, about the most effective manner to minimize political corruption in the United States. A thoroughgoing investigation of the issue sug-gests that a complex amalgam of circumstances may be required to introduce honesty into public business. Ronald Wraith and Edgar Simpkins note that the observation of the diarist Samuel Pepys, a minor Naval Department official, was characteristic of seventeenth century British officeholders; "One bribe did so cheer my heart that I could eat no victuals almost for dinner; for joy think how God do bless us, every day more and more."[5] The interpretation in Pepys's mind that he had received the bribe as a divine beneficence is not without its irony. "What were the factors which led Britian, a country as corrupt as any, to achieve in a particular century a standard of public integrity which is perhaps without precedent?" Wraith and Simpkins ask. They offer the following inter-pretation:

> Merchants and manufacturers had prospered and become wealthy by their own hard work and skill; a significant portion of them were professedly religious, and all of them, as the century advanced, lived under the influence of the strict, if often harsh morality of the Victorian age. . . . (M)any of them turned in middle

age to seek that peculiar combination of power and status which is accorded in Britain to those who engage in unpaid public service; their wealth was important because it put them beyond criticism and beyond temptation.... They were immensely *responsible* people. In considering solid, middle-class Victorian respectability today it is fashionable to emphasize the smugness and hypocrisy which were its darker side, and to pay too little tribute to its enduring achievement, particularly in the creation of a sense of public duty.[6]

Whether personal wealth truly inoculates public officials against corruption is arguable; that a social ethos of honesty is important for political honesty seems likely. Americans expect their political leaders to be devious; and the leaders tend not to disappoint them.

The readings in this section provide samples of major forms of political white-collar crime. The first piece, by John Gardiner, a political scientist, indicates the intimate relationships that often exists between political corruption and other forms of criminal activity, particularly those concerned with "victimless crimes," such as gambling and prostitution. As Gardiner points out, elected officials in American cities often enter into collusive arrangements with the law enforcement officials to allow illegal activities to proceed unmolested. The city studied by Gardiner—Reading, Pennsylvania—was run very much like those municipalities whose ventures into kickbacks, bribes, padded payrolls, fund misappropriation, the issuance of fraudulent licenses, and similar practices, were so vividly exposed by Lincoln Steffens in *Shame of the Cities* (1904).[7]

A case study of political bribery constitutes the next reading. It provides details of the investigation of Spiro Agnew, at the time vice president of the United States, for eliciting and accepting bribes while head of the county government in Baltimore. Particularly noteworthy in this case was the fact that Agnew continued to accept from Maryland contractors after he was installed as vice president. His explanation that he required the funds in order to live in a style appropriate to his public office and position offers some insight into the self-concept that allowed Agnew to act as he did. In addition, of course, it was alleged (and it appeared to be true) that Agnew was behaving no differently than many of his predecessors in office. The fact that the vice president was allowed to plead *nolo contendere* to a single charge of income-tax violation in exchange for a sentence of unsupervised probation, constitutes one of the more controversial aspects of the case. The reading details the reasoning of the persons who entered into the bargaining procedure. The thought processes of the prosecutor's team, as described by two journalists who covered the Agnew case, offers insight into the bias and condescension with which traditional offenders, in contrast to Agnew, are regarded:

Men under investigation (in the Agnew case) were called "bad men."... (T)he prosecutors employed terms like these to condition themselves for the job at hand —mean nasty work that often entailed sending a man to jail. It was one thing to dispose of a mugger in that fashion, but quite another thing when it came to men very much like themselves—college-educated, middle-class, articulate. These were not street people, but men with roots in the community. The humiliation of jail was total and absolute. It destroyed families, careers, and the men themselves.[8]

While Agnew escaped jail, the men who had supplied the information that had led to his downfall were sentenced to prison terms of one year and eighteen months. That they had paid the bribes to Agnew led the *Wall Street Journal* to the wry observation that apparently "it's more blessed to receive than to give."[9]

The subsequent reading, by Russell Baker, a political satirist, provides a bittersweet comment on the subject of political white-collar crime. Tongue in cheek, Baker observes that there would be no point to putting ex-President Nixon in prison because Nixon was too old to "profit from it and repay the country with the long career at crime necessary to amortize the high cost of prison education." In a sly way, Baker raises a host of questions regarding proper methods for dealing with white-collar crime offenders; he also touches upon some of the more vicious biases in present penal policy which serves, he notes, "to provide storage space for poor people."

Baker's serio-comic presentation is followed by John Silber's review of the implications of the treatment of Vice President Agnew and, in particular, of former President Nixon. Stressing that Nixon had been pardoned without being accused formally, Silber maintains that the national interests would have been better served by a thorough airing and discussion of every aspect of the Watergate crimes.

The most dramatic instance of political white-collar crime in the history of the United States, the Watergate conspiracies, is discussed in detail in the reading by Kirkpatrick Sale. The complex web of social and personal interconnections among principals in the case and the methods for illegal exchange of money parallel on a national, much grander scale, the petty corruption that Gardiner found in the Pennsylvania city he studied. The Watergate crimes are political white-collar crimes of such an extraordinary character in many ways, perhaps the most interesting of which is that they appeared in large measure to be dictated not by a quest for personal wealth (though the wealth accumulated in the course of their incumbency by some of the participants, and most notably the president, was considerable), but by an intense desire to retain power. That desire seemed to be based on a conviction that their continuation in office clearly was in the best interest of the country—and had to be achieved at almost any cost. Perhaps the most intriguing aspect of the Watergate crimes was the avalanche of evidence that became available when it was discovered that the president had had most of his conversations, including many related to the conspiracy, tape-recorded. It may be doubted that we ever again will be exposed to such rare insights into the manner in which political power can be, and was being, used in a criminal fashion.

As the trials of the Watergate conspirators were drawing to a close in mid-December 1974, Walter Lippmann, one of the most highly respected commentators in the United States on political life, died at the age of eighty-five. Obituaries included some of Lippmann's more pointed comments on public office, two of which are especially pertinent to matters related to political white-collar crimes:

> *On the Duty of Officials:* Those in high places are more than the administrators of government bureaus. They are more than the writers of laws. They are the custodians of a nation's ideals, of the beliefs it cherishes, of its permanent hopes, of the faith which makes a nation out of a mere aggregation of individuals. They are unfaithful to that trust when by word or example they promote a spirit that is complacent, evasive, and acquisitive.[10]

> *On Codes of Conduct:* There is no mechanical gadget by which the moral level of public life can be maintained. There is no spasm of popular righteousness which will raise it much for very long. All depends on the code of conduct which is fashionable. All depends on the working rules of behavior which the leading and conspicuous men and women in a society practice because they believe them, which most of the others conform with as a matter of course. . . .[11]

## Notes

1. See, for example, Donald J. Newman, "Public Attitudes Toward A Form of White-Collar Crime," *Social Problems*, 4 (January, 1957), pp. 228–232; Don C. Gibbons, "Crime and Punishment: A Study in Social Attitudes"; *Social Forces* 47 (June, 1969), pp. 391–397; Peter H. Rossi, Emily Waite, Christine E. Bose, and Richard E. Berk, "The Seriousness of Crimes: Normative Structure and Individual Differences," *American Sociological Review*, 39 (April, 1974), pp. 224–237.

2. Robert M. Carroll, Steven M. Pine, Cindy J. Cline, and Bruce R. Kleinhans, "Judged Seriousness of Watergate-Related Crimes," *Journal of Psychology*, 86 (March, 1974), pp. 235–239.

3. James T. Wooten, "Voters in Rural New England Apathetic and Cynical," *New York Times*, October 10, 1974, p. 22.

4. Mark J. Green, James M. Fallows, and David Zwick, *Who Runs Congress? The President, Big Business or You?* (New York: Bantam, 1972), p. 131.

5. Cited in Ronald Wraith and Edgar Simpkins, *Corruption in Developing Countries* (New York: Norton, 1964), p. 120.

6. *Ibid.,* p. 166.

7. Lincoln Steffens, *Shame of the Cities;* see also Justin Kaplan, *Lincoln Steffens: A Biography* (New York: Simon and Schuster, 1974).

8. Richard M. Cohen and Jules Witcover, *A Heartbeat Away: The Investigation and Resignation of Spiro T. Agnew* (New York: Viking, 1974), p. 71.

9. *Wall Street Journal*, December 30, 1974.

10. *New York Times*, December 15, 1974, p. 17.

11. *Ibid.*

# 14

# THE POLITICS OF CORRUPTION
# IN AN AMERICAN CITY

*John A. Gardiner*

## OFFICIAL CORRUPTION

Textbooks on municipal corporation law speak of at least three varieties of official corruption. The major categories are nonfeasance (failing to perform a required duty at all), malfeasance (the commission of some act which is positively unlawful), and misfeasance (the improper performance of some act which a man may properly do). During the years in which Irv Stern was running his gambling operations, Wincanton officials were guilty of all of these. Some residents say that Bob Walasek came to regard the mayor's office as a brokerage, levying a tariff on every item that came across his desk. Sometimes a request for simple municipal services turned into a game of cat and mouse, with Walasek sitting on the request, waiting to see how much would be offered, and the "petitioner" waiting to see if he could obtain his rights without having to pay for them. Corruption was not as lucrative an enterprise as gambling, but it offered a tempting supplement to low official salaries.

Reprinted from *Task Force Report: Organized Crime*. The President's Commission on Law Enforcement and Administration of Justice (1967), pp. 67–70, 74–76.

*Nonfeasance.* Irv Stern saw to it that Wincanton officials would ignore at least one of their statutory duties, enforcement of the State's gambling laws. Bob Walasek and his cohorts also agreed to overlook other illegal activities. Stern preferred not to get directly involved in prostitution; Walasek and Police Chief Dave Phillips tolerated all prostitutes who kept up their protection payments. One madam, controlling more than 20 girls, gave Phillips *et al.* $500 each week; one woman employing only one girl paid $75 each week that she was in business. Operators of a carnival in rural Alsace County paid a public official $5000 for the privilege of operating gambling tents for 5 nights each summer. A burlesque theater manager, under attack by high school teachers, was ordered to pay $25 each week for the privilege of keeping his strip show open.

Many other city and county officials must be termed guilty of nonfeasance, although there is no evidence that they received payoffs, and although they could present reasonable excuses for their inaction. Most policemen began to ignore prostitution and gambling completely after their reports of offenses were ignored or superior officers told them to mind their own business. State policemen, well informed about city vice and gambling conditions, did nothing unless called upon to act by local officials. Finally, the judges of the Alsace County Court failed to exercise their power to call for State Police investigations. In 1957, following Federal raids on horse bookies, the judges did request an investigation by the State Attorney General, but refused to approve his suggestion that a grand jury be convened to continue the investigation. For each of these instances of inaction, a tenable excuse might be offered—the beat patrolman should not be expected to endure harassment from his superior officers, State police gambling raids in a hostile city might jeopardize State-local cooperation on more serious crimes, and a grand jury probe might easily be turned into a "whitewash" in the hands of a corrupt district attorney. In any event, powers available to these law enforcement agencies for the prevention of gambling and corruption were not utilized.

*Malfeasance.* In fixing parking and speeding tickets, Wincanton politicians and policemen committed malfeasance, or committed an act they were forbidden to do, by illegally compromising valid civil and criminal actions. Similarly, while State law provides no particular standards by which the mayor is to make promotions within his police department, it was obviously improper for Mayor Walasek to demand a "political contribution" of $10,000 from Dave Phillips before he was appointed chief in 1960.

The term "political contribution" raises a serious legal and analytical problem in classifying the malfeasance of Wincanton officials, and indeed of politicians in many cities. Political campaigns cost money; citizens have a right to support the candidates of their choice; and officials have a right to appoint their backers to noncivil service positions. At some point, however, threats or oppression convert legitimate requests for political contributions into extortion. Shortly after taking office in the mid-1950s, Mayor Gene Donnelly notified city hall employees that they would be expected "voluntarily" to contribute 2 per cent of their salary to the Democratic Party. (It might be noted that Donnelly never forwarded any of these "political contributions" to the party treasurer.) A number of salesmen doing business with the city were notified that companies which had supported the party would receive favored treatment; Donnelly notified one salesman that in light of a proposed $81,000 contract for the purchase of fire engines, a "political contribution" of $2000 might not be inappropriate. While neither the city hall employees nor the salesmen had rights to their positions or their contracts, the "voluntary" quality of their contributions seems questionable.

One final, in the end almost ludicrous, example of malfeasance came with Mayor Donnelly's abortive "War on the Press." Following a series of gambling raids by the Internal Revenue Service, the newspapers began asking why the local police had not participated in the raids. The mayor lost his temper and threw a reporter in jail. Policemen were instructed to harass newspaper delivery trucks, and 73 tickets were written over a 48-hour period for supposed parking and traffic violations. Donnelly soon backed down after national news services picked up the story, since press coverage made him look ridiculous. Charges against the reporter were dropped, and the newspapers continued to expose gambling and corruption.

*Misfeasance.*   Misfeasance in office, says the common law, is the improper performance of some act which a man may properly do. City officials must buy and sell equipment, contract for services, and allocate licenses, privileges, etc. These actions can be improperly performed if either the results are improper (e.g., if a building inspector were to approve a home with defective wiring or a zoning board to authorize a variance which had no justification in terms of land usage) or a result is achieved by improper procedures (e.g., if the city purchased an acceptable automobile in consideration of a bribe paid to the purchasing agent). In the latter case, we can usually assume an improper result as well—while the automobile will be satisfactory, the bribe giver will probably have inflated the sale price to cover the costs of the bribe.

In Wincanton, it was rather easy for city officials to demand kickbacks, for State law frequently does not demand competitive bidding or permits the city to ignore the lowest bid. The city council is not required to advertise or take bids on purchases under $1000, contracts for maintenance of streets and other public works, personal or professional services, or patented or copyrighted products. Even when bids must be sought, the council is only required to award the contract to the lowest responsible bidder. Given these permissive provisions, it was relatively easy for council members to justify or disguise contracts in fact based upon bribes. The exemption for patented products facilitated bribe taking on the purchase of two emergency trucks for the police department (with a $500 campaign contribution on a $7500 deal), three fire engines ($2000 was allegedly paid on an $81,000 contract), and 1500 parking meters (involving payments of $10,500 plus an $880 clock for Mayor Walasek's home). Similar fees were allegedly exacted in connection with the purchase of a city fire alarm system and police uniforms and firearms. A former mayor and other officials also profited on the sale of city property, allegedly dividing $500 on the sale of a crane and $20,000 for approving the sale, for $22,000, of a piece of land immediately resold for $75,000.

When contracts involved services to the city, the provisions in the State law regarding the lowest responsible bidder and excluding "professional services" from competitive bidding provided convenient loopholes. One internationally known engineering firm refused to agree to kickback in order to secure a contract to design a $4.5 million sewage disposal plant for the city; a local firm was then appointed, which paid $10,700 of its $225,000 fee to an associate of Irv Stern and Mayor Donnelly as a "finder's fee." Since the State law also excludes public works maintenance contracts from the competitive bidding requirements, many city paving and street repair contracts during the Donnelly-Walasek era were given to a contributor to the Democratic Party. Finally, the franchise for towing illegally parked cars and cars involved in accidents was awarded to two garages which were then required to kickback $1 for each car towed.

The handling of graft on the towing contracts illustrates the way in which minor violence and the "lowest responsible bidder" clause could be used to keep bribe payers in line. After Federal investigators began to look into Wincanton corruption, the owner of one of the garages with a towing franchise testified before the grand jury. Mayor Walasek immediately withdrew his franchise, citing "health violations" at the garage. The garageman was also "encouraged" not to testify by a series of "accidents"—wheels would fall off towtrucks on the highway, steering cables were cut, and so forth. Newspaper satirization of the "health violations" forced the restoration of the towing franchise, and the "accidents" ceased.

Lest the reader infer that the "lowest responsible bidder" clause was used as an escape valve only for corrupt purposes, one incident might be noted which took place under the present reform administration. In 1964, the Wincanton School Board sought bids for the renovation of an athletic field. The lowest bid came from a construction company owned by Dave Phillips, the corrupt police chief who had served formerly under Mayor Walasek. While the company was presumably competent to carry out the assignment, the board rejected Phillips' bid "because of a question as to his moral responsibility." The board did not specify whether this referred to his prior corruption as chief or his present status as an informer in testifying against Walasek and Stern.

One final area of city power, which was abused by Walasek *et al.*, covered discretionary acts, such as granting permits and allowing zoning variances. On taking office, Walasek took the unusual step of asking that the bureaus of building and plumbing inspection be put under the mayor's control. With this power to approve or deny building permits, Walasek "sat on" applications, waiting until the petitioner contributed $50 or $75, or threatened to sue to get his permit. Some building designs were not approved until a favored architect was retained as a "consultant." (It is not known whether this involved kickbacks to Walasek or simply patronage for a friend.) At least three instances are known in which developers were forced to pay for zoning variances before apartment buildings or supermarkets could be erected. Businessmen who wanted to encourage rapid turnover of the curb space in front of their stores were told to pay a police sergeant to erect "10-minute parking" signs. To repeat a caveat stated earlier, it is impossible to tell whether these kickbacks were demanded to expedite legitimate requests or to approve improper demands, such as a variance that would hurt a neighborhood or a certificate approving improper electrical work.

All of the activities detailed thus far involve fairly clear violations of the law. To complete the picture of the abuse of office by Wincanton officials, we might briefly mention "honest graft." This term was best defined by one of its earlier practitioners, State Senator George Washington Plunkitt who loyally served Tammany Hall at the turn of the century.

There's all the difference in the world between [honest and dishonest graft]. Yes, many of our men have grown rich in politics. I have myself. I've made a big fortune out of the game, and I'm gettin' richer every day, but I've not gone in for dishonest graft—blackmailin' gamblers, saloonkeepers, disorderly people, etc.—and neither has any of the men who have made big fortunes in politics.

There's an honest graft, and I'm an example of how it works. I might sum up the whole thing by sayin': "I seen my opportunities and I took 'em."

Let me explain by examples. My party's in power in the city, and it's goin' to undertake a lot of public improvements. Well, I'm tipped off, say, that they're going to lay out a new park at a certain place.

I see my opportunity and I take it. I go to that place, and I buy up all the land I can in the neighborhood. Then the board of this or that makes its plan public, and there is a rush to get my land, which nobody cared particular for before.

Ain't it perfectly honest to charge a good price and make a profit on my investment and foresight? Of course, it is. Well, that's honest graft.[1]

While there was little in the way of land purchasing—either honest or dishonest—going on in Wincanton during this period, several officials who carried on their own businesses while in office were able to pick up some "honest graft." One city councilman with an accounting office served as bookkeeper for Irv Stern and the major bookies and prostitutes in the city.

Police Chief Phillips' construction firm received a contract to remodel the exterior of the largest brothel in town. Finally one councilman serving in the present reform administration received a contract to construct all gasoline stations built in the city by a major petroleum company; skeptics say that the contract was the quid pro quo for the councilman's vote to give the company the contract to sell gasoline to the city.

*How Far Did It Go?*   This cataloging of acts of nonfeasance, malfeasance, and misfeasance by Wincanton officials raises a danger of confusing variety with universality, of assuming that every employee of the city was either engaged in corrupt activities or was being paid to ignore the corruption of others. On the contrary, both official investigations and private research lead to the conclusion that there is no reason whatsoever to question the honesty of the vast majority of the employees of the city of Wincanton. Certainly no more than 10 of the 155 members of the Wincanton police force were on Irv Stern's payroll (although as many as half of them may have accepted petty Christmas presents—turkeys or liquor). In each department, there were a few employees who objected actively to the misdeeds of their superiors, and the only charge that can justly be leveled against the mass of employees is that they were unwilling to jeopardize their employment by publicly exposing what was going on. When Federal investigators showed that an honest (and possibly successful) attempt was being made to expose Stern-Walasek corruption, a number of city employees cooperated with the grand jury in aggregating evidence which could be used to convict the corrupt officials.

Before these Federal investigations began, however, it could reasonably appear to an individual employee that the entire machinery of law enforcement in the city was controlled by Stern, Walasek, *et al.*, and that an individual protest would be silenced quickly. This can be illustrated by the momentary crusade conducted by First Assistant District Attorney Phil Roper in the summer of 1962. When the district attorney left for a short vacation, Roper decided to act against the gamblers and madams in the city. With the help of the State Police, Roper raided several large brothels. Apprehending on the street the city's largest distributor of punchboards and lotteries, Roper effected a citizen's arrest and drove him to police headquarters for proper detention and questioning. "I'm sorry, Mr. Roper," said the desk sergeant, "we're under orders not to arrest persons brought in by you." Roper was forced to call upon the State Police for aid in confining the gambler. When the district attorney returned from his vacation, he quickly fired Roper "for introducing politics into the district attorney's office."

If it is incorrect to say that Wincanton corruption extended very far vertically—into the rank and file of the various departments of the city—how far did it extend horizontally? How many branches and levels of government were affected? With the exception of the local Congressman and the city treasurer, it seems that a few personnel at each level (city, county, and State) and in most offices in city hall can be identified either with Stern or with some form of freelance corruption. A number of local judges received campaign financing from Stern, although there is no evidence that they were on his payroll after they were elected. Several State legislators were on Stern's payroll, and one Republican councilman charged that a high-ranking State Democratic official promised Stern first choice of all Alsace County patronage. The county chairman, he claimed, was only to receive the jobs that Stern did not want. While they were later to play an active role in disrupting Wincanton gambling, the district attorney in Hal Craig's reform administration feared that the State Police were on Stern's payroll, and thus refused to use them in city gambling raids.

Within the city administration, the evidence is fairly clear that some mayors and councilmen received regular payments from Stern and divided kickbacks on city purchases and sales. Some key subcouncil personnel frequently shared in payoffs affecting their particular departments—the police chief shared in the gambling and prostitution payoffs and received $300 of the $10,500 kickback on parking meter purchases. A councilman controlling one department, for example, might get a higher percentage of kickbacks than the other councilmen in contracts involving that department.

## PUBLIC ATTITUDES TOWARD GAMBLING AND CORRUPTION

A clean city, a city free of gambling, vice, and corruption, requires at least two things—active law enforcement and elected officials who oppose organized crime. . . . If the level of law enforcement in a community is tied to local voting patterns, we must look more closely at the attitudes and values of Wincanton residents. First, how much did residents know about what was going on? Were the events which have been discussed previously matters of common knowledge or were they perceived by only a few residents? Second, were they voting for open gambling and corruption; were they being duped by seemingly honest candidates who became corrupt after taking office; or were these issues irrelevant to the average voter, who was thinking about other issues entirely? Our conclusions about these questions will indicate whether long-range reform can be attained through legal changes (closing loopholes in the city's bidding practices, expanding civil service in the police department, ending the "home rule" policy of the State police, etc.) or whether reform must await a change in popular mores.

*Public Awareness of Gambling and Corruption.* In a survey of Wincanton residents conducted recently,[2] 90 percent of the respondents were able correctly to identify the present mayor, 63 percent recognized the name of their Congressman, and 36 percent knew the Alsace County district attorney. Seventy percent identified Irv Stern correctly, and 62 percent admitted that they did recognize the name of the largest madam in town. But how much did the people of Wincanton know about what had been going on—the extent and organization of Irv Stern's empire, the payoffs to city hall and the police, or the malfeasance and misfeasance of Bob Walasek and other city officials? Instead of thinking about simply "knowing" or "not knowing," we might subdivide public awareness into several categories—a general awareness that gambling and prostitution were present in the city, some perception that city officials were protecting these enterprises, and finally a specific knowledge that officials X and Y were being paid off. These categories vary, it will be noticed, in the specificity of knowledge and in the linkage between the result (e.g., presence of gambling or corruption) and an official's action.

Public awareness of wrongdoing was probably least widespread in regard to corruption—kickbacks on contracts, extortion, etc. Direct involvement was generally limited to officials and businessmen, and probably few of them knew anything other than that they personally had been asked to pay. Either from shame or from fear of being prosecuted on bribery charges or out of unwillingness to jeopardize a profitable contract, those who did pay did not want to talk. Those who refused to pay usually were unable to substantiate charges made against bribes so that exposure of the attempt led only to libel suits or official harassment. As we have seen, the newspapers and one garage with a towing contract did talk about what was going on. The garageman lost his franchise and suffered a series of "accidents"; the newspapers found a reporter in jail and their trucks harassed by the police. Peter French, the district attorney under Walasek and Donnelly, won a libel suit (since reversed on appeal and dismissed) against the papers after they stated that he was protecting gamblers. Except for an unsuccessful citizen suit in the mid-1950s seeking to void the purchase of fire trucks (for the purchase of which Donnelly received a $2000 "political contribution") and a newspaper article in the early

1960s implying that Donnelly and his council had received $500 on the sale of a city crane, no evidence—no specific facts—of corruption was available to the public until Phillips was indicted several years later for perjury in connection with the towing contracts.

Returning then to the three categories of public knowledge, we can say that even at the lowest level—general perception of some form of wrongdoing—awareness was quite limited (except among the businessmen, most of whom live and vote in the suburbs). Specific knowledge—this official received this much to approve that contract—was only available after legislative hearings in the early 1950s and the indictment of Phillips in the early 1960s; on both occasions the voters turned to reform candidates.

If, therefore, it is unlikely that many residents of Wincanton had the second or third type of knowledge about local gambling or corruption (while many more had the first type) during the time it was taking place, how much do they know now—after several years of reform and a series of trials—all well-covered in the newspapers revealing the nature of Stern-Donnelly-Walasek operations? To test the extent of specific knowledge about local officials and events, respondents in a recent survey were asked to identify past and present officials and racketeers and to compare the Walasek and Whitton administrations on a number of points.

Earlier, we noted that 90 percent of the 183 respondents recognized the name of the present mayor, 63 percent knew their Congressman (who had been in office more than 10 years), and 36 percent knew the district attorney. How many members of the Stern organization were known to the public? Seventy percent recognized Stern's name, 63 percent knew the head of the numbers bank, 40 percent identified the "bagman" or collector for Stern, and 31 percent knew the operator of the largest horsebook in town. With regard to many of these questions, it must be kept in mind that since many respondents may subconsciously have felt that to admit recognition of a name would have implied personal contact with or sympathy for a criminal or a criminal act, these results probably understate the extent of public knowledge. When 100 of the respondents were asked "What things did Mr. Walasek do that were illegal?," 59 mentioned extortion regarding vice and gambling, 2 mentioned extortion on city contracts, 7 stated that he stole from the city, 8 that he fixed parking and speeding tickets, 4 that he was "controlled by rackets," and 20 simply stated that Walasek was corrupt, not listing specific acts.

Even if Wincantonites do not remember too many specific misdeeds, they clearly perceive that the present Whitton administration has run a cleaner town than did Walasek or Donnelly. When asked to comment on the statement, "Some people say that the present city administration under Mayor Whitton is about the same as when Mayor Walasek was in office," 10 percent said it was the same, 74 percent said it was different, and 14 percent didn't know. When asked why, 75 respondents cited "better law enforcement" and the end of corruption; only 7 of 183 felt that the city had been better run by Walasek. Fifty-eight percent felt the police force was better now, 22 percent thought that it was about the same as when Walasek controlled the force, and only 7 percent thought it was worse now. Those who felt that the police department was better run now stressed "honesty" and "better law enforcement," or thought that it was valuable to have an outsider as commissioner. Those who thought it was worse now cited "inefficiency," "loafing," or "unfriendliness." It was impossible to tell whether the comments of "unfriendliness" refer simply to the present refusal to tolerate gambling or whether they signify a more remote police-public contact resulting from the "professionalism" of the commissioner. (In this regard, we might note that a number of policemen and lawyers felt that it had been easier to secure information regarding major crimes when prostitution and gambling were tolerated. As one former captain put it, "If I found out that some gangster was in town that I didn't know about, I raised hell with the prostitutes for not telling me.")

Comparing perceptions of the present and former district attorneys, we also find a clear preference for the present man, Thomas Hendricks, over Peter French, but there is a surprising increase in "Don't knows." Thirty-five percent felt the district attorney's office is run "differently" now, 13 percent said it is run in the same way, but 50 percent did not know. Paralleling this lack of attitudes toward the office, we can recall that only 36 percent of the respondents were able to identify the present incumbent's name, while 55 percent knew his more flamboyant predecessor. Of those respondents who saw a difference between the two men, 51 percent cited "better law enforcement" and "no more rackets control over law enforcement."

In addition to recognizing these differences between past and present officials, the respondents in the recent survey felt that there were clear differences in the extent of corruption and gambling. Sixty-nine percent disagreed with the statement, "Underworld elements and racketeers had very little say in what the Wincanton city government did when Mr. Walasek was mayor"; only 13 percent disagreed with the same statement as applied to reform Mayor Whitton.

# Notes

1. William L. Riordan, *Plunkitt of Tammany Hall* (New York: E. P. Dutton, 1963), p. 3.
2. This survey was conducted by eight female interviewers from the Wisconsin Survey Research Laboratory, using a schedule of questions requiring forty-five to seventy-five minutes to complete. Respondents were selected from among the adults residing in housing units selected at random from the Wincanton city directory. One hundred eighty-three completed interviews were obtained.

# 15

## AGNEW AND NIXON: THREE VIEWS

*James M. Naughton*
*John Crewdson*
*Ben Franklin*
*Christopher Lydon*
*Agie Solpukas*

*Russell Baker*

*John R. Silber*

## HOW AGNEW BARTERED HIS
## OFFICE TO KEEP FROM GOING TO PRISON

*James M. Naughton* et al.

It started with a casual remark, over lunch in Baltimore, late in the fall of 1972.

Robert Brown, director of the local Internal Revenue Service intelligence unit, mentioned a curious matter to George Beall, the United States Attorney. The intelligence unit had been poking into the income tax returns of Maryland officials and some of them "don't jibe," said Mr. Brown.

With equal nonchalance, Mr. Beall replied that he had heard rumors of local officials taking kickbacks from government contractors. Perhaps, the two men agreed, it was time to seek a connection between the tax returns and the rumors.

The investigation centered in suburban Baltimore County, where a Democrat, N. Dale Anderson, succeeded Mr. Agnew as the county executive in 1967. On Dec. 4, Mr. Beall had United States District Judge

Reprinted from *The New York Times*, October 23, 1973, © 1973 by The New York Times Company. Reprinted by permission.

C. Stanley Blain—who had been Vice President Agnew's chief of staff until his appointment to the bench in 1971—impanel a Federal grand jury.

The objectives were modest. Maybe they would catch "a couple of building inspectors" on the take, Mr. Beall thought. He assigned the case to three young assistants—Barnet D. Skolnik, Russell T. Baker Jr. and Ronald S. Liebman.

## AGNEW HEARD RUMORS

In January, they subpoenaed truckloads of official records from Baltimore County. By February, the county seat, Towson, was alive with speculation about the inquiry and rumors of it reached Mr. Agnew. He was startled, but outwardly unconcerned. He had done nothing wrong in his tenure there, he confided to friends.

Then the prosecutors traced the suspicious pattern of payoffs to two contractors who had long been associates of Mr. Agnew: Jerome B. Wolff, who had served as a public works staff man to County Executive Agnew, state roads commissioner under Governor Agnew and science adviser to Vice President Agnew, and Lester Matz, a partner in a consulting firm that had had many dealings with Mr. Agnew's county and state administrations.

The two contractors were alarmed. They warned Mr. Agnew that his name would be dragged into the investigation if it were not cut short.

One account, from an Agnew associate, is that the two men approached the Vice President directly last spring but Mr. Agnew told them he had nothing to fear and would not intervene.

## AGNEW REASSURANCE

Another version—which the prosecutors in Baltimore were exploring as the basis for a possible obstruction of justice charge against Mr. Agnew —was more involved. It was that Mr. Matz and Mr. Wolff had sent their message through I. H. Hammerman, a wealthy Maryland mortgage banker who had begun an Agnew-for-President movement for his close friend with "Spiro of '76" bumper stickers. Mr. Agnew was said to have sent back a rejoinder, paraphrased by one prosecutor:

"Don't worry. It's going to be stopped. You'll be indicted, but what's an indictment? You can beat it. The prosecutors will be kicked upstairs and it will end."

Whichever version was more correct, Mr. Agnew decided in April that he had to have legal advice. He got in touch with Charles W. Colson, the former White House special counsel. It was a curious choice. Mr.

Colson was himself coming under investigation by the Senate Watergate committee for his activities on behalf of President Nixon and had gone so far as to take a lie detector test to demonstrate that he was not involved in the Watergate burglary on June 17, 1972.

Mr. Colson met a number of times with Mr. Agnew. He also is known to have discussed the situation with the President. He asked his law partner, Judah Best, to get in touch with United States Attorney Beall.

Just before Easter, on April 19, Mr. Best went to Baltimore to declare that Mr. Agnew was concerned that "people were putting pressure on him to stop the investigation," and he wanted Mr. Beall to know that the last thing the Vice President "wanted to do in the middle of Watergate was to cover up."

As he later recalled it:

"I explained to Beall that I represented the Vice President, that the Vice President had heard these stories that he'd better stop the investigation or they'd make charges about him, and also that we'd heard about the dubious loyalties and lack of discretion of people on his (Beall's) staff."

## SKOLNIK PURSUED IT

The last remark was a reference to Mr. Skolnik, the most expert of the three assistant prosecutors on corruption cases—"I have an instinct for going after public officials who take cash in envelopes," he later boasted—but a liberal Democrat who had taken a leave from the prosecutor's office to work in the unsuccessful 1972 Presidential campaign of Senator Edmund S. Muskie, Democrat of Maine.

It was Mr. Skolnik who pursued the investigation until it touched on Mr. Agnew, a point that later would lead one of the Vice President's strategists to complain that Mr. Beall, a Republican whose father had been and brother was a United States Senator, had "lost control" of the inquiry.

In April, though, Mr. Agnew had yet to be implicated. Mr. Beall told the Vice President's lawyer that there was nothing to warrant any suggestion that Mr. Agnew was involved, said that he understood the delicacy of the situation and agreed to keep Mr. Best advised of the progress of the case.

Through June, Mr. Best kept telephoning Mr. Beall every 10 days or so and getting the same report: don't worry.

They didn't. Mr. Agnew discussed with his staff the prospect of another trip abroad on behalf of the White House. He submitted to a series of interviews in which he was able to note that he alone, among the officials closest to the President, had escaped any hint of involvement in the burgeoning Watergate scandal.

## THREE WERE PRESSING

But Mr. Skolnik and his two colleagues were pressing hard with the tactic that prosecutors employ to get lesser figures to implicate higher-ups.

"The train is at the station," they would warn a potential criminal defendant. "Lots of people are getting on. Room is running out. Time is also running out. The train may leave at any moment."

On June 4, the Baltimore County administrator, William E. Fornoff, succumbed to the tactic and gave the prosecutors detailed allegations that led to a subsequent grand jury indictment of Dale Anderson. Unknown to the Vice President, however, Fornoff gave no information involving him.

But Fornoff's actions apparently threatened Mr. Wolff and Mr. Matz. On June 11, almost simultaneously, they reached the prosecutors and started talking. By the end of June, the case against Vice President Agnew had begun to take shape.

*No More Smiles.*   The routine call from Judah Best to George Beall, in early July did not elicit the routine assurance. Instead, the United States Attorney told Mr. Agnew's lawyer, "It would be beneficial if we didn't talk again."

To Mr. Best, the implication was clear. "All smiles ended in early July."

It was universal, among those involved. On July 3, Mr. Beall and his three assistants came to Washington to alert Attorney General Elliot L. Richardson to the important new turn in the case.

"Boy, do we have bad news for you," one of them said as they entered the office of the nation's top law enforcement official.

## RICHARDSON'S CONCERN

They outlined the charges: For a decade, up to last December, Mr. Agnew had accepted, perhaps even solicited, cash payments from contractors in return for official favors.

Mr. Richardson listened, leaned back in his chair when the prosecutors had finished, and lit up a cigar. It was the eve of Independence Day. The Attorney General immediately cast the situation in its most broad and serious context. What was at stake, he remarked, was "the continuing capacity of the nation to govern itself."

All during the previous week, John W. Dean 3d, the former White House legal counsel, had been testifying to the Senate Watergate committee that President Nixon was an active participant in the Watergate cover-up.

Beyond that, Mr. Richardson voiced concern—which he would repeat many times over the next three months—that Mr. Agnew was one step away from becoming President of the United States.

"The President's plane could go down tomorrow," the Attorney General kept saying. "There could be an assassin's bullet. He could die tomorrow. Here we have a Vice President under a cloud."

He told the Baltimore prosecutors to proceed. They expected, as one of them later put it, "some midnight phone calls" to order that they direct the investigation away from the Vice President. The calls never came.

Much later, after Mr. Agnew had resigned, an associate attributed Mr. Agnew's denouement to the turmoil that Watergate had stirred in the Nixon Administration.

"If it hadn't been for Watergate," he said, "this whole thing would have been manageable. We wouldn't have had Richardson in the Justice Department, for one thing. I sure as hell would rather have dealt with Kleindienst"—former Attorney General Richard G. Kleindienst.

The point was not that Mr. Kliendienst might have been induced to cover up the case. It was that he might have understood better than Mr. Richardson—a Boston Brahmin whose politics had never depended upon others' wealth—how Mr. Agnew could rationalize a political life-style in which secret gifts from others were considered necessary for survival.

From the outset of the case against him through his televised explanation of his resignation last Monday, Mr. Agnew insisted that he was innocent of any wrongdoing, that he had never violated a public trust in return for political contributions.

For Mr. Agnew, it was all essential to survival, a basic platform from which he could continue to pursue higher office. Having entered big time politics without benefit of wealth, he felt constant pressure to live up to the standards of his wealthier peers.

He accepted groceries from a supermarket executive. His restaurant tabs were picked up by Mr. Hammerman. He used funds given to him when he was Governor to stock a wine cellar. When he traveled as Vice President to Palm Springs, Calif., everything was paid for him there by Frank Sinatra or Bob Hope. Early this year he moved into a $190,000 home with a $610,000 mortgage—and could not afford new draperies.

As one of his closest associates stated it, Mr. Agnew felt that "you can't go to (political) rallies if you don't have shoes, and gasoline in the car."

But as the Agnew supporters suspected, Attorney General Richardson took the view—as did the prosecutors in Maryland—that what the Vice President was accused of was illegal and immoral.

"How can he stay in office?" Mr. Richardson asked colleagues in one Justice Department meeting. "I couldn't do it."

*From X to Y to Z.*   On the last day of July, George Beall telephoned Judah Best and asked him to come to Baltimore. Mr. Best asked if he could do so in a few days, but the United States Attorney said, "You'd better make it tomorrow."

When Mr. Best entered Mr. Beall's office the next day, Aug. 1, the three other prosecutors already were there. Mr. Beall asked, "Do you want to sit with your back to the wall?"

"If it's all the same to you," Mr. Best answered, "I'd rather sit by the window."

Mr. Beall handed him a letter advising Mr. Best that the Vice President was under investigation for possible violations of the Federal criminal code and internal revenue statutes. Mr. Best read it, folded it up and without a word, left the office.

He drove back to Washington and made arrangements through Mr. Colson to see the Vice President, who was then in New York, the next day. Then another partner, David I. Shapiro, telephoned to the New York law firm of Paul, Weiss, Rifkind, Garrison & Wharton to ask Jay H. Topkis, a specialist in tax fraud cases, to join in the defense.

"We've got a very high government official we'd like you to defend," Mr. Shapiro said.

There was a pause at his end of the telephone conversation and then he told Mr. Topkis, "Well, no, not quite *the* highest."

Mr. Topkis agreed and added Martin London of the New York firm to the defense team. From that point on, in many telephone conversations about defense strategy, the lawyers referred to the Vice President only as "the client" and spoke in what they later described as a "highly eliptical" manner. They suspected that the Government would tap their phones.

The three principal defense lawyers—Messrs. Best, Topkis and London—had their first meeting with Mr. Agnew on the morning of Aug. 6, in the Vice President's suite in the Executive Office Building.

The meeting lasted all day. In the afternoon, Mr. Agnew's telephone rang. He picked it up, then announced: "It's Richardson. He's coming over."

The Attorney General joined them and recited the case as it then stood. It consisted of allegations by Mr. Matz and Mr. Wolff and by Allen Green, the principal in a large engineering company, that they had funneled thousands of dollars to Mr. Agnew on a regular basis in exchange for favors.

*Purgatory.*   The messages had been coming with some regularity from Mr. Hammerman. Mr. Agnew would answer the phone and an intermediary would say, "We may be in trouble."

Then came the day in August when there was a final, shocking message: "You may be in big trouble."

There were no more cryptic calls after that, and the Vice President knew what that meant: even Mr. Hammerman had turned on him. But he set out to win vindication. The process was complicated by the suddenness with which the case against him had become an open fight, in full view of the public. Before it would end, he would describe it as a "purgatory."

The same day that Mr. Richardson outlined to Mr. Agnew the government's evidence against him, the Vice President learned that someone had already outlined part of it to Jerry Landaur of The Wall Street Journal.

With the aid of the lawyers, he prepared a brief statement acknowledging that he was being investigated and proclaiming innocence of any violations of law.

On Aug. 8, Mr. Agnew conducted a news conference at which he called the charges against him "damned lies," pledged cooperation with the prosecutors and said he had absolutely nothing to hide."

It was the first step in an intricate campaign to place pressure on the President and, through him, on the Department of Justice.

As one official knowledgeable about Mr. Agnew's strategy deliberations characterized it, the news conference was intended to draw a sharp contrast between a cooperative Vice President and a President who was withholding Watergate tapes from the Senate and Government investigators. Second, it was intended to "use the press, in the classic sense, to counter the other side's use of the press" through leaks of evidence against the Vice President. Finally, it was meant to be a warning to the President: "We're going to fight; we're not going to be pushed around."

Mr. Nixon and Mr. Agnew never became close personally.

When the two senior officials of the United States Government met in private they were uncomfortable with one another. Cordial, yes. Respectful, always, but never fully candid. When the Agnew scandal became a public property it was doubly so. Mr. Nixon at first gave periodic and seemingly begrudged expressions of public confidence in Mr. Agnew. Later he began volunteering the statement that no improprieties had been cited—while Mr. Agnew was Vice President—a qualification that later proved to be erroneous.

The White House kept insisting, after each of a series of private meetings between the President and Vice President, that no requests had been made by Mr. Nixon for the resignation of the man he twice had picked for his heir apparent. Most Washington skeptics automatically disbelieved it. Curiously enough, it was true, strictly speaking.

*No Deal.* The President discussed the criminal case with the Vice President on Sept. 1. He reportedly wanted Mr. Agnew to resign, but recoiled from the task of making a direct appeal.

Instead, he sent an agent to see the Vice President some time during the first few days of September. An Agnew associate said that it was Bryce

N. Harlow, a gentle but politically streetwise counselor to the President who had developed a close relationship with Mr. Agnew during the 1970 campaign but was closest of all to Mr. Nixon.

Mr. Harlow described the severity of the charges against Mr. Agnew. He suggested that a resignation might be best, "for the good of the country." And he alluded to an understanding in the White House that the consequences for Mr. Agnew should be made minimal in return for an act of patriotism.

From the outset, Mr. Agnew expressed interest in the proposal but would stand and fight if any such proposal involved the risk of imprisonment. It was, said one of the half-dozen people with whom he consulted about the overture, "very, very important to him the most important thing of all that he not go to prison." He continued to profess his innocence, but he understood that resignation would be taken as a token of guilt and a presumption of guilt might well be a prelude to conviction and jail.

On Sept. 14, Mr. Agnew asked his closest confidant in the Senate, Barry Goldwater of Arizona, to meet with him. He told the Senator, whose support for him had rallied other American conservatives, that he was seriously weighing a Presidential request for his resignation.

Mr. Goldwater told the Vice President that was fine if he were guilty. If not—as Mr. Agnew assured him—then he should fight it to the end.

Later that morning, Senator Goldwater telephoned Mr. Harlow and was harshly critical of the request and the pressure it represented. The Senator then flew to his home in Phoenix.

To the Senator's surprise, Mr. Harlow arrived by jet in Phoenix not long afterwards, accompanied by J. Fred Buzhardt Jr., the president's special counsel on Watergate. The purpose of their journey was to dissuade the senator from continuing to support Mr. Agnew.

## RESENTED PUBLICITY

For an hour, the two Presidential assistants outlined the evidence, but Mr. Goldwater told them it contained nothing he had not already seen in the newspapers, a fact he resented nearly as much as Mr. Agnew for its prejudicial impact on the Vice President's defense. In his customary blunt style, Mr. Goldwater said that he did not care if Mr. Agnew was "as guilty as John Dillinger"—what mattered was that he was not getting fair treatment from the Department of Justice.

But Mr. Agnew was already secretly beginning to try to make a satisfactory bargain with Justice. Each side withheld from the opposite a private fear that prosecution could be disastrous: the Government lawyers because they thought it inevitable that one or more jurors would shrink from convicting a Vice President, Mr. Agnew's attorneys because they were uncertain that jurors would accept a centention that their client had abided by a code of ethics, however questionable, that was standard in Maryland politics.

## BUZHARDT WAS BROKER

Each side had a fundamental demand that was to imperil the negotiations. Mr. Agnew would not go to prison; the Baltimore prosecutors insisted that he should. The Government had to be able to avoid cover-up charges by publishing the core of its evidence; Mr. Agnew's lawyers wanted some opportunity to insist on his innocence and thus salvage some dignity.

Mr. Buzhardt played the role of broker to get the two sides to the bargaining table. Who instructed him to do so remains unclear, but to Assistant Attorney General Petersen, "it was clear where he was from. It was clear that the quicker it could be resolved the better the President would like it." But Mr. Buzhardt made no suggestions. He didn't have to. When the two sets of lawyers met the first time on Sept. 13, Judah Best made a startling proposal.

"My line was," he later reminisced, "I want an end of this, an end of the investigation. And his resignation is part of it. Let's cut a deal. A nolo plea (nolo contendere, or no contest, the legal equivalent of a plea of guilt without the admission) to a one-count information. No jail term. And he'll resign. And I want to save this man's honor to the extent I can."

Henry Petersen was "dumfounded." He had encountered nothing like it in 25 years of the Justice Department. "When a guy comes in and wants to plead before indictment, you've got him whipped," he said. "That's extraordinary in itself."

But the senior law enforcement officials wrangled for five days over whether to accept. The arguments were ferocious. Mr. Richardson sat at the head of a large conference table with five aides and the four Baltimore prosecutors shouting at one another. Mr. Skolnik in particular demanded stern retribution, a prison term. Others argued about the impact of a deal on the public image of a Justice Department already soiled by Watergate. Everyone worried about the political implications, the effect on legal institutions from a Vice President copping a plea vs. the damage to the nation and the Republican party from a bitter and long public prosecution.

The Attorney General refereed for the most part, but periodically he would chime in with the same insistent theme: Mr. Agnew must not become President. Mr. Nixon had been hospitalized with viral pneumonia in July. And, a colleague of Mr. Richardson's said, the Attorney General "was very worried about Nixon—he might be impeached, assassinated, he was not in the best psychological condition."

On Wednesday, Sept. 22, it leaked into print that plea bargaining was under way. Mr. Best denied it; Justice waffled. And Mr. Agnew called it off.

"No," he told his lawyers, "it's impossible. We're negotiating in a posture where I'm plea bargaining. I'm innocent, and the public perception must be that I'm innocent."

*Pressure.* On Sept. 23, the Vice President set up a legal defense fund. On Sept. 25, he urged the House of Representatives to conduct a full, public inquiry that would give him an opportunity to vindicate himself. On Sept. 26, House Speaker Carl Albert shelved the request. On Sept. 27, the Baltimore prosecutors began presenting evidence against Mr. Agnew to the grand jury. On Sept. 28, Mr. Agnew's lawyers filed suit in the Federal courts to block the grand jury action, contending that the constitution forbade the indictment of a Vice President and that news leaks had irreparably damaged the prospect of a fair trial.

## BID TO HOUSE

On Sept. 29, the Vice President vowed in a Los Angeles speech not to resign even if indicted and accused the Justice Department of trying to "destroy" his career. On Oct. 3, Judge Hoffman granted Mr. Agnew unparalleled authority to subpoena prosecutors and journalists to find the sources of news leaks. On Oct. 5, the Justice Department asserted in a legal memorandum that a President could not be indicted but a Vice President could.

It occurred with such breathtaking rapidity and mounting intensity that the nation seemed confronted with not merely another but a whole series of new legal, constitutional and political crises. The cascade of developments was, in fact, the public product of a strategy to strengthen Mr. Agnew's hand at the secret bargaining table or, failing there, to build a foundation for a long-drawn-out effort in the courts.

The bid for a House inquiry—an open invitation to impeachment— was the most excruciating of the pressure tactics. It was designed to pose a risk to a besieged President that the derelict constitutional machinery of impeachment would be overhauled for an Agnew case and, oiled, humming and ready to perform, be available for use against Mr. Nixon himself.

The legal argument that Mr. Agnew could not be indicted in office contained a threat of a Supreme Court ruling that might also set a precedent for the Presidency.

The legal and oratorical charges that the Justice Department was systematically leaking damning accusations against Mr. Agnew were meant to generate public support for his role as an underdog and thus put more heat on the prosecutors.

An admirer once credited Mr. Agnew with an uncanny ability to compartmentalize his activities, erecting watertight barriers that kept some of his closest associates from knowledge of what equally close aides were doing on his behalf.

Only three other persons were aware of Mr. Agnew's strategy of escalating pressure. They were Arthur J. Sohmer, the Vice President administrative assistant; Major General John M. Dunn, his military aide; and Mary Ellen Warner, Mr. Agnew's confidential secretary.

The message, later summarized by a marveling admirer of the strategy, was basic:

"We need help. Wanted help. Demanded help."
The White House got the message.

*The Bargain.*   Within days of Mr. Agnew's Sept. 29 attack in Los Angeles against the Justice Department and his vow to stand and fight, a channel of communication that none of the participants would specify but one called "bizarre" fed a response to Mr. Agnew from the White House: resume the bargaining and this time it will work.

J. Marsh Thomson, the Vice President's spokesman, was advising newsmen that Mr. Agnew would deliver another stern rebuke to the prosecutors on Oct. 4 at a Republican party banquet in Chicago. But a day earlier, Mr. Thomson was suddenly ordered to make himself totally unavailable to news outlets. The speech turned out to be unfettered praise of the President, with only a cryptic reference to the Baltimore investigation.

"A candle is only so long and eventually it goes out," the Vice President told a mystified Chicago audience.

The next day, Mr. Agnew told Mr. Best, "I think they're ready to negotiate."

Once again the broker was Mr. Buzhardt and it was implicit for whom he was acting. As Mr. Petersen stated it, "The President would be a blithering idiot if he weren't trying to exert some role in this thing. It's his administration! He had both a political interest and a constitutional interest in getting a resolution of the situation."


## SETTLED ON WORDING

Late on Friday, Oct. 5, Mr. Best caught a plane to Miami to meet with Mr. Buzhardt, who was at nearby Key Biscayne with the President's entourage. From midnight until 3 A.M. Saturday, in Mr. Best's room at the Marriott Hotel, they settled on the wording of a statement in which Mr. Agnew would acknowledge evading income taxes in 1967, and they reached an "ironclad agreement" that the Vice President could see the summary of the evidence against him before it was published.

"The key," Mr. Best said, "was Agnew's capacity to deny it."

But the question of punishment still had to be settled, and that would mean involving a Federal judge in the private negotiations.

On Columbus Day, Oct. 8, Judge Hoffman met from 5 to 7 P.M. in the Old Colony Motel, across the Potomac River from the capital in Alexandria, Va., with three representatives from each side: Messrs. Petersen, Beall and Skolnik for the Government and Messrs. Topkis, London and Best for the Vice President. The tentative agreement was outlined, but Mr. Agnew's lawyers wanted a decision on the sentence they could expect, and Judge Hoffman refused to make any commitment without a recommendation from the Attorney General's office.


## COULDN'T AGREE ON PENALTY

Mr. Petersen said he could not give a recommendation, and the meeting broke up with resolution still eluding the negotiators.

The Government could not agree on the punishment it wished to exact. The argument broke out again and it became apparent, in the words of one source, that they would have to "trample on Skolnik" to get his support for a recommendation of leniency.

At 8:45 that night, Mr. Petersen was driving home from the office. On his car radio he heard part of a speech by Secretary of State Kissinger to Pacem in Terris, a conference on the search for world peace.

"A presumed monopoly on truth obstructs negotiation and accommodation," Mr. Kissinger was saying. "Good results may be given up in the quest for ever-elusive ideal solutions." Policy makers, he said moments later, must understand "the crucial importance of timing. Opportunities cannot be hoarded; once past, they are usually irretrievable."

The next morning, Mr. Petersen had his secretary type copies of two pertinent pages from Mr. Kissinger's text. The Assistant Attorney General gave them to the Baltimore prosecutors and told Mr. Skolnik, "We can bring him (Mr. Agnew) to his knees. There's no doubt about that. The question is, should we?"

Disgrace, he said, would be sufficient without sending the Vice President to prison.

Later that day, Oct. 9, the negotiations resumed before Judge Hoffman. This time, however, they were at the Justice Department. Attorney General Richardson was present and he was prepared to recommend against a prison sentence.

"It is my understanding," Mr. Richardson told the judge, "that for you to give a guarantee you need an affirmative recommendation from me. Judge, if it's a must, you've got it."

"If I've got it, okay, I will commit myself," Judge Hoffman replied. It was a bargain.

# ON FLUNKING PRISON

*Russell Baker*

Most of the debate about whether it is fitting to jail an ex-President is so high-flown that one feels a bit timid about injecting some realism into it.

It is with considerable diffidence, therefore, that I suggest that the whole debate is silly. Those arguing for jail say no man can be beyond the law, while those against it say it would be a terrible thing for the country to lock up a man who has been President and, anyhow, his unscheduled departure from the White House is punishment enough.

Nobody has yet asked the central question: Is locking the fellow up going to do any good?

If we look at the American prison system, the overwhelming logic of this conclusion becomes manifest. The American prison is primarily an educational institution. We send young men to prison and they come out finished criminals, just as we send other young men to Yale and turn them into bankers.

A constant supply of criminals turned out by our prisons contributes to economic health by maintaining full employment in the police and the judicial industries, enriching lawyers and insurance companies, keeping social workers occupied and supporting large government bureaucracies.

Offering the benefits of prison education to former Presidents, however, makes little sense. To begin with, they will invariably be too old to profit from it and repay the country with the long career at crime necessary to amortize the high cost of prison education.

When I last saw the figures, the Federal Government was paying more to maintain a man in prison per year than it would cost to send him to Harvard. For an education as expensive as that, society is entitled to some assurance that he is going to be able to repay his debt to its prison-related industries.

The average ex-President will be in his late fifties or more probably, in his sixties before he even enters prison. By the time he comes out, his useful criminal life will be negligible. No insurance company in the land would bet against actuarial odds like these.

One secondary purpose of prison is to provide storage space for poor people. In the criminal, legal and judicial classes, it is an established principle that the less wealth a felon has, the more time he must serve.

This has the incidental political value of holding down the unemployment statistics, but the main reason for it is that poor people, as all the data prove, are far more likely to go into crime than the well-to-do and, therefore, far more likely to profit from the benefits of prison's criminal education.

Former Presidents will almost invariably be far too well-heeled to qualify. If admission to prison were conducted like admission to Ivy League colleges, with a lot of hocus-pocus testing to determine a candidate's chances of succeeding, former Presidents would be so obviously doomed to failure that prisons would reject them without the courtesy of an interview at the admitting office.

Does it make the slightest sense for the country to spend more than the cost of a Harvard education on men like ex-Presidents whose very wealth must prevent them from ever making first-rate criminals of themselves?

The other secondary purpose of prison is to silence people whose political opinions are obnoxious to society but who insist, nevertheless, on airing them. Prison protects us from having to be harangued by people we disagree with. Timothy Leary, war resisters, black militants, nudists, practicing Christians and others of that stripe.

No man who has been President of the United States could conceivably qualify for prison on these terms, since no matter how grave his offense we are not likely to concede that we could have ever elected a man of unorthodox mind.

When we consider, then, what prison in America is truly about, the question whether former Presidents should go is easily answered. The answer is no. They are totally unqualified.

# THE THICKET OF LAW
# AND THE MARSH OF CONSCIENCE

*John R. Silber*

Elementary legal traditions, such as that sanction should follow conviction of a crime, have not been observed. This part of the rule of law was clearly compromised in statements by former Attorney General Richardson at the time of Mr. Agnew's resignation. He remarked at the time: "I am fairly

Copyright © by *Harvard Magazine*, 77 (November, 1974), pp. 15–18.

convinced that in all circumstances leniency was justified. . . . I am keenly aware of the historical magnitude of the penalties inherent in the Vice President's resignation from his high office and his acceptance of a judgment of conviction for a felony. . . . Each individual will have to make up his or her mind about the justice of this result. I believe it is just, fair, and honorable."

Richardson's statement reveals the sharp decline of our expectation of our leaders. We are to be satisfied if a politician pays for his crime by removal from office and payment of a fine; that is, by denying him the opportunity to continue his criminal activity and by taxing its proceeds. If the fox will wipe the feathers from his mouth, the fox may leave the chicken house with impunity. He has suffered enough by being asked to leave. This is perhaps adequate as a political solution to the political problem of removing a putative felon from the Presidential succession. But Richardson confounds policy with justice and says of the arrangement, "I believe it is just, fair, and honorable." The national mood of cynicism was thus seen to erode even the sensibilities of the man who from the standpoint of personal integrity was one of the few redeeming members of the Nixon Administration. Fortunately, the Maryland supreme court resisted this cynicism. In disbarring Mr. Agnew, the court held: "It is difficult to feel compassion for an attorney who is so morally obtuse that he consciously cheats for his own pecuniary gain that government he has sworn to serve, completely disregards the words of the oath he uttered when he was first admitted to the bar, and absolutely fails to perceive his professional duty to act honestly in all matters." In this case, at long last, responsibility entailed consequence, and sanction followed conviction.

But the essential deficiency remained: it became increasingly apparent in the reluctance to move against the President. This action was retarded not only by cynicism, but by a genuine, though ill-conceived, concern that no one should injure the office of the President of the United States. On this point we are all finally reassured. Subsequent events showed us that there is no way that anyone can injure or detract from the office of the President as long as we hold all incumbents to the very highest standards of moral, legal, and political rectitude. To hold the incumbents of this office to anything less would in fact have been the most serious way to impair if not destroy the office.

At last even Mr. Nixon's most loyal supporters realized that his conduct had been grotesquely incommensurate with the minimum demands of the office, and Mr. Nixon himself was brought to understand that he faced certain removal from office and that resignation was more advantageous to him than conviction following impeachment.

With the accession of a new and unblemished President, the dignity and respect of the office were instantly restored. And the Ford Administration moved swiftly to regain the confidence and respect of the people by its explicit affirmation of the rule of law and the subordination of every citizen to it. Regrettably, Mr. Ford held to this principle for no more than a month. Following the dictates of a conscience that although honest is far from wise, he pardoned a citizen who had neither been indicted for nor convicted of any crime. When Mr. Nixon went to bed on Saturday night, he was, in the eyes of the law, an innocent man. By Sunday evening, he was a pardoned criminal. The judgment that he had committed crimes was made by Mr. Ford alone, without benefit of any judicial proceedings. Such an act is an executive equivalent of the bills of attainder that our Constitution specifically prohibits Congress from passing.

The President has impulsively and carelessly cut a great road through the law to "shut and seal this book [of Watergate]," to "write the end of it." With this laudable intent, President Ford laid flat every law that applied to Richard M. Nixon between January 20, 1969, and August 9, 1974. The winds of lawlessness and anarchy now blow about Mr. Ford, and where will he hide? Having exempted Mr. Nixon from the rule of law, how shall he stand upright in the winds of precedent?

When Mr. Ford says that his conscience should be superior to the Constitution, he does no more than articulate the classical rationale for civil disobedience. But this may guide his personal and private behavior only. If citizen Ford finds that a higher law tells him to disobey the laws of men, and he is willing to take the legal consequences, a decent respect for the rights of conscience will allow citizen Ford to disobey the law and suffer the consequences. But President Ford must be bound to no law higher than the Constitution. He ought to have considered that restraint before accepting nomination as Vice President.

Instead of expecting more of those to whom much has been given, President Ford, following Richardson's unfortunate precedent, has held that far less shall be expected of a President of the United States than is expected from a Boston housewife concerned for the safety of her children. He has excused Mr. Nixon from the consequences of bribery, of burglary, of income-tax fraud, of the appropriation of public funds for personal use, of the misuse of the F.B.I., the C.I.A., and the I.R.S., and of the obstruction of justice. He has said, following Richardson's rule, that merely to deny a person continuation in such misconduct is enough. Can this be the law of God? It is not the law of an enlightened community.

Mr. Ford has said that he acted for the good of the country and to preserve the credibility of its institutions. But in fact he has proclaimed to the world his lack of faith in these institutions, for he tells us that they could not have provided Richard Nixon with a fair trial without subjecting him to cruel and unusual punishment. He also confesses his doubt in the ability of the American people to endure the ordeal of trying an ex-President.

Mr. Ford told us that only he could write "The End" on what he called the American tragedy of Watergate. Mr. Ford is wrong, for only the law can put an end to Watergate. But that end could be swiftly accomplished even now, were Mr. Nixon to sit down with the Prosecutor, agree on charges, plead guilty, and thus complete the legal process. Mr. Nixon's health problems do not demand a suspension of the rule of law. The rule of law is not inherently inhumane, and humane men can administer it without overthrowing it. There are already adequate and humane procedures for dealing with the case of anyone physically unable to stand trial. As soon as Mr. Nixon admits his guilt to properly drawn charges, President Ford's pardon restores our expectation of equal justice under law and mercifully closes the book of Watergate for Mr. Nixon.

As things now stand, Mr. Nixon has gained what he sought so long in vain, what had been denied him by the Supreme Court itself: a special place in the legal system of the United States. President Ford has given Mr. Nixon what no other President ever gave to any alleged criminal: a blanket pardon for *unspecified* crimes without even the formality of an indictment or a confession of guilt. President Ford has overturned the precedent set by the high court in its tapes decision and replaced it with a new one: no future President need worry about facing the legal consequences for any crimes he may wish to commit, as long as he takes care in selecting his Vice President.

At his inauguration President Ford told the American people: "Fellow citizens, the long nightmare of Watergate is over." But he seems not to have understood what the nightmare was. Not that a President or ex-President might go on trial, but rather that he might *deserve* to go on trial. Not that an ex-President might go to jail, but that an ex-President might *deserve* to go to jail. That was the nightmare of Watergate. To this Mr. Ford has added a new nightmare. Not that an ex-President might need to be pardoned or that mercy might dictate his being pardoned, but that he should be pardoned prior to any indictment or acknowledgment of guilt on the grounds that defects in our legal institutions and public instability and impatience require it.

The nightmare of Watergate is not satisfactorily resolved by the addition of another nightmare. It was the desire of the American people to prevent obstruction of justice that brought Mr. Ford with such swiftness into the Presidential office. The national interest will not be served by his inadvertently completing what he was called to prevent.

The President said that he wanted to spare the country further degradation. By his action he has done one of the few things that could have increased the degradation of Watergate. It was degrading for the country to have a President who directed a criminal conspiracy. It was degrading to have that President wrap himself in the flag and lie and lie and lie to the American people. It was degrading to see that President and his underlings slander and libel the press and the members of the House Judiciary

Committee. All of these were degradation. But there could have been only honor for the nation in Mr. Nixon's having become at last, like all other citizens, subject to the rule of law. Mr. Ford has substituted for this honor yet another degradation.

There is certainly nothing in Mr. Nixon's behavior to warrant special treatment. Despite his incessant attempts to blame Watergate on the press, to say he was hounded from office by his enemies, and to attribute his resignation to a loss of a political base in Congress, we must now see that he was personally responsible for what his successor has called the nightmare. Had he in fact been willing to get the story out in June 1972, or even following the election in November, there would have been a Watergate affair, but it would not have immobilized the government and distracted the people from the serious substantive problems at hand. It was Mr. Nixon's own formula to speak of Watergate getting in the way of the people's business. Mr. Nixon has shown no contrition for what he has done to this country. He has not even shown any contrition for his complicity in the ruin of the lives of those whom he involved in his crimes. Some of them were originally honest men too foolish to understand that not even the dictates of conscience allow the President of the United States to place himself or his subordinates above the law and to order the commission of crimes. His own insistence upon his innocence and upon treating these crimes as mere errors of judgment shows how little Mr. Nixon at this point merits pardon. Once Mr. Nixon acknowledges the claims of justice, the mercy and pardon may follow unstrained.

Mr. Agnew has recently claimed that because he was not tried he is therefore in fact innocent of crimes. Mr. Nixon is likely to make similar good use of the fact that through the pardon process he has become, in the words of the Supreme Court decision that governs the granting of pardons, "a new man."

The government should now publish in full transcripts of *all* the Watergate-related tapes, without any deletion. The American people have a right to know exactly what has been done to them in the last five years. We are strong enough to bear the shock and to learn from it. If the President believes that we are not, and must be shielded from the truth, he will join his predecessor in believing that we are like children. Such contempt for the people is offensive under any government, and especially so in a democracy.

Complete information as to the full nature of the Watergate tragedy is essential if we are to repair the damage done to our institutions by Gerald R. Ford. For he has temporarily established as legal the principle that an ex-President of the United States is in fact a superior being who can be exempted for the period of his Presidency from the rule of law.

# 16

# THE WORLD BEHIND WATERGATE

*Kirkpatrick Sale*

The bedfellows politics makes are never strange; it only seems that way to those who have not watched the courtship. In Richard Nixon's case, notwithstanding his presence in national politics for the last twenty-five years, those courtships have remained remarkably unexamined—or, when examined, remarkably misunderstood—and as a result the bedfellows he has acquired have remained unusually obscure both to the public and to the political pundits who are supposed to conjure with such things. Certain obvious relationships, to be sure, have been given attention—the back-scratching of Nixon and his old friend and Pepsico chairman Donald Kendall, for example,[1] the latest evidence of which is Washington's gift of the Soviet soft-drink franchise to Pepsi-Cola. But the wider pattern of his associations, the character of his power base, remains essentially obscure. . . .

The Nixonian bedfellows, the people whose creed the President expresses and whose interests he guards, are, to generalize, the economic sovereigns of America's Southern rim, the "sunbelt" that runs from Southern California, through Arizona and Texas, down to the Florida keys.

They are for the most part new-money people, without the family fortunes and backgrounds of Eastern wealth (Rockefellers, DuPonts, etc.), people whose fortunes have been made only in the postwar decades, mostly in new industries such as aerospace and defense contracting, in oil, natural gas, and allied businesses, usually domestic rather than international, and in real-estate operations during the postwar sunbelt population boom.

They are "self-made" men and women, in the sense that they did not generally inherit great riches (though of course in another sense they are government-made, depending, as in oil and aerospace, on large favors from Washington, but they hardly like to think of it that way), and they tend to a notable degree to be politically conservative, even retrograde, usually anti-union, anti-black, anti-consumer, and anti-regulation, and quite often associated with professional "anti-communist" organizations. Whether because of the newness of their position, their frontier heritage, or their lack of old-school ties, they tend to be without particular concerns about the niceties of business ethics and morals, and therefore to be connected more than earlier money would have thought wise with shady speculations, political influence-peddling, corrupt unions, and even organized crime.

The political ascendancy of these Southern-rim people—those whom Carl Oglesby once called "the cowboys," as distinct from "the yankees" of old Eastern money—has taken place coincidentally with their economic growth in the last generation. Their power on a state level was solidified a decade or so ago, and they made certain inroads to national influence with Johnson's assumption of the presidency in 1963.[2] But it was not until the election of Richard Nixon in 1968 . . . that the Southern-rim bedfellows were firmly installed in the bedrooms of political power in Washington. It is a fitting symbol of this that Nixon has established White Houses at the two extremes of the Southern rim, San Clemente and Key Biscayne. . . .

One rough measure of the political ascendancy of the cowboys is the number of them who actually occupy high positions in Washington. Of the four members of what Nixon likes to call his "super-super cabinet," three of them—the three with the highest authority in domestic affairs (the fourth is Kissinger)—are from the Southern rim: Roy Ash (California: millionaire defense contractor), John Ehrlichman (California, out of Seattle: lawyer, politico), and Bob Haldeman (California: PR man). On the cabinet level there are Anne Armstrong (Texas: Republican politico), Claude Brinegar (California: Union Oil executive), Frederick Dent (South Carolina: textile millionaire), Richard Kleindienst (Arizona: Goldwater crony), and Caspar Weinberger (California: Republican politico and ex-Reagan aide).

Of the five Nixon nominees to the Supreme Court, three (Rehnquist, Carswell, and Haynesworth) were wool-died Southern-rim conservatives and one (Powell) was a right-wing Virginian who was also a director of oil and gas corporations. The key appointments to the increasingly powerful Republican National Committee have all been from the Southern-rim—co-chairpersons George Bush (Texas: oil company co-founder) and Janet Johnston (California: rancher) and general counsel Harry Dent (South Carolina: lawyer, ex-GOP state head). The rim influence is here so strong that there have even been published complaints from Mid-western Republicans about a "Southern Mafia."[3]

And peppered throughout the government are such key cowboys as press secretary Ronald Ziegler (California: public relations), Frederic Malek, second-in-command of the budget (South Carolina: tool-manufacturing millionaire), Commissioner of Education John Ottina (California: defense industry consultant), Director of Communications Herbert Klein (California: Copley Press executive), Deputy Secretary of Defense William Clements (Texas: oil millionaire), Assistant Agriculture Secretary Robert Long (California: Bank of America executive), Undersecretary of State William Casey (a New Yorker, but director and counsel of a Southern-rim agribusiness corporation).... And on and on, scores more throughout the top levels of the Administration, not even balanced this term by very many liberals and Easterners.

A second measure of cowboy penetration is their preponderance among Nixon's major financial supporters. Though the loopholed campaign-spending laws permit only partial identification of the top money men, it seems clear at least that the chief sources of Nixon's campaign finances—and therefore presumably the people whose interests the President will try to keep dominant—are independent oil producers, defense contractors, right-wing unions, rich conservative businessmen, and various Southern-rim manufacturers. This does not mean, of course, that the more traditional sources of Republican money, such as the old-money families and yankees new and old throughout the financial world, have been thoroughly displaced or no longer make big contributions, but only that their position is being steadily narrowed and their importance therefore steadily decreased.

Oil money, for example, has always found its way into politics, as much from the old corporations with chiefly international interests as from the new independents who have sprung up along the Southern rim.[4] But it has been the latter who have been most important in Nixon's career, from such supporters as Union Oil, Superior Oil, and Texas ultra-conservative H. L. Hunt, who helped finance his early campaigns, through California right-winger Henry Salvatori, the Texas Murchison family, and at least a third of the backers in the 1952 "slush fund." In this last campaign there were some large contributions from old oil—Richard Mellon Scaife (Gulf Oil, among other interests) gave $1 million, the Phipps family (Texaco among others) gave at least $55,000—but the striking fact is the number of domestic oil donors, rimsters or with rim interests, people like Kent Smith (Lubrizol, $244,000), Francis Cappeart (Southern oil and agribusiness, $174,000), John Paul Getty (Getty Oil, $97,000), John J. Shaheen (Shaheen Natural Resources, $100,000), Elisha Walker (Petroleum Corporation of America, $100,000), Max Fisher (Marathon Oil, $60,000), the O'Connor family (Texas Oil, $60,000), and the Osea Wyatt family (Coastal States Gas, $41,000).[5]

Other major sources of support in the last campaign can be traced, too, and they follow the same general pattern: some sizable donors from the old-money families and new-money Easterners, but surprising strength from the Southern rim. Among the largest donors with defense interests last year were yankees like Arthur Watson (IBM, $303,000) and Saul Steinberg (Leasco, $250,000), but they were matched by the rimsters, people like Charles and Sam Wyly (Dallas computer company, $172,000), Thomas Marquez (Electronic Data Systems, Dallas, $88,000), Howard Hughes (Hughes Tool, etc., Houston, $100,000), Ling-Temco-Vought (Texas, $60,000), and Litton Industries ($18,000).

Southern-rim new-money businessmen included Walter T. Duncan (Texas, real estate, $305,000), Sam Schulman (California, National General conglomerate, $257,000), John and Charles Williams (Oklahoma manufacturers, $98,000), M. B. Seretean and Eugene Barwick (Southern textile manufacturers, $200,000), Anthony Rossi (Florida, Tropicana, $100,000), C. Arnholt Smith (California financier, $50,000), and L. B. Maytag (Florida, National Airlines, $50,000). Donors among the major organizations include three with extensive rim contracts, the Texas-based Associated Milk Producers ($782,000), and the two right-wing unions, the Seafarers (with direct oil and agribusiness links, $100,000) and the Teamsters (with heavy investments from Southern California and Las Vegas to Miami, an estimated $100,000).

Perhaps an even more revealing measure of the rimsters' influence is their dominance of the Nixon inner circle. Now their numbers are hardly legion, because this President is an essentially friendless man, a distrustful person with few close cronies, but the few that exist are, almost to a man (no women), from the sunbelt states. The only visible exceptions are Donald Kendall and Secretary of State William Rogers, both solid Easterners, and even they are new-money, up-from-poverty types.

The rest are people like Southern California businessmen Jack Drown, Ray Arbuthnot and C. Arnholt Smith, California politician Robert Finch (a friend, apparently, even after his fall from office), and four men who seem to be closest of all to the President: Herbert Kalmbach, a rich Los Angeles lawyer who is the President's personal counsel and was his chief fund raiser during 1971; John Connally, the oil-tied Texas politician who is Nixon's financial guru and reportedly his choice as successor; Murray Chotiner, the California lawyer who has been with Nixon since the beginning and during 1971 and 1972 was with him in the White House; and Bebe Rebozo, the Florida millionaire who is reckoned to be the most intimate of all with the President. All of these are fairly typical Southern rimsters, all are new-money people, all are well-off, and all of them (except maybe Finch) are politically conservative. Most disturbing of all, several of these people have had the taint, and sometimes the full stigma, of scandal around them.

This last attribute deserves somewhat more attention, for it is inevitably one of the most striking features of the political cowboys and one with very serious implications for our national life. Without going into a full portrait of the noisome character of so much of the Southern rim—home of well-established organized-crime centers in such places as Las Vegas, New Orleans, and Miami, the last having lately become a veritable Marseilles—one can still note that many of Nixon's closest friends from this region are, to a remarkable and unhealthy degree, guilty of improprieties in business, a certain disregard for public trust, a general lack of ethical sophistication, or in some cases direct association with criminal figures. To cite a few examples:

Herbert Kalmbach has been identified as one of the five people in charge of funds for the million-dollar Republican operation to sabotage the Democratic campaign last year,[6] and according to the FBI he personally gave Republican funds to Donald Segretti, the California lawyer who by all accounts (none denied) was the West Coast leader of that operation;[7] Kalmbach has also been identified in sworn court papers as the strong-man in the Republicans' efforts to squeeze some $700,000 out of the large milk producers in return for a government-approved price raise.[8]

Connally, whose service on behalf of rich Texas oilmen has been well documented, was attorney for Texas millionaire Sid Richardson when he engineered a million-dollar payment to Texas oil-man Robert Anderson in the mid-Fifties;[9] and while governor of Texas he trickily denied the fact that he had received at least $225,000 from the multimillion-dollar Richardson estate,[10] a payment that was possibly in violation of the Texas constitution.

Chotiner has also had a career of slimy dealings ever since he first invented the Pink-Lady attack on Helen Gahagan Douglas: between 1949 and 1952 he handled some 221 gambler-bookmaker cases in Los Angeles;[11] he was instrumental in getting a deportation order rescinded for Philadelphia mobster Marco Reginelli in the 1950s;[12] in 1956 the McClellan Senate committee investigated his role as attorney for a convicted clothing racketeer and exposed (but did not fully explore) his influence-peddling activities in Washington;[13] and most recently he has acknowledged in court papers his own role in the milk scandal by admitting he intervened with Ehrlichman and others in the White House to get the price increase for the milk producers and subsequently arranged the channeling of their contributions to the Nixon campaign.[14]

Whatever else you want to say about these presidential pals, they hardly seem to be the kind that Billy Graham, let's say, should approve of.

Rebozo, the inscrutable man who is closest of all to Nixon—the latest example of his intimacy being the donation of his $100,000 Bethesda home to Julie Nixon Eisenhower—deserves a somewhat closer examination here, for in some ways he personifies the cowboy type.[15] Rebozo, Cuban-born of American parents, grew up in relative poverty, and at the start of World War II he was a gas-station operator in Florida. With the wartime tire shortage Rebozo got it into his head to expand his properties and start a recapping business, so he got a loan from a friend who happened to be on the local OPA tire board (a clear conflict of interest)[16] and before long was the largest recapper in Florida. In 1951, he met Richard Nixon on one of the latter's trips to Miami and the two seem to have hit it off: both the same age, both quiet, withdrawn, and humorless, both aggressive success-hunters, both part of the new Southern-rim milieu.

Rebozo later expanded into land deals and in the early 1960s established the Key Biscayne Bank, of which he is president and whose first savings-account customer was Nixon. This bank in 1968 was the repository of stolen stocks, originally taken and channeled to the bank by organized-crime sources. Rebozo clearly suspected there was something dubious about these stocks (he even told an FBI agent that he had called up Nixon's brother Donald to check on their validity), but he subsequently sold them for cash, even after an insurance company circular was mailed out to every bank listing them as stolen.[17] Small wonder that the bank was thereupon sued by the company which had insured those stocks. (The case was eventually tried before a Nixon-appointed federal judge, James Lawrence King, who himself had some interesting banking experience as a director in 1964 of the Miami National Bank, cited by the *New York Times* [December 1, 1969, p. 42] as a conduit for the Meyer Lansky syndicate's "shady money" from 1963 to 1967. King decided against the insurance company, but the case is now being appealed to a higher court.)

At about the same time as the stolen stocks episode came the shopping-center deal. Rebozo, by now a very rich man, still managed to get a loan out of the federal Small Business Administration—one of five which he somehow was lucky enough to secure in the 1960s, perhaps because of his friendship with ex-Senator George Smathers (who had been on the Senate Small Business Committee and who wrote the SBA to help Rebozo get another loan), or perhaps because the Miami officer of the SBA also happened to be a close friend of Rebozo's and a stockholder in his bank. This, coupled with the fact that Rebozo never fully disclosed his business dealings in making applications to the SBA, led *Newsday,* in a prominent editorial, to denounce the SBA for "wheeling and dealing . . . on Rebozo's behalf,"[18] and it led Representative Wright Patman to accuse the SBA publicly of wrongdoing in making Rebozo a "preferred customer."[19]

With one of the SBA grants Rebozo proceeded to build an elaborate shopping center, to be leased to members of the right-wing Cuban exile community, and he let out the contracting bid for that to one "Big Al" Polizzi, a convicted black marketeer and a man named by the Federal Bureau of Narcotics as "one of the most influential members of the underworld in the United States."[20]

Rather unsavory, all that, if not precisely criminal, and a rather odd career for an intimate of our moralistic President. But Nixon seems not to mind. In fact he has even gone in with Rebozo on at least one of his deals, a Florida real-estate venture called Fisher's Island Inc., in which Nixon invested some $185,891 around 1962, and which he sold for exactly twice the value, $371,782, in 1969. It seems to have been a peculiarly shrewd deal, since the going rate for Fisher's Island stock had not in fact increased by a penny during those years and certainly hadn't doubled for anyone else—but happily for the stockholders, Nixon shortly thereafter signed a bill paving the way for $7 million worth of federal funds for the improvement of the Port of Miami, in which Fisher Island just happens to be located.[21] In any case, that's small enough potatoes for a man in Nixon's position, and seems to reflect the fact that, no matter how many rich wheeler-dealers he has around him, Nixon himself is not out to make a vast personal fortune as his predecessor did.

But the unsavoriness surrounding Bebe Rebozo does not stop there. For in the mid-1960s Rebozo was also a partner in a Florida real-estate company with one Donald Berg, an acquaintance of Nixon's and the man from whom Nixon bought property in Key Biscayne less than a mile from the Florida White House. This same Donald Berg, who has been linked with at least one associate of mobster Meyer Lansky, has a background so questionable that after Nixon became President the Secret Service asked him to stop eating at Berg's Key Biscayne restaurant.[22] Finally, according to Jack Anderson, Rebozo was "involved" in some of the real-estate deals of Bernard Barker—the former CIA operative who was the convicted payoff man for the Watergate operation.[23] . . .

Mention of Bernard Barker brings up the Watergate scandal, perhaps even more interesting because it is so complicated and revealing of the interlocking relations along the Southern rim. We are far from knowing all the details as yet, but an examination of the people known to have been involved does provide a clear window on the Nixon milieu.

Watergate, and at least some of the other operations against the Democrats and radical political groups last year, was paid for by cowboy money. Most of it came from Texas oil, channeled through Nixon fundraiser Robert Allen (Gulf Resources),[24] "laundered" in a Mexican bank, and then carried to Republican finance chairman Maurice Stans by an executive of Penzoil.[25] The rest came from a Minneapolis "soybean king," Dwayne Andreas,[26] with a home and investments in Florida and ties to Southern money, and was delivered to Stans by a crony of Andreas's with Florida investments of his own.[27] The money stayed for a time in Stan's safe and then was deposited in a Miami bank for Bernard Barker, Rebozo's business associate, a man who had worked for the CIA, had been paymaster of the Bay of Pigs operation, was close to the anti-Castro–pro-Batista Cuban community in Miami, and masterminded at least three forays by Cuban emigres to attack antiwar protesters in Washington last spring.[28]

Barker was paymaster this time around, too, and personally recruited three others, all of whom subsequently pleaded guilty at the Watergate trial: Eugenio Martinez, another old CIA operative and a real-estate business partner of Barker's, and also vice president of another real-estate firm with whom both Nixon and Rebozo have done business;[29] Frank Sturgis, a CIA operative, who lost his citizenship at one time for his Caribbean gun-running activities (first for Castro in 1958, then against him in 1962), and organizer of a "Cubans for Nixon" demonstration at Miami Beach last year;[30] and Virgilio Gonzalez, also a CIA operative in on the Bay of Pigs, and a member of a right-wing anti-Castro organization run by the same people who ran the "Cubans for Nixon" operation both last year and in 1968.

These four men were guided in their operations by at least three others with close connections to the Nixon inner circle, all of whom have been convicted for their part in Watergate: Gordon Liddy, a former FBI agent who had worked on espionage matters in the White House under Ehrlichman, who was assigned by White House counsel John Dean to Nixon's Committee to Re-elect the President (CRP), and who thereupon, according to trial testimony, set up the Republican sabotage campaign; James McCord, a twenty-year CIA agent with extensive contacts among the anti-Castro community, who was "security coordinator" for the CRP and who says that Dean cleared him for the job;[31] and Howard Hunt, another career CIA agent (chief operations officer for the Bay of Pigs) and former White House consultant, who became a CRP operative in 1971. Having spooks right in the White House seems bad enough, but the sorry trail goes on—in fact goes on for two more steps.

The first step involves at least three other men besides Dean who were White House aides to Nixon: Charles Colson, Hunt's supervisor at the White House and head of a White House anti-Democrat committee known as the "attack group";[32] Gordon Strachan, a Haldeman assistant who (according to an FBI file) was the chief link to the reported California saboteur, Donald Segretti, and according to the *New York Times* was the White House contact for the Watergate people;[33] and Dwight

Chapin, another White House Californian and Haledman aide who, according to L. Patrick Gray III, transmitted funds to his old college friend Segretti, mostly through—here he is again—Herbert Kalmbach.[34] (In the recent hearsay testimony of McCord to the Senate Watergate Committee Haldeman himself is said to have known "what was going on" at CRP.)

The second step leads to two men close to Nixon, personally and professionally, CRP treasurer Stans and CRP chairman John Mitchell. Though things get pretty shadowy at this point—partly because Nixon's FBI hasn't investigated much here—it seems obvious that both men condoned the anti-Democratic operations, and trial testimony indicates that both men approved specific payments to spy-master Liddy out of Stan's own office safe.[35] In addition, Mitchell as CRP chairman was so implicated in the scandal—not least by his loquacious wife, who complained of John's "dirty things"—that he resigned his CRP position in July; it has since emerged that he met daily with McCord while running the CRP and according to McCord was the "overall boss" of the operation.[36]

Stans, who stayed on, has since been shown to be directly involved in at least one other piece of chicanery having to do with a secret $200,000 campaign gift he accepted in cash from Arthur Vesco of Investors Overseas Service (heavily invested, incidentally, in the Bahamas), a man then (and now) being sued by the SEC for having "spirited away" some $224 million from four mutual funds.[37]

There can be little doubt finally that the entire sabotage campaign was at least tacitly approved, if not actually orchestrated, by the President himself—a conclusion which subsequent presidential actions seem only to confirm, from the hasty attempt at a "no-one-was-involved" coverup to the testy erection of "executive privilege" barriers. And so there it is: from the top level of the government, through two of Nixon's closest advisers and the "California Mafia" in the White House, through CIA career men and right-wing Miami exiles, down to Florida businessmen and Texas oil millionaires. This is the world of the thirty-seventh President. . . .

The purpose of examining all of this is not, of course, to sling more mud on a figure already as splattered as a happy hippopotamus, but to try to clarify the shadowy world of Nixon's bedfellows and to examine the extent of what is almost a second government, an unofficial but very important nexus of power behind the acknowledged civics-textbook institutions. This second government, as we have begun to see, is a combination of vast and complicated interlocking forces, pulling in the CIA here and organized crime there, using politicians one time and emigre thugs the next, which seems to regard government as a tool for financial enrichment, and is to a large extent financed by and working to the benefit of the newer exploitative businesses, chiefly in the Southern rim.

Perhaps because they are new to the game, perhaps because they just feel they can get away with it, the more recent operatives of this second government seem to have been a little clumsy, inadvertently supplying several revealing glimpses into their world.[38]

Take the Soviet wheat deal, a bonanza for certain American shippers and agricultural middlemen, oddly enough with Republican ties. Or the cost-plus banditry which such defense giants as Litton and Ling-Temco-Vought have been allowed to get away with. Or the funny dealings of Under Secretary of State and former SEC chairman William Casey, who is one of seventeen defendants in a $2.1 million federal damage suit, charged, in the words of the court-appointed trustee, with "self-dealings among themselves for their own personal self-gain but to the utmost detriment and damage" to a Southern rim agribusiness corporation which went bankrupt a week after Casey was nominated for the SEC.[39] Or the charges against California businessman and former Assistant Attorney General Robert Mardian, a leader of Nixon's CRP whom McCord has linked to Watergate and whom the *New York Times* has accused of getting confidential information from the Justice Department to use in the Republican campaign.[40]

Or the findings of "profound immorality and corruption" by a non-partisan investigating committee of the Argentine legislature against Texan William Clements, now Deputy Secretary of Defense, for his very profitable role in a multimillion dollar oil deal, a deal in which he was partners with one man who is suing him for fraudulent conspiracy and two others who have skipped the U.S. to avoid paying taxes on their profits.[41] Or the neat little deal by which Director of the Budget Roy Ash and a partner in 1969 traded twenty-two acres of land in California with the Federal Bureau of Lands for 14,145 acres of government-owned land in Nevada,[42] or his even neater dumping of some $2.6 million worth of Litton stock in 1970, not long before it became public that Litton's shipbuilding program was in deep trouble and the price of the stock dropped by half, the implications of which are now being looked into by the SEC.[45] Or, . . . but just wait until tomorrow morning's paper.

All of these glimpses into the world of the second government—and they are obviously only tip-of-the-iceberg glimpses—suggest that there are important operations going on beyond the reach of ordinary citizens or of party politics, in many ways beyond even the control of Congress. And though these operations involve men at the top levels of government, they do not seem to indicate any great attachment to democratic processes, as the acknowledged campaign to sabotage one major political party bears witness, or to the constitutional exercise of foreign policy, as the acknowledged attempt to forestall Allende makes clear. Who knows what other schemes ITT may be hatching right now in some other part of the world? Who knows what other secret plans the Republican party has ready to serve its own narrow purposes? . . .

The real trouble with such . . . stains . . . is that they are very hard to wash off your hands. Some liberals, clucking with glee over the new Watergate disclosures, might like to believe that the power of the Southern rimsters is going to vanish after Nixon and his immediate friends leave office. As I read it, however, this power is not likely to be washed away with a new administration, no matter what party it comes from, for the entrenched position of the Southern rim in the American economy is not likely to diminish—indeed, seems most likely to increase—in the decades to come. . . .

## Notes

1. Evidence of their cozy relationship may be found in Leonard Lurie, *The Running of Richard Nixon* (New York: Coward, McCann and Geoghegan, 1972) and Earl Mazo and Stephen Hess, *Nixon* (New York: Harper and Row, 1968).

2. Johnson's assumption of power had several consequences beyond the enthronement of a man heavily in political debt to conservative Texas oil, among them the squelching of the Bobby Baker and TFX-Convair (Dallas) investigations, the exercise of American pressure to forestall a threatened nationalization of American oil interests in Argentina, and the reversal of Kennedy's announced plans to begin withdrawing troops from Vietnam.

3. *New York Times*, March 27, 1973, p. 27.

4. There are several valuable surveys of the effect of oil on politics among the best of which are Ronald Dugger, *Atlantic*, September, 1969; Robert Enger, *The Politics of Oil* (New York: Macmillan, 1961); Erwin Knoll, *New York Times Magazine*, March 8, 1970; Morton Mintz and Jerry S. Cohen, *America, Inc.* (New York; Dial, 1971), chapters 4 and 5; Robert Sherrill, *The Accidental President* (New York: Grossman, 1967), and Michael Tanzer, *The Political Economy of International Oil and the Underdeveloped Countries* (Boston: Beacon, 1969).

5. These figures are from the Citizens Research Foundation of Princeton, New Jersey, a group that tries to keep track of all the sources of campaign money. They are generally only estimates and often represent only a small part of what was actually given. Other major oil donors and fund-raisers on the CRF lists include Arthur E. Johnson (Midwest Oil), Thomas Pappas (ESSO-Pappas), the Pew family (Sun Oil), William Liedtke (Pennzoil), J. A. Vickers (Vickers Petroleum), and H. W. McCollum, Philip Kramer, and J. D. Callender (Amerada Hess).

6. *New York Times*, February 11, 1973.

7. Senate Hearings, March 7, 1973; *New York Times*, March 8, 1973, p. 1.

8. *New York Times*, January 11, 1973, p. 1.

9. Robert Sherrill, *op. cit.*, pp. 122, 236. The payment was to compensate Anderson for an anticipated salary cut he would take as vice-president on the 1966 ticket, for which his Texas oil friends were then pushing.

10. *New York Times*, February 1, 1971, p. 1; February 3, 1971, p. 1.

11. Drew Pearson's column, May 1, 1956, distributed by Bell Syndicate; Drew Pearson and Jack Anderson, *USA: Second Class Power* (New York: Simon and Schuster, 1958), p. 281.

12. Jeff Gerth, *SunDance*, November–December, 1972, p. 66.

13. McClellan Committee hearings, *Textile Procurement in the Military Services*, 21 (May 3, 1956), pp. 1563–1602.

14. *New York Times*, January 28, 1973, p. 12.

15. Rebozo's career has been examined in at least three recent studies which also spell out other unsavory aspects of Nixon's Florida connections in the fall of 1971 (available as a "Special Report" from *Newsday*, 550 Stewart Avenue, Garden City, New York 11530); a New Leftish magazine called *SunDance* (1913 Fillmore Street,

San Francisco, California 94115) ran an article by journalist Jeff Gerth in its November–December 1972 issue; and the North American Congress on Latin America (Box 57, Cathedral Station, New York, New York 10025) published a booklet on Nixon's links to organized crime and the Watergate affair in October, 1972. In constructing this portrait of Rebozo, as in other sections in this article, I have also used the copious and careful researches of Peter Dale Scott.

16. A violation of OPA guideline 3C-118; *SunDance*, November–December, 1972, p. 35.

17. *Newsday*, "Special Report," *op. cit.*, pp. 16–20.

18. The exposé of Rebozo's dealings with the SBA was in *Ibid.*, pp. 9–15 and the editorial on p. 43.

19. *Ibid.*, p. 10.

20. *Ibid.*, p. 14.

21. Fisher's Island details are to be found in Lurie, *op. cit.*, pp. 305–308; *Newsday*, "Special Report," *op. cit.*, pp. 42–43; and *SunDance*, *op. cit.*, p. 64.

22. *Newsday*, "Special Report," *op. cit.*, pp. 40–42. Two mortgages on a part of the property Nixon bought from Berg were held, from 1967 to 1971, by Arthur Desser, a Florida real-estate operator who was another director of the Miami National Bank during the time it was a Lansky syndicate conduit. Nixon let this property go unrecorded in the Dade County Clerk's office for four years, until the mortgages were paid off in March 1971, presumably because he wanted no public record of his connection with a man like Desser (*SunDance*, *op. cit.*, p. 64).

23. See Jack Anderson's Washington column for weekly newspapers, United Features Syndicate, June 26, 1972.

24. Which the Nixon re-election committee acknowledged March 9, 1973, in returning $100,000 to Allen; *New York Times*, March 10, 1973, p. 1.

25. *Ibid.*, and *Times*, October 23, 1972, pp. 23–30.

26. See "Report of the General Office of Federal Elections to the Comptroller General of the United States, Audit of the Finance Committee to Re-elect the President," issued by the U.S. General Accounting Office, August 26, 1972.

27. To get an idea of how complicated Southern-rim contacts can be, try this. Andreas's crony, Kenneth Dahlberg, a Nixon fund-raiser, was also a director of a Florida bank whose co-chairman was a major stockholder in an investment group called Penphil and who has benefited enormously from Penphil's favors. Penphil has since been accused by a congressional committee of helping to bankrupt the Penn Central Railroad, and two of its organizers and one of its key shareholders have been indicted for criminal conspiracy in manipulating more than $85 million of Penn Central investments for their own personal profit (*New York Times*, January 5, 1972, p. 1).

Among Penphil's major investments were a Florida gas company, two Florida banks, and a Dallas investment corporation, which also owned a California real-estate operation—a rather neat sweep of the Southern rim. This last outfit, Macco Corporation, had—are you ready?—Herbert Kalmbach as its vice-president and Maurice Stans as an investor with stock options that turned out to be worth $570,000. How's that for full cricle? The Penphil story is told in full in Joseph R. Daughen and Peter Blinzen, *The Wreck of the Penn Central* (Boston: Little, Brown, 1971), pp. 148–175. For the role of the congressional committee, see House Committee on Banking and Currency, *The Penn Central Failure and the Role of Financial Institutions*, Staff Report, January 3, 1972.

28. *New York Times*, March 19, 1973; *Time*, October 23, 1972; NACLA booklet, p. 24 (see footnote 15).

29. *SunDance*, *op. cit.*, p. 36.

30. Senate Committee of the Judiciary, *Communist Threat to the United States Through the Caribbean*, Hearings, 1965, pp. 918–920, 946, 951, 963–964; *New York Times*, June 28, 1972; NACLA, p. 24; *Washington Post* June 18, 1972. Sturgis (then using the name Fiorini) was also involved in a scheme—aborted by the Miami police —to supply arms for a Nicaraguan rebellion in 1959, using planes bought in his name originally for Castro (Senate Hearings, pp. 963–964); that same year he also flew a

plane over Havana to drop anti-Castro leaflets, provoking a major diplomatic incident (*New York Times*, October 3, 1959, p. 12).

31. Dean's assignment of Liddy emerged from testimony at the Gray hearings (e.g., *New York Times*, March 10, 1973, p. 1 and *Newsweek*, March 19, 1973, p. 21). Trial testimony was reported in *New York Times*, January 24, 1973, p. 1. *New York Times*, April 7, 1973, reported his "clearing" McCord.

32. *The Washington Post*, February 8, 1973, p. 1. Colson has produced his own private lie detector test claiming that, in spite of McCord's impression, he was not involved specifically in Watergate. *New York Times* reported, however, that, "The examination did not deal with the campaign of espionage and disruption that was reportedly directed from the White House. . . ." (April 7).

33. FBI file, *Time*, October 23, 1972; *New York Times*, February 7, 1973, p. 1.

34. FBI testimony, reported by Gray, *New York Times*, March 8, 1973; Kalmbach, *supra*.

35. *New York Times*, January 24, 1973, p. 1; March 18, 1973, Section 4, p. 1.

36. *New York Times*, March 20, 1973, p. 1.

37. *New York Times*, February 28, 1973, p. 1., and March 2, 1973, p. 15.

38. Even one of the old operators of this type has recently misstepped. ITT, which has been quietly cozy with the CIA since World War II, recently had to acknowledge its attempt to pay a million dollars to the White House and the CIA to prevent Allende's election in Chile, and this followed not long after its public embarrassment in being caught bribing and armtwisting to pave the way for its multibillion dollar Hartford Insurance merger.

39. *New York Times*, January 18, 1973, p. 10; *Wall Street Journal*, January 16, 1973, p. 1.

40. *New York Times*, October 13, 1972.

41. *New York Times*, December 21, 1972.

42. *New York Times*, December 4, 1972.

43. Representative Les Aspin, *Nation*, February 26, 1973; *New York Times*, January 24, 1973, p. 6.

# VI

# CONTROVERSY REGARDING WHITE-COLLAR CRIME

White-collar crime is clearly established today as a legitimate area of criminological and criminal law investigation and theorizing. Many universities, in fact, offer specific courses devoted to the subject, and the work of Ralph Nader and his colleagues has formed a bridge between academic interests and popular debate regarding the extent and character of business, professional, and political offenses, and the kinds of responses that ought to be mounted to deter and, perhaps, simply punish such behavior.

There remain, however, a considerable array of pressing intellectual concerns associated with the study of white-collar crime. In particular, work on the subject has been characterized for too long by semantic quarrels. Case studies of white-collar crime and/or white-collar criminals, conducted from behavioral science perspectives, are notably rare, particularly when compared to the massive amount of space devoted to traditional kinds of criminal actors and activities in social science journals, with their focus on statistical analyses, biographical and participant-observer materials, and psychological evaluations.

In part, the absence of a greater amount of substantive work on white-collar crime can be traced to the difficulties involved in applying standard methodological approaches to the study of economic offenses. A more fundamental problem lies in the continuing absence of conceptual clarity and consensus in regard to white-collar crime, a condition which has tended to stifle creative and replicative research. Paradoxically, this confusion was built into the concept of white-collar crime by Sutherland when he introduced the term into the literature. By failing to specify precisely and fully what it was that he was concerned with, Sutherland left the door wide open for a barrage of speculative attempts to refine and redefine white-collar crime. Nonetheless, the definitional debates have not prevented scholars from examining specific white-collar crime offenses. Such work, indeed, has constituted the bulk of material in this volume. It proceeds on the progmatic view that everybody pretty much knows what is meant by white-collar crime. The advantage of such a pragmatic focus is that it allows important work to get done; its disadvantage is that it fails to establish rigorous definitions which might lead more readily to cumulative, interrelated patterns of investigation.

Taken together, the readings in this last section provide a solid basis for definitional advance in white-collar crime. The readings address head-on the most important definitional issues and offer a wide variety of opinions and facts to buttress their positions. Ultimately, intensive study of statutory provisions and review of the behaviors they proscribe and fail to proscribe, plus historical analyses, and elaborate case studies, will have to be conducted to provide the groundwork for determination of the "proper" definition of many of the behaviors now grouped as "white-collar crime." It must be understood, however, that definitions are only ways of organizing phenomena; they are neither "correct" nor "wrong." Their adequacy can be judged only in terms of how satisfactorily they serve to advance specified ends, ends which themselves may change with changing social or personal values.

If, for instance, the goal were to stimulate definitional debate, Sutherland's rather nebulous definitions of white-collar crime were marvelously attuned to the task. If the aim were to create an esthetically satisfying typology of mutually exclusive and homogeneous categories of white-collar crime, then Sutherland clearly fell short of this goal. Definitions may also be judged in terms of their ability to stimulate research; to fit coherently into larger frameworks of knowledge; to serve as vehicles for change; to carve out comfortable realms of inquiry, or in terms of a variety of other purposes. Each individual must decide for himself or herself (and intellectual subgroups for themselves) whether or not a given definition satisfies criteria that are deemed important. The nonscientific implications of definitions should never be underestimated: Note, for example, the extraordinary consequences which ensued from social agreement (based on the flimsiest of scientific support) that the "best" way of defining divisions of the human group was in terms of three major "races" based on skin color.

Readers will observe that the authors of the following selections are apt to strike a posture of disingenuous innocence while vigorously pursuing their points, as if they cannot quite understand how it is that others are unable to comprehend the self-evident position that they put forward. The authors are usually members of either the legal profession or the sociological discipline, with one foot firmly planted in their area of major concentration and the other less securely rooted in or seeking out the second area. In particular, the authors are persons conversant to a noteworthy degree with two fields of knowledge who tend to snipe at members of one with specialized information and insights from the other.

The Sutherland-Tappan debate opens the section. Sutherland's knowledge of law was not formidable, but he had enough command of it to offer forceful arguments regarding logical flaws in a professional approach often so bound up in day-to-day pursuits and so committed to historical precedent that it is apt to blur the distinction between the defined and the definitive. Both Sutherland and Tappan, it might be noted, are rather agile at paraphrasing opposing views, so that such views stand in their least attractive and least persuasive form when they are finally marshaled for rebuttal.

The tenacious and inexorable nature of Sutherland's polemical steamroller commands respect. Obviously irritated by criticism of his earlier work, Sutherland sets out to demonstrate that white-collar crime truly is "crime." Perhaps the most treacherous moment in his presentation occurs when he argues that civil fines are really the same as criminal fines except that the stigma of criminality has been extracted from them. It is, of course, true that all fines involve deprivation and that they therefore penalize, under whatever guise. If, however, civil fines are to be regarded as equivalent to criminal sanctions, except for the removal of stigma, then Sutherland would appear obligated to maintain that any official sanction involving loss or hurt is a criminal sanction. Justice Earl Warren in *Trop v. Dulles*, in fact, enunciated essentially this view, with the observation that "inquiry must be directed to substance" and that "a statute that prescribes the consequences that will befall one who fails to abide by these regulatory provisions is a penal law." "Even a clear legislative classification of a statute as nonpenal," Warren wrote, "would not alter the fundamental nature of a plainly penal statute."[1]

Therefore, it is not Sutherland's position that is necessarily out of line; his default lies in not grappling with its extraordinarily far-reaching implications for the study not only of crime and deviance, but also of virtually all forms of human activity that may result in retaliatory actions.

Sutherland is also apt to regard the generally more benign treatment accorded to white-collar offenders in contrast to traditional offenders as at least partially traceable to class and behavioral homogeneity between the authorities and the white-collar violators, a conclusion of considerable interest but one not clearly demonstrated. Certainly it is true that during the Depression period in the United States the prosecution of business firms increased considerably, perhaps, as Sutherland maintains, because business was in a period of its lowest status. Nonetheless, capital punishment of traditional property offenders, for example, also increased markedly during the same period.[2] It may be that it is something more fundamental and pervasive than the status of business that conditions the ebbs and flows of prosecutory actions against white-collar offenders.

More than any other scholar, Paul W. Tappan (1911–1964) incessantly called cirminologists to task for their neglect of legal concerns in their work. Tappan, who had earned a doctorate in both law and sociology, spent the major portion of his career at New York University before moving to the University of California in Berkeley, a few years before his death. Tappan spearheaded campaigns against sexual psychopath statutes[3] (a crusade, incidentally, in which his most notable intellectual companion was Sutherland)[4] and iniquitous and euphemistic practices in juvenile courts, which he believed (and the Supreme Court subsequently—in the *Gault* decision in 1967—so held)[5] were violative of due process of law.

The Tappan article forcefully states a position that only comes to peripheral grips with Sutherland's work, despite the illusion it creates of a penetrating rebuttal. Tappan is notably effective in documenting the varying definitions that Sutherland accorded to white-collar crime, and he marks the tendency to group together as criminal all forms of behavior by a person who, in his colorful language, may be "a boor, a sinner, a moral leper, or the devil incarnate" but who, despite this, need not be a criminal. But when he comes to the core of his differences with Sutherland, Tappan sidesteps direct confrontation. For one thing, Tappan moves from Sutherland to concentrate his attack on Harry E. Barnes and Negley K. Teeters, authors of a fire-eating criminological textbook that makes no pretense of scientific exactitude or analysis.[6] More important, Tappan avoids adjudication of precisely what is criminal and what is not, the issue that preoccupied Sutherland. Sutherland probably would not have disputed Tappan's theme that white-collar crime should in fact be violative of criminal statutes; it is that the two different (though Tappan's precise position is unclear) on what it is that is a criminal statute.

The article by Richard Quinney represents an attempt to move beyond the Sutherland-Tappan debate by specifying different kinds of white-collar crime. Quinney suggests that white-collar crime might be seen as merely one form of a group of offenses which can best be regarded as "occupational crime," law violations committed in the course of legitimate occupations.

Quinney's piece on criminal violations by pharamacists (reprinted earlier in this volume) represented a summary of his doctoral dissertation. Further research and speculation convinced Quinney, some years after he had published the piece included in this section, that crime itself is largely a matter of definitions imposed upon behavior of others by individuals and groups in power who seek to enhance their own hegemony and to amass even greater wealth. Quinney came to view the enactment of criminal penalties against certain forms of predatory professional, business, or political behavior as largely the result of efforts by the strongest segments of the society to keep their competitors under control. In addition, such white-collar crime statutes might at times serve as minor concessions aimed at placating unrest and indignation in the larger society, without making any fundamental alterations in its basic structure. Quinney, a professor of sociology, spent several years away from academic life, contemplating and writing, trying to spell out in several books the details of the Marxian political position to which he had been persuaded, in part as a consequence of his earlier studies of white-collar crime.[7]

Other writers have followed Quinney's quest for more careful categorization of forms of white-collar offenses.[8] Most recently, Harold Pepinsky has attempted to use the idea of "exploitation" as the analytical tool to differentiate acts which ought or ought not be viewed as "crime."[9] Pepinsky regards white-collar crime as merely one form of exploitation. Marshall B. Clinard and Quinney, in a revision of their book, *Criminal Behavior Systems*, further pursue the idea of occupational crime, and observe that many acts labeled as "white-collar crime" by Sutherland are committed by persons in blue collars (e.g., in working-class positions) and in other strata of the social system.[10]

The final two readings focus on issues of control of white-collar crime. The central question here regards deterrence, since few persons are concerned with trying to "rehabilitate" white-collar offenders (a matter of some interest itself, given the considerable belief in the inexorable nature of commitment of traditional crime, and the transient nature of involvement in white-collar crime). The regulatory weapons for dealing with white-collar crime include a diverse armamentarium, such as licensing, searches and inspections, injunctions, cease and desist orders, publicity, and civil sanctions. The relative utility of each of these diverse responses is barely understood as yet.

The first of the articles in the section about these problems is by Sanford H. Kadish, a professor of law at the University of California in Berkeley. Besides representing legal writing at its very best, the reading thrusts the study of white-collar crime directly into the mainstream of economic considerations and views it in a much broader perspective than has usually been the case.

It may be that the chronological age of academic concern with white-collar crime or the social class position of the scholars concerned with the subject is largely responsible for its curious disjunction with other work on crime. In the early writings traditional crimes were considered patently malevolent and authors concentrated their attention upon distinguishing offenders from "normal" persons. Invective was commonplace and self-righteousness pervasive. Subsequently, writers were apt to take a more neutral stand toward violations and violators. Following this—and the matter is very much at this point today—sophisticated inquiry has been directed toward elimination of criminal sanctions against certain kinds of offenses (such as homosexual behavior between consenting adults, drunkenness, and abortion).

White-collar crime studies, appearing late on the scene, have mainly traveled through only the earlier stages of inquiry. Sutherland, most notably, was apt to regard white-collar violations rather uncritically as acts which society chose to outlaw, and deservedly so, though he was too perceptive not to be aware that such decisions were at least arguable. It was merely that he chose not to argue them. Most other writers totally bypass ideological and pragmatic issues underlying the delineation of white-collar offenses.

It is noteworthy that Kadish served as a general consultant to the President's Commission on Law Enforcement and Administration of Justice during 1966 and 1967 and helped to fashion the commission's stand regarding the decriminalization of a variety of offenses presently coming within the criminal codes.[11] His article on white-collar crime attempts to address the same kinds of questions that were asked to statutes outlawing acts because of moral considerations. Kadish raises a number of teasing issues. He wants to know, for example, how much deterrence is involved in the stigma presumably attached to criminal conviction for economic violations. He picks away at the prevalent view that white-collar crime statutes are poorly enforced because of congruence between the values of the enforcers and the violators by suggesting that the very existence of the laws despite "the ardent protests of important economic interests in the past thirty years is some evidence that (business) is not all-powerful." He also challenges the view that business interests are united in monolithic consensus.

How the same set of facts may be variously interpreted is clearly shown by Kadish's reasoning concerning public response to white-collar offenses. The relative degree of public indifference to such behavior, he maintains, is the product neither of insensitivity nor of business machinations, but rather inheres in the relative absence of moral approbrium in the acts themselves. Most writers appear to believe that the community should be outraged by white-collar crime; Kadish views as more important the stipulated fact that the public is not outraged. In the absence of such public indignation, he is hesitant to favor use of criminal sanctions, though he grants that campaigns calculated to create a sense of outrage might be in order. Kadish is particularly concerned with the "danger of debilitating the moral impact of the criminal conviction and hence decreasing the overall effectiveness of the criminal law."

Many of Kadish's points are given a critical re-examination in the final chapter, written by Harry V. Ball, a sociologist, and Lawrence M. Friedman, a law professor.

Ball and Friedman find little utility in Kadish's attempt to isolate and distinguish a class of offenses labeled "economic crimes," and they are adept at putting on display a plethora of statutes whose contents, depending upon a point of view, may be considered economic, common law, or health and safety measures. Much of their discussion is occupied with attempts to qualify the broad generalizations of the Kadish presentation. Ball and Friedman make telling points with empirical illustrations of the fluidity of some of Kadish's observations when elements of the defined ingredients are given specific rather than general content. They falter at times, however, in their attempt to amalgamate white-collar offenses with a broader range of criminal actions and, almost inadvertently, seem to regard economic crimes as a behavioral entity of some kind, about which important things may be said.

The reading by Ball and Friedman presents warnings that both summarize and herald scholarship regarding white-collar crime. Their concluding cautionary note states a thesis to which other writers have often turned. The search for general theories of crime is a futile exercise, Ball and Friedman maintain. Intellectual advance in the understanding of all human behavior represents the most pressing necessity for sound comprehension of criminal behavior. In criminological research, attempts must be made to determine distinguishing characteristics of the legislative and social history of crimes such as murder, trespass, and corporate monopoly, and characterstics of persons who commit such offenses. In essence, their call is a statement of fundamental demands of intelligent inquiry, whose essential but elusive quality is so well indicated by the range of results and viewpoints represented throughout the present volume.

## Notes

1. *Trop v. Dulles* 356 U.S. 86 (1958).

2. E. P. Evans, *The Criminal Prosecution and Capital Punishment of Animals* (London: Heinemann, 1906).

3. Paul W. Tappan, "The Sexual Psychopath—A Civic Responsibility," *Journal of Social Hygiene*, 35 (November, 1949), pp. 354–368.

4. Edwin H. Sutherland, "The Sexual Psychopath Laws," *Journal of Criminal Law and Criminology*, 40 (January–February, 1950), pp. 534–554; idem, "The Diffusion of Sexual Psychopath Laws," *American Journal of Sociology*, 56 (September, 1950), pp. 142–148.

5. *In Re Gault* 387 U.S. 1 (1967).

6. Harry E. Barnes and Negley K. Teeters, *New Horizons in Criminology* (Englewood Cliffs, N.J.: Prentice-Hall, 1943).

7. Richard Quinney, *Critique of Legal Order* (Boston: Little, Brown and Company, 1974); idem, ed., *Criminal Justice in America: A Critical Understanding* (Boston: Little, Brown, 1974).

8. Gerald D. Robin, "White-Collar Crime and Employee Theft," *Crime and Delinquency*, 20 (July, 1974), pp. 251–262.

9. Harold E. Pepinsky, "From White Collar Crime To Exploitation: Redefinition of a Field," *Journal of Criminal Law and Criminology*, 65 (June, 1974), pp. 225–233.

10. Marshall B. Clinard and Richard Quinney, *Criminal Behavior Systems: A Typology*, 2nd ed. (New York: Holt, Rinehart and Winston, 1973), pp. 187–223.

11. Sanford H. Kadish, "The Crisis of Overcriminalization," *Annals of American Academy of Political and Social Science*, 374 (November, 1967), pp. 157–170. For an exchange between a sociologist and a philosopher on some of these issues see Edwin H. Schur and Hugo A. Bedau, *Crimes Without Victims* (Englewood Cliffs, N.J.: Prentice-Hall, 1974).

# 17

# IS "WHITE-COLLAR CRIME" CRIME?

*Edwin H. Sutherland*

The argument has been made that business and professional men commit crimes which should be brought within the scope of the theories of criminal behavior.[1] In order to secure evidence as to the prevalence of such white-collar crimes, an analysis was made of the decisions by courts and commissions against the seventy largest industrial and mercantile corporations in the United States under four types of laws: namely, antitrust, false advertising, National Labor Relations, and infringement of patents, copyrights, and trademarks. This resulted in the finding that 547 such adverse decisions had been made, with an average of 7.8 decisions per corporation and with each corporation's having at least one.[2] Although all of these were decisions that the behavior was unlawful, only forty-nine, or 9 per cent, of the total were made by criminal courts and were *ipso facto* decisions that the behavior was criminal. Since not all unlawful behavior is criminal behavior, these decisions can be used as a measure of criminal behavior only if the other 498 decisions can be shown to be decisions that the behavior of the corporations was criminal.

Reprinted from *American Sociological Review*, 10 (April, 1945), pp. 132–139, by permission of The American Sociological Association.

This is a problem in the legal definition of crime and involves two types of questions: May the word "crime" be applied to the behavior regarding which these decisions were made? If so, why is it not generally applied and why have not the criminologists regarded white-collar crime as cognate with other crime? The first question involves semantics, the second interpretation or explanation.

A combination of two abstract criteria is generally regarded by legal scholars as necessary to define crime; namely, legal description of an act as socially injurious and legal provision of a penalty for the act.[3]

When the criterion of legally defined social injury is applied to these 547 decisions, the conclusion is reached that all of the classes of behaviors regarding which the decisions were made are legally defined as socially injurious. This can be readily determined by the words in the statutes—"crime" or "misdemeanor" in some, and "unfair," "discrimination," or "infringement" in all the others. The persons injured may be divided into two groups: first, a relatively small number of persons engaged in the same occupation as the offenders or in related occupations; and, second, the general public either as consumers or as constituents of the general social institutions which are affected by the violations of the laws. The antitrust laws are designed to protect competitors; they are also designed to protect the institution of free competition as the regulator of the economic system and thereby to protect consumers against arbitrary prices, as well as being designed to protect the institution of democracy against the dangers of great concentration of wealth in the hands of monopolies. Laws against false advertising are designed to protect competitors against unfair competition and also to protect consumers against fraud. The National Labor Relations Law is designed to protect employees against coercion by employers and also to protect the general public against interferences with commerce due to strikes and lockouts. The laws against infringements are designed to protect the owners of patents, copyrights, and trademarks against deprivation of their property and against unfair competition, and also to protect the institution of patents and copyrights which was established in order to "promote the progress of science and the useful arts." Violations of these laws are legally defined as injuries to the parties specified.

Each of these laws has a logical basis in the common law and is an adaptation of the common law to modern social organization. False advertising is related to common-law fraud, and infringement to larceny. The National Labor Relations Law, as an attempt to prevent coercion, is related to the common-law prohibition of restrictions on freedom in the form of assault, false imprisonment, and extortion. For at least two centuries prior to the enactment of the modern antitrust laws, the common law was moving against restraint of trade, monopoly, and unfair competition.

Each of the four laws provides a penal sanction and thus meets the second criterion in the definition of crime, and each of the adverse decisions under these four laws (except certain decisions under the infringement laws to be discussed later) is a decision that a crime was committed. This conclusion will be made more specific by analysis of the penal sanctions provided in the four laws.

The Sherman antitrust law states explicitly that a violation of the law is a misdemeanor. Three methods of enforcement of this law are provided, each of them involving procedures regarding misdemeanors. First, it may be enforced by the usual criminal prosecution, resulting in the imposition of fine or imprisonment. Second, the Attorney General of the United States and the several district attorneys are given the "duty" of "repressing and preventing" violations of the law by petitions for injunctions, and violations of the injunctions are punishable as contempt of court. This method of enforcing a criminal law was an invention and, as will be described later, is the key to the interpretation of the differential implementation of the criminal law as applied to white-collar criminals. Third, parties who are injured by violations of the law are authorized to sue for damages, with a mandatory provision that the damages awarded be three times the damages suffered. These damages in excess of reparation are penalties for violation of the law. They are payable to the injured party in order to induce him to take the initiative in the enforcement of the criminal law and in this respect are similar to the earlier methods of private prosecutions under the criminal law. All three of these methods of enforcement are based on decisions that a criminal law was violated and, therefore, that a crime was committed; the decisions of a civil court or a court of equity as to these violations are as good evidence of criminal behavior as is the decision of a criminal court.

The Sherman Antitrust Act has been amended by the Federal Trade Commission Law, the Clayton Law, and several other laws. Some of these amendments define violations as crimes and provide the conventional penalties, but most of the amendments do not make the criminality explicit. A large proportion of the cases which are dealt with under these amendments could be dealt with instead under the original Sherman Act, which is explicitly a criminal law. In practice, the amendments are under the jurisdiction of the Federal Trade Commission, which has authority to make official decisions as to violations. The commission has two principal sanctions under its control: the stipulation and the cease and desist order. The commission may, after the violation of the law has been proved, accept a stipulation from the corporation that it will not violate the law in the future. Such stipulations are customarily restricted to the minor or technical violations. If a stipulation is violated or if no stipulation is accepted, the commission may issue a cease and desist order; this is equivalent to a court's injunction except that violation is not punishable as contempt. If the commission's desist order is violated, the commission may apply to the court for an injunction, the violation of which is punishable as contempt. By an amendment to the Federal Trade Commission Law in the Wheeler-Lea Act of 1938, an order of the commission becomes "final" if not officially questioned within a specified time and thereafter its violation is punishable by a civil fine. Thus, although certain interim procedures may be used in the enforcement of the amendments to the antitrust law, fines or imprisonment for contempt are available if the interim procedures fail. In this respect, the interim procedures are similar to probation in ordinary criminal cases. An unlawful act is not defined as criminal by the fact that it is punished, but by the fact that it is punishable. Larceny is as truly a crime when the thief is placed on probation as when he is committed to prison. The argument may be made that punishment for contempt of court is not punishment for violation of the original law and that, therefore, the original law does not contain a penal sanction. This reasoning is specious, since the original law provides the injunction with its penalty as a part of the procedure for enforcement. Consequently, all of the decisions made under the amendments to the antitrust law are decisions that the corporations committed crimes.[4]

The laws regarding false advertising, as included in the decisions under consideration, are of two types. First, false advertising in the form of false labels is defined in the Pure Food and Drug Act as a misdemeanor and is punishable by a fine. Second, false advertising generally is defined in the Federal Trade Commission Act as unfair competition. Cases of the second type are under the jurisdiction of the Federal Trade Commission, which uses the same procedures as in antitrust cases. Penal sanctions are available in antitrust cases, as previously described, and are similarly available in these cases of false advertising. Thus, all of the decisions in false advertising cases are decisions that the corporations committed crimes.

The National Labor Relations Law of 1935 defines a violation as "unfair labor practice." The National Labor Relations Board is authorized to make official decisions as to violations of the law and, in case of violation, to issue desist orders and also to make certain remedial orders, such as reimbursement of employees who had been dismissed or demoted because of activities in collective bargaining. If an order is violated, the board may apply to the court for enforcement and a violation of the order of the court is punishable as contempt. Thus, all of the decisions under this law, which is enforceable by penal sanctions, are decisions that crimes were committed.

The methods for the repression of infringements vary. Infringements of a copyright or a patented design are defined as misdemeanors, punishable by fines. No case of this type has been discovered against the seventy corporations. Other infringements are not explicitly defined in the statutes on patents, copyrights, and trademarks as crimes, and agents of the state are not authorized by these statutes to initiate actions against violators of the law. Nevertheless, infringements may be punished in either of two ways: First, agents of the state may initiate action against infringers under the Federal Trade Commission Law as unfair competition and they do so, especially against infringers of copyrights and trademarks; these infringements are then punishable in the same sense as violations of the amendments to the antitrust laws. Second, the patent, copyright, and trademark statutes provide that the damages awarded to injured owners of those rights may be greater than (in one statute as much as threefold) the damages actually suffered. These additional damages are not mandatory, as in the Sherman Antitrust Law, but on the other hand they are not explicitly limited to wanton and malicious infringements. Three decisions against the seventy corporations under the patent law and one under the copyright law included awards of such additional damages and on that account were classified in the tabulation of decisions as evidence of criminal behavior of the corporations. The other decisions, seventy-four in number, in regard to infringements were classified as not conclusive evidence of criminal behavior and were discarded. However, in twenty of these seventy-four cases the decisions of the court contain evidence which would be sufficient to make a *prima facie* case in a criminal prosecution; evidence outside these decisions, which may be found in the general descriptions of practices regarding patents, copyrights, and trademarks, justifies a belief that a very large proportion of the seventy-four cases did, in fact, involve willful infringement of property rights and might well have resulted in the imposition of a penalty if the injured party and the court had approached the behavior from the point of view of crime.

In the preceding discussion, the penalties that are definitive of crime have been limited to fine, imprisonment, and punitive damages. In addition, the stipulation, the desist order, and the injunction, without references to punishment for contempt, have the attributes of punishment. This is evident both in that they result in some suffering on the part of the corporation against which they are issued and also in that they are designed by legislators and administrators to produce suffering. The suffering is in the form of public shame, as illustrated in more extreme form in the colonial penalty of sewing the letter *T* on the clothing of the thief. The design is shown in the sequence of sanctions used by the Federal Trade Commission. The stipulation involves the least publicity and the least discomfort, and it is used for minor and technical violations. The desist order is used if the stipulation is violated and also if the violation of the law is appraised by the commission as willful and major. This involves more public shame; this shame is somewhat mitigated by the statements made by corporations, in exculpation, that such orders are merely the acts of bureaucrats. Still more shameful to the corporation is an injunction issued by a court. The shame resulting from this order is sometimes mitigated and the corporation's face saved by taking a consent decree.[5] The corporation may insist that the consent decree is not an admission that it violated the law. For instance, the meat packers took a consent decree in an antitrust case in 1921, with the explanation that they had not knowingly violated any law and were consenting to the decree without attempting to defend themselves because they wished to cooperate with the government in every possible way. This patriotic motivation appeared questionable, however, after the packers fought during almost all of the next ten years for a modification of the decree. Although the sequence of stipulation, desist order, and injunction indicates that the variations in public shame are designed, these orders have other functions as well, especially a remedial function and the clarification of the law in a particular complex situation.

The conclusion in this semantic portion of the discussion is that 473 of the 547 decisions are decisions that crimes were committed. This conclusion may be questioned on the ground that the rules of proof and evidence used in reaching these decisions are not the same as those used in decisions regarding other crimes, especially that some of the agencies which rendered the decisions did not require proof of criminal intent and did not presume the accused to be innocent. These rules of criminal intent and presumption of innocence, however, are not required in all prosecutions under the regular penal code and the number of exceptions is increasing. In many states a person may be committed to prison without protection of one or both of these rules on charges of statutory rape, bigamy, adultery, passing bad checks, selling mortgaged property, defrauding a hotel keeper, and other offenses.[6] Consequently, the criteria that have been used in defining white-collar crimes are not categorically different from the criteria used in defining other crimes, for these rules are abrogated both in regard to white-collar crimes and other crimes, including some felonies. The proportion of decisions rendered against corporations without the protection of these rules is probably greater than the proportion rendered against other criminals, but a difference in proportions does not make the violations of law by corporations categorically different from the violations of law by other criminals. Moreover, the difference in proportion, as the procedures actually operate, is not great. On the one side, many of the defendants in usual criminal cases, being in relative poverty, do not get good defense and consequently secure little benefit from these rules; on the other hand, the commissions come close to observing these rules of proof and evidence although they are not required to do so. This is illustrated by the procedure of the Federal Trade Commission in regard to advertisements. Each year it examines several hundred thousand advertisements and appraises about 50,000 of them as probably false. From the 50,000 it selects about 1,500 as patently false. For instance, an advertisement of gum-wood furniture as "mahogany" would seldom be an accidental error and would generally result from a state of mind which deviated from honesty by more than the natural tendency of human beings to feel proud of their handiwork.

The preceding discussion has shown that these seventy corporations committed crimes according to 473 adverse decisions and has also shown that the criminality of their behavior was not made obvious by the conventional procedures of the criminal law, but was blurred and concealed by special procedures. This differential implementation of the law as applied to the crimes of corporations eliminates, or at least minimizes, the stigma of crime. This differential implementation of the law began with the Sherman Antitrust Law of 1890. As previously described, this law is explicitly a criminal law and a violation of the law is a misdemeanor no matter what procedure is used. The customary policy would have been to rely entirely on criminal prosecution as the method of enforcement. But a clever invention was made in the provision of an injunction to enforce a criminal law; this was not only an invention, but also a direct reversal of previous case law. Also, private parties were encouraged by treble damages to enforce a criminal law by suits in civil courts. In either case, the defendant did not appear in the criminal court, and the fact that he had committed a crime did not appear in the face of the proceedings.

The Sherman Antitrust Act, in this respect, became the model in practically all the subsequent procedures authorized to deal with the crimes of corporations. When the Federal Trade Commission Bill and the Clayton Bill were introduced in Congress, they contained the conventional criminal procedures; these were eliminated in committee discussions, and other procedures which did not carry the external symbols of criminal process were substituted. The violations of these laws are crimes, as has been shown above, but they are treated as though they were not crimes, with the effect and probably the intention of eliminating the stigma of crime.

This policy of eliminating the stigma of crime is illustrated in the following statement by Wendell Berge, at the time assistant to the head of the antitrust division of the Department of Justice, in a plea for abandonment of the criminal prosecution under the Sherman Antitrust Act and the authorization of civil procedures with civil fines as a substitute.

> While civil penalties may be as severe in their financial effects as criminal penalties, yet they do not involve the stigma that attends indictment and conviction. Most of the defendants in antitrust cases are not criminals in the usual sense. There is no inherent reason why antitrust enforcement requires branding them as such.[7]

If a civil fine were substituted for a criminal fine, a violation of the antitrust law would be as truly a crime as it is now. The thing which would be eliminated would be the stigma of crime. Consequently, the stigma of crime has become a penalty in itself, which may be imposed in connection with other penalties or withheld, just as it is possible to combine imprisonment with a fine or have a fine without imprisonment. A civil fine is a financial penalty without the additional penalty of stigma, while a criminal fine is a financial penalty with the additional penalty of stigma.

When the stigma of crime is imposed as a penalty, it places the defendant in the category of a criminal and he becomes one according to the popular stereotype of "the criminal." In primitive society "the criminal" was substantially the same as "the stranger,"[8] while in modern society "the criminal" is a person of less-esteemed cultural attainments. Seventy-five per cent of the persons committed to state prisons are probably not, aside from their unesteemed cultural attainments, "criminals in the usual sense of the word." It may be excellent policy to eliminate the stigma of crime in a large proportion of cases, but the question at hand is why the law has a different implementation for white-collar criminals than for others.

Three factors assist in explaining this differential implementation of the law: the status of the businessman, the trend away from punishment, and the relatively unorganized resentment of the public against white-collar criminals. Each of these will be described.

First, the methods used in the enforcement of- any law are an adaption to the characteristics of the prospective violators of the law, as appraised by the legislators and the judicial and administrative personnel. The appraisals regarding businessmen, who are the prospective violators of the four laws under consideration, include a combination of fear and admiration. Those who are responsible for the system of criminal justice are afraid to antagonize businessmen; among other consequences, such antagonism may result in a reduction in contributions to the campaign funds needed to win the next election. Probably much more important is the cultural homogeneity of legislators, judges, and administrators with businessmen. Legislators admire and respect businessmen and cannot conceive of them as criminals; that is, businessmen do not conform to the popular stereotype of "the criminal." The legislators are confident that these businessmen will conform as a result of very mild pressures.

This interpretation meets with considerable opposition from persons who insist that this is an egalitarian society in which all men are equal in the eyes of the law. It is not possible to give a complete demonstration of the validity of this interpretation but four types of evidence are presented in the following paragraphs as partial demonstration.

The Department of Justice is authorized to use both criminal prosecutions and petitions in equity to enforce the Sherman Antitrust Act. The department has selected the method of criminal prosecution in a larger proportion of cases against trade unions than of cases against corporations, although the law was enacted primarily because of fear of the corporations. From 1890 to 1929, the Department of Justice initiated 438 actions under this law with decisions favorable to the United States. Of the actions against business firms and associations of business firms, 27 per cent were criminal prosecutions; while of the actions against trade unions, 71 per cent were criminal prosecutions. This shows that the Department of Justice has been comparatively reluctant to use a method against business firms which carries with it the stigma of crime.

The method of criminal prosecution in enforcement of the Sherman Antitrust Act has varied from one presidential administration to another. It has seldom been used in the administrations of the presidents who are popularly appraised as friendly toward business; for example, McKinley, Harding, Coolidge, and Hoover.

Businessmen suffered their greatest loss of prestige in the Depression which began in 1929. It was precisely in this period of low status of businessmen that the most strenuous efforts were made to enforce the old laws and enact new laws for the regulation of businessmen. The appropriations for this purpose were multiplied several times and persons were selected for their vigor in administration of the laws. Of the 547 decisions against the seventy corporations during their life careers (which have averaged about forty years) 63 per cent were rendered in the period of 1935 to 1943, that is, during the period of the low status of businessmen.

The Federal Trade Commission Law states that a violation of the antitrust laws by a corporation shall be deemed to be, also, a violation by the officers and directors of the corporation. However, businessmen are practically never convicted as persons, and several cases have been reported (such as the "6 per cent case" against the automobile manufacturers) in which the corporation was convicted and the persons who direct the corporation were all acquitted.[9]

A second factor in the explanation of the differential implementation of the law as applied to white-collar criminals is the trend away from reliance on penal methods. This trend advanced more rapidly in the area of white-collar crime than of other crime because—due to the recency of the statutes—it is least bound by precedents and also because of the status of businessmen. This trend is seen in the almost complete abandonment of the most extreme penalties of death and physical torture; in the supplanting of conventional penal methods by nonpenal methods, such as probation and the case work methods which accompany probation. These decreases in penal methods are explained by a series of social changes: the increased power of the lower socioeconomic class upon which most of the penalties were previously inflicted; the inclusion within the scope of the penal laws of a large part of the upper socioeconomic class, as illustrated by traffic resulted in increased understanding and sympathy; the failure of penal methods to make substantial reductions in crime rates; and the weakening hold on the legal profession and others of the individualistic and hedonistic psychology, which had placed great emphasis on pain in the control of behavior. To some extent overlapping those just mentioned is the fact that punishment, which was previously the chief reliance for control in the home, the school, and the church, has tended to disappear from those institutions, leaving the state without cultural support for its own penal methods.[10]

White-collar crime is similar to juvenile delinquency in respect to the differential implementation of the law. In both cases, the procedures of the criminal law are modified so that the stigma of crime will not attach to the offenders. The stigma of crime has been less completely eliminated from juvenile delinquents than from white-collar criminals because the procedures for the former are a less complete departure from conventional criminal procedures, since most juvenile delinquents come from a class with low social status, and because the juveniles have not organized to protect their good names. Because the juveniles have not been successfully freed from the stigma of crime, they have been generally held to be within the scope of the theories of criminology and, in fact, provide a large part of the data for criminology; because the external symbols have been more successfully eliminated from white-collar crimes, white-collar crimes have generally not been included within these theories.

A third factor in the differential implementation of the law is the difference in the relation between the law and the mores in the area of white-collar crime. The laws under consideration are recent and do not have a firm foundation in public ethics or business ethics; in fact, certain rules of business ethics, such as the contempt for the "price chiseler," are generally in conflict with the law. These crimes are not obvious, as is assault and battery, and can be appreciated readily only by persons who are expert in the occupations in which they occur. A corporation often violates a law for a decade or longer before the administrative agency becomes aware of the violation; in the meantime the violation may have become accepted practice in the industry. The effects of a white-collar crime upon the public are diffused over a long period of time and perhaps over millions of people, with no person's suffering much at a particular time. The public agencies of communication do not express and organize the moral sentiments of the community as to white-collar crimes in part because the crimes are complicated and not easily presented as news, but probably in greater part because these agencies of communication are owned or controlled by the businessmen who violate the laws and because these agencies are themselves frequently charged with violations of the same laws. Public opinion in regard to picking pockets would not be well organized if most of the information regarding this crime came to the public directly from the pick-pockets themselves.

This third factor, if properly limited, is a valid part of the explanation of the differential implementation of the law. It tends to be exaggerated and become the complete explanation in the form of a denial that white-collar crimes involve any moral culpability whatever. On that account it is desirable to state a few reasons why this factor is not the complete explanation.

The assertion is sometimes made that white-collar crimes are merely technical violations and involve no moral culpability (i.e., violation of the mores) whatever. In fact, these white-collar crimes, like other crimes, are distributed along a continuum in which the *mala in se* are at one extreme and the *mala prohibita* at the other.[11] None of the white collar crimes is purely arbitrary, as is the regulation that one must drive on the right side of the street, which might equally well be that one must drive on the left side. The Sherman Antitrust Law, for instance, is regarded by many persons as an unwise law and it may well be that some other policy would be preferable. It is questioned principally by persons who believe in a more collectivistic economic system; namely, the communists and the leaders of big business, while its support comes largely from an emotional ideology in favor of free enterprise which is held by farmers, wage-earners, small-business men, and professional men. Therefore, as appraised by the majority of the population it is necessary for the preservation of American institutions and its violation is a violation of strongly entrenched moral sentiments.

The sentimental reaction toward a particular white-collar crime is certainly different from that toward some other crimes. This difference is often exaggerated, especially as the reaction occurs in urban society. The characteristic reaction of the average citizen in the modern city toward burglary is apathy unless he or his immediate friends are victims or unless the case is very spectacular. The average citizen, reading in his morning paper that the home of an unknown person has been burglarized by another unknown person, has no appreciable increase in blood pressure. Fear and resentment develop in modern society primarily as the result of the accumulation of crimes as depicted in crime rates or in general descriptions, and this develops both as to white-collar crimes and other crimes.

Finally, although many laws have been enacted for the regulation of occupations other than business, such as agriculture or plumbing, the procedures used in the enforcement of those other laws are more nearly the same as the conventional criminal procedures, and law-violators in these other occupations are not so completely protected against the stigma of crime as are businessmen. The relation between the law and the mores tends to be circular. The mores are crystallized in the law and each act of enforcement of the laws tends to re-enforce the mores. The laws regarding white-collar crime, which conceal the criminality of the behavior, have been less effective than other laws in re-enforcement of the mores.

## Notes

1. Edwin H. Sutherland, "White-Collar Criminality," *American Sociological Review*, 5 (February, 1940), pp. 1–12; and "Crime and Business," *Annals of the American Academy of Political and Social Science*, 217 (September, 1941), pp. 112–118.

2. Cf., Edwin H. Sutherland, *White Collar Crime* (New York: Dryden Press, 1949), pp. 15–182.

3. The most thorough analysis of crime from the point of view of legal definition is Jerome Hall, *Principles of Criminal Law* (Indianapolis: Bobbs-Merrill, 1947).

4. Some of the antitrust decisions were made against meat packers under the Packers and Stockyards Act. The penal sanctions in this act are essentially the same as in the Federal Trade Commission Act.

5. The consent decree may be taken for other reasons, especially because it cannot be used as evidence in other suits.

6. Livingston Hall, "Statutory Law of Crimes, 1887–1936," *Harvard Law Review*, 50 (February, 1937), pp. 616–653.

7. Wendell Berge, "Remedies Available to the Government under the Sherman Act," *Law and Contemporary Problems*, 7 (January, 1940), p. 111.

8. On the role of the stranger in punitive justice, see Ellsworth Faris, "The Origin of Punishment," *International Journal of Ethics*, 25 (October, 1914), pp. 54–67; George H. Mead, "The Psychology of Punitive Justice," *American Journal of Sociology*, 23 (March, 1918), pp. 577–602.

9. The question may be asked, "If businessmen are so influential, why did they not retain the protection of the rules of the criminal procedure?" The answer is that they lost this protection, despite their status, on the principle, "You can't eat your cake and have it, too."

10. This trend away from penal methods suggests that the penal sanction may not be a completely adequate criterion in the definition of crime.

11. An excellent discussion of this continuum is presented by Jerome Hall, "Prolegomena to a Science of Criminal Law," *University of Pennsylvania Law Review*, 89 (March, 1941), pp. 563–569.

# 18

# WHO IS THE CRIMINAL?

*Paul W. Tappan*

What is crime? As a lawyer-sociologist, the writer finds perturbing the current confusion on this important issue. Important because it delimits the subject matter of criminological investigation. A criminologist who strives to aid in formulating the beginnings of a science finds himself in an increasingly equivocal position. He studies the criminals convicted by the courts and is then confounded by the growing clamor that he is not studying the real criminal at all, but an insignificant proportion of nonrepresentative and stupid unfortunates who happened to have become enmeshed in technical legal difficulties. It has become a fashion to maintain that the convicted population is no proper category for the empirical research of the criminologist. Ergo, the many studies of convicts which have been conducted by the orthodox, now presumably outmoded criminologists, have no real meaning for either descriptive or scientific purposes. Off with the old criminologies, on with the new orientations, the new horizons!

This position reflects in part at least the familiar suspicion and misunderstanding held by the layman sociologist toward the law. To a large

Reprinted from *American Sociological Review*, 12 (February, 1947), pp. 96–102, by permission of The American Sociological Association.

extent it reveals the feeling among social scientists that not all antisocial conduct is proscribed by law (which is probably true), that not all conduct violative of the criminal code is truly antisocial, or is not so to any significant extent (which is also undoubtedly true). Among some students the opposition to the traditional definition of crime as law violation arises from their desire to discover and study wrongs which are absolute and eternal rather than mere violations of a statutory and case law system which vary in time and place; this is essentially the old metaphysical search for the law of nature. They consider the dynamic and relativistic nature of law to be a barrier to the growth of a scientific system of hypotheses possessing universal validity.[1]

Recent protestants against the orthodox conceptions of crime and criminal are diverse in their views; they unite only in their denial of the allegedly legalistic and arbitrary doctrine that those convicted under the criminal law are the criminals of our society and in promoting the confusion as to the proper province of criminology. It is enough here to examine briefly a few of the current schisms with a view to the difficulties at which they arrive.

I

A number of criminologists today maintain that mere violation of the criminal law is an artificial criterion of criminality, that categories set up by the law do not meet the demands of scientists because they are of a "fortuitous nature" and do not "arise intrinsically from the nature of the subject matter."[2] The validity of this contention must depend, of course, upon what the nature of the subject matter is. These scholars suggest that, as a part of the general study of human behavior, criminology should concern itself broadly with all antisocial conduct, behavior injurious to society. We take it that antisocial conduct is essentially any sort of behavior which violates some social interest. But what are these social interests? Which are weighty enough to merit the concern of the sociologist, to bear the odium of crime? What shall constitute a violation of them—particularly where, as is so commonly true in our complicated and unintegrated society, these interests are themselves in conflict? Roscoe Pound's suggestive classification of the social interests served by law is valuable in a juristic framework, but it solves no problems for the sociologist who seeks to depart from legal standards in search of all manner of antisocial behavior.

However desirable may be the concept of socially injurious conduct for purposes of general normation or abstract description, it does not define what is injurious. It sets no standard. It does not discriminate cases, but merely invites the subjective value judgments of the investigator. Until it is structurally embodied with distinct criteria or norms—as is now the case in the legal system—the notion of antisocial conduct is useless for purposes of research, even for the rawest empiricism. The emancipated criminologist reasons himself into a *cul de sac*: having decided that it is footless to study convicted offenders on the ground that this is an artificial category—though its membership is quite precisely ascertainable, he must now conclude that, in his lack of standards to determine antisociality, though this may be what he considers a real scientific category, its membership and its characteristics are unascertainable. Failing to define antisocial behavior in any fashion suitable to research, the criminologist may be deluded further into assuming that there is an absoluteness and permanence in this undefined category, lacking in the law. It is unwise for the social scientist ever to forget that all standards of social normation are relative, impermanent, variable, and that they do not, certainly the law does not, arise out of mere fortuity or artifice.[3]

## II

In a differing approach certain other criminologists suggest that "conduct norms" rather than either crime or antisocial conduct should be studied.[4] There is an unquestionable need to pursue the investigation of general conduct norms and their violation. It is desirable to segregate the various classes of such norms, to determine relationships between them, and to understand similarities and differences between them as to the norms themselves, their sources, methods of imposition of control, and their consequences. The subject matter of this field of social control is in a regrettably primitive state. It will be important to discover the individuals who belong within the several categories of norm-violators established and to determine then what motivations operate to promote conformity or breach. So far as it may be determinable, we shall wish to know in what way these motivations may serve to insure conformity to different sets of conduct norms, how they may overlap and reinforce the norms or conflict and weaken the effectiveness of the norms.

We concur in the importance of the study of conduct norms and their violation and, more particularly, if we are to develop a science of human behavior, in the need for careful research to determine the psychological and environmental variables which are associated etiologically with nonconformity to these norms. However, the importance of the more general subject matter of social control or "ethology" does not mean that the more specific study of the law-violator is nonsignificant. Indeed, the direction of progress in the field of social control seems to lie largely in the observation and analysis of more specific types of nonconformity to particular, specialized standards. We shall learn more by attempting to determine *why* some individuals take human life deliberately and with premeditation, *why* some take property by force and others by trick than we shall in seeking at the start a universal formula to account for any and all behavior in breach of social interests. This broader knowledge of conduct norms may conceivably develop through induction, in its inevitably very generic terms, from the empirical data derived in the study of particular sorts of violations. Also, our more specific information about the factors which lie behind violations of precisely defined norms will be more useful in the technology of social control. Where legal standards require change to keep step with the changing requirements of a dynamic society, the sociologist may advocate—even as the legal profession does—the necessary statutory modifications, rather than assume that for sociological purposes the conduct he disapproves is already criminal, without legislative, political, or judicial intervention.

## III

Another increasingly widespread and seductive movement to revolutionize the concepts of crime and criminal has developed around the currently fashionable dogma of "white-collar crime." This is actually a particular school among those who contend that the criminologist should study antisocial behavior rather than law violation. The dominant contention of the group appears to be that the convict classes are merely our "petty" criminals, the few whose depredations against society have been on a small scale, who have blundered into difficulties with the police and courts through their ignorance and stupidity. The important criminals, those who do irreparable damage with impunity, deftly evade the machinery of justice, either by remaining "technically" within the law or by exercising their intelligence, financial prowess, or political connections in its violation. We seek a definition of the white-collar criminal and find an amazing diversity, even among those flowing from the same pen, and observe that characteristically they are loose, doctrinaire, and invective. When Professor Sutherland launched the term, it was applied to those individuals of upper socioeconomic class who violate the criminal law, usually by breach of trust, in the ordinary course of their business activities.[5] This original usage accords with legal ideas of crime and points moreover to the significant and difficult problems of enforcement in the areas of business crimes, particularly where those violations are made criminal by recent statutory enactment. From this fruitful beginning, the term has spread into vacuity, wide and handsome. We learn that the white-collar criminal may be the suave and deceptive merchant prince or "robber baron," that the existence of such crime may be determined readily "in casual conversation with a representative of an occupation by asking him, 'What crooked practices are found in your occupation?' "[6]

Confusion grows as we learn from another proponent of this concept that, "There are various phases of white-collar criminality that touch the lives of the common man almost daily. The large majority of them are operating within the letter and spirit of the law" and that "In short, greed, not need, lies at the basis of white-collar crime."[7] Apparently, the criminal may be law-obedient but greedy; the specific quality of his crimes is far from clear.

Another avenue is taken in Professor Sutherland's more recent definition of crime as a "legal description of an act as socially injurious and legal provision of penalty for the act."[8] Here he has deemed the connotation of his term too narrow if confined to violations of the criminal code; he includes by a slight modification conduct violative of any law, civil or criminal, when it is "socially injurious."

In light of these definitions, the normative issue is pointed. Who should be considered the white-collar criminal? Is it the merchant who, out of greed, business acumen, or competitive motivations, breaches a trust with his consumer by "puffing his wares" beyond their merits, by pricing them beyond their value, or by ordinary advertising? Is it he who breaks trust with his employees in order to keep wages down, refusing to permit labor organization or to bargain collectively, and who is found guilty by a labor relations board of an unfair labor practice? May it be the white-collar worker who breaches trust with his employers by inefficient performance at work, by sympathetic strike or secondary boycott? Or is it the merchandiser who violates ethics by undercutting the prices of his fellow merchants? In general these acts do not violate the criminal law. All in some manner breach a trust for motives which a criminologist may (or may not) disapprove for one reason or another. All are within the framework of the norms of ordinary business practice. One seeks in vain for criteria to determine this white-collar criminality. It is the conduct of one who wears a white collar and who indulges in occupational behavior to which some particular criminologist takes exception. It may easily be a term of propaganda. For purposes of empirical research or objective description, what is it?

Whether criminology aspires one day to become a science or a repository of reasonably accurate descriptive information, it cannot tolerate a nomenclature of such loose and variable usage. A special hazard exists in the employment of the term, "white-collar criminal," in that it invites individual systems of private values to run riot in an area (economic ethics) where gross variation exists among criminologists as well as others. The rebel may enjoy a veritable orgy of delight in damning as criminal most anyone he pleases; one imagines that some experts would thus consign to the criminal classes any successful capitalistic businessman; the reactionary or conservative, complacently viewing the occupational practices of the business world, might find all in perfect order in this best of all possible worlds. The result may be fine indoctrination or catharsis achieved through blustering broadsides against the "existing system." It is not criminology. It is not social science. The terms "unfair," "infringement," "discrimination," "injury to society," and so on, employed by the white collar criminologists cannot, taken alone, differentiate criminal and non-criminal. Until refined to mean certain specific actions, they are merely epithets.

Vague, omnibus concepts defining crime are a blight upon either a legal system or a system of sociology that strives to be objective. They allow judge, administrator, or—conceivably—sociologist, in an undirected, freely operating discretion, to attribute the status "criminal" to any individual or class which he conceives nefarious. This can accomplish no desirable objective, either politically or sociologically.[9]

Worse than futile, it is courting disaster, political, economic, and social, to promulgate a system of justice in which the individual may be held criminal without having committed a crime, defined with some precision by statute and case law. To describe crime the sociologist, like the lawyer-legislator, must do more than condemn conduct deviation in the abstract. He must avoid definitions predicated simply upon state of mind or social injury and determine what particular types of deviation, in what directions, and to what degree shall be considered criminal. This is exactly what the criminal code today attempts to do, though imperfectly of course. More slowly and conservatively than many of us would wish—that is in the nature of legal institutions, as it is in other social institutions as well. But law has defined with greater clarity and precision the conduct which is criminal than our antilegalistic criminologists promise to do; it has moreover promoted a stability, a security and dependability of justice through its exactness, its so-called "technicalities," and its moderation in inspecting proposals for change.


IV


Having considered the conceptions of an innovating sociology in ascribing the terms "crime" and "criminal," let us state here the juristic view: Only those are criminals who have been adjudicated as such by the courts. Crime is an intentional act in violation of the criminal law (statutory and case law), committed without defense or excuse, and penalized by the state as a felony or misdemeanor. In studying the offender there can be no presumption that arrested, arraigned, indicted, or prosecuted persons are criminals unless they also be held guilty beyond a reasonable doubt of a particular offense.[10] Even less than the unconvicted suspect can those individuals be considered criminal who have violated no law. Only those are criminals who have been selected by a clear substantive and a careful adjective law, such as obtains in our courts. The unconvicted offenders of whom the criminologist may wish to take cognizance are an important but unselected group; it has no specific membership presently ascertainable. Sociologists may strive, as does the legal profession, to perfect measures for more complete and accurate ascertainment of offenders, but it is futile simply to rail against a machinery of justice which is, and to a large extent must inevitably remain, something less than entirely accurate or efficient.

Criminal behavior as here defined fits very nicely into the sociologists' formulations of social control. Here we find *norms* of conduct, comparable to the mores, but considerably more distinct, precise, and detailed, as they are fashioned through statutory and case law. The agencies of this control, like the norms themselves, are more formal than is true in other types of control: The law depends for its instrumentation chiefly upon police, prosecutors, judges, juries, and the support of a favorable public opinion. The law has for its *sanctions* the specifically enumerated punitive measures set up by the state for breach, penalties which are additional to any of the sanctions which society exerts informally against the violator of norms which may overlap with laws. Crime is itself simply the breach of the legal norm, a violation within this particular category of social control; the criminal is, of course, the individual who has committed such acts of breach.

Much ink has been spilled on the extent of deterrent efficacy of the criminal law in social control. This is a matter which is not subject to demonstration in any exact and measurable fashion, any more than one can conclusively demonstrate the efficiency of a moral norm.[11] Certainly the degree of success in asserting a control, legal or moral, will vary with the particular norm itself, its instrumentation, the subject individuals, the time, the place, and the sanctions. The efficiency of legal control is sometimes confused by the fact that, in the common overlapping of crimes (particularly those *mala in se*) with moral standards, the norms and sanctions of each may operate in mutual support to produce conformity. Moreover, mere breach of norm is no evidence of the general failure of a social control system, but indication rather of the need for control. Thus, the occurrence of theft and homicide does not mean that the law is ineffective, for one cannot tell how frequently such acts might occur in the absence of law and penal sanction. Where such acts are avoided, one may not appraise the relative efficacy of law and mores in prevention. When they occur, one cannot apportion blame, either in the individual case or in general, to failures of the legal and moral systems. The individual in society does undoubtedly conduct himself in reference to legal requirements. Living "beyond the law" has a quality independent of being nonconventional, immoral, sinful. Mr. Justice Holmes has shown that the "bad man of the law"—those who become our criminals—are motivated in part by disrespect for the law or, at the least, are inadequately restrained by its taboos.

From introspection and from objective analysis of criminal histories one can not but accept as axiomatic the thesis that the norms of criminal law and its sanctions do exert some measure of effective control over human behavior; that this control is increased by moral, conventional, and traditional norms; and that the effectiveness of control norms is variable. It seems a fair inference from urban investigations that in our contemporary mass society, the legal system is becoming increasingly important in constraining behavior as primary group norms and sanctions deteriorate. Criminal law, crime, and the criminal become more significant subjects of sociological inquiry, therefore, as we strive to describe, understand, and control the uniformities and variability in culture.

We consider that the "white-collar criminal," the violator of conduct norms, and the antisocial personality are not criminal in any sense meaningful to the social scientist unless he has violated a criminal statute. We cannot know him as such unless he has been properly convicted. He may be a boor, a sinner, a moral leper, or the devil incarnate, but he does not become a criminal through sociological name calling unless politically constituted authority says he is. It is footless for the sociologist to confuse issues of definition, normation, etiology, sanction, agency and social effects by saying one thing and meaning another.

V

To conclude, we reiterate and defend the contention that crime, as legally defined, is a sociologically significant province of study. The view that it is not appears to be based upon either of two premises: first, that offenders convicted under the criminal law are not representative of all criminals and, second, that criminal law violation (and, therefore, the criminal himself) is not significant to the sociologist because it is composed of a set of legal, nonsociological categories irrelevant to the understanding of group behavior and/or social control. Through these contentions to invalidate the traditional and legal frame of reference adopted by the criminologist, several considerations, briefly enumerated below, must be met.

1. *Convicted criminals as a sample of law violators:*

a. Adjudicated offenders represent the closest possible approximation to those who have in fact violated the law, carefully selected by sieving of the due process of law; no other province of social control attempts to ascertain the breach of norms with such rigor and precision.

b. It is as futile to contend that this group should not be studied on the grounds that it is incomplete or nonrepresentative as it would be to maintain that psychology should terminate its description, analysis, diagnosis, and treatment of deviants who cannot be completely representative as selected. Convicted persons are nearly all criminals. They offer large and varied samples of all types; their origins, traits, dynamics of development, and treatment influences can be studied profitably for purposes of description, understanding, and control. To be sure, they are not necessarily representative of all offenders; if characteristics observed among them are imputed to law-violators generally, it must be with the qualification implied by the selective processes of discovery and adjudication.

c. Convicted criminals are important as a sociological category, furthermore, in that they have been exposed and respond to the influences of court contact, official punitive treatment, and public stigma as convicts.

2. *The relevance of violation of the criminal law*:

a. The criminal law establishes substantive norms of behavior, standards more clear-cut, specific, and detailed than the norms in any other category of social controls.

b. The behavior prohibited has been considered significantly in derogation of group welfare by deliberative and representative assembly, formally constituted for the purpose of establishing such norms; nowhere else in the field of social control is there directed a comparable rational effort to elaborate standards conforming to the predominant needs, desires, and interests of the community.

c. There are legislative and juridical lags which reduce the social value of the legal norms; as an important characteristic of law, such lag does not reduce the relevance of law as a province of sociological inquiry. From a detached sociological view, the significant thing is not the absolute goodness or badness of the norms but the fact that these norms do control behavior. The sociologist is interested in the results of such control, the correlates of violation, and in the lags themselves.

d. Upon breach of these legal (and social) norms, the refractory are treated officially in punitive and/or rehabilitative ways, not for being generally antisocial, immoral, unconventional, or bad, but for violation of the specific legal norms of control.[12]

e. Law becomes the peculiarly important and ultimate pressure toward conformity to minimum standards of conduct deemed essential to group welfare as other systems of norms and mechanics of control deteriorate.

f. Criminals, therefore, are a sociologically distinct group of violators of specific legal norms, subjected to official state treatment. They and the noncriminals respond, though differentially, of course, to the standards, threats, and correctional devices established in this system of social control.

g. The norms, their violation, the mechanics of dealing with breach constitute major provinces of legal sociology. They are basic to the theoretical framework of sociological criminology.

## ADDENDUM

A special class of cases that illustrates very well both the problem of definition and of legal policy is that of so-called "white-collar crime." Much attention has been devoted to such "crime" in recent years, and properly so, for peculiarly difficult problems of public policy as well as causation and treatment are involved in this area.[13] However, there is possibly less consistency involved in analyses of white-collar "criminality" than there is in any other category of crime. The white-collar criminologists represent one particular group among those who contend that the criminologist should study antisocial behavior rather than criminal law violation as such.[14] In seeking definitions of white-collar crime, one finds a rather remarkable diversity, but characteristically the definitions are loose and sometimes doctrinaire.

Unfortunately, norms of proper behavior in the economic fields of production, distribution, and advertising have been difficult to develop, partly because the commercial revolution took place so rapidly. Drawing lines between efficient and practical competitive behavior by the sharp but skilled and honest businessman, on the one hand, and the criminal practices of the dishonest and overpowerful, on the other, has proved extremely difficult. Interpretations and enforcement of the modern laws directed against various forms of white-collar crime have revealed the complex and controversial character of such policy, in part but not entirely by any means, because of the wealth and power of many of those who are brought to trial. The excessive tolerance that has developed for a loose economic and political morality is also at fault to a great extent. Unlike most forms of crime, white-collar depredations commonly have a diffused impact upon many in the society but little direct or obvious injury to single individuals. Moreover, and this is a peculiarly subtle problem, much of the white-collar conduct disapproved by some criminologists does have economic value. Often the policy question is one of balancing gain and loss from the behavior involved. Finally, it should be noted that our court and correctional systems have little to offer in the way of effective treatment, training, or even of deterrence in the handling of individuals of the sort here involved.

Our definitions of crime cannot be rooted in epithets, in minority value judgments or prejudice, or in loose abstractions. Within a system of justice under law, crime must be defined quite precisely and in accordance with the explicit formulations of the legislature. Such crime will not include all behavior that is antisocial, for reasons that we have noted, nor even all conduct that should be made criminal.

## Notes

1. For the manner in which the legal definition of the criminal is avoided by prominent sociological scholars through amazingly loose, circumlocutory description, see, for instance, Florian Znaniecki, "Social Research in Criminology," *Sociology and Social Research*, 12 (March, 1928), p. 307.

2. See, for example, Thorsten Sellin, *Culture Conflict and Crime* (New York: Social Science Research Council, 1938), pp. 20–21.

3. An instance of this broadening of the concept of the criminal is the penchant among certain anthropologists to equate crime with taboo. See, especially, Bronislaw Malinowski, *Crime and Custom in Savage Society* (New York: Harcourt, Brace, 1926), and "A New Instrument for the Interpretation of Law—Especially Primitive," *Yale Law Journal*, 51 (June, 1942), pp. 1237–1254. Compare William Seagle, "Primitive Law and Professor Malinowski," *American Anthropologist*, 39 (April–June, 1937), pp. 275–290, and *The Quest for Law* (New York: Knopf, 1941); Karl N. Llewellyn and E. Adamson Hoebel, *The Cheyenne Way: Conflict and Case Law in Primitive Jurisprudence* (Norman, Okla.: University of Oklahoma Press, 1941); and Hoebel, "Law and Anthropology," *Virginia Law Review*, 32 (June, 1946), pp. 835–854.

4. Sellin, *op. cit.*, pp. 25ff.

5. Edwin H. Sutherland, "Crime and Business," *Annals of the American Academy of Political and Social Science*, 217 (September, 1941), pp. 112–118.

6. Edwin H. Sutherland, "White-Collar Criminality," *American Sociological Review*, 5 (February, 1940), pp. 1–12.

7. Harry Elmer Barnes and Negley K. Teeters, *New Horizons in Criminology* (Englewood Cliffs, N.J.: Prentice-Hall, 1943), pp. 42–43.

8. Edwin H. Sutherland, "Is 'White Collar Crime' Crime?" *American Sociological Review*, 10 (April, 1945), pp. 132–139.

9. In the province of juvenile delinquency we may observe already the evil that flows from this sort of loose definition in applied sociology. See Roscoe Pound, "Introduction," in Pauline V. Young, *Social Treatment in Probation and Delinquency* (New York: McGraw-Hill, 1937), pp. xxiii–xxxi. See also Paul W. Tappan, *Delinquent Girls in Court* (New York: Columbia University Press, 1947); and "Treatment without Trial," *Social Forces*, 24 (March, 1946), pp. 306–311.

10. The unconvicted suspect cannot be known as a violator of the law, to assume him so would be in derogation of our most basic political and ethical philosophies. In empirical research it would be quite inaccurate, obviously, to study all suspects or defendants as criminals.

11. For a detailed consideration of the efficacy of legal norms, see Jerome Michael and Herbert Wechsler, "A Rationale of the Law of Homicide," *Columbia Law Review*, 37 (May, 1937), pp. 701–761, and 37 (December, 1937), pp. 1261–1325.

12. For other expositions of this view, see articles by Jerome Hall: "Prolegomena to a Science of Criminal Law," *University of Pennsylvania Law Review*, 89 (March, 1941), pp. 549–580; "Criminology and a Modern Penal Code," *Journal of Criminal Law and Criminology*, 27 (May–June, 1936), pp. 1–16; and "Criminology," in Georges Gurvitch and Wilbert E. Moore, editors, *Twentieth-Century Sociology* (New York: Philosophical Library, 1945), pp. 342–365.

13. The author wishes to make it clear here, since there has been some misconstruction of his view in literature on the subject, that he believes white-collar crime, properly and precisely defined, to be not only a legitimate but an important phase of criminological inquiry. He deplores the loosely normative connotations that have been attached to the concept by some of Sutherland's interpreters, and he believes that they have resulted in some confusion so far as needed empirical research in this area is concerned.

14. Barnes and Teeters, *op. cit.*, 3d ed. (1959).

# 19

# THE STUDY OF WHITE-COLLAR CRIME: TOWARD A
# REORIENTATION IN THEORY AND RESEARCH

*Richard Quinney*

White-collar crime as a unique form of illegal behavior has received a
great deal of attention since Sutherland introduced the concept in his 1939
presidential address to the American Sociological Society.[1] White-collar
crime—the violation of criminal law by a person of high socio-economic
status in the course of occupational activity—has been focused upon in
several ways. For instance, a number of research studies of white-collar
crime have been initiated;[2] the legal character of the violations has been
questioned;[3] the sociological relevance of the concept has been doubted;[4]
the theoretical and research significance of the concept has been indicated;[5] critiques and summaries have been written;[6] and in most criminology textbooks considerable space has been devoted to a discussion of
white-collar crime.[7] Most important to the field of criminology, use of the
concept of white-collar crime has led to the reexamination of the grounds
on which generalizations about crime and criminals are made. Although
controversy still occurs, the majority of criminologists regard white-collar
crime as a legitimate subject for criminological research.

Because the validity of white-collar crime as a form of crime has
been a subject of severe controversy, the question of conceptual clarity

Reprinted by special permission of the *Journal of Criminal Law, Criminology, and
Police Science.* Copyright © 1964 by the Northwestern University School of Law, Vol.
55, No. 2.

has largely been ignored. . . . In addition to the lack of conceptual clarity, a satisfactory explanation of the diverse behaviors subsumed under the concept does not exist. These difficulties are to be expected since the search for a causative theory of white-collar crime has been hampered by a number of problems which have also impeded the study of other forms of crime. Two principal problems have been (1) unit of analysis, and (2) level of explanation. A discussion of these problems as they apply particularly to the study of white-collar crime will aid to clarify the concept of white-collar crime and also will provide suggestions for a reorientation in theory and research.

## UNIT OF ANALYSIS

The first problem stems from the fact that the legal category of crime includes many different kinds of behavior, and it follows that it is unlikely that the different behaviors are subject to a common explanation. Several writers have attempted to correct this difficulty by delineating various behaviors within the legal definition of criminal behavior.[8] Law violators have been placed into behavior units that are more homogeneous than those provided in the legal definitions.

Arguments for the delineation of types of white-collar crime have been made on several occasions. Aubert noted a few years ago that, similar to the concept of crime, white-collar crime probably covers a range of behaviors and each type of behavior may need a different causal explanation.[9] Recently, Bloch and Geis in their criminology textbook, which concentrates on behavior systems of crime, noted in regard to white-collar crime that the concept has come to cover a vast array of illegal behaviors and that "it is apparent that more rigid procedures to distinguish categories of white-collar offenses will have to be undertaken to render the classification of maximum scientific worth."[10] As a starting point in delineating types of white-collar crime, Bloch and Geis suggested that it might be desirable to separate white-collar crimes committed (1) by individuals( e.g., lawyers, doctors), (2) by employees against the corporation (e.g., embezzlers), and (3) by policy-making officials for the corporation (as in the recent antitrust cases).

In a somewhat different manner, Geis in a recent article, after recommending that white-collar crimes be grouped into forms of behaviors that analytically resemble one another both in their manifestation and in terms of the ingredients which appear to enter into their origin, suggested that the concept of white-collar crime be restricted to "corporate violations." He concluded that "unless the concept of white-collar crime is restricted, in line with the above or similar ideas, it will continue to remain prey to the legitimate criticisms of numerous scholars . . . , and it will continue to be so broad and indefinite as to fall into inevitable desuetude."[11]

It is apparent, then, that such efforts to distinguish categories of white-collar crime, or to restrict the definition of white-collar crime itself, must be undertaken in order to give the concept any scientific utility. Various principles of classification should be considered. Possible classifications could include such factors as a more elaborate indication of the kind of occupation and the source of employment, the position of the occupation in the occupational structure, the occupational role or roles of the offender, and the institutional nature of the occupation or organization (political, business, industrial, medical, etc.). Also, classifications could be based on the nature and recency of the law itself and the relation of the offense to societal values. An additional consideration is the possibility of a multi-dimensional classification.[12]

However, before white-collar typologies can be developed, a more pressing problem must be faced and that is that the concept of white-collar crime today rather indiscriminately covers a diverse, wide, and oftentimes uncertain and inconsistent range of behaviors. The result is that we are not entirely certain what behaviors constitute white-collar crime. This is due in part to Sutherland's definition and to his own subsequent use of the concept.[13] The research and writing of others on the subject have done little to clarify the concept. We remain uncertain as to (1) the importance of the social status of the offender, (2) the exact meaning of occupational activity, and (3) the possibility of including deviant behaviors which are not strictly legal violations.

*Social Status of the Offender.*   Sutherland conceptually limited white-collar crime to violation of the criminal laws regulating occupations by persons who are "respectable" or of the "upper socioeconomic class." His reason for emphasizing social status was primarily for the purpose of illustation of white-collar crime to a particular status group may be of historical significance in the reformation of criminological theory, it appears to have little theoretical merit today, except to point to procedural differences in the administration of justice. Newman, in his critique of white-collar crime, suggested that "farmers, repairmen, and others in essentially nonwhite collar occupations, could through such illegalities as watering milk for public consumption, making unnecessary 'repairs' on television sets, and so forth, be classified as white-collar violators."[14] Such an expansion of the concept to include all violations that occur in the course of occupational activity—regardless of the offender's social status—would increase the utility of the concept. It would then be advisable to change the term to *occupational crime.*

*Occupational Activity.*   The exact meaning of occupational activity is drawn into question when one reviews the writings on white-collar crime. One cannot quarrel with the fact that the study of such offenses as embezzlement, price fixing, over-pricing in time of war, misrepresentation in advertising, unfair labor practices, and medical fee-splitting involve behaviors that occur directly in the course of one's occupational activities. It is another thing, however, to include certain forms of such acts as income tax evasion, rent control violation, and violation of welfare compensation laws in the category of occupational crime.[15] These latter behaviors usually do not strictly occur in the course of occupational activity, except, for example, in the case of income tax evasion which is carried out for a corporation or in the case of rent control violation when it can be established that one pursues renting as an occupation. The important point here is that the behavior must be directly related to the violator's occupational activities if it is to be included in white-collar crime or occupational crime. Such precision will reduce conceptual problems in future theory and research.

*Crime and Deviant Behavior.* Those who have argued against the inclusion of white-collar crime in criminology have stressed that the violations are not crimes because they are not in violation of the traditional criminal code and, what is more, that the violations are not crimes because the offenders are not usually convicted in a court of criminal law.[16] The advocates of the concept of white-collar crime have argued that the behaviors are nevertheless in violation of laws and regulations which contain provisions for punishment. They also argue that the fact that cases are usually processed differently is of no scientific interest, at least for the purpose of explanation.[17]

Although the controversy no longer seems to be of primary concern, ambiguities arise because some writers on white-collar crime, Sutherland included, have been interested in behaviors which are not punishable by law, for example, "sharp" business practices and contract violation. It is important that only behaviors which are punishable by law be included in the concept of white-collar crime (or occupational crime). On the other hand, the student of occupational crime could gain much by focusing on any deviations in occupational activity, be they criminal or not. It would be valuable, then, to employ the concept of *occupational deviation*. In keeping with recent conceptualization of deviant behavior in general, occupational deviation represents departures from expectations that are shared and recognized as legitimate within an occupation.[18] Occupational deviation includes all occupational behavior that violates the institutionalized expectations of an occupation, that is, deviant behavior that occurs in the course of occupational activity. It should be made explicit at all times, however, whether or not the behavior in question is criminal as well as a deviation from occupational norms.[19]

By thus expanding the concept beyond the limits set by legal definitions, but still noting if the behaviors are illegal or not, it would be possible to handle the heretofore unmanageable fact that violations of the legal norms are not necessarily violations of other (non-legal) norms. Because many of the white-collar crimes are in violation of laws and regulations recently enacted, they may not yet be a part of the normative structure of the occupation. These laws and regulations are often imposed by outsiders and thus are not necessarily held as binding by the occupational incumbents themselves. Although the violation of the laws and regulations is defined as crime, it is often the case that an occupational norm is not broken. In fact, the white-collar offender is likely at most to regard himself as a lawbreaker rather than a criminal.[20] Even the public is unlikely to regard the violation of such laws as crime. These laws do not have their basis in other norms, occupational or otherwise, and the offenses are only bad because they are prohibited (*mala prohibita* rather than *mala in se*).[21]

Therefore, a shift of the concept of occupational deviation would allow researchers to investigate actual departures from occupational norms without having to rely upon the otherwise necessary inference that violations of legal norms are also deviations from occupational norms. It would also be possible to study occupational deviations that have not been formalized into law. A range of other problems would be opened by the use of the concept, such as the relationship between law-making and law-breaking, the acceptance of legal norms and the process by which they are incorporated into the occupation, resistance to laws by particular occupational members and the factors associated with resistance, competing occupational norms, redefintion of occupational roles, and occupational change.

*Figure 1. Relationship Between Occupational Behavior, Occupational Crime, and Occupational Deviation*

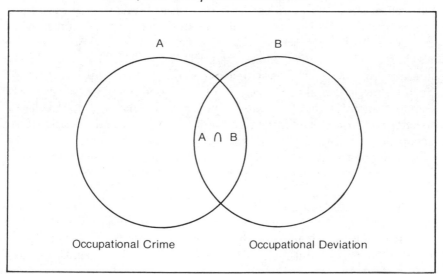

In addition to occupational crime and deviation, there are several different orders of behavior which are made obvious when both the violation of legal norms and deviation from occupational norms are considered together and in relation to occupational behavior in general. Each type of behavior presents the researcher with a different set of problems for investigation. Figure 1 is an attempt at a graphic presentation of the relationship between the violation of legal norms and deviation from occupational norms in the larger framework of occupational behavior. It should be kept in mind, however, that the circles representing occupational deviation and occupational crime could assume varying positions in the diagram and are likely to do so in reality. There is the possibility, for example, that the circles could be either mutually exclusive or equivalent, as well as vary in the degree of overlap. Also, either circle could contain the other, or one or both circles could be nonexistent. The circles can, of course, vary in size in relation to the universe of discourse. Nevertheless, the diagram as shown probably presents the most common situation. The circle A represents behavior in violation of laws and regulations governing an occupation (occupational crime). The behaviors in B are the deviations from occupational norms (occupational deviation). The intersection of A and B represents criminal violations which are also deviations from occupational norms (or those occupational deviations which have also been defined as crime)—possibly called *criminal occupational deviation.* Other combinations could also be of theoretical interest. For example, in notation form, AUB represents all behaviors which are either in violation of a criminal law or a deviation from an occupational norm; $A - (A \cap B)$ includes behaviors which are in violation of the law but do not deviate from an occupational norm; similarly, $B - (A \cap B)$ includes deviations from occupational norms which have not been defined as crime; $\Omega - B$ (or c [B]) represents behaviors that do not deviate from occupational norms, while $\Omega - A$ (or c [A]) represents behaviors which are not in violation of laws regulating the occupation; and $\Omega - (AUB)$ (or c [AUB]) includes behaviors that do not depart from either criminal laws or occupational norms. Such distinctions could continue until the possibilities are exhausted. The important point is that there are a number of different orders of behavior in reference to the combination of criminal violation and deviation from occupational norms. It follows that researchers must always make clear what order of behavior they are trying to describe and explain. The theories in turn will vary according to the particular behavior (or unit of analysis) in question.

Another interesting observation arises when the criminologist views the relationship between legal norms and occupational norms. There is the special case in which most of the occupational behaviors are defined as criminal by persons outside of the occupation. To the incumbents, however, the behaviors may be legitimate according to their own standards, yet there are entirely different behaviors which they regard as occupational deviations.[22] These are the illegitimate (and usually illegal) occupations which are organized around criminal activity. Crime is pursued by the members as a career and as a regular day-by-day means of livelihood, as in the case of professional theft and the various forms of organized crime.[23] These criminal occupations are known to have their own norms and deviations. The criminal code, for example, presents the professional criminal with the rules that one criminal should not inform on another and that there should be an honest division of the loot with partners in crime. The study of occupational crime and occupational deviation among these illegitimate occupations would certainly present the researcher with two separate and distinct behaviors. Of course, it is not unlikely that the criminal behaviors of illegitimate occupations are also supported by some legitimate occupations.[24]

There is also the fact that in some occupations deviations become institutionalized for certain segments of the occupation or even for most members in particular situations. There may be cases in which there are patterned evasions of occupational norms. Alternative norms may exist which are followed by some members.[25] Also, it is known that certain occupational behaviors which are usually regarded as deviant are legitimate in certain situations.[26] There is, in addition, the fact that occupations are in a constant process of change, and occupational deviation (and sometimes crime) is a necessary concomitant of occupational change. The deviant or criminal is often an innovator. Occupational deviation and crime can be an indication of the development of new occupational norms.[27] It can therefore be seen that in the process of occupational change, definitions of both occupational deviation and occupational crime pational crime.

Thus, because the concept of white-collar crime does not accurately purport what criminologists always desire to study, it is suggested that rather than restrict the area of investigation to a narrow range of illegal behavior, the various orders of behavior should be specified. Such specification is necessary in order to assure future progress in both theory and research. Particularly valuable for study is the behavior noted in the concept of occupational deviation which includes all deviant behaviors committed in the course of occupational activity, yet at the same time the legal status of the specific deviations should be considered. Distinguishing the different orders of behavior is a step in the delineation of homogeneous behavioral units for the purpose of explanation. It is likely, in reference to the problem which follows, that the level of explanation employed will depend upon the particular behavioral unit under study.

## LEVEL OF EXPLANATION

The problem of level of explanation has caused a great deal of con-fusion in criminology. Theories have differed from one another not only because some have been valid and others have not been, but because they have merely been on different levels. Cressey, in the introduction to his study of embezzlement, identified two levels in the sociological explana-tion of crime: "The first kind of theory deals with social learning. The data are the specific behaviors of persons, and the task is to identify the process or processes by which a person becomes a criminal. In the other type of theory the data are the social statistics of crime, and the aim is to account for variations in crime rates."[28]

Sutherland, on the same occasion that he introduced the concept of white-collar crime, offered his theory of differential association as an ex-planation of the process by which a person becomes a white-collar criminal. Since that time most of the studies of white-collar crime have employed differential association as an explanation of the behavior. The theory, however, has been only partially successful in explaining white-collar criminality. For example, even though Clinard in his study of the black market concluded that most of the violations appeared to have their ori-gins in behavior learned in association with others, he noted that the theory was limited because it could not adequately explain why some individuals who are familiar with the techniques of violation and also fre-quently associate with persons familiar with techniques of violation do not engage in such practices. In addition, Clinard noted that the theory did not consider the variety of roles played by the individual, the early asso-ciations, the independent invention of a complex technique for violations which are extraordinarily simple, nor the individual's personality pattern.[29]

Also critical of differential association, Cressey in his study of em-bezzlement seriously questioned the usefulness of the theory in explaining some types of crime. It was found that contacts with criminal behavior patterns were not necessary for the learning of techniques of trust violation and that the specific sources of rationalizations for trust violation could not be identified precisely. Cressey found it necessary to conclude that "it is doubtful that it can be shown empirically that the differential associa-tion theory applies or does not apply to crimes of financial trust violation or even to other kinds of criminal behavior."[30] It remains questionable then, whether or not differential association as utilized thus far can state precisely the process by which a person becomes a criminal. Further re-finement of this level of explanation, however, might be attempted in future studies of specific types of occupational crime and deviation.

Sutherland originally presented his theory of differential association in nine propositions on two pages of the 1939 Third Edition of his well-established textbook in criminology. Only slight modifications, primarily in terminology, were made in subsequent editions.[31] As Cressey has recently pointed out, numerous errors have arisen in the interpretation of the theory because readers have not understood what Sutherland apparently was trying to say.[32] An important interpretative error, according to Cressey, is that of assuming that Sutherland's theory deals only with the process by which a person becomes a criminal. However, an examination of Sutherland's writing clearly indicates that he was greatly, if not primarily, concerned with organizing and integrating the factual information about crime rates.[33] This conclusion is supported by the fact that Sutherland proposed the concept of "differential social organization" or "differential group organization" as a complementary concept to differential association in order to account for variations in rates of crime. The essential idea in differential social organization is that in a multi-group or heterogeneous type of social organization, alternative and likely inconsistent standards of conduct are possessed by the various segments.[34] The conception that crime (or deviant behavior in general) is structured and that there are strains for crime in a social organization is also found in another sociological tradition, that of functionalism.[35] Both approaches attempt to account for variations in rates of crime between or within social organizations.

Consideration should be given to the explanation of rates of criminal behavior in occupations, a level of analysis which has been ignored in the study of white-collar crime. However, even given this level, it is likely that the orientation will be so general that it can serve only as an organizing principle, as seems to be the case with differential association. In fact, it may be suggested that differential social organization be employed as a general orientation. It would thus turn research in the direction of attempting to account for variations in rates of crime among different occupations or among segments within an occupation. The particular social organization of the occupation in question would determine the further specification of the theory.[36]

A glaring omission in criminology is the failure to use a level of explanation based on the criminal law itself. The study of white-collar crime, however, has forced some criminologists to realize that the criminal law should be considered as well as the behavior in violation of the law. As Aubert has noted in reference to white-collar crime, "The recent concern among social scientists with white-collar crime tends to bring long-neglected relationships between criminal behavior, criminal law, penal sanctions, and social structure into focus. The unexpected and somehow deviant nature of many recent laws defining white-collar crimes has made it natural to ask for an explanation of the norms themselves and not only of their infringements. As soon as this happens new theoretical vistas are immediately opened."[37] It seems obvious, then, that an urgent need in the study of occupational crime, and crime in general, is research that explicitly takes the nature of particular criminal laws into consideration in the explanation of specific types of crime. The discussion above, and accompanying diagram, in reference to the relationship between criminal law and occupational norms could provide a framework for the formulation of such a research problem.

The idea that criminal law is important in the study of crime was noted some time ago by Michael and Adler. They forcefully stated at one point that "if crime is merely an instance of conduct which is proscribed by the criminal code it follows that the criminal law is the formal cause of crime."[38] It is only the criminal law that gives any behavior its quality and criminality. And, as Jeffery has been arguing more recently, attention must be turned to the study of criminal law, not the criminal, in order to determine why a particular behavior is defined as crime.[39] The study of the conditions in society by which certain behaviors become defined as criminal may be important in explanation of the resulting criminal behaviors. It is probably the case, for example, that in some occupations certain behaviors have been a part (possibly deviant) of the occupation for some time, but the fact that for some reason a law was established suddenly made the behaviors criminal. The point is that the relationship between social structure, criminal law, occupational norms, and criminal behavior should be given further consideration. This level of analysis, as well as others, should be attempted in future study of the specific orders of behavior that are related to violations of the criminal law and deviations from occupational norms.

## CONCLUSION

Although there has been considerable interest and activity in the study of white-collar crime, the development of the area has been hampered by a number of problems that have not been made explicit. The concept has remained unclear because criminologists have subsumed different behaviors under the term. In addition, writers have varied on the amount of emphasis given to the social status of the offender, have employed different meanings of occupational activity, and have lacked consistency in designating the illegal nature of the offenses. Because the concept includes a wide range of behaviors, it becomes necessary to delineate more homogeneous units for the purpose of explanation. Several distinct orders of behavior become evident when the relationship between criminal behavior and occupational deviation is considered. Finally, it is important that different levels of explanation be employed in future studies of occupational crime and deviation.

*Notes*

1. Edwin H. Sutherland, "White-Collar Criminality," *American Sociological Review*, 5 (February, 1940), pp. 1–12.
2. Significant studies are those of Marshall B. Clinard, *The Black Market* (New York: Holt, Rinehart and Winston, 1952); Donald R. Cressey, *Other People's Money* (Glencoe, Ill.: Free Press, 1953); Frank E. Hartung, "White-Collar Offenses in the Wholesale Meat Industry in Detroit," *American Journal of Sociology*, 56 (July, 1950), pp. 25–34; and Edwin H. Sutherland, *White Collar Crime* (New York: Dryden Press, 1949).
3. Robert G. Caldwell, "A Re-examination of the Concept of White-Collar Crime," *Federal Probation*, 22 (March, 1958), p. 30; and Paul W. Tappan, "Who Is the Criminal?" *American Sociological Review*, 12 (February, 1947), pp. 96–102.
4. Ernest W. Burgess, "Comment" on Frank E. Hartung's "White-Collar Offenses in the Wholesale Meat Industry in Detroit," *American Journal of Sociology*, 56 (July, 1950), pp. 32–33.
5. Frank E. Hartung, "White-Collar Crime: Its Significance for Theory and Practice," *Federal Probation*, 17 (June, 1953), pp. 31–36.
6. Donald L. Newman, "White-Collar Crime," *Law and Contemporary Problems*, 23 (Autumn 1958), pp. 735–753; George Vold, *Theoretical* Criminology (New York: Oxford University Press, 1958), pp. 243–261.
7. For example see Harry Elmer Barnes and Negley K. Teeters, *New Horizons in Criminology*, 3d ed. (Englewood Cliffs, N.J.: Prentice Hall, 1959), pp. 3–57; Herbert A. Bloch and Gilbert Geis, *Man, Crime and Society* (New York: Random House, 1962), pp. 379–404; Walter K. Reckless, *The Crime Problem* (New York: Appleton-Century-Crofts, 1961), pp. 207–229; and Donald R. Taft, *Criminology* (New York: Macmillan, 1956), pp. 250–256.
8. Marshall B. Clinard, *Sociology of Deviant Behavior*, 2d ed. (New York: Holt, Rinehart and Winston, 1963), pp. 195–264; Marshall B. Clinard and Andrew L. Wade, "Toward the Delineation of Vandalism as a Sub-type of Juvenile Delinquency," *Journal of Criminal Law, Criminology and Police Science*, 48 (January–February, 1958), p. 493; Donald R. Cressey, "Criminal Research and the Definition of Crimes," *American Journal of Sociology*, 56 (1951), pp. 546–551; Cressey, *Other People's Money*; Don Gibbons, "Prospects and Problems of Delinquent Typology," *Sociological Inquiry*, 32 (Spring, 1962), p. 235; Don Gibbons and Donald L. Garrity, "Definition and Analysis of Certain Criminal Types," *Journal of Criminal Law, Criminology and Police Science*, 53 (March, 1962), pp. 27–35; Don C. Gibbons and Donald L. Garrity, "Some Suggestions for the Development of Etiological and Treatment Theory in Criminology," *Social Forces*, 38 (October, 1959), pp. 51–58; Jack P. Gibbs, "Needed: Analytical Typologies in Criminology," *Southwestern Social Science Quarterly*, 40 (March, 1960), pp. 321–329; John W. Kinch, "Continuities in the Study of Delinquent Types," *Journal of Criminal Law, Criminology and Police Science*, 53 (September, 1962), pp. 323–328; John W. Kinch, "Self-Conceptions of Types of Delinquents," *Sociological Inquiry*, 32 (Spring, 1962), p. 228; Alfred R. Lindesmith and H. Warren Dunham, "Some Principles of Criminal Typology," *Social Forces*, 19 (March, 1941), pp. 307–314; Reckless, *op. cit.*, pp. 75–229; and Clarence Schrag, "A Preliminary Criminal Typology," *Pacific Sociological Review*, 4 (Spring, 1961), pp. 11–16.
9. Vilhelm Aubert, "White-Collar Crime and Social Structure," *American Journal of Sociology*, 58 (November, 1952), pp. 263–271.
10. Bloch and Geis, *op. cit.*, p. 379.
11. Gilbert Geis, "Toward a Delineation of White-Collar Offenses," *Sociological Inquiry*, 32 (Spring, 1962), p. 171.
12. For a multi-dimensional classification in regard to juvenile delinquency see Gibbons, *op. cit.*
13. See Donald R. Cressey, "Foreword" to Edwin H. Sutherland, *White Collar Crime* (New York: Holt, Rinehart and Winston, 1961), p. vii; and Geis, *op. cit.*, pp. 160–161.
14. Newman, *op. cit.*, p. 737. See also Bloch and Geis, *op. cit.*, p. 402.

15. For studies of these behaviors see Elmer Irey and William J. Slocum, *The Tax Dodgers* (New York: Greenberg, 1948); Harry V. Ball, "Social Structure and Rent-Control Violations," *American Journal of Sociology*, 65 (May, 1960), pp. 598–604; and Erwin O. Smigel, "Public Attitudes Toward 'Chiseling' with Reference to Unemployment Compensation," *American Sociological Review*, 18 (February, 1953), pp. 59–67.

16. Caldwell, *op. cit.*; and Tappan, *op. cit.*

17. See Edwin H. Sutherland, "Is 'White-Collar Crime' Crime?" *American Sociological Review*, 10 (April, 1945), pp. 132–139.

18. Albert K. Cohen, "The Study of Social Disorganization and Deviant Behavior," in Robert K. Merton, Leonard Broom and Leonard S. Cottrell, Jr., eds., *Sociology Today* (New York: Basic Books, 1959), pp. 461–484.

19. Donald J. Newman had recently stated that, because deviation is similar behaviorally to the violation of legal norms, deviation must be considered along with conventional legal violations in testing etiological hypotheses. Donald J. Newman, "Legal Norms and Criminological Definitions," in Joseph S. Roucek, ed. *Sociology of Crime* (New York: Philosophical Library, 1961), pp. 55–89. The pioneer statement of extending criminology beyond legal definitions is in Thorsten Sellin, *Culture, Conflict and Crime* (New York: Social Science Research Council, 1938).

20. Clinard, *Sociology of Deviant Behavior*, *op. cit.*, pp. 263–264; and Clinard, *Black Market*, p. 236.

21. See the classical article by Richard C. Fuller, "Morals and the Criminal Law," *Journal of Criminal Law and Criminology*, 32 (March–April, 1942), p. 624. Also Clinard, *Sociology of Deviant Behavior*, pp. 152–153.

22. A discussion of the norms of deviant groups is found in Edwin M. Lemert, *Social Pathology* (New York: McGraw-Hill, 1951), pp. 49–51.

23. Edwin H. Sutherland, *The Professional Thief* (Chicago: University of Chicago Press, 1937); Clinard, *Sociology of Deviant Behavior*, pp. 259–291; and Reckless, *op. cit.*, pp. 153–206.

24. See Vold, *op. cit.*, pp. 220–242.

25. A discussion of alternative norms and patterned evasion of norms in general is found in Robin M. Williams, *American Society* (New York: Knopf, 1960), especially Chapter 10.

26. Joseph Bensman and Israel Gerver, "Crime and Punishment in the Factory: The Function of Deviancy in Maintaining the Social System," *American Sociological Review*, 28 (August, 1963), pp. 588–598.

27. Lewis A. Coser, "Some Functions of Deviant Behavior and Normative Flexibility," *American Journal of Sociology*, 68 (September, 1962), pp. 172–181; Herbert Menzel, "Innovation, Integration and Marginality," *American Sociological Review*, 25 (1960), pp. 704–713; and Robert K. Merton, *Social Theory and Social Structure*, rev. ed., (Glencoe, Ill.: Free Press, 1957), pp. 131–194.

28. Cressey, *op. cit.*, pp. 11–12.

29. Marshall B. Clinard, "Criminological Theories of Violations of Wartime Regulations," *American Sociological Review*, 11 (June, 1946), pp. 258–270.

30. Donald R. Cressey, "Application and Verification of the Differential Association Theory," *Journal of Criminal Law, Criminology and Police Science*, 43 (May–June, 1952), pp. 43–52.

31. Edwin H. Sutherland and Donald R. Cressey, *Principles of Criminology*, 6th ed. (Chicago: Lippincott, 1960), pp. 74–81.

32. Donald R. Cressey, "Epidemiology and Individual Conduct: A Case from Criminology," *Pacific Sociological Review*, 3 (Fall, 1960), pp. 47–58.

33. As particularly seen in Edwin H. Sutherland, "Development of the Theory," in *The Sutherland Papers* (Bloomington: Indiana University Press, 1956), pp. 13–29.

34. Sutherland and Cressey, *op. cit.*, pp. 79–80, 82–85.

35. See especially Robert K. Merton, "Social Structure and Anomie," *American Sociological Review*, 3 (October, 1938), pp. 672–682, and Talcott Parsons, *The Social System* (Glencoe, Ill.: Free Press, 1951), pp. 249.

36. This strategy was taken in Earl R. Quinney's recent research, Earl Richard Quinney, "Occupational Structure and Criminal Behavior: Prescription Violation by Retail Pharmacists," *Social Problems*, 11 (Fall, 1963), pp. 179–185.

37. Aubert, *op. cit.*, p. 264.

38. Jerome Michael and Mortimer J. Adler, *Crime, Law, and Social Science* (New York: Harcourt, Brace, and Company, 1933), p. 5.

39. Stated in several places by Clarence R. Jeffery especially in, "The Structure of American Criminological Thinking," *Journal of Criminal Law, Criminology and Police Science*, 46 (January–February, 1956), p. 658. A similar idea is found in George B. Vold, "Some Basic Problems in Criminological Research," *Federal Probation*, 17 (March, 1953), p. 37.

# 20

# SOME OBSERVATIONS ON THE USE OF CRIMINAL SANCTIONS IN ENFORCING ECONOMIC REGULATIONS

*Sanford H. Kadish*

Those who have had occasion to look for answers to the problems of the use of sanctions, taken to include the whole range of official modes of securing compliance with norms of conduct, have commonly agreed for some time now that there are few to be found. In view of the antiquity of the legal experience, which for the most part has always entailed the use of sanctions of one kind or another, this is a remarkable verdict. Indeed, works written at the turn of the eighteenth century by Jeremy Bentham[1] are still the basic works in the area, a sobering observation which could scarcely be made of more than a handful of subjects of inquiry. In this state of affairs it is not surprising that we are largely ignorant of the impact of the penal sanction, which is only one aspect of the larger problem of sanctions, and still less so that we know little about the use of the penal sanction in an area of relatively recent development—economic regulatory legislation. These are only sectors of a much larger unexplored terrain.

Moreover, unnecessary confusion has become an ally of ignorance

Reprinted from the *University of Chicago Law Review*, 30 (Spring, 1963), pp. 423–449.

in impeding understanding of these areas. Because strong ideological differences separate the proponents and opponents of economic regulation, judgments about the effect of penal sanctions in achieving compliance tend to turn upon judgments about the merits of the substantive regulation. Liberally oriented social scientists, otherwise critical of the case made for the deterrent and vindicatory uses of punishment of ordinary offenders, may be found supporting stern penal enforcement against economic violators.[2] At the same time conservative groups, rarely foes of rigorous punishment for ordinary offenders, appear less sanguine for the criminal prosecution when punishment of business offenders is debated.[3]

This statement of the underdeveloped state of the art is by no means designed as an introduction to an ambitious effort to close the ancient gap in understanding. Quite the contrary, it is meant rather to excuse the modest ambit of these observations. What I would like to accomplish is to outline the special characteristics of economic regulatory legislation relevant to the use of the criminal sanction, to indicate what implications they have for effective use of the criminal law, and to suggest relevant concerns in the use of this sanction beyond the goal of enforcing the specific regulatory norm.

# I

The kind of economic regulations whose enforcement through the criminal sanction is the subject of this inquiry may be briefly stated: those which impose restrictions upon the conduct of business as part of a considered economic policy. This includes such laws as price-control and rationing laws, antitrust laws, and other legislation designed to protect or promote competition or prevent unfair competition, export controls, small-loan laws, securities regulations, and, perhaps, some tax laws. Put to one side, therefore, are regulations directly affecting business conduct that are founded on interests other than economic ones; for example, laws regulating the conduct of business in the interest of public safety and general physical welfare. Also to one side are laws indirectly affecting business conduct by their general applicability; for example, embezzlement, varieties of fraud, and related white-collar offenses.

The class of regulations so defined possesses several characteristics that have a direct bearing upon the uses and limits of the criminal sanction as a means of achieving compliance. The first is the very feature suggested as the identifying characteristic of such legislation; that is, the nature of the interest protected. Certainly the use of criminal sanctions to protect interests of an economic character is not a contemporary departure. The extension of the classic larceny offense by courts and legislatures to embrace fraud, embezzlement, and similar varieties of misappropriation that threatened newly developing ways of transacting business is a well-documented chapter in the history of the criminal law.[4] Indeed, the process continues today.[5] But there is an important difference between the traditional and expanded property offenses and the newer economic regulatory offenses, a difference reflecting the shift from an economic order that rested on maximum freedom for the private entrepreneur to one committed to restraints upon that freedom. The traditional property offenses protect private property interests against the acquisitive behavior of others in the furtherance of free private decision.[6] The newer offenses, on the other hand, seek to protect the economic order of the community against harmful use by the individual of his property interest. The central purpose, therefore, is to control private choice, rather than to free it. But the control imposed (and this too has significance) is not total, as it would be in a socialistic system. Private economic self-determination has not been abandoned in favor of a wholly state-regulated economy. Indeed, the ideal of free enterprise is maintained, the imposed regulations being regarded as necessary to prevent that ideal from consuming itself. Whether the criminal sanction may safely and effectively be used in the service of implementing the large-scale economic policies underlying regulatory legislation of this kind raises fundamental questions.

A second relevant feature of these laws concerns the nature of the conduct restrained. Since it is not criminal under traditional categories of crime and, apart from the regulatory proscription, closely resembles acceptable aggressive business behavior, the stigma of moral reprehensibility does not naturally associate itself with the regulated conduct.[7] Moreover, the conduct is engaged in by persons of relatively high social and economic status; since it is motivated by economic considerations, it is calculated and deliberate rather than reactive; it is usually part of a pattern of business conduct rather than episodic in character; and it often involves group action through the corporate form.

The third noteworthy attribute of this legislation is the role provided for the criminal sanction in the total scheme of enforcement. Typically, the criminal penalty is only one of a variety of authorized sanctions which may include monetary settlements, private actions (compensatory or penal), injunctions, inspections, licensing, required reporting, or others. Its role, therefore, is largely ancillary and takes either or both of two forms. On the one hand, the criminal penalty may serve as a means to insure the functioning of other sanctions, as, for example, penalties for operating without a license or without prior registration or reporting. On the other hand, the criminal sanction may serve as a separate and supplementary mode of enforcement by directly prohibiting the conduct sought to be prevented, as in the Sherman Antitrust Act. Furthermore, implicit in the legislative scheme is the conception of the criminal sanction as a last resort to be used selectively and discriminatingly when other sanctions fail. In some legislation, of course, the message of selective enforcement is explicit in the law. Finally, the responsibility for investigation, detection, and initiating prosecution is often vested in a specialized agency or other body rather than left with the usual institutions for policing and prosecuting criminal violations. Moreover, these bodies commonly are not specialized organs of criminal enforcement, but are the agencies broadly charged with administering the legislative scheme.

This statement of the relevant features of the laws under inquiry, in terms of the interest protected, the behavior regulated, and the contemplated role of the criminal penalty, is not meant to suggest that these laws are ultimately unique in the problems they raise for criminal enforcement. Apart from the nature of the interest protected, most, if not all, of these characteristics may be found in other areas of the criminal law. And even though the nature of the interest protected is by definition unique, many of the problems it poses, such as making morally neutral behavior criminal, are common to other areas as well. All that is suggested is that if one asks, "What problems are raised for the effective use of the criminal sanction as a mode of achieving compliance in this area?" the beginnings of an answer are to be found in these congeries of characteristics. It remains now to suggest what bearing they have.

II

I propose to deal with the relevance of these characteristics in terms of three major problems: the problem of defining the proscribed conduct, the problem of corporate criminality and the problem of moral neutrality.

*The Problem of Defining the Proscribed Conduct.* The fact that the protected interest is the preferred functioning of the economic system and entails only partial restriction upon the operation of American business bears directly upon the task of defining the proscribed behavior with sufficient specificity to meet the requirement of fair notice generally applicable to criminal legislation. Where the criminal sanction is used to police other enforcement devices (as, for example, when it becomes criminal to market a security issue without registration or to do business without a license), the standard is met without difficulty. But the requirement of specificity is notably difficult of fulfillment where the crime itself purports to define the substantive economic behavior sought to be avoided. A notable example is the Sherman Antitrust Act's prohibition of "restraint of trade or commerce" and "illegal monopolization." Only to a small degree, if at all, is the difficulty remediable by better draftsmanship. As Thurman Arnold observed, "Antitrust policy touches fields and boundaries which recede as you approach them and disappear each time you try to stake them out."[8] The reason for this arises from several sources: First, the economic policy is itself unclear, constituting largely a vague aspiration for a proper balance among competing economic goals.[9] Second, illegality must turn on judgments that are essentially evaluative in character, rather than upon purely factual determinations. Third, the inevitable development of novel circumstances and arrangements in the dynamic areas under regulation would soon make precise formulations obsolete, even to the limited extent they proved feasible. . . .[10]

The requirement in an otherwise unconstitutionally vague definition of criminal conduct that the defendant must be shown to have acted willfully or knowingly has sometimes been held to remedy the defect of definition. Thus the Supreme Court found no unfairness in convicting a motor company for failing to reroute their explosive-laden truck "as far as practical, and where feasible" to avoid congested areas, where it was necessary to prove that this was done "knowingly"[11] or in convicting a taxpayer for attempting to evade taxes by making "unreasonable" deductions for commissions paid to stockholders as compensation for service, where the action was taken "willfully."[12] A requirement that the defendant have intentionally committed the act with a full and correct understanding of the factual circumstances is of no help to a defendant faced with an unclear definition of the conduct forbidden. On the other hand, however vague the line between what is permissible and what is criminal, where the actor is aware that his conduct falls squarely within the forbidden zone he is in no position to complain.[13] "A mind intent upon willful evasion is inconsistent with surprised innocence."[14] Apparently, therefore, it is *scienter* in this sense, that is, knowledge by the actor that he is violating the law, which is held in these cases to eliminate the vagueness problem. Yet this premise probably affords defenses to a larger group than intended, since a defendant who knew nothing of the existence of the law would be in as good a position as one who did not know that his action came within its terms.[15] If the prosecution must prove that the defendant knew his conduct fell within the terms of the law, it could hardly do so without proof as well that he knew of its existence. A legislature, however, could presumably resolve the semantic impasse by making it a defense that the defendant did not know his acts fell within its terms or perhaps, more narrowly, that he could not reasonably know it, though not a defense simply that he did not know of the law's existence.

Another approach to mitigating the difficulties of a vague formulation is through administrative choice of cases to prosecute. If the enforcement agency initiates criminal prosecution solely where the meaning of the statute has become acceptably clear through judicial interpretation, the unfairness of the original unclarity may be thought adequately reduced. An example is the announced policy of the Department of Justice to institute criminal prosecutions for Sherman Antitrust Act violations only where there is a per se violation, such as price fixing, a violation accompanied by a specific intent to restrain competition or monopolize, the use of predatory practices, or where the defendant has before been convicted of a Sherman Antitrust Act violation. This approach, unlike the legislative requirement of *scienter*, is of no avail where the vagueness of the statutory formulation renders the law constitutionally unenforceable. It is also dependent upon the existence of means other than criminal prosecutions to develop clarifying interpretation. In the Sherman Antitrust Act this is provided through the civil suit as a parallel means of enforcing the identical standard of conduct. This, in turn, however, may be a mixed blessing. One of the purposes of looseness and generality in the formulation of the standard is to create a flexibility that will allow judicial interpretation to keep pace with the changes in the character of the area under regulation. Courts may prove understandably reluctant to sustain expansive, although desirable, interpretations where the consequence will be to subject defendants to criminal as well as civil sanctions.

There are several alternatives to civil litigation as a means of producing clarifying interpretation. The most obvious is to delegate to the responsible administrative agency the authority to issue so-called "legislative regulations" in implementation of the statutory scheme. Providing criminal penalties for violations of these regulations then eliminates the vagueness problem to the extent of the clarity of the regulation. There is still, to be sure, a requirement of some specificity in the legislative standard from which the agency derives its authority. But this raises the different, though related, issue of delegation of powers, where requirements of specificity are considerably less than those applicable to criminal statutes. The declaratory order, in which the agency renders an advisory judgment on the legality of a contemplated course of action, is another possibility. This has utility both in providing further clarification of the applicability of regulations and in rendering interpretive guidance of the law when it, rather than a regulation, is the direct source of the prohibition. Section 5 of the Administrative Procedure Act provides a precedent for such an order, although the use authorized therein is considerably more limited than it might be.

Still another alternative is flatly to prohibit certain kinds of activity, except where an administrative agency, interpreting and applying general legislative standards, expressly allows it, as by issuing a license. The criminal penalty may then be imposed for the clearly defined offense of engaging in the activity without authorization. This, of course, is to use the criminal sanction, as previously suggested, as a means of enforcing another, noncriminal sanction. It is readily usable in such narrow areas as marketing securities or engaging in other particular types of business. It is impractical where the thrust of the prohibition goes to ways of conducting any and all kinds of business, as in the Sherman Act.

*The Problem of Corporate Criminality.* Conduct reached by economic regulatory legislation is typically group conduct often engaged in through the corporate form. This raises the formidable issue of corporate criminality. From the legislative viewpoint, the principal questions are twofold. First, what difficulties beset enforcement agencies in affixing criminal liability upon responsible actors where the principal violator is the corporation? Second, in any event, what are the possibilities of effective enforcement through the imposition of criminal penalties upon the corporation itself?

Fixing criminal liability upon the immediate actors within a corporate structure generally poses no special problem. But the immediate actors may be lower echelon officials or employees who are the tools rather than the responsible originators of the violative conduct. Where the corporation is managed by its owners, the task of identifying the policy formulators is not acute. But where the stock of the corporation is widely held, the organization complex and sprawling, and the responsibility spread over a maze of departments and divisions, then there may be conspicuous difficulties in pinpointing responsibility on the higher echelon policy-making officials.[16] The source of the difficulty is the conventional requirement that to hold one person criminally liable for the acts of another he must have participated in the acts of the other in some meaningful way, as by directing or encouraging them, aiding in their commission, or permitting them to be done by subordinates whom he has power to control. The difficulty is exemplified in the now famous antitrust prosecution of the electrical equipment manufacturers. Here the high policy makers of General Electric and other companies involved escaped personal accountability for a criminal conspiracy of lesser officials that extended over several years to the profit of the corporations, despite the belief of the trial judge and most observers that these higher officials either knew of and condoned these activities or were willfully ignorant of them.[17]

It cannot be known to what extent this legal obstacle to convicting the policy initiators actually reduces the efficacy of the criminal sanction in achieving compliance. Certainly, it would prove more significant in those areas, like antitrust, where giant corporations are the principal targets of the law, than in areas where they are not. But other factors may be more influential in preventing widescale successful prosecution of individual corporate officials under the antitrust laws; for example, there have been strikingly few convictions of corporate officials, even of officials of closely held corporations and the lesser officials of large, public corporations.

At all events, one means of reducing the difficulty would be to alter by statute the basis of accountability of corporate directors, officers, or agents. An amendment, for example, of the antitrust law was recently proposed which would have changed the present basis of accountability (that such persons "shall have authorized, ordered or done" the acts) to make it suffice that the individual had knowledge or reason to know of the corporate violation and failed to exercise his authority to stop or prevent it. This falls short of outright vicarious liability, since accountability is made to turn on fault in not knowing and acting rather than on a relationship simpliciter. Essentially it makes a negligent omission the basis of accountability. Still, a standard of accountability resting on precisely how much the far-flung operations of a nationwide corporation an official should reasonably be aware of approaches vicarious liability in its indeterminateness, since neither the common experience of the jury nor even specialized experience affords substantial guidance. In effect, it introduces an element of uncertainty concerning accountability into laws that often, like the Sherman Antitrust Act, are already marked by uncertainty concerning the conduct forbidden. . . .

Fixing criminal liability upon the corporation itself has posed fewer legal obstacles in the enforcement of regulatory legislation. The earlier conceptual difficulties of ascribing criminal intent to a fictitious entity have been largely removed by the developing law. And whatever doubt may exist is readily met by expressly providing for corporate liability in the regulatory statute. But the problem of corporate accountability—that is, when the entity is liable for conduct of its agents at various levels of responsibility—is analogous to the problem of holding corporate officials accountable for the acts of lesser agents. It has been resolved more sweepingly in the case of the entity. For acts of its high managerial agents, it is, by definition, accountable since a corporation cannot act by itself. For the acts of its lesser agents, the tendency has been, at least in the regulatory offenses, to hold the corporation accountable for the acts of employees within the scope of their employment or while acting as employees. Whether the consequential imposition of vicarious responsibility upon the corporate entity, as well as upon shareholders, is justified raises the question of the deterrent efficacy of convicting and fining the corporate entity.

The case for corporate criminality rests presumably upon the inadequacy of the threat of personal conviction upon the individual actors. As said earlier, difficulties of proof under legal principles of accountability have interfered with effective prosecution of high corporate officials. And the commonly observed jury behavior of convicting the corporate defendant while acquitting the individual defendants, even where proof is apparently strong, further supports the case for the alternate sanction. Moreover, "there are probably cases in which the economic pressures within the corporate body are sufficiently potent to tempt individuals to hazard personal liability for the sake of company gain, especially where the penalties threatened are moderate and where the offense does not involve behavior condemned as highly immoral by the individual's associates."[18]

Yet the question remains of the effectiveness of corporate criminality as a supplementary deterrent.

The only two practically available modes of imposing criminal sanctions upon the corporate defendant are through the stigma of conviction and the exaction of a fine. The former, classified by Bentham as the "moral or popular" sanction, operates, as he suggested, through the adverse reactions to the conviction of persons in the community.[19] Whether there is any substantial moral opprobrium attached to violation of economic regulatory legislation (even where individuals are convicted) I defer until later. Assuming there is, can it be said to have any appreciable significance when directed to a corporate entity? There is no substantial empirical basis for answering this question.[20] It seems unlikely that whatever moral stigma may attach to a convicted corporation would be felt in any effectual way by the corporate individuals, especially in large corporations where responsibility is diffused. On the other hand, the point has been made[21] (though denied as well)[22] that the corporate stigma may operate as a deterrent by impairing the reputation of the corporation in its business operations and hence adversely affecting its economic position. Until there is more to go on, one can only guess at the validity of this observation, though there is reason to expect that the impact of the conviction would operate differentially, depending on the size of the corporation, the extent of competition and the dominance of its market position, the degree to which its conviction attracted public notice, and the like.

The exaction of a corporate fine serves in part to give color to the moral stigma of conviction. Insofar as this is its role, its value depends upon the existence and power of the stigma to deter. On the other hand, the use of the corporate fine apart from the stigma of conviction raises no issue peculiar to the criminal sanction, since civil fines afford identical deterrent possibilities. Whether it would prove effective to increase the economic hazard of misconduct by authorizing higher fines than those now commonly authorized depends on such considerations as the general ability of the corporation to recoup its losses through its pricing policy and the likelihood that courts would impose the higher fines. An alternative recently proposed would substitute for the fine a governmental proceeding designed to compel the corporation to disgorge the profits attributable to its violation. These alternatives raise substantial questions concerning sanctions, but not the criminal sanction, strictly speaking.

*The Problem of Moral Neutrality.* Viewed in the large, the characteristic of the conduct typically proscribed by economic regulatory legislation most relevant for the purposes of criminal enforcement is that it is calculated and deliberative and directed to economic gain.[23] It would appear, therefore, to constitute a classic case for the operation of the deterrent strategy. Nonetheless, it is a widely shared view that the strategy has not worked out in fact, that the criminal sanction has not proved a major weapon for achieving compliance. Part of the explanation may be attributable to the difficulties of enforcement suggested above, such as the resistance to vaguely defined standards of criminality, the difficulty of fixing culpability upon high corporate officials, and the muffled and absorbable impact of corporate criminal sanctions. But it is likely that other factors play a more dominant role.

A common explanation of the failure of the criminal sanction is simply that the powerful business interests affected do not want these laws enforced and employ their power and position in American life to block vigorous enforcement. Influence is exercised over the legislatures to keep enforcement staffs impoverished and sanctions safely inefficacious. Enforcement officials, as prospective counsel for business interests, and judges, as former counsel, identify with these interests and resist criminal enforcement. Moreover, news media, under the control of these same groups, work to create hostility to these laws and their vigorous enforcement and sympathy for the violators. In short, "those who are responsible for the system of criminal justice are afraid to antagonize businessmen. . . . The most powerful group in medieval society secured relative immunity from punishment by 'benefit of clergy,' and now our most powerful group secures relative immunity by 'benefit of business.' "[24]

It would be dogmatic to assert that influences of this kind do not exist, but it may be doubted that they play a dispositive role. Business surely constitutes a powerful interest group in American life; but the profusion of regulatory legislation over the ardent protests of important economic interests in the past thirty years is some evidence that it is not all-powerful. Opposing forces have been able to marshal considerable public sentiment against a variety of business practices. Moreover, it is perhaps an oversimplification to identify all business as united in monolithic opposition. There is less a single business interest than a substantial variety of business interests. What then, in addition to business propaganda and influence, has accounted for the failure of the criminal sanction? Or, if we must have a villain, how has it been that business, which has not always gotten its way, has been this successful in devitalizing the use of that sanction?

It is a plausible surmise that the explanation is implicated in another feature of the behavior regulated by these laws; namely, that it is not generally regarded as morally reprehensible in the common view, that, indeed, in some measure it is the laws themselves that appear bad or, at least, painful necessities, and that the violators by and large turn out to be respectable people in the respectable pursuit of profit. It is not likely that these popular attitudes are wholly products of a public-relations campaign by the affected business community. The springs of the public sentiment reach into the national ethos, producing the values that the man of business himself holds, as well as the attitude of the public toward him and his activities. Typically, the conduct prohibited by economic regulatory laws is not immediately distinguishable from modes of business behavior that are not only socially acceptable, but also affirmatively desirable in an economy founded upon an ideology (not denied by the regulatory regime itself) of free enterprise and the profit motive. Distinctions there are, of course, between salutary entrepreneurial practices and those which threaten the values of the very regime of economic freedom. And it is possible to reason convincingly that the harms done to the economic order by violations of many of these regulatory laws are of a magnitude that dwarf in significance the lower-class property offenses. But the point is that these perceptions require distinguishing and reasoning processes that are not the normal governors of the passion of moral disapproval, and they are not dramatically obvious to a public long conditioned to responding approvingly to the production of profit through business shrewdness, especially in the absence of live and visible victims. Moreover, in some areas, notably the antitrust laws, it is far from clear that there is consensus even by the authors and enforcers of the regulation—the legislators, courts and administrators—on precisely what should be prohibited and what permitted, and the reasons therefor. And as Freund observed, "If a law declares a practice to be criminal, and cannot apply its policy with consistency, its moral effect is necessarily weakened."[25]

The consequences of the absence of sustained public moral resentment for the effective use of the criminal sanction may be briefly stated. The central distinguishing aspect of the criminal sanction appears to be the stigmatization of the morally culpable.[26] At least, it tends so to be regarded in the community. Without moral culpability, there is in a democratic community an explicable and justifiable reluctance to affix the stigma of blame. [27] This perhaps is the basic explanation, rather than the selfish machinations of business interests, for the reluctance of administrators and prosecutors to invoke the criminal sanction, the reluctance of jurors to find guilt, and the reluctance of judges to impose strong penalties. And beyond its effect on enforcement, the absence of moral opprobrium interferes in another more subtle way with achieving compliance. Fear of being caught and punished does not exhaust the deterrent mechanism of the criminal law. It is supplemented by the personal disinclination to act in violation of the law's commands, apart from immediate fear of being punished. One would suppose that especially in the cast of those who normally regard themselves as respectable, proper, and law-abiding the appeal to act in accordance with conscience is relatively great. But where the violation is not generally regarded as ethically reprehensible, either by the community at large or by the class of businessmen itself, the private appeal to conscience is at its minimum and being convicted and fined may have little more impact than a bad selling season.[28]

Are there modes of dealing with these consequences of making morally neutral behavior criminal? A commonly suggested remedy for inadequate enforcement is a campaign of strict enforcement aided by strengthened prosecution staffs and, perhaps, more severe penalties. But to the extent that the deficiency in enforcement is attributable to the moral inoffensiveness of the behavior, the major limitation of such a call to arms is that it is addressed to the symptom rather than the cause. How will legislatures be convinced to expend substantial sums for criminal enforcement or prosecutors to go for the jugular or courts and juries to cooperate in the face of a fundamental lack of sympathy for the criminal penalty in this area? Enlarged resources for prosecution may well afford staff enthusiasts an opportunity for more vigorous enforcement, but one may doubt that it can achieve more than a minor flurry of enforcement.[29]

An attack on the cause, insofar as moral neutrality is the cause, would presumably require a two-pronged program: one directed at the obstacle of popular nullification; the other at inculcating the sentiment of moral disapproval in the community. Each, of course, would inevitably have an effect upon the other. The former might proceed, not simply by allocating greater enforcement resources, but by arrangements that would reduce the traditional discretionary authority of the various bodies involved in criminal law enforcement. For example, the decision to prosecute might be exclusively centered in the agency responsible for the whole regulatory program; conservative legal interpretation might be dealt with by authorizing agency-interpretative regulations which are made relevant in criminal prosecutions; the temporizing of juries might be avoided by eliminating, where possible, jury trials; the judge's sentencing discretion might be curtailed by mandatory minimum penalties. There is, of course, the substantial task of persuading legislatures to abjure the traditional mediating institutions of the criminal law in an area where, the moral factor's being largely absent, they might be thought to have their historic and most useful function to perform. But if enacted, one might reasonably suppose that such legal arrangements could result in a somewhat more frequent and rigorous use of the criminal sanction and a heightening of the deterrent effect of the law.

The other prong of the program, the cultivation of the sentiment of moral disapproval, is perhaps closer to the heart of the matter. To some extent, the more frequent enforcement and the more stringent punishment of violators may tend to serve this objective, as well as its more direct in terrorem purposes, especially where cases are selected for enforcement with this end in view.[30] Whether a governmentally mounted campaign should be employed as well to give widespread publicity to successful convictions and to shape the public conscience in other ways may be questioned from various viewpoints, but it surely would be consistent with the basic strategy of using criminal sanctions in these areas.

How effective a campaign of selected prosecutions and attendant publicity would prove in creating a changed climate is problematical. Certainly one can not confidently deny that the spectacle of frequent conviction and severe punishment may play a role in molding the community's attitudes toward the conduct in question. Experience offers uncertain guidance. Tax evasion has a history that provides some support. We have come a considerable distance, though not all the way,[31] from the day when an English judge could observe from the bench, "there is not behind taxing laws, as there is behind laws against crime, an independent moral obligation."[32] The change was accompanied in this country by a gradual tightening of the criminal sanction. In 1924, tax evasion was upgraded from a misdemeanor to a felony and maximum imprisonment raised from one to five years; reforms in 1952 converted the criminal prosecution from a tax recovery device and weapon against the professional racketeer to a means of general deterrence of tax evasion by widespread and selected enforcement against all levels of violators.[33] While the tax evasion prosecution is still something of a special case, the record of successful prosecution has become genuinely impressive and the tax-evasion conviction a sanction of some consequence. Experience such as this, however, gives little more than support for the plainly plausible assumption that criminal enforcement may play some part. One can not be sure of the extent to which other factors, not necessarily present in areas other than tax, created the conditions for optimum use of the criminal sanction as a moralizing weapon or, indeed, of the extent to which other influences rather than, or in addition to, the criminal sanction, produced the changed climate. . . .

III

I have reserved for last those issues and concerns that arise out of goals other than the effectiveness of the criminal sanction in achieving compliance. Those which most prominently compete for consideration are, first, the sentiment of fundamental fairness—in a word, justice; and, second, the retention of the vitality of the criminal law in its traditional sphere of application. They come into play in connection with two aspects of the use of the criminal law to enforce economic regulatory laws; namely, the loosening of minimum requirements for culpability in the cause of enforcement efficiency and the criminalizing and punishing of behavior that does not generally attract the sentiment of moral reprobation.

*Requirements of Culpability.* At several points, attention has been called to the obstacles to effective prosecution created by certain conventional requirements of the criminal law; for example, the requirement of specificity in defining the prohibited conduct and the requirement of minimum conditions of accountability in holding persons responsible for the acts of others. Whatever basis these requirements have in the area of traditional crime, may they properly be diluted or dispensed with in the area of economic regulatory crime? The issue is fundamentally the same as that posed by the use of strict criminal liability, though, interestingly enough, this appears to have been much less commonly employed in economic regulation than in those controls on business directed to public health and safety.

The case for the irrelevance of these traditional requirements is reflected in the observation of a trust-buster of an earlier generation: "The rights of the accused, which are of the utmost importance where liberty of an individual is in jeopardy, are irrelevant symbols when the real issue is the arrangement under which corporations in industry compete."[34] In essence, the concept is that the purpose behind the criminal sanction in this area is not penalization, but regulation. Unlike the area of conventional crime against person and property, where criminalization serves to reassure the community, to express condemnation, and to set in motion a corrective or restraining regime, as well as to deter proscribed behavior, here the concern is solely with this last factor. "[T]he problem of responsibility is not the general social phenomenon of moral delinquency and guilt, but the practical problem of dealing with physical conditions and social or economic practices that are to be controlled."[35]

A countervailing consideration commonly adduced in discussions of strict liability is equally applicable where culpability requirements are otherwise withdrawn by statutes that do not adequately announce what is prohibited or that impose varieties of vicarious responsibility. Absent these requirements, it cannot be said except in a strictly formal sense that the actor made a choice to commit the acts prohibited. Hence, it is said that the law has no deterrent function to perform, offering no lesson to the actor or to other persons beyond the Pickwickian instruction that even if he does the best he can or anyone could to comply with the law, he may nonetheless be punished. Yet the argument does not quite persuade, for it may as plausibly be argued that the consequence of dispensing with the requirement of proof of culpability eases the task of the enforcing authorities, rendering successful prosecution more likely and, by discouraging insistence on trial and simplifying the issues when trials are held, enhances the efficiency of prosecution. In a word, certainty of conviction is increased. This may readily exert an added deterrent force upon the actor faced with a choice, since the chances of escaping punishment for a culpable choice, intentional or negligent, are decreased. And even where there is no immediate choice, the effect could sometimes be to influence persons to arrange their affairs to reduce to a minimum the possibilities of accidental violation; in short, to exercise extraordinary care.

Further, the persistent use of such laws by legislatures and their strong support by persons charged with their enforcement make it dogmatic to insist they can not deter in these ways.

Closer, perhaps, to the core of the opposition to dispensing with culpability is the principle that it is morally improper and ultimately unsound and self-defeating to employ penal sanctions with respect to conduct that does not warrant the moral condemnation that is implicit, or that should be implicit, in the concept of a crime. The issue is whether these considerations are adequately dealt with by the contention that laws dispensing with culpability are directed to regulation rather than penalization.

The contention plainly proves too much. If the sole concern is a nonreprobative deterrent threat, then it follows that the sanction should be drastic and certain enough to overcome the motive of economic gain, and not necessarily that the sanction should be criminal. Civil fines, punitive damages, injunctions, profit-divestiture programs, or other varieties of noncriminal sanctions would thus appear to offer equivalent possibilities of enforcing the regulatory scheme. Indeed, these alternatives might enhance the possibilities, since proof and evidentiary requirements are more onerous in criminal prosecutions than in civil suits. The conclusion appears difficult to resist that insistence on the criminal penalty is attributable to a desire to make use of the unique deterrent mode of the criminal sanction, the stigma of moral blame that it carries. If so, the argument of regulation rather than penalization turns out in the end to be only a temporary diversion that does not escape the need to confront the basic issue: the justice and wisdom of imposing a stigma of moral blame in the absence of blameworthiness in the actor.

So far as the issue of justice is concerned, once having put the moral question the footing becomes unsteady. Is the moral difficulty inconsequential, requiring simply the side-stepping of an otherwise useful symbol that happens to stand in the way of attaining immediately desirable goals? Does it yield to a pragmatic evaluation in terms of an estimate of the soundness of departing from principle to some degree in particular cases in order to attain goals of greater consequence?[36] Does it present an insuperable objection entailing commitment to values of such profundity that compromise is unthinkable? For present purposes it is perhaps enough to put the questions, though three points may be suggested: First, the starkness of the moral issue is to some degree assuaged by regarding laws dispensing with culpability as empowering enforcement officials to use their discretion to select for prosecution those who have in their judgment acted culpably. Plainly, however, the issue is not escaped since it remains to justify dispensing with the safeguards of trial on this single and crucial issue. Second, the recognition of the moral impasse does not necessarily require agreement that the criminal *law* should use its weapons for the purpose of fixing moral obloquy upon transgressors. It is sufficient that it is broadly characteristic of the way criminal conviction operates in our society. Third, and in consequence, the moral difficulty exists only so long as and to the extent that criminal conviction retains its aura of moral condemnation. The impasse lessens to the extent that the element of blame and punishment is replaced by a conception of the criminal process as a means of social improvement through a program of morally neutral rehabilitation and regulation. (Though such a development has important implications which I mean to return to shortly.)

Concerning the issue of ultimate wisdom, the point frequently made respecting strict liability is equally applicable to the dilution of these aspects of culpability typically at issue in economic regulatory legislation. The dilution is not readily confined within the narrow area for which it was designed, but tends to overflow into the main body of conventional crimes. The distinction between offenses that regulate and those that penalize in the traditional sense proves inadequate to divide the waters. For example, traditional concepts of liability in the main body of criminal law tend to receive a new and diluted form when construed as part of a regulatory statute. Moreover, the habituation of courts and legislatures to crimes dispensing with culpability in the regulatory area may readily dull legislative and judicial sensitivity to the departures from minimum culpability requirements already fixed in the main body of the criminal law. . . .

*The Criminalization of Morally Neutral Conduct.* But let it be assumed that the traditional grounds of culpability have been adhered to so that the defendant can fairly be held accountable for a choice to violate the economic prohibition. May there be costs, even so, in terms of principle and other goals, in employing the criminal sanction where the violative behavior does not attract in the community the moral disapprobation associated with a criminal conviction? How different and how similar are the considerations involved in dispensing with culpability? The question is the obverse of an aspect of the relation between criminal law and morals which has been much considered—the use of the criminal law to prohibit and condemn behavior that is widely (either actually or formally) viewed as morally reprehensible, where secular interests, in the sense of concerns beyond the immorality of individuals, do not exist.[37] Here the issue is the use of the criminal sanction to prohibit and condemn behavior that threatens secular interests, but that is not regarded as fundamentally and inherently wrong.

The central consequence of diluting or eliminating requirements of culpability is, as suggested, the criminalization and punishment of persons who cannot be said to warrant the condemnation thereby imported. It is this consequence that gives rise to the hard question of principle and practical consequences. In a sense a similar consequence follows from punishing conduct that is not itself blameworthy, even when culpably engaged in: Persons are stigmatized with conviction for conduct not regarded as deserving the moral stigma. The problem of principle, however, is of considerably smaller dimension, since the choice to act in defiance of the criminal prohibition may be regarded as in some measure furnishing an independently adequate ground for condemnation. (Yet it is necessary to add that the ground exists only in cases where the culpability requirements are extended to include knowledge or culpable disregard of the existence of the prohibition, an extension only occasionally made in regulatory legislation.)

The danger of debilitating the moral impact of the criminal conviction and hence decreasing the overall effectiveness of the criminal law can not readily be put aside. As Henry Hart has noted, "The criminal law always loses face if things are declared to be crimes which people believe they ought to be free to do, even willfully."[38] It may be mitigated to a degree by maintaining a proper proportion in the punishment authorized for various offenses in accordance with the moral culpability of the behavior. The limitations of such a strategy are, first, that there is always a strong pressure to raise authorized penalties when violations become widespread or conspicuous and, second, that there is an irreducible minimum in the moral condemnation comported by conviction of crime. Such considerations have led one observer to "decry the trend toward an increasingly undiscriminating employment of this branch of the law, and to repudiate the suggestion that criminal law should be applied more extensively in the areas of ordinary economic relationships."[39]

Of course, it may be answered that the conviction of violators of laws of this character serves as a means of moral instruction to the community; in short, that the onus of conviction is transferred to the behavior prohibited. That there will be a transference would appear quite likely, but that it should necessarily or generally be expected to involve imparting moral onus to the behavior rather than moral indifference to the conviction is considerably less so. The more widely the criminal conviction is used for this purpose and the less clear the immorality of the behavior so sanctioned, the more likely would it appear that the criminal conviction will not only fail to attain the immediate purpose of its use, but will degenerate in effectiveness for other purposes as well.

There is another cost not paralleled in the dilution of culpability requirements. The behavior under discussion involves restraints upon the free operation of business without at the same time denying commitment to a free enterprise system. The demarcation of the line between the legitimate, indeed the affirmatively desirable, and the illegitimate in business conduct is continually in flux and subject to wide controversy in the community. To say there is no complete consensus on what business decisions should be regulated and what left free of regulation is to say what is minimally true. It would not follow from this that a legislature should abstain from enacting such controls as command a majority. But the appropriateness of the criminal sanction as a means of enforcing the imposed control is another matter. I have already suggested that the criminal remedy in this situation tends to be ineffective and destructive of its overall utility as a sanctioning device. Here the point is different. To the extent it is effective in generating strong moral commitments to the regulatory regime it supports, it has the dangerous potential of introducing a rigidification of values too soon, of cutting off the debate, or at least restricting the ease of movement to new positions and a new consensus.[40] This seems to me the wisdom of Allen's caveat that "the function of the criminal law in these areas is not to anticipate but to reflect and implement the consensus already achieved in the community."[41]

A word in conclusion on lines of legislative action. The widescale abandonment of the criminal sanction in those areas where its cost is excessive is as unlikely as it is desirable. Legislative habit and the simple logic of here-and-now expediency have a compulsion not to be denied by contemplation of long-range consequences in areas removed from the immediate target of legislative concern. A more acceptable and hence more fruitful course is the development of means of reducing the costs of the use of the criminal sanction in economic regulations, which do not demand that it be abandoned altogether. If such means exist, one would expect they would be found in ways of dealing with the central fact principally responsible for the predicament, the irreducible core of condemnation in a criminal conviction. One possible approach is to institutionalize a system of gradation of convictions, just as systems of grading punishment have long been a part of the law. There is no adequate basis for accomplishing this under present law. The distinction between offenses *mala prohibita* and *mala in se* carries something of the flavor, but it is an informal rather than an institutionalized distinction and lacks any clear meaning. The felony-misdemeanor distinction has an established statutory basis. However, the categories have largely lost significance in distinguishing degrees of blameworthiness, some misdemeanors embracing crimes of serious moral import and some felonies embracing relatively minor transgressions. Moreover, there is need for a category of offense carrying considerably less weight than a misdemeanor. The petty-offense category, which appears in many statutes, is essentially a petty misdemeanor, retaining its label as a crime and being punishable with imprisonment. In those cases in which the label has been removed, the substance (that is, provision for imprisonment) has not. The Model Penal Code has attempted to meet the inadequacies of existing law by adding to its three categories of crime (felonies, misdemeanors, and petty misdemeanors) a separate noncriminal category designated a "violation," which is punishable only by a sentence of fine (under $500 or any higher amount equal to double the pecuniary gain made by the offender) or civil penalty and which does not "give rise to any disability or legal disadvantage based on conviction of a criminal offense." The design of this proposal "reflects the purpose of the code to employ penal sanctions only with respect to conduct warranting the moral condemnation implicit in the concept of a crime." Since strict liability even for crimes properly so regarded presents the same problem, the same solution is applied by treating crimes committed without culpability as "violations."

While the idea is novel in American law, German law has for some years adopted an approach similar to that proposed by the Model Penal Code. Separate from a three-level classification of crimes, properly so called (*Straftat*), is another category of offense, the "regulatory violation" (*Ordnungswidrigkeit*). These regulatory violations are not punishable by imprisonment. A fine is the sole available sanction, indeed a fine which bears a special designation (*Geldbusse*, literally "monetary repentance") as opposed to the penal fine (*Geldstrafe*, literally "monetary punishment"). These fines are not registered in the punishment registry and are imposed at the first instance by the responsible administrative agency subject to the right of the violator to object and to be tried in the courts.

The feasibility of using the category of regulatory violation for sanctioning economic regulation is, of course, the principal issue. Here the German experience may offer some evidence for decision. Unfortunately, there appear to be no empirical studies of the relative effectiveness of its use in Germany. But to judge from the statute books, it is the typical noncivil sanction for economic misconduct. All antitrust violations, for example, are regulatory violations, as are violations of other restrictions upon economic behavior, such as certain behavior prohibited by the foreign trade law, laws governing the operation of loan banks, laws governing the closing of shops, transportation rate laws, and other laws. Particularly suggestive is the strategy used in connection with certain kinds of economic offenses as a means of individualizing the determination of whether a defendant's behavior is to be treated as a crime or a regulatory violation. For violations of certain price-control laws, import restrictions, and unlawful overcharging, a legislative determination of the appropriate category of the offense is withheld in favor of a judicial determination in each case. The law requires an offense under these laws to be dealt with as a regulatory violation unless the nature either of the conduct or of the defendant warrants dealing with it as a crime. It is a crime when the conduct "by virtue of its scope or consequences is likely to prejudice the goals of the economic system, especially those of market or price regulations" or when the defendant is a "repeated or professional violator or acts in culpable selfishness or otherwise irresponsibly, and by his conduct shows that he lacks respect for the public interest in the protection of the economic system, especially of the market or price regulations." With all their vagueness these provisions suggest a need in any system that employs a noncriminal category of violation and uses it to deal with economic violations, for a flexible device whereby violations may, with changed public sentiment and in consideration of the extremity of the circumstances, be raised to the category of crime.

One can hardly say that this approach through a *tertium quid* is the clear answer to the problem of using criminal sanctions to enforce economic restrictions. There are many imponderables with respect to its effectiveness both as a preventive and as a means of reducing the costs of an indiscriminate use of the criminal sanction. On the side of preventive effectiveness, is the reprobative association of a genuine criminal conviction a needed weapon of enforcement? Would the semicriminal category of offense convey enough of a sense of wrongness to perform its tasks? Can these laws be enforced efficiently enough without such associations? Is the loss of the power to imprison a substantial loss? Does what is left of the criminal process still provide efficiencies not available in the pure civil remedy? Will the regulatory offense prove politically acceptable to legislators and administrators as an alternative to outright criminalization? On the side of reducing costs, how much will it help that a new label has been created so long as the criminal process is used or that imprisonment is not available as a sanction, when in fact it is rarely used anyway? And finally, is whatever is lost in effectiveness worth what is gained in other respects? One cannot be dogmatic in answering these questions. But one can, I think, insist that these are the kinds of questions which must be asked about this alternative as well as others if we are to escape the limited options inherited from different days in the use of the criminal sanction.

# Notes

1. See, for example, Jeremy Bentham, *An Introduction to the Principles of Morals and Legislation* (Oxford, 1789).

2. Harry Elmer Barnes and Negley K. Teeters, *New Horizons in Criminology*, 3d ed. (Englewood Cliffs, N.J.: Prentice-Hall, 1959), p. 43; Marshall B. Clinard, *The Black Market: A Study of White-Collar Crime* (New York: Holt, 1952), p. 243; George Bernard Shaw, *The Crime of Imprisonment* (New York: Philosophical Library, 1946), p. 34; Edwin H. Sutherland and Donald R. Cressey, *Principles of Criminology*, 5th ed. (Philadelphia: Lippincott, 1955). Feelings sometimes run high; see, for example, Edwin H. Sutherland, *White Collar Crime* (New York: Dryden Press, 1949), p. 85: "This change in the economic system from free competition to private collectivism has been produced largely by the efforts of businessmen. Although they have not acted *en masse* with a definite intention of undermining the traditional American institutions, their behavior has actually produced this result."

3. See *Wall Street Journal* (February 7, 1961).

4. For example, Jerome Hall, *Theft, Law, and Society*, 2d ed. (Indianapolis: Bobbs-Merrill, 1952).

5. Compare *People* v. *Ashley*, 42 Cal.2d 246, 267 P.2d 271 (1954), with *Chaplin* v. *United States*, 157 F.2d 697 (D.C. Circ. 1946).

6. Cf. J. Willard Hurst, *Law and the Conditions of Freedom in the Nineteenth Century* (Madison: University of Wisconsin Press, 1956), p. 21.

7. But see Sutherland, *op. cit.*, p. 45.

8. Quoted in John T. Cahill, "Must We Brand American Business by Indictment as Criminal?" in American Bar Association, Section on Antitrust Law, *Proceedings* (Chicago: American Bar Association, 1952), p. 30.

9. Robert H. Jackson and Edward Dumbauld, "Monopolies and the Courts," *University of Pennsylvania Law Review*, 86 (January, 1938), p. 237: "[I]t must be confessed that there is no consistent or intelligible policy embodied in our law by which public officials and businessmen may distinguish bona fide pursuit of industrial efficiency from an illicit program of industrial empire building." See *ibid.* at p. 232, quoting Senator Wagner: "Half of the laws enacted by Congress represent one school of thought, the other half another. No one can state authoritatively what our national policy is."

10. Hermann Mannheim, *Criminal Justice and Social Reconstruction* (London: Routledge, 1946), p. 159.

11. *Boyce Motor Lines* v. *United States*, 342 U.S. 337 (1952).

12. *United States* v. *Ragen*, 314 U.S. 513 (1942).

13. See *Screws* v. *United States*, 325 U.S. 91, 103–104 (1945).

14. *United States* v. *Ragen*, 314 U.S. 513, 524 (1942).

15. Cf. *Boyce Motor Lines* v. *United States*, 342 U.S. 337, 345 (1952) (Justice Jackson, dissenting).

16. See Richard A. Whiting, "Antitrust and the Corporate Executive," *Virginia Law Review*, 47 (October, 1961), p. 931; Alan M. Dershowitz, "Increasing Community Control over Corporate Crime," *Yale Law Journal*, 71 (December, 1961), p. 291.

17. See Myron W. Watkins, "Electrical Equipment Antitrust Cases–Their Implications for Government and for Business," *University of Chicago Law Review*, 29 (Autumn, 1961), p. 106.

18. Model Penal Code, Section 2.07, comment at pp. 148–149 (Tentative Draft No. 4, 1955).

19. Bentham, *op. cit.*, p. 25 (1907 ed.).

20. See Victor H. Kramer, "Criminal Prosecutions for Violations of the Sherman Act: In Search of a Policy," *Georgetown Law Journal*, 48 (Spring, 1960), p. 539.

21. Wolfgang Friedmann, *Law in a Changing Society* (Berkeley, Calif.: University of California Press, 1959), p. 196; Glanville Williams, *Criminal Law: The General Part*, 2d ed. (London: William Stevens, 1961), pp. 863–864.

22. Dershowitz, *op. cit.*, p. 287, fn. 5.

23. But see Robert E. Lane, "Why Business Men Violate the Law," *Journal of Criminal Law, Criminology, and Police Science*, 44 (July, 1953), pp. 151–165.

24. Sutherland, *op. cit.*, pp. 46–47.

25. Ernst Freund, *Legislative Regulation* (New York: Commonwealth Fund, 1932), p. 253.

26. See Henry M. Hart, Jr., "Aims of the Criminal Law," *Law and Contemporary Problems*, 23 (Summer, 1958), p. 404.

27. Mannheim, *op. cit.*, pp. 167–168: "Emile Durkheim has pointed out that 'the only common characteristic of all crimes is that they consist . . . in acts universally disapproved of by members of each society . . . crime shocks sentiments which, for a given social system, are found in all healthy consciences.' Although this requirement of universal disapproval may appear somewhat exaggerated, there can be no doubt that without the backing of at least the major part of the community legislation, in a democracy, must fail."

28. In his study of OPA regulation, Clinard concluded that punishment was largely ineffective beyond causing business to adopt shrewd manipulative evasions. He concluded that control required "the voluntary compliance with the regulations of society by the vast majority of the citizens." Clinard, *op. cit.*, p. 261. See also George B. Vold, *Theoretical Criminology* (New York: Oxford University Press, 1958), p. 257.

29. The short-lived Arnold era of vigorous criminal antitrust enforcement is a case in point. See Thurman Arnold, "Antitrust Law Enforcement, Past and Future," *Law and Contemporary Problems*, 7 (Winter, 1940), pp. 5–23.

30. *Cf.* OPA Manual, quoted by George H. Dession, *Criminal Law, Administration and Public Order* (Charlottesville, Va.: Michie Casebook, 1948), p. 200.

31. Congressman Thomas J. Lane of Massachusetts was convicted and imprisoned for tax evasion. He was renominated and re-elected to the House the next fall (*The New York Times* [October 17, 1962]). But having regard to Mayor Curley's experiences, Massachusetts may be a rather special case.

32. Mannheim, *op. cit.*, p. 146.

33. See Joseph H. Murphy, "Criminal Income Tax Evasion," *Northwestern University Law Review*, 48 (July–August, 1953), pp. 317–341, for a description of the reforms. As to the effects of the reforms, see Robert M. Schmidt, "Current Department of Justice Criminal Income Tax Policies," *Taxes*, 38 (April, 1960), pp. 299–311.

34. Assistant Attorney General Wendell Berge, quoted in Attorney General's National Committee to Study the Antitrust Laws, *Report* (Washington, D.C.: Government Printing Office, 1955), p. 353.

35. Freund, *op. cit.*, p. 302; Friedman, *op. cit.*, p. 198.

36. Holmes believed that the objective standard of criminal liability which disregards the personal peculiarities of the actor demonstrates that the existence of moral wrong is not a condition of punishment (Oliver Wendell Holmes, *The Common Law* [Boston: Little, Brown, 1923], p. 45). He found support for this in the proposition that "no society has ever admitted that it could not sacrifice individual welfare to its own existence" (*Ibid.*, p. 43). *Cf.* Richard A. Wasserstrom, "Strict Liability in the Criminal Law," *Stanford Law Review*, 12 (July, 1960), p. 739.

37. See the debate between Lord Devlin and Professor Hart in Patrick Devlin, *The Enforcement of Morals* (London: Oxford University Press, 1959); and H. L. A. Hart, *Law, Liberty, and Morality* (Stanford, Calif.: Stanford University Press, 1963).

38. See Hart, "Aims of the Criminal Law," *op. cit.*, p. 418.

39. Paul W. Tappan, *Crime, Justice, and Correction* (New York: McGraw-Hill, 1960), pp. 15–16. For a suggestive discussion of alternative ways of achieving favorable business sentiment, see Robert E. Lane, *The Regulation of Businessmen: Social Conditions of Government Economic Control* (New Haven, Conn.: Yale University Press, 1954), pp. 118–130.

40. The danger of the use of the criminal law to destroy a repugnant philosophy is exemplified in the revealing observation of Barnes and Teeters, *op. cit.*, p. 49: "White-collar crime flows from a competitive economy and philosophy that reveres success based almost exclusively on money. The job of the courts of justice, legislators, and a regenerated public is to wipe out this insidious philosophy before it is too late." *Cf.* Oliver Wendell Holmes, *Speeches* (Boston: Little, Brown, 1913), p. 101: "As law embodies beliefs that have triumphed in the battle of ideas and then have translated themselves into action, while there is still doubt, while opposite convictions still keep a battle front against each other, the time for law has not come; the notion destined to prevail is not yet entitled to the field."

41. Francis A. Allen, "Offenses against Property," *Annals of the American Academy of Political and Social Science*, 339 (January, 1962), p. 76.

# 21

# THE USE OF CRIMINAL SANCTIONS IN THE
# ENFORCEMENT OF ECONOMIC LEGISLATION:
# A SOCIOLOGICAL VIEW

*Harry V. Ball and*
*Lawrence M. Friedman*

Concern over the use of criminal sanctions in the enforcement of business legislation is by no means new.... Two recent prosecutions have intensified the discussion.... In *United States* v. *McDonough Co.* one president and three vice presidents of several comparatively small garden-tool manufacturing firms received ninety-day jail sentences and a fine of $5,000 for deliberate price fixing and market rigging. The defendants entered pleas of *nolo contendere*. The government felt that a fine would be "a sufficient deterring factor"; the defendants . . . [pointed] out that no jail sentence had been imposed in *nolo contendere* cases during the fifty-nine-year life of the Sherman Antitrust Act. The judge ignored both the government and the defendants. His position was that Congress would not have provided for imprisonment in the original act and retained it thereafter unless that penalty was intended to be used whenever a sentencing court believed jail sentences proper.

Reprinted from an article first published in the *Stanford Law Review*, 17 (January, 1965), pp. 197–223. Copyright 1965 by the Board of Trustees of the Leland Stanford Junior University.

In the second and more famous case, the *Electrical Equipment Antitrust Cases*, the government demanded jail sentences in several instances. Moreover, the prosecutor asked the court to refuse pleas of *nolo contendere* from the individual defendants. The government argued that acceptance of such pleas "would neither foster respect for the law nor vindicate the public interest" in the light of the fact that the grand jury's indictments "charge violations of rigging and price fixing as serious as any instances ever charged in the more than half a century life of the Sherman Act." The judge agreed. The sentences imposed included, in addition to fines and probation, seven sentences to imprisonment for thirty days and thirty-one suspended sentences for various periods.

Many major newspapers paid little or no attention to the convictions and sentences;[1] some critics of the prosecution saw "ominous overtones" in the fact that men had been sent to jail for "something that has been going on for years as an accepted business practice";[2] and a convicted president of one of the twenty-nine accused corporations questioned the right of the government to enact such "regulations," much less to send a person to jail for their violation and asserted that "price stabilization" was an essential element of "free enterprise."[3]

Perhaps these price-fixing (price-stabilizing) and market-rigging (market-stabilizing) cases are not typical of the broader class of criminal-penal laws regulating business. The defendants knew they were violating the law, they acted in secret collusion, huge sums of money were involved, and the Justice Department strove mightily to equate the conduct in the second case to a fraud against the government. Quite different are mine-run violations of regulations affecting business, especially those involving strict liability where intentional violation is not an essential element of the crime. These may raise more clearly the problem of what Kadish has called "moral neutrality."[4] The issue is whether severe criminal sanctions ought to be imposed on those who violate the legal but not the moral code. In the view of Kadish and others, a key factor in any discussion of the propriety and effectiveness of the use of criminal sanctions in enforcing business regulations is the relationship between prevailing morality and the norms of the criminal law. Are economic crimes *morally* wrong? If they are, should men be sent to jail for committing them?

First, when we speak of using criminal sanctions, we may be referring to more than one meaning of the term use. One may distinguish between (1) authorization by the legislature of the employment of criminal sanctions, and (2) their application by the administrator. That is, the law may be said to "use" a sanction when a statute authorizes its use; in a second sense, the sanction is "used" only when it is actually applied. Discussing antitrust laws, for example, one might debate whether it is proper to append criminal sanctions for violations of the regulations at all; and even those who concede that it is proper may question whether it is right to unsheath the sword in particular cases. Thus, those who are distressed because even a small proportion of the implicated officials of the electrical industry were imprisoned are probably opposed to any authorization of criminal sanctions in regulating business affairs; they can hardly argue that these particular offenders merited any special leniency. On the other hand, persons who complain because criminal sanctions are rarely invoked in mine-run antitrust cases and who look upon this as an indication of favoritism to "white-collar criminals" are questioning the administration of the sanctions while conceding—or even urging—the propriety of their authorization. . . .

Second, what do we mean by term "criminal sanctions"? Statutes aimed at economic regulation often provide multiple, alternative sanctions. Sometimes mandatory sequences of use are prescribed. The sanctions may include cease and desist orders (enforced through contempt proceedings), injunctive divestiture proceedings, awards of damages or treble damages, monetary fines or forfeitures (which may or may not involve imprisonment for nonpayment), seizures of goods, revocations of business or occupational licenses, prison sentences, and probation with a threat of fine or imprisonment for the violation of probation. Of these, some classes of fines, direct imprisonment, and probation with threat of fine or imprisonment for the violation of the conditions of probation are generally considered "criminal" sanctions.

However, fines or money forfeitures are widely used also as sanctions in actions formally classified as "civil proceedings." Criminologists generally approve of the use of fines as a sanction for violation of laws punishing deliberate, calculated, antisocial "profit making," because the fine divests the violator of his profits; it is a penalty which plausibly can be said to deter profit-making misconduct. However, this defense of the propriety of the fine fails to distinguish a criminal fine from a civil forfeiture or from treble damages or other forms of punitive damages, which may also deter. One may, of course, ask whether money penalties are appropriate sanctions against a business organization; and there are other subsidiary questions; for example, should the state or the victim receive the money? But such questions are irrelevant to a discussion of whether the sanction of a money penalty should be "civil" or "criminal." Therefore, when one asks whether certain conduct should be subject to criminal sanctions, one is not asking whether the conduct should be subject to a money penalty. The civil law "punishes" breach of contract and torts with damage awards, but no one imagines that money damages here are criminal sanctions. For these reasons we are eliminating the fine or money penalty from our consideration of criminal sanctions.

When discussion is directed to the question of the use of "criminal" sanctions, then, the issues raised are essentially these: (1) Must the evidence establish the defendant's guilt beyond a reasonable doubt, and shall the defendant be entitled to all the procedural safeguards of criminal law? (2) Shall the defendant and his conduct be publicly labeled as criminal? (3) Shall the defendant, upon conviction, be subject to imprisonment or conditional probation with the threat of loss of liberty for violation of the conditions?

Finally, what is the meaning in this context of "economic regulation"? Kadish feels there is more than one kind of economic regulation and limits his discussion of enforcement problems to regulations "which impose restrictions upon the conduct of business as part of a considered economic policy." Kadish certainly has the right to specify types of regulation, and for his purposes they may constitute a unitary category. However, his reasons for isolating them—the uniqueness of the protected interest and their origin as part of a considered economic policy—cannot be defended upon empirical grounds. Let us test some of his examples in the light of his claimed differentiae.

For Kadish, the economic crime par excellence is the antitrust violation. The text of the Sherman Antitrust Act reflected legislative awareness of existing common-law doctrine concerning restraint of trade.[5] The enactment of a much-debated federal criminal statute on the subject owed more to political forces and theories operating in the late nineteenth century than it did to economic theory, policy, or ideology. The primary interest involved was and is "the emergence of the modern corporate organization as presenting a problem in the distribution of power," the continuing problem of individual freedom of choice, and the functioning of democratic processes in a society where large corporations had tremendous wealth and power, including political power. The basic problem has been and is "that of the control of the conduct of the business organization rather than a problem of preserving 'competition.'" This was clearly recognized at the time of the enactment of the Sherman Antitrust Act by proponents and opponents alike. William Graham Sumner, for example, opposed "federal interference" because he was firmly convinced that industrial "bigness" was economically desirable[6] and that government was too weak to resist being taken over by a business plutocracy if it sought to interfere with the trusts.[7] Arguably, considered economic policy entered the picture when the courts rejected arguments based on bigness per se and explicitly read the concepts of reasonableness and control into federal antitrust law.[8] "Dissolution is not a penalty but a remedy" to be employed only "if the industry will . . . need it for its protection."[9] Economic policy in its purest form entered the arena not as the primary purpose of the legislation but as an alleviation against its strictness in the face of good faith on the part of the regulated. Much of the vagueness of antitrust regulation must be ascribed not to efforts to restrict business but to efforts to prevent the use of the "political" Sherman Antitrust Act to hamstring productive efficiency.

Laws regulating maximum prices or rents represent the same basic situation. They are necessary to restrict the power of persons to use property in ways contrary to the public interest because some emergency condition has eliminated the freedom of the normal market. The crisis situation is viewed as a general threat to national health, safety, and welfare—even survival. In such a situation, extraordinary powers are assumed by the agents of the politically organized community against, for example, "speculative, unwarranted, and abnormal increases in rents; exactions of unjust, unreasonable, oppressive rents and rental agreements; overcrowding occupation of uninhabitable dwellings; speculative, manipulative, and disruptive practices by landlords of housing accommodations; and other acts and conditions endangering the public health, safety, welfare and morals" of the community. . . . Private housing has, in the legislature's opinion, become vested with a public interest.

The preceding suggests the difficulty of maintaining Kadish's claimed distinction between "economic" laws which are part of "considered economic policy" and "economic" laws relating to health and physical safety. In which category, for instance, belong the laws limiting the employment or the hours of work of women and children? These were propounded as health laws, to be sure, but another important factor was a considered economic policy giving job preference to male heads of households over the competition of women and children.[10] In general, "considered economic policy" and health and safety factors are inextricably bound together in the history of all types of regulation. For example, occupational licensing and similar laws are curious mixtures of economic policy and health and safety measures. The Wisconsin barber statute makes it unlawful "for any barber to use any instrument or article that has not been disinfected in accordance with . . . sanitary standards"; but the statute makes it equally unlawful to "advertise a definite price for any barbering service by means of displaying a sign containing such prices so that the same is visible to persons outside the barbershop." The two sections of this law are, to be sure, analytically separable; but the whole statute is animated by one spirit, in which an economic aim (protecting barbers from competitors) is mixed with a public-welfare aim (improving sanitary conditions of public barbershops).

In short, Kadish's attempt to distinguish the "economic" from other forms of regulation produces numerous inconsistencies. Thus, a rent-control law directed against unjust rents is viewed by Kadish as referring to morally neutral behavior and as part of a considered economic policy; a tenement-house law that requires minimum standards of quality, regardless of the amount of rent, is presumably a health measure. In similar fashion, that part of most rent-control laws which makes it criminal for a landlord to seek to evict an existing tenant under certain circumstances would also be a regulation of morally neutral behavior. But how would

Kadish classify an "open occupancy" statute that makes it criminal for a landlord to discriminate on the basis of race in the initial selection of tenants?

Moreover, it is even difficult to distinguish Kadish's "pure" form of economic crimes from his "traditional property offenses." These offenses, such as robbery, blackmail, forgery, and passing worthless checks, were intended, in his words, to protect property interests "against the acquisitive behavior of others," so as to further "free private decisions." To say that the traditional property offenses protect property (and thus aid private decisions) begs the question. These offenses are part of the system by which the legal order defines what objects and interests a particular social system chooses to protect as property. All social systems protect property as they define it; in so doing they map out what types of economic exchanges are protected (these they further) and what types are not (these they discourage). In our present society, you may induce a young lady to break her date and instead to go out with you on Saturday night. This is no crime (so long as she is over a certain age and you do not entice her from her family for immoral purposes) nor does it give her initial date a basis for civil action, for he had no property right in her agreement to attend the movies with him. In fact, you, the aggressor, have the benefit of the protection of the law from any physical intimidation by the first young man to keep you from "stealing his girl." But it is a crime to steal a wristwatch, a ten-dollar bill, or the sexual privileges of another man's wife. The noncriminality of inducing a girl to break a date (in legal terms, the fact one cannot have a property interest in a rendezvous) frees private citizens to engage in vigorous courtships and vigorous competition for eventual wives and sweethearts. Laws against adultery prevent or attempt to control the exercise of "free private decisions" in competition for sexual privileges by establishing property rights. Aultery is a form of trespass.

The traditional property offenses take their definition of property from the underlying assumptions of a given society and seek to use the criminal law to channel economic behavior along lines consistent with these assumptions. Therefore, they are arguably the product of considered economic policy, though so rooted in the social order that no one actually bothers much to consider them. The traditional criminal law has always aimed at regulating economic exchanges in the broadest sense. . . .

So, for example, you are not allowed to make a person buy his reputation (blackmail). The criminality of blackmail represents a social judgment that one may not manipulate as an income-producing asset knowledge about another person's past; you may not sell to that person forbearance to use your knowledge of his guilt. If, on the other hand, you acquire knowledge of a person's illustrious ancestry or use in business the skills necessary to ascertain the ancestry of others, you may set yourself up as a genealogist and bargain with others on the basis of your skill or information. The difference between a genealogist and a blackmailer—between a genteel and a criminal profession—reflects a difference in the notions of legitimate exchange within our society. In other societies, of course, the criminal law adopts a quite different definition of what is and what is not a legitimate exchange.

Even within our own society, subtle distinctions are made among types of economic exchange that are criminal, those which lead to civil penalties only, and those which lead to no penalties at all, but are positively encouraged by the legal order. The distinctions may at times appear anomalous. In Wisconsin if you give a worthless check to a tavern owner, you may be criminally responsible for your act, even though you are drunk on liquor he has sold you and even though he continues to sell liquor to you on the strength of the "credit" of your check. If, however, you buy liquor on open credit from this same tavern owner, he may not even collect his debt from you through regular civil court processes. Credit sales of liquor are against public policy, and liquor debts, like gambling debts, are unenforceable. However, much of the apparent anomaly of this situation is reduced when the researcher finds that it is also criminal for a tavern owner knowingly to serve a certified alcoholic or allow him to be served.

In short, Kadish's attempt to distinguish the "traditional property offenses" from his pure "economic policy" offenses turns out to be an instance of circular reasoning. The basic difference is presumably found in the fact that the traditional offenses are naturally associated with a "stigma of moral reprehensibility," while the economic offenses are "morally neutral." But he asserts that the traditional offenses possess this natural association in part precisely because they are criminal under traditional categories of crime. This seems to mean at its core that his "morally neutral" conduct is so simply because it is newly proscribed behavior. Kadish adds, however, that the new crimes are morally neutral also because they "closely resemble acceptable aggressive business behavior." But the key word here is "acceptable." Throughout one finds the hidden assumptions that business conduct not included in traditional property offenses was by definition not considered unethical or morally reprehensible, and, conversely, that all conduct proscribed by traditional property offenses is currently considered unethical or morally reprehensible. But this is precisely one of the central issues to be discussed in considering the relationship between popular morality and the criminal law relative to economic regulation.

This means that defining a pure category of economic crimes is of little value to a sociological examination of the use of criminal sanctions regulating economic transactions. It is more fruitful to begin with a broader inquiry: How does any given legal regulation affect the conduct of business and businessmen, what is its relationship in this regard to the prevailing morality, and what are the implications of this relationship to the use (in both senses) of criminal sanctions?

In pursuing this inquiry, we do not assume that there are any pure "economic crimes." Some criminal statutes, like the Sherman Antitrust Act, regulate the conduct of businessmen exclusively or almost so. Others, like price-control laws, regulate business transactions and control the conduct of both businessmen and nonbusinessmen, for example, consumers. Still others only rarely have special relevance to a businessman in the conduct of his business; e.g., laws against murder. To deny that there is a category of pure economic crimes is not to say that laws against murder and laws against monopoly do not reflect different social forces in their inception, diffusion, moral basis, and enforceability. But it does mean that these matters should be resolved by empirical evidence and not by definition.

## LEGAL REGULATION, BUSINESS CONDUCT, AND PREVAILING MORALITY

We have shown the futility of looking for pure economic crimes and have framed our inquiry in terms of the relationship between specific legal regulations, business conduct, prevailing morality, and criminal sanctions.

By "prevailing morality" we mean the current attitudes of the public (or any relevant portion of the public) toward given courses of conduct in specified circumstances. The circumstances must be given close attention. For example, a study of various samples of the population of Akron, Ohio, in the mid-1930s indicated that prevailing opinion did not believe it "wrong" for West Virginia coal miners to steal coal from inoperative mines for their own use, though it was thought "wrong" if the theft were for resale for profit.[1] It was overwhelmingly recognized that in both instances the taking was a crime. On the other hand, the populace believed it "wrong" for a corporation to close its plant and move to another community because of a strike, though it was widely recognized that such a course of action was legal. As one might expect, the opinions varied with the position of the individual in the social structure of the community.

Clearly, it is important to learn which segments of the population determine the prevailing morality on any given issue. In discussions of what "ought" to be the relationship between morality and criminal law, a number of different, supposedly important "publics" have been designated. Some writers have placed special emphasis upon enforcement administrators, especially judges, while others have spoken in vague terms; e.g., of the offender's "fellowmen."[12] Kadish appears to be talking mostly about the public of the "regulated." Another writer has referred to "ma jority feelings of disgust or revulsion in the community."[13] Another has, in addition to distinguishing the administrators, sought to divide citizens into the regulated, the militant regulators, and the indifferent.[14] At least it is clear that communities, in generating standards of morality, are not to be considered as sets of isolated individuals; rather, communities are made up of persons of varying statuses and group memberships.

What is the evidence concerning the relationship between compliance with economic regulation and approval or disapproval of the regulation by the regulated? Here the general regulation of a specified area of conduct should be distinguished from particular rules or restrictions in effect at a particular point in time. We shall first consider attitudes toward general regulation. This is a relevant consideration, since the degree of approval reflects the attitude of the regulated toward the moral justification of the regulation.

The few empirical studies that have been made fail to indicate any simple relationships between the general attitudes of businessmen toward a given area of regulation and the willingness or propensity of businessmen to violate the regulations. . . .[15] These studies make only a negative point, that compliance and noncompliance are not wholly determined by whether persons subject to regulation approve of it, that is, whether they deem the regulation consistent with their moral code. The extent to which compliance is related to approval, however, ought to be taken into account. Regulatory laws are directed toward businessmen . . . and businessmen constitute the "public" within which compliance must be measured. To be sure, there is a wider "public" for purposes of measuring support for enforcement. Thus, complete and intransigent refusal by businessmen to obey might lead to more than collapse of regulation; severe social conflict might result if the narrower "public" (businessmen) refused to obey regulatory laws widely supported by the broader "public" (the general population). Moreover, the studies indicate that "disapproval" of laws by the regulated does not necessarily result in defiance and rebellion. Grumbling acceptance of the income tax, food and drug laws, and the Clayton Act may serve the purposes of the legal order perfectly well; wild enthusiasm . . . is not necessary.

Empirical evidence tends, therefore, to show that moral approval by the regulated is not a necessary condition of general compliance. It is also true that general compliance—even coupled with deep public moral support—does not of itself mean that application-use of criminal sanctions (as defined above) is an appropriate technique to ensure achievement of the social ends underlying given regulations with maximum efficiency. This fact is often recognized in discussion of certain sexual crimes, such as adultery, fornication, and consensual homosexuality. The general public condemns such sexual conduct, and most people comply with the law. Yet arguments are continually and powerfully advanced against punishing these acts through criminal processes. These arguments will be familiar to most readers. Essentially, it is argued that enforcement does more harm than good; for example, it encourages blackmail, snooping, arbitrary and unfair punishment of unlucky or unpopular offenders, and overzealous police work.

What underlies these arguments can be highlighted by considering a less flamboyant example, nonsupport of children. Here too the failure of the criminal law bears directly on the problem of economic regulation and the criminal process. Our "prevailing morality" does, of course, condemn a person's willful failure to provide support for his children.... Most people sacrifice heavily to provide advantages for their children, and judges in good conscience vigorously denounce offenders. Yet the problem of nonsupport shows no sign of vanishing. Correctional administrators complain that child-support offenders fill too many jail cells; welfare administrators do not want to require mothers receiving Aid-to-Dependent-Children benefits to take legal action against nonsupporting fathers, feeling that such action would handicap their programs. Increasingly, law and administration seek devices to induce public condemnation of nonsupport with noncriminal sanctions (or at least without felony conviction). Here again, the use of criminal sanctions does not seem to provide an adequate solution to problems raised by conduct clearly condemned by prevailing morality.

It is easy to see why the "use" of criminal sanctions (in our second sense of "use") may actually impede the attainment of the ends supported by public policy and morality. The criminal law is more than a set of propositions, more than a moral code, more than a catalog of rights and wrongs. A set of precepts and definitions lies at the heart of the criminal law; but criminal law is also a technique, a mechanism; and it is administered through highly organized institutions. Criminal justice does not consist only of penal statutes, it is also judges, bailiffs, sheriffs, policemen, district attorneys, jails, workhouses, courtrooms, files, fingerprints.... Any realistic discussion of the application-use of criminal sanctions must take into account the impact on the accused of one of the law's most effective sanctions: the bringing of the accused into contact with the enforcement institutions of the criminal law. The difficulty with the use of criminal sanctions in child-support cases... its repressive and cumbersome techniques may interfere with the goals of persuasion, negotiation, and voluntary compliance on the part of the erring father.

This does not mean that making an act formally criminal may not have, in some cases, subtle aftereffects. Labeling conduct as "criminal" may change the public attitude toward the man who breaks the law as well as the attitudes of those who are themselves tempted to break the law. We shall examine these aftereffects later. For the present, it is enough to note that there is no necessary connection between the label "crime" and public morality nor between the forces which tend to induce compliance with statutory precepts. Criminal law, particularly as it relates to economic crime, is a set of techniques to be manipulated for social ends.

The history of criminal law is in fact a history of the reasons why techniques of criminal law enforcement have been brought to bear in particular areas to advance social goals. One factor dictating the use of criminal sanctions has been unduly ignored in most treatments of crime. This is the fact that the cost of enforcing the criminal law is borne by the state and that the initiation of criminal process and its administration are conducted by servants of the state. This is, in fact, a major social distinction between criminal and noncriminal law. To say that breach of contract is not a crime is not a statement about the morality of breach of contract, though we may consider breach of contract highly immoral under certain circumstances. Liability for breach of contract in the twentieth century has been imposed in some situations where the prior law did not impose liability, because of popular feelings that certain kinds of breach of contract are "unfair" (that is, immoral) and should therefore give rise to liability. The use of the concept of "unjust enrichment" affords a good illustration. The noncriminal nature of breach of contract means that the initial decision to "punish" a man who breaches his contract lies in the private sector and is, in fact, the exclusive decision of the man whose contract has been breached. In addition, once the aggrieved party decides to pursue his action in court, he must bear the expenses himself (though he hopes to recover some of them if he wins). He must hire his own lawyer and make ararngements to pay him. The state provides judges and courtrooms as a service, but the state has no interest in whether the plaintiff chooses to terminate his case before judgment or whether he chooses to levy execution on the goods of the defendant after judgment. The victim of theft, on the other hand, docs not hire the state to punish the thief. It is generally true of theft that the state will not prosecute unless a private citizen complains. But there are many areas of criminal law where this is not so. Murder is an obvious example.

We do not suggest that the only difference between criminal law and noncriminal law is that the former has socialized the process of enforcement, but this is an important distinction between the two areas, particularly with respect to economic regulation. Often the morality or immorality of proscribed conduct has little to do with whether the law labels the conduct criminal or leaves enforcement in private hands.

A striking example is usury. In Wisconsin, for example, usury was considered a socially dangerous and immoral practice by most of the population, as far as we can judge, through most of the nineteenth century.[16] It was not, however, a crime. It was discouraged by severe civil penalties under some of the statutes; under one statute, based on a New York model, the usurer was barred from recovering either principal or interest and thus might lose the entire amount of his loan. Common statutory provisions called for treble damages, as in modern antitrust law. Provisions for punitive or multiple damages tend to encourage (and are meant to encourage) private enforcement. But since usury was punished only by civil sanctions, penalties inured to the private citizen who pursued his remedy. He made the choice of suing or not suing, and he saw the matter through the courts.

In 1895, usury was made a crime in Wisconsin, punishable by fine. It would be a rash assumption to say that usury became a crime because in 1895 a heightened sense of the immorality of usury suddenly gripped the public. The true explanation is more subtle. In the Middle West of the nineteenth century, usury has been primarily a problem of the rate of interest on farm mortgages. By the turn of the century, it became pre-eminently a problem of urban consumption loans. Those who suffered from usury were unable to handle enforcement themselves because of their social and economic status. Loans were small; the borrowers were in large measure landless urban workers, many of them foreign-born. By contrast, the farmers in the 1850s and 1860s had had a larger voice in the affairs of the community and had been willing, to judge from court records, to enforce the usury laws. Making usury a crime was thus a legislative judgment that it was best to socialize remedial action, not because of the immorality of usury, but because under existing social conditions civil enforcement had failed.

Lending money at interest is an economic act, and usury is an economic wrong under the law of the American states. The historical development just related demonstrates that the progression from civil to criminal sanctions does not necessarily represent any change in the moral status of the act proscribed. Usury was stamped with immorality both before and after it was made criminal in Wisconsin. . . .

Statute books are filled with economic crimes whose congruence with popular morality is either completely absent or so muted that one need not consider it. Take, for example, the Wisconsin statute which makes it a crime for any publicly supported hospital to "furnish to its inmates or patrons . . . any oleomargarine." Offenders are liable to fine "not to exceed $200 or imprisoned in the county jail not to exceed six months, for the first offense"; for subsequent offenses, fines may range up to $500, with imprisonment "not less than thirty days nor more than six months." The origins and purposes of the statute are perfectly obvious, but it is dubious to assert that it arose out of popular morality; and whether the public brands the purveyor of oleomargarine to patients in public (as opposed to private) hospitals with any special obloquy is even more dubious. Another Wisconsin statute forbids the sale of baking powder unless the label lists the ingredients, is printed "in the English language, with black ink, in type not smaller than eight point, bold-faced, Gothic capitals," and contains "the name and address of the manufacturer of such baking powder, and the words: 'This baking powder is composed of the following ingredients and none other.'" This crime bears the same penalties as the crime of giving oleomargarine to hospital patients. There may be considerable popular revulsion against the selling of poisonous or harmful or deceptive foods, but surely neither before nor after the passage of the act were there any deep well-springs of disgust against selling imported baking powder with a French label in small typefaces or printed in green ink instead of black. The purpose of the act is regulatory; as in the case of the criminal usury law, administrative considerations probably led to the choice of criminal sanctions. Theoretically, the state could give the buyer of baking powder that did not conform to statutory standards a civil action for damages or the right to rescind his purchase. This would certainly fail to accomplish the purpose of the statute, since the buyer of a small amount of baking powder would never bother to sue the seller. The criminal law is here used as an administrative technique, as a way of socializing the costs of enforcement, which are too great for individuals profitably to bear.

Frequently, however, the general criminal processes will prove too cumbersome and inefficient to attain the state's policy goals. The next step is to vest responsibility for enforcement and administration in an administrative agency. Although mislabeling of baking powder formally remains a crime in Wisconsin, one can be fairly certain that enforcement and policing of baking-powder labels (if any) are carried out by the staff of the appropriate executive department or agency, not by the distinct attorneys of the various counties.

The shift to administrative enforcement takes place partly because criminal sanctions drag with them all the traditional safeguards surrounding the defendant. Proof beyond a reasonable doubt, trial by jury, and other forms of protection are required. The socialization of remedies thus has the dysfunctional result of making large-scale enforcement difficult for reasons irrelevant to the purpose of making the proscribed acts criminal. Thus, transfer to an administrative agency is likely to occur as soon as such an agency is available. The criminal sanctions remain as threats—they are "used" in the sense of being authorized, but no longer "used" in the sense of wholesale application to offenders.

It is not, however, only the administrators of economic regulation who sharply distinguish between their authorization to invoke criminal sanctions and the selective application of these sanctions. We are coming more and more to recognize how highly selective is the process by which criminal sanctions are actually invoked. Even classic crimes of violence and immorality—murder, robbery, arson—are "administered" by public officials. Often only flagrant cases receive the full treatment. But the full treatment also serves as a threat to induce compliance by voluntary means. . . . Statutes creating administrative regulation often admit frankly that vast discretion is vested in the administrators—they use such terms as "public interest," "convenience," and "necessity." Although the traditional criminal law does not specify that enforcement is selective, this difference is largely a matter of form. Statues which set up administrative agencies are almost never content to give these agencies rule-making and civil-enforcement power; the statutes almost invariably add to a catch-all section making violation of the statute or of the rules and regulations of the agency a crime. . . .

The purpose of providing for criminal sanctions is at least twofold. First, it adds dimension to the full treatment available. This strengthens the agency's position by giving it one more weapon. Flagrant, unpopular violators of the law or the rules can be told they may go to jail, or at least face the obloquy, the annoyance, the physical restraints of the criminal process. Secondly, the criminal section of the statute enables the agency to use, when necessary, the general law enforcement machinery of the state. Of course the agency will invoke criminal sanctions only in exceptional cases. A criminal trial is a slow process, heavily laden with procedural safeguards for the defendant. It is not only the business community which is chary of criminal sanctions; the administrators themselves avoid them for the same reasons that lead welfare workers to deplore excessive use of criminal law in nonsupport cases.

## INTERACTIONS BETWEEN CRIMINAL LAW AND BUSINESS CONDUCT

Historically, growth in the number of regulatory crimes represents a broadening of the techniques for the enforcement of state policy. Nevertheless, the word "crime" has symbolic meaning for the public, and the criminal law is stained so deeply with notions of morality and immorality, public censure and punishment, that labeling an act criminal often has consequences that go far beyond mere administrative effectiveness. . . . Imprisonment or threat of imprisonment and the public stigma of the criminal process are the real issues about which the discussion of criminal sanctions in regulating business revolves. It is generally accepted today that fear of criminal prosecution is an effective deterrent to businessmen, professional men, and the middle class.[17]

The very effectiveness of criminal sanctions in restraining the behavior of businessmen accounts in large part for the concern over the use of criminal-penal sanctions in regulating business. Businessmen abhor the idea of being branded a criminal. Society does not particularly care whether murderers and rapists like being branded as criminals, but businessmen, after all, form a large, respectable, and influential class in our society.

Therefore, effectiveness of the penal sanction in this case leads to pressure against use of the sanction. . . . But rules acquire legitimacy through being adopted in the regular processes utilized in society for making rules. The legitimacy of rules derives from the use of a standardized process of adoption, as much as or more than from the subject matter with which the rules deal. Americans in general accept the proposition that it is "wrong" to violate the law, even if they feel the law acts unwisely when it prohibits certain conduct. The very fact that a criminal statute has been enacted by the legislature is a powerful factor in making the proscribed conduct illegitimate in the eyes of a potential actor, even when the actor disagrees with the purpose of the law. . . .

The difficulty of categorizing the behavior of businessmen as criminal or noncriminal does not mean that [acts such as] restraint of trade cannot be a "crime" in the same sense as burglary—the electrical price-fixing case, for one, proves that it can. The defendants, in effect, put on masks, jimmied open windows, and stole the people's money. . . . For the mine-run economic crime, it is easy to see why the sanctions of the criminal law are not often employed. The nonuse of criminal sanctions to enforce antitrust laws, for example, is a consequence of the institutionalizing of a program which was originally the product of genuine popular outrage. The clamor against "the trusts" can be compared with the clamor against sex criminals, murderers, and those who plant bombs in airplanes. Ultimately, however, state and federal governments created enforcement and administrative agencies staffed with personnel who tended to treat with some understanding the problems of the businessmen. . . . Even when antitrust law is vigorously enforced through civil sanctions (e.g., cease and desist orders), the choice of such civil sanctions reflects the fact that the administrators are able to sympathize with the business position; they readily separate the "conduct" from the "person.". . . (This genuine sympathy is above and apart from another, admittedly potent, factor inducing sympathetic behavior; namely, the fact that regulators often end up in the employ of the companies they formerly regulated.)

Thus the "moral neutrality" of regulatory crimes arises out of a number of factors to which writers like Kadish may give insufficient weight. The businessman can hardly be blamed for failing to sense as an abhorrent crime the commission of an act which is forbidden in . . . a regulatory statute in which criminal sanctions have been authorized but which historically have not been used except in flagrant cases. Nor can he be blamed for failing to sense as "criminal" acts made criminal only in order to socialize the remedial process. But tensions and conflicts arise because of lack of understanding of these facts by the broader public and because, as noted above, the authorization of criminal sanctions may initiate a process of interaction between law and prevailing morality.

Some general features of this process of interaction are worthy of note here. The aim of regulatory law is to secure compliance by the regulated. Criminal sanctions are a technique to ensure compliance. Compliance, however, can be viewed in two lights: short- and long-run compliance. When a program of economic regulation is adopted, the attention of the legislature is usually fixed on problems of short-run compliance. The symbolic value of law as law, the fact that most people want to obey the law and will do so, has important consequences for long-run compliance. American social scientists generally agree that social sanctions can be employed deliberately to modify modes of social action—not only overt behavior, but also cognitive, affective, and conative attitudes. Less technically put, social sanctions can be used to change beliefs, attitudes, and personal values and goals; they can effectuate policy considerations by influencing what a person thinks he ought to do or what he wants to do in a particular situation. . . . Some authorities have suggested that administrative regulation is an especially useful tool for bringing about social change: it permits detailed specification of required conduct, it can modify the rules to plug loopholes as attempts at evasion appear, and it has great flexibility to adopt tactics and allocate resources toward enforcement of its regulations.[18]

Underlying these propositions is the assumption that people tend to think that what they do is the right thing to do, even if they began to do so because they were forced to. Eventually, they begin to expect similar conduct from others and, indeed, are eager to impose it upon others. As conduct becomes formalized, it lays an ideological basis for the extension of similar social norms to situations that are perceived in "analogous" terms. Ironically, some of the participants in the electrical price-fixing case reported that they first experienced price fixing when they served as industry representatives in federal price-control programs during World War II.[19] Less dramatically, filing income tax returns and carrying drivers' licenses have become so commonplace that the public probably accepts these "customs" and, by and large, believes strongly that they are proper.

Other social scientists, however, disagree with the proposition that people learn to want to do what they have to do. Bendix, for example, stresses how variable are the effects of coercion on personality.[20] How a person will react to a requirement that he do something he thinks wrong and does not want to do depends on his whole arsenal of psychological resources. Certainly people are not sheep; the countless revolutions and civil wars of human history are proof enough that law does not always convert its subjects. But surely there is some tendency for persons to provide "public justification" for what they are actually doing.[21] Thus, the public morality must be under some pressure to correspond with required conduct. We should not be surprised to find an intergenerational "drift" toward increased moral justification of required conduct.

The phenomenon of intergenerational drift is probably particularly important in the case of "economic crimes." A major factor in determining whether this drift toward justification takes place is the extent to which public officials appreciate the distinction between criminal law as technique and criminal law as a reflection of popular morality. Again we may use the antitrust laws as an example of economic legislation which arose out of profound and passionate feelings of public outrage. The passion which attended the birth of the Sherman Antitrust Act has certainly subsided. Yet antitrust laws have not become dead letters, because they have been handed over to federal agencies which have increasingly buttressed the statutes with relatively precise regulations and have built up bureaucratic structures to enforce these laws. Business, for its part, has learned to live with the antitrust laws, whatever reservations business has as to the wisdom of these laws. The businessman knows generally that these laws exist; he is accustomed to consult lawyers who advise him on the legality of proposed mergers and acquisitions; he frequently modifies his behavior in ways which take the laws into account.

Some criminal statutes, however, have become dead letters because they have not become highly institutionalized. When the moral outrage which set them in motion subsides, they lose their vitality. The classic case is that of the colonial blue laws. These laws were vigorously enforced because the society which created them believed in them passionately: Men informed on their neighbors; local courts and magistrates rigorously enforced laws against Sabbath breaking, adultery, card playing, disobedience to parents, and fornication.[22] Formal administrative techniques were neither needed nor used; the whole society involved itself in seeking out violators and bringing them before the bar of public opinion and legal punishment. When the passion subsided, the laws ceased to be enforced, since there was no administrative structure charged with enforcement.

The electrical price-fixing cases are unusually interesting in that they seem to foreshadow a rebirth of passion in the relatively colorless field of antitust law. The wide publicity, the newspaper harangues, the human interest stories and the rash of lawsuits which followed in their wake certainly dramatized the antitrust laws and disturbed many businessmen. In the price-fixing case—as in "show trials" in general—the criminal law was used, whether deliberately or not, to influence behavior by the use of the mechanisms of law enforcement most open to public view—the preachments of the prosecutors, the sermons delivered by the judge. The public participated in these trials, directly (on grand juries, for example) and indirectly as spectators, newspaper readers, and radio and television audiences. The effect sought in such cases is twofold: first, to warn and deter those who might violate the law; second, to rekindle in the public a sense of the immorality of the defendants' acts. But it was the quality of flagrancy and stealth, combined with the magnitude of the crime, which made a "crackdown" possible. And at the same time it alerted the business community and its apologists to the dangers inherent in the mere authorization of criminal sanctions. This danger lies in the discretion vested in the administrators—the danger of selective use of these powerful sanctions for reasons not justified on grounds of administrative efficiency. It is precisely the same danger which some have seen in the "misuse" of tax law to put gangsters in jail, the abuse of laws against fornication, the application of trespass laws against Negro sit-in demonstrators, and the "persecution" of Communists through the use of laws which originally had nothing to do with Communism. But these are problems not peculiar to regulatory crimes; they are problems of government generally and of bureaucracy generally, the general problem of fairness in the use of administrative discretion.

It is equally clear that these are not problems peculiar to the use of criminal sanctions, since similar problems are raised by the variable administration of zoning laws, the "unfairness" of the licensing process, and the inequities involved in government subsidies and penalties in general. The sanctions (positive and negative) which are available to a legal system range in a continuum from cash grants on one end to death in the electric chair on the other. Historical and social realities dictate the authorization and application of sanctions (criminal and civil) in legal regulations, depending upon the ends to be achieved, the class of persons to be affected, and the behavior sought to be influenced. At every point in the process of choosing and using sanctions questions are raised—moral questions, empirical questions, questions of ends and means. Criminology in general has given up the search for general theories of "crime" and general theories of "criminal sanctions." This is all to the good; what is needed is not a theory of "crime" (let alone a theory of "economic crime") but theories of human behavior. It is not likely (at least at this stage of the development of social science) that a theory will be found to describe and predict human behavior accurately enough to fit the murderer, the corporate monopolist, the mislabeler of baking powder, and the trespasser on public grass (to mention only "criminals"). Discussions of the use of sanctions in economic regulation—whether the discussants are lawyers or social scientists—ought properly to begin by delineating exactly what sanctions and types of economic regulation are under debate.

# Notes

1. "When the Story Broke," *New Republic,* 144 (February 20, 1961), p. 7.
2. Quoted in John Herling, *The Great Price Conspiracy* (Washington, D.C.: Robert B. Luce, 1962), pp. 291–297.
3. Quoted in John G. Fuller, *The Gentleman Conspirators* (New York: Grove Press, 1962), p. 14.
4. Sanford H. Kadish, "Some Observations on the Use of Criminal Sanctions in Enforcing Economic Regulations," *University of Chicago Law Review,* 30 (Spring, 1963), p. 423.
5. See Kenneth Carlston, *Law and Structures of Social Action* (London: William

Stevens, 1956), p. 194; William L. Letwin, "Congress and the Sherman Antitrust Law, 1887–1889," *University of Chicago Law Review*, 23 (Winter, 1956), pp. 240–247.

6. William Graham Sumner, "The Concentration of Wealth: Its Economic Justification," in Stow Persons, ed., *Social Darwinism: Selected Essays* (Englewood Cliffs, N.J.: Prentice-Hall, 1963), p. 153.

7. Sumner, "Democracy and Plutocracy," in *ibid.*, pp. 143–149.

8. See *Standard Oil Co.* v. *United States*, 221 U.S. 1, 60 (1911); *United States* v. *American Tobacco Co.*, 221 U.S. 106, 179 (1911); *United States* v. *Corn Prods. Ref. Co.*, 234 F.: 964 (So. Dist. N.Y. 1916).

9. *United States* v. *Aluminum Co. of America*, 148 F.2d 416, 446 (2d Circ. 1945).

10. John R. Commons and John B. Andrews, *Principles of Labor Legislation*, 4th ed. rev. (New York: Harper & Row, 1936), p. 97.

11. Alfred W. Jones, *Life, Liberty and Property: A Study of Conflict and a Measurement of Conflicting Rights* (New York: Octagon Books, 1964).

12. Henry M. Hart, Jr., "Aims of the Criminal Law," *Law and Contemporary Problems*, 23 (Summer, 1958), p. 437.

13. Graham Hughes, "Morals and the Criminal Law," *Yale Law Journal*, 71 (March, 1962), p. 682.

14. Karl N. Llewellyn, *Jurisprudence: Realism in Theory and Practice* (Chicago: University of Chicago Press, 1962), p. 403.

15. Robert E. Lane, *The Regulation of Businessmen: Social Conditions of Government Economic Control* (New Haven, Conn.: Yale University Press, 1954); Harry V. Ball, "Social Structure and Rent Control Violations," *American Journal of Sociology*, 65 (May, 1960), pp. 598–604.

16. See generally Lawrence M. Friedman, "The Usury Laws of Wisconsin: A Study in Legal and Social History," *Wisconsin Law Review* (July, 1963), pp. 515–565.

17. See Llewellyn, *op. cit.*, pp. 403–404.

18. Arnold Rose, "The Use of Law to Induce Social Change," *Transactions of the 3d World Congress of Sociology*, 6 (1956), p. 52; Jack Greenberg, *Race Relations and American Law* (New York: Columbia University Press, 1959), pp. 1–30.

19. Richard Austin Smith, "The Incredible Electrical Conspiracy," *Fortune*, 63 (April, 1961), p. 136.

20. Reinhard Bendix, "Compliant Behavior and Individual Personality," *American Journal of Sociology*, 58 (November, 1952), p. 302.

21. See generally, Jack W. Brehm and Arthur R. Cohen, *Explorations in Cognitive Dissonance* (New York: Wiley, 1962).

22. See generally, George L. Haskins, *Law and Authority in Early Massachusetts* (New York: Macmillan, 1960).

# BIBLIOGRAPHY

Akers, Ronald L. "White-Collar Crime: Crime in Business, Occupations, and Professions." In *Deviant Behavior: A Social Learning Approach*, pp. 177–192. Belmont, Ca.: Wadsworth, 1973.

Allen, Brandt R. "Computer Fraud." *Financial Executive*, 39 (May, 1971), pp. 38–43.

Apel, Hans. "The Scope and Significance of Economic Misrepresentation." *Journal of Economics and Sociology*, 21 (January, 1962), pp. 77–90, and 21 (April, 1962), pp. 173–188.

Areeda, Phillip. *Antitrust Analysis: Problems, Text, and Cases.* 2d. ed. Boston: Little, Brown, 1974.

Bacon, Seldon D. "Review of Sutherland, *White Collar Crime*." *American Sociological Review*, 15 (April, 1950), pp. 309–310.

Bane, Charles A. *The Electrical Equipment Conspiracy: The Treble Damage Actions.* New York: Federal Legal Publications, 1973.

Barmash, Isadore, ed. *Great Business Disasters: Swindlers, Bunglers, and Frauds in American Industry.* Chicago: Playboy Press, 1972.

Bauer, Bertrand N. "Truth in Lending; College Students' Opinions of Caveat Emptor, 'Fraud and Deception'." *American Business Law Journal*, 4 (Fall, 1966), pp. 156–161.

Bayley, David H. "The Effects of Corruption in a Developing Nation." *Western Political Science Quarterly*, 19 (December, 1966), pp. 719–732.

Becker, Joseph M. *The Problem of Abuse in Unemployment Benefits.* New York: Columbia University Press, 1953.

Bensman, Joseph, and Gerver, Israel. "Crime and Punishment in the Factory: The Function of Deviancy in Maintaining the Social System." *American Sociological Review*, 28 (August, 1963), pp. 588–598.

Berckhauer, Friedrich H. *Wirtschaftsdelinquenz: Eine Bibliographie.* Freiburg: Max Planck–Institut, 1975.

Bernard, Viola W. "Why People Become Victims of Medical Quackery." *American Journal of Public Health*, 55 (August, 1965), pp. 1142–47.

Bickel, Alexander M. "Watergate and the Legal Order." *Commentary*, 57 (January 1974), pp. 19–25.

Binder, Markus. "Weisse-Kragen-Kriminalität." *Kriminalistik* (Hamburg), 16 (June, 1962), pp. 251–255.

Black, Hillel. *The Watchdogs of Wall Street*. New York: Morrow, 1962.

Bloch, Herbert A., and Geis, Gilbert. *Man, Crime, and Society*, pp. 299–323. 2d. ed. New York: Random House, 1970.

Bork, Robert H. "Legislative Intent and the Policy of the Sherman Act." *Journal of Law and Economics*, 9 (October, 1966), pp. 7–48.

Breit, William, and Elzinga, Kenneth G. "The Instruments of Antitrust Enforcement." *Emory Law Journal*, 23 (Fall, 1974), pp. 945–961.

Brooks, John Nixon. *Business Adventures*. New York: Weybright and Talley, 1969.

Bromberg, Walter. *Crime and the Mind*, pp. 377–400. New York: Macmillan, 1965.

Browning, Frank, ed. *In the Marketplace: Consumerism in America*. San Francisco: Canfield Press, 1972.

Bryant, Clifton D. *Deviant Behavior: Occupational and Organizational Bases*. Chicago: Rand McNally, 1974.

Caldwell, Robert G. "A Re-Examination of the Concept of White-Collar Crime." *Federal Probation*, 22 (March, 1958), pp. 30–36.

Caplovitz, David. *The Poor Pay More: Consumer Practice of Low-Income Families*. New York: The Free Press, 1963.

————. "The Merchant and the Low-Income Consumer." *Jewish Social Studies*, 27 (January, 1965), pp. 45–53.

Carlin, Jerome E. *Lawyer's Ethics: A Survey of the New York City Bar*. New York: Russell Sage Foundation, 1966.

Carroll, Robert M., Pine, Steven M., Cline, Cindy J., and Kleinhans, Bruce R. "Judged Seriousness of Watergate-Related Crimes." *Journal of Psychology*, 86 (March, 1974), pp. 235–239.

Carper, Jean. *Not with a Gun*. New York: Grossman, 1973.

Carson, W. G. "White-Collar Crime and the Enforcement of Factory Legislation." *British Journal of Criminology*, 10 (October, 1970), pp. 383–398.

Cash, Norman E. "Crime and the Corporation." *Conference Board Record*, 6 (August, 1969), pp. 11–13.

*Caveat Emptor*. New York: Arno Press, 1976.

Chambliss, William J. "Types of Deviance and the Effectiveness of Legal Sanctions." *Wisconsin Law Review* (Summer, 1967), pp. 703–719.

Chambliss, William J. "Vice, Corruption, Bureaucracy, and Power." *Wisconsin Law Review*. (1971), 4: 1150–73.

Chapman, Dennis. "Social Class and the Differential Distribution of Immunity." In *Sociology and the Stereotype of the Criminal*, pp. 54–96. London: Tavistock, 1968.

Childs, Marquis W., and Cater, Douglass. *Ethics in a Business Society*. New York: Harper & Row, 1954.

Chilson, Francis. "Corporate Ethics and White-Collar Crime." *Drug and Cosmetic Industry Journal*, 113 (November, 1973), pp. 89–90.

Clement, W. *The Canadian Corporate Elite: An Analysis of Economic Power*. Toronto: McClelland and Stewart, 1975.

Clinard, Marshall B. *The Black Market: A Study of White-Collar Crime*. New York: Holt, 1952.

————. "White-Collar Crime." *International Encyclopedia of the Social Sciences*, pp. 483–90. New York: Macmillan, 1968.

————, and Abbott, Daniel J. *Crime in Developing Countries*, pp. 50–57. New York: Wiley, 1973.

————, and Quinney, Richard. *Criminal Behavior Systems: A Typology*, pp. 187–223. 2d. ed. New York: Holt, Rinehart, and Winston, 1973.

Cohen, Albert, Lindesmith, Alfred and Schuessler, Karl, eds. *The Sutherland Papers* Bloomington: Indiana University Press, 1956.

Cohen, Richard E. "Justice Report/Legislation for 'White-Collar Crime' May Evoke Controversy at Code Hearings." *National Journal*, 5 (April 14, 1973), pp. 535–545.

Cohen, Sheldon S. "Morality and the American Tax System." *George Washington Law Review*, 34 (June, 1966), pp. 839–845.

Cook, Fred J. *The Corrupted Land: The Morality of Modern America.* New York: Macmillan, 1966.

Conklin, John E., and Smigel, Erwin O. "Norms and Attitudes Toward Business-Related Crimes." Paper presented at the Symposium on Studies of Public Experience, Knowledge and Opinion of Crime and Justice. Washington, D.C.; Bureau of Social Science Research, 1972.

"Consumerism and Corporate Responsibility." *Journal of Contemporary Issues*, 1 (December, 1973), pp. 2–31.

"Corporate Criminal Liability." *Northwestern University Law Review*, 68 (November–December, 1973), pp. 870–892.

Cosson, J., *Les Industriels de la fraude fiscale* Paris: Sevil, 1971.

Cox, Archibald. "Watergate and the U.S. Constitution." *British Journal of Law and Society*, 2 (Summer, 1975), pp. 1–13.

Cozby, Paul C. "Student Reactions to Agnew's Resignation: Inconsistency Resolution in Another Natural-Occurring Event." *Sociometry*, 37 (September, 1974), pp. 450–457.

Cressey, Donald R. *Other People's Money: The Social Psychology of Embezzlement.* New York: The Free Press, 1953.

———. Foreword to *White-Collar Crime* by Edwin H. Sutherland, pp. iii–xii. New York: Holt, 1961.

"Criminal Liability of Corporations." *McGill Law Review*, 10 (1964), pp. 142–157.

Curtis, S. J. "A Look at Business Crime Today and Tomorrow." *Police*, 8 (September–October 1963), pp. 26–29.

Demaris, Ovid. *Dirty Business.* New York: Harper & Row, 1974.

Dershowitz, Alan M. "Increasing Community Control over Corporate Crime: A Problem in the Law of Sanctions." *Yale Law Journal*, 71 (September, 1961), pp. 289–306.

Destler, Chester. "Wealth Against Commonwealth: 1894–1944." *American Historical Review*, 50 (October 1944), pp. 49–72.

Dickinson, William B. "Business Morality." *Editorial Research Reports* 1 (June 12, 1961).

Dirks, Raymond L., and Gross, Leonard. *The Great Wall Street Scandal.* New York: McGraw-Hill, 1974.

Dunfee, Thomas W., and Gleim, Irvin N. "Criminal Liability of Accountants: Sources and Policies." *American Business Law Journal*, 9 (Spring, 1971), pp. 1–20.

"Economic Crimes—The Proposed New Federal Criminal Code." *Business Lawyer*, 27 (November, 1971), pp. 177–193.

Edelhertz, Herbert. *The Nature, Impact and Prosecution of White Collar Crime.* Washington, D.C.: Government Printing Office, 1970.

Edgerton, Henry W. "Corporate Criminal Responsibility." *Yale Law Journal*, 36 (April, 1927), pp. 827–844.

Egan, Bowes. "Criminal Economic Law and Consumer Protection." *Journal of Business Law* (England), 26 (January, 1967), pp. 26–31.

Eliasberg, Wladimir. "Corporation and Bribery." *Journal of Criminal Law*, 42 (September–October, 1951), pp. 317–331.

Emerson, Thomas I. "Review of Sutherland, *White Collar Crime*." *Yale Law Journal*, 59 (January, 1950), pp. 581–585.

Erikson, Walter R. *Price Fixing Under the Sherman Act: Case Studies in Conspiracy.* Ph.D. Dissertation, Michigan State University, 1965.

Erskine, Hazel. "The Polls: Corruption in Government." *Public Opinion Quarterly*, 37 (Winter, 1973–74), pp. 628–644.

Falk, Richard A., Kolko, Gabriel, and Lifton, Robert Jay. *Crimes of War.* New York: Vintage, 1971.

Farr, Robert. *The Electronic Criminals.* New York: McGraw-Hill, 1975.

Feifer, George. "Russia Shoots Its Business Crooks." *New York Times Magazine*,

May 2, 1965, pp. 32–33, 111–12.

Fellmeth, Robert C. *The Interstate Commerce Omission* (New York: Grossman, 1970).

Fien, C. C. "Corporate Responsibility Under Criminal Law: A Study of the *Mens Rea*." *Manitoba Law Review*, 5 (1973), pp. 422–439.

Fisse, Brent. "The Use of Publicity as a Criminal Sanction Against Business Corporations." *Melbourne University Law Review*, 8 (June, 1971), pp. 107–150.

Francis, Joseph. "Criminal Responsibility of the Corporation." *Illinois Law Review*, 18 (January, 1924), pp. 305–323.

Friedrich, C. J. *The Pathology of Politics: Violence, Betrayal, Corruption, Secrecy and Propaganda*. New York: Harper & Row, 1972.

Fuller, John G. *The Gentlemen Conspirators: The Story of Price-Fixers in the Electrical Industry*. New York: Grove Press, 1962.

Fuller, Richard C. "Morals and the Criminal Law." *Journal of Criminal Law and Criminology*, 32 (March–April, 1942), pp. 624–630.

Gardiner, John A. *The Politics of Corruption: Organized Crime in an American City*. New York: Russell Sage Foundation, 1970.

Geis, Gilbert. "Avocational Crime." In Daniel Glaser, ed., *Handbook of Criminology*, pp. 273–298. Chicago: Rand-McNally, 1974.

———. "Deterring Corporate Crime." In Ralph Nader and Mark J. Green, eds., *Corporate Power in America*, pp. 182–197. New York: Grossman, 1973.

———. "Criminal Penalties for Corporate Criminals." *Criminal Law Bulletin*, 8 (June 1972), pp. 377–92.

———. "Toward a Delineation of White-Collar Offenses." *Sociological Inquiry*, 32 (Spring, 1962), pp. 160–171.

———. "Upperworld Crime." In Abraham S. Blumberg, ed., *Current Perspectives on Criminal Behavior*, pp. 114–37. New York: Knopf, 1974.

———. "Victimization Patterns in White-Collar Crime." In Israel Drapkin and Emilio Viano, eds. *Victimology: A New Focus*. Vol. 5. Lexington, Mass.: Lexington Books, 1975.

———, and Edelhertz, Herbert. "Criminal Law and Consumer Fraud." *American Criminal Law Review*, 11 (Summer, 1973), pp. 989–1010.

Gentry, Curt. *The Vulnerable Americans*. Garden City, N.Y.: Doubleday, 1966.

Gibbons, Don C. "Crime and Punishment: A Study in Social Attitudes." *Social Forces*, 47 (June, 1969), pp. 391–397.

Gibney, Frank, *The Operators*. New York: Harper & Row, 1960.

Glenn, Michael K. "The Crime of 'Pollution': The Role of Federal Water Pollution Criminal Sanctions." *American Criminal Law Review*, 11 (Summer, 1973), pp. 835–882.

Goff, Colin H. "Corporate Crime in Canada." Unpublished Master's thesis. University of Calgary, Alberta, Canada, Department of Sociology, 1976.

Goldman, M. M. *You Pay and You Pay: An Expose of the Respectable Racketeers*. New York: Howell, Soskin, 1941.

Goode, M. "Corporate Conspiracy: Problems of *Mens Rea* and the Parties to the Agreement." *Dalhousie Law Journal*, 2 (February, 1975), pp. 121–156.

Goodman, Margaret. "Does Political Corruption Really Help Economic Development?" *Polity*, 7 (Winter, 1974), pp. 143–162.

Goodman, Walter. *All Honorable Men: Corruption and Compromise in American Life*. Boston: Little, Brown, 1963.

Gordon, David M. "Capitalism, Class and Crime in America." *Crime and Delinquency*, 19 (April, 1973), pp. 163–168.

Green, Mark J., Moore, Beverly C., Jr., and Wasserstein, Bruce. *The Closed Enterprise System*. New York: Grossman, 1972.

Green, R. A. "Indications as to the Real Nature of the Criminal Responsibility of Corporations." *Victoria University of Wellington Law Review*, 6 (February, 1971), pp. 85–97.

Gross, Llewellyn. *Symposium on Sociological Theory*, pp. 531–564. New York: Harper & Row, 1959.

*Grundfragen der Wirtschaftskriminalität.* Wiebader, Bundekriminaamt, 1963.
Hadden, Tom. "The Origins and Development of Conspiracy to Defraud." *American Journal of Legal History,* 11 (January, 1967), pp. 25–40.
Hadlick, Paul E. *Criminal Prosecution Under the Sherman Antitrust Act.* Washington, D.C.: Ramsdell, 1939.
Haeger, John D., and Weber, Michael P., eds. *The Bosses.* St. Charles, Mo.: Forum Press, 1974.
Hanawalt, Barbara A. "Fur Collar Crime: The Pattern of Crime Among the Fourteenth Century English Nobility." *Journal of Social History,* 8 (Summer, 1975), pp. 1–17.
Hannay, William M. Introduction to *American Criminal Law Review,* 11 (Summer, 1973), pp. 817–819.
Hartung, Frank E. "Common and Discrete Values." *Journal of Social Psychology,* 38 (August, 1953), pp. 3–22.
———. "White-Collar Crime: Its Significance for Theory and Practice." *Federal Probation,* 17 (June, 1953), pp. 31–36.
Harward, Donald W., ed. *Crisis in Confidence: The Impact of Watergate.* Boston: Little, Brown, 1974.
Hay, George A., and Kelly, Daniel. "An Empirical Survey of Price Fixing Conspiracies." *Journal of Law and Economics,* 17 (April, 1974), pp. 13–38.
Hazard, Leland. "Are Big Businessmen Crooks?" *The Atlantic,* 208 (November, 1961), pp. 57–61.
Heidenheimer, Arnold J. *Political Corruption: Readings in Comparative Analysis.* New York: Holt, Rinehart and Winston, 1970.
Heilbroner, Robert, ed. *In the Name of Profit.* Garden City, N.Y.: Doubleday, 1972.
Herling, John. *The Great Price Conspiracy: The Story of Anti-Trust Violations in the Electrical Industry.* Washington, D.C.: Luce, 1962.
Hewitt, William H. "Combatting the White-Collar Criminal." *Law and Order* 11 (February, 1963), pp. 14–16.
Hills, Stuart L. *Crime, Power and Morality.* (Scranton, P.: Chandler, 1971), pp. 145–202.
Insalata, S. John "Deceptive Business Practices: Criminals in Cuff Links." *Vital Speeches of the Day,* 29 (May 15, 1963), pp. 473–475.
Iseman, Robert H. "The Criminal Responsibility of Corporate Officials for Pollution of the Environment." *Albany Law Review,* 37 (1971) 1: 61–96.
Jackson, Charles O. *Food and Drug Legislation in the New Deal.* Princeton, N.J.: *Princeton University Press,* 1970.
James, Leslie. "Bribery and Corruption in Commerce." *International and Comparative Law Quarterly,* 11 (July, 1962), pp. 880–886.
Jaspan, Norman, and Black, Illel. *The Thief in the White Collar.* Philadelphia: Lippincott, 1960.
Josephson, Mathew. *The Robber Barons: The Great American Capitalists, 1861–1901.* New York: Harcourt, Brace, 1934.
Kahn, E. J., Jr. *Fraud.* New York: Harper & Row, 1972.
Kellens, Georges. *Banqueroute et banqueroutiers.* Paris: Dessart et Mardaga, 1974.
———, "Du 'Crime en Col Blanc' au Delit de Chevalier." *Annales de la faculte de droit de Liège,* 30 (1968), pp. 60–124.
———, Le Crime en col blanc: sa place dans une criminologie économique." *Revue de science criminelle et de droit penal comparé,* 4 (October–November, 1974), pp. pp. 807–821.
Kinter, Earl A. *A Primer on the Law of Deceptive Practices: A Guide for the Businessman.* New York: Macmillan, 1971.
Kline, George L. "Economic Crime and Punishment." *Survey,* 57 (October, 1965), pp. 67–72.
Kohli, Suresh, ed. *Corruption in India.* New Delhi: Chetana Publications, 1975.
Kohlmeier, Louis M., Jr. *The Regulators.* New York: Harper & Row, 1969.
Korner, Waldemar, "Die misbräuchliche Erlangung der Gasölbetriebsbeihilfe." Faculty of Law dissertation, University of Mainz, 1968.

Kostelanetz, Boris. *Tax Frauds*. New York: Practicing Law Institute, 1975.

Kwan, Quon Y. Ponnusamy Rajeswaran, Parlor, Brian P., and Amir, Menachem. "The Role of Criminalistics in White-Collar Crime." *Journal of Criminal Law*, 62 (September, 1971), pp. 434–439.

Laite, W. E. *The United States vs. William Laite*. Washington, D.C.: Acropolis Books, 1972.

Lane, Robert E. *The Regulation of Business: Social Conditions of Government Economic Control*. (New Haven, Conn.: Yale University Press, 1954.

Lang, Gladys Engel, and Lang, Kurt. "Van Doren as Victim: Student Reaction." *Studies in Public Communications*, 3 (Summer, 1961), pp. 50–58.

Leigh, Leonard H. *The Criminal Liability of Corporations in English Law*. London: Weidenfeld & Nicolson, 1969.

Levens, E. "101 White-Collar Criminals." *New Society*, 78 (March 26, 1964), pp. 6–8.

Lever, Harry, and Young, Joseph. *Wartime Racketeering*. New York: Putnam & Sons, 1945.

Lieberman, Jethro K. *How the Government Breaks the Law*. New York: Penguin, 1974.

Lockard, Duanne. "The 'Great Tradition' of American Corruption." *New Society*, 24 (May 31, 1973), pp. 486–488.

Lundberg, Ferdinand. *The Rich and the Super-Rich*. New York: Lyle Stuart, 1968.

Lyon, Charles S. "The Crime of Income Tax Fraud: Its Present Status and Function." *Columbia Law Review*, 53 (April, 1953), pp. 476–503.

Maltz, Michael. "Policy Issues in Organized Crime and White-Collar Crime." In John A. Gardiner and Michael Mulkey, eds., *Crime and Criminal Justice*, pp. 73–92. Lexington, Mass.: Lexington Books, 1975.

Maccaulay, Stewart. "Changing A Continuing Relationship Between A Large Corporation and Those Who Deal With It: Automobile Manufacturers, Their Dealers, and The Legal System." *Wisconsin Law Review* (Summer–Fall, 1965), pp. 483–575, 740–858.

McDonald, B. "Criminality and the Canadian Anti-Combines Laws." *Alberta Law Review*, 9 (1975), pp. 67–95.

Maddock, Charles S. "The Proposed Criminal Code: Business Lawyer Beware." *Business Lawyer*, 29 (April, 1974), pp. 711–722.

————. "Criminal Prosecutions under the Investment Company Act of 1940 and the Investment Advisers Act." *Boston College Industrial and Commercial Law Review*, 13 (April, 1973), pp. 1257–1273.

Mannheim, Hermann. *Comparative Criminology*. Vol. 2, pp. 469–498. London: Routledge, 1965.

————. *Social Aspects of Crime in England Between the Wars*, pp. 186–210. London: G. Allen, 1940.

Mathews, Arthur F. "Criminal Prosecutions under the Federal Securities Laws and Related Statutes: The Nature and Development of SEC Criminal Cases." *George Washington Law Review*, 39 (July, 1971), pp. 901–970.

Mayer, Joseph. "Watergate Flimflam." *Social Science*, 49 (Spring, 1974), pp. 99–103.

McShane, Paul. "War on White-Collar Crime," *Penthouse*, 3 (November, 1971), pp. 32–35.

Meltsner, Michael, and Schrag, Philip G. *Public Interest Advocacy*. Boston: Little, Brown, 1974.

Meyer, John C. "An Action-Orientation Approach to the Study of Occupational Crime." *Australian and New Zealand Journal of Criminology*, 5 (March, 1972), pp. 35–48.

Mintz, Morton, and Cohen, Jerry S. *America, Inc.: Who Owns and Operates the United States*. New York: Dial, 1971.

Molotch, Harvey. "Oil in Santa Barbara and Power in America." In William J. Chambliss, ed., pp. 297–323. *Sociological Readings in the Conflict Perspective*, Reading, Mass.: Addison Wesley, 1973.

Morgenthau, Robert. "Equal Justice and Problem of White-Collar Crime." *Conference Board Record*, 6 (August, 1969), pp. 17–20.

Morris, Albert. *Criminology*, pp. 152–58. New York: Longmans, Green, 1939.

Morris, Joe, Scott. "Environmental Problems and the Use of Criminal Sanctions." *Land and Water Law Review*, 7 (1972), 1: 421–31.

Mosher, Frederick C. *Watergate: Implications for Responsible Government*. New York: Basic Books, 1974.

Mueller, Gerhard O. W. *"Mens Rea* and the Corporation: A Study of the Model Penal Code Position on Corporate Criminal Liability." *University of Pittsburgh Law Review*, 19 (Fall, 1957), pp. 21–50.

Murphy, Joseph H. "Criminal Income Tax Evasion." *Northwestern University Law Review*, 48 (July–August, 1953), pp. 313–341.

Nader, Ralph. "Business Crime." In David Sanford, ed., *Hot War on the Consumer*, pp. 138–140. New York: Pitman, 1969.

––––––. "Violence of Omission." *Nation*, February 10, 1969.

National Chamber of Commerce. *A Handbook on White-Collar Crime*. Washington, D.C.: Chamber of Commerce of the United States, 1974.

Newman, Donald J. "The Agnew Plea Bargain." *Criminal Law Bulletin*, 10 (January–February, 1974), pp. 85–90.

––––––. "Public Attitudes Toward a Form of White-Collar Crime." *Social Problems*, 4 (January, 1953), pp. 228–232.

Normandeau, André, "Les Deviation en affaires et la "Crime en col blanc," *Revue internationale de criminologie et de police technique*, 19 (October–December, 1965), pp. 247–58.

O'Keefe, Jr., Daniel F., and Shapiro, Marc H. "Personal Criminal Liability Under the Food, Drug and Cosmetic Act—The *Dotterweich* Doctrine." *Food, Drug, Cosmetic Law Journal*, 30 (January, 1975), pp. 5–78.

Ogren, Robert W. "The Ineffectiveness of the Criminal Sanction in Fraud and Corruption Cases: Losing the Battle Against White-Collar Crime." *American Criminal Law Review*, 11 (Summer, 1973), pp. 959–988.

Ottenberg, Miriam. *The Federal Investigators*. Englewood Cliffs, N.J.: Prentice-Hall, 1962.

Packer, Herbert L. *The Limits of the Criminal Sanction*, pp. 345–363. Stanford, Calif.: Stanford University Press, 1968.

Paulus, Ingeborg. *The Search for Pure Food: A Sociology of Legislation in Britain*. London: M. Robertson, 1975.

Pavarini, Massimo. "Ricerca in Terma Di: Criminalita Economica." *La Questione Criminale*, 1 (September–December, 1975), pp. 537–545.

Pearce, Frank. "Crime, Corporations and the American Social Order." In Ian Taylor and Laurie Taylor, eds., *Politics and Deviance*, pp. 13–41. Baltimore: Penguin, 1973.

Pepinsky, Harold E. "From White-Collar Crime to Exploitation: Redefinition of a Field." *Journal of Criminal Law and Criminology*, 65 (June, 1974), pp. 225–233.

President's Commission on Law Enforcement and Administration of Justice. *The Challenge of Crime in a Free Society*, pp. 47–49. Washington, D.C.: Government Printing Office, 1967.

––––––. *Crime and Its Impact—An Assessment*, pp. 102–115. Washington, D.C.: Government Printing Office, 1967.

Reed, John P., and Reed, Robin S. "Doctor, Lawyer, Indian Chief: Old Rhymes and New on White-Collar Crime." *The Australian and New Zealand Journal of Criminology*, 7 (September, 1974), pp. 145–156.

Riis, Roger, and Patric, John. *Repairmen Will Get You If You Don't Watch Out*. Garden City, N.Y.: Doubleday, 1942.

Rimann, Bernhard R., *Wirtschaftskriminalität, die Unterswchung bei Wirtschaftsdelikten*. Unpublished Ph.D. dissertation, University of Zurich, 1973.

Robins, Gerald D. "White-Collar Crime and Employee Theft." *Crime and Delinquency*, 20 (July, 1974), pp. 251–262.

Roebuck, Julian B. and Hunter, Robert B. "Medical Quackery as Deviant Behavior." *Criminology*, 8 (May, 1970), pp. 46–62.

Rose-Ackerman, Susan. "The Economics of Corruption." *Journal of Public Economics,* 4 (1975), pp. 187–203.
Rosenberg, Kenyon. *Watergate: An Annotated Bibliography.* Littleton, Cal.: Libraries Unlimited, 1975.
Ross, Edward A. *Sin and Society: An Analysis of Latter-Day Iniquity.* Boston: Houghton Mifflin, 1907.
Rossi, Peter, H., Waite, Emily, Rose, Christine E., and Berk, Richard E. "The Seriousness of Crimes: Normative Structure and Individual Differences." *American Sociological Review,* 39 (April, 1974), pp. 224–237.
Sanford, David, ed. *Hot War on the Consumer.* (New York: Pitman, 1969).
Schafer, Herbert, ed., *Wirtschaftskriminalität.* Hamburg: Steintor, 1967.
Schmidt, Peter, *Die trügerische Reklame.* Faculty of Law dissertation, University of Kiel, 1965.
Schneider, Hans, J., "Wirtschaftskriminalität in Kriminologischer und Strafrechtlichersicht." *Juristenzeitung,* 27 (August 18, 1972), pp. 461–467.
Schrag, Philip G. "On Her Majesty's Secret Service: Protecting the Consumer in New York City." *Yale Law Journal,* 80 (July, 1971), pp. 1529–1602.
Schur, Edwin H. *Our Criminal Society,* pp. 158–90. Englewood Cliffs, N.J.: Prentice-Hall, 1969.
Schwartz, Richard D. and Orleans, Soyna. "On Legal Sanctions." *University of Chicago Law Review,* 34 (Winter, 1967), pp. 274–300.
Schwenk, Edmund H. "The Administrative Crime, Its Creation and Punishment by Administrative Agencies." *Michigan Law Review,* 42 (August, 1943), pp. 51–86.
Scott, James. *Comparative Political Corruption.* Englewood Cliffs, N.J.: Prentice-Hall, 1972.
Seider, Maynard. "American Big Business Ideology: A Content Analysis of Executive Speeches." *American Sociological Review,* 39 (December, 1974), pp. 802–815.
Seymour, J. and North, Whitney. *Fighting White-Collar Crime.* New York: Office of the United States Attorney for the Southern District of New York, 1972.
Shapiro, Susan. "A Background Paper on White Collar Crime: Considerations of Conceptualization and Future Research." Unpublished paper, Yale University, 1976.
Sherman, Lawrence W., ed. *Police Corruption: A Sociological Perspective.* (Garden City, N.Y.: Anchor, 1974).
Sherwin, Robert. "White-Collar Crime, Conventional Crime and Merton's Deviant Behavior Theory." *Wisconsin Sociologist,* 2 (Spring, 1963), pp. 7–10.
Shoemaker, Donald, and South, Donald R. "White-Collar Crime." In Clifton D. Bryant, ed., *Deviant Behavior,* pp. 189–200. Chicago: Rand-McNally, 1974.
Smigel, Erwin O., and Ross H. Laurence, eds. *Crimes Against Bureaucracy.* New York: Van Nostrand Reinhold, 1970.
Smith, Richard A. "The Incredible Electrical Conspiracy." *Fortune,* 63 (April, 1961), pp. 132–137, and 63 (May, 1961), pp. 161–164.
Snodgrass, Jon. "Edwin Hardin Sutherland (1883–1950)." In *The American Criminological Tradition: Portraits of Men and Ideology in a Discipline.* Ph.D. dissertation, University of Pennsylvania, 1972, pp. 218–308.
Sobel, Lester A., ed. *Money and Politics.* New York: Facts on File, 1974.
Sorenson, Robert C. "Review of Sutherland, *White-Collar Crime." Journal of Criminal Law, Criminology and Police Science,* 41 (May–June, 1950), pp. 80–82.
Spencer, John C. "White-Collar Crime." In Tadeusz Grygier, Howard Jones, and John C. Spencer, eds., *Criminology in Transition,* pp. 251–64. London: Tavistock, 1965.
Staats, Steven J. "Corruption in the Soviet System." *Problems of Communism,* 21 (January–February, 1972), pp. 40–47.
Steele, Eric H. "Fraud, Dispute and the Consumer: Responding to Consumer Complaints." *University of Pennsylvania Law Review,* 123 (May, 1975), pp. 1107–1186.
Steinberg, Harris. "The Defense of the White-Collar Accused." *American Criminal Law Quarterly,* 3 (Spring, 1964), pp. 129–138.
Stevenson, Russell B. "Corporations and Social Responsibility: In Search of the Corporate Soul." *George Washington Law Review,* 42 (May, 1974), pp. 709–736.

Stocker, Frederick D., and Ellickson, John C. "How Fully Do Farmers Report Their Incomes?" *National Tax Journal,* 12 (June, 1959), pp. 116–126.

Stone, Christopher D. *Where the Law Ends.* New York: Harper & Row, 1975.

Surface, William. *Inside Internal Revenue.* New York: Coward-McCann, 1967.

Sutherland, Edwin H. *On Analyzing Crime.* Ed. by Karl Schuessler. Chicago: University of Chicago Press, 1973.

———. *White Collar Crime.* New York: Dryden, 1949.

———. "Crime and Business." *Annals of the American Academy of Political and Social Science.* 217 (September, 1941), pp. 112–118.

———. "The White-Collar Criminal." In Vernon C. Branham and Samuel B. Kutash, eds., *Encyclopedia of Criminology,* pp. 511–515. New York: Philosophical Library, 1949.

Thayer, George. *Who Shakes the Money Tree?: American Campaign Practices from 1789 to the Present.* New York: Simon and Schuster, 1974.

Tiedemann, Klause, ed. *Die Verbrechen in der Wirtschaft.* Karlsruhe: C. F. Muller, 1970.

Tompkins, Dorothy C. *White-Collar Crime—A Bibliography.* Berkeley Institute of Governmental Studies, University of California, 1967.

Teufel, Manfred. "Zur Kriminologie der Wirtschaftsdelikte." *Archiv für Kriminologie,* 155 (1975), pp. 129–147.

Uffelman, John. "Corporate Criminal Liability in Oregon: State v. Pacific Power and the New Oregon Criminal Code." *Oregon Law Review,* 51 (Spring, 1972), pp. 587–595.

Usitalo, Paavo. *White-Collar Crimes and Status Selectivity in the Law Enforcement System.* Helsinki: Institute of Sociology, University of Helsinki, 1969.

Vaughan, Diane, and Carlo, Giovanna. "The Appliance Repairman: A Study of Victim-Responsiveness and Fraud." *Journal of Research on Crime and Delinquency,* July, 1975, pp. 153–161.

Viner, Jacob. "An Intellectual History of Laissez Faire." *Journal of Law and Economics,* 3 (October, 1960), pp. 45–69.

Vold, George B. *Theoretical Criminology,* pp. 245–61. New York: Oxford University Press, 1958.

Wagner, Walter. *The Golden Fleecers.* Garden City, N.Y.: Doubleday, 1967.

Walton, Clarence C., and Cleveland, Frederick W., Jr., *Corporations on Trial: The Electrical Cases.* Belmont, Ca.: Wadsworth, 1964.

Weinberg, Arthur, and Weinberg, Lila. *The Muckrakers.* New York: Simon and Schuster, 1961.

Welsh, R. S. "The Criminal Liability of Corporations." *Law Quarterly Review,* 62 (October, 1946), pp. 345–365.

Wheeler, Stanton. "Trends and Problems in the Sociological Study of Crime." *Social Problems,* 23 (June, 1976), pp. 526–534.

"White-Collar Crime." *Barron's,* March 30, 1970, pp. 1, 5.

"White-Collar Crime: Huge Economic and Moral Drain." *Congressional Quarterly Weekly Report,* 29 (May 7, 1971), pp. 1047–1049.

Whitman, Howard. "Why Some Doctors Should be in Jail." *Collier's,* 132 (October 30, 1953), pp. 23–27.

Wilson, James Q. "Corruption Is Not Always Scandalous." *New York Times Magazine,* pp. 52–54 ff.

Wise, David. *The Politics of Lying: Government Deception, Secrecy and Power.* New York: Random House, 1973.

Wraith, Ronald, and Simpkins, Edgar. *Corruption in Developing Countries.* London: G. Allen, 1963.

Yeager, Matthew, G. "The Gangster as White-Collar Criminal: Organized Crime and Stolen Securities." *Issues in Criminology,* 8 (Spring, 1973), pp. 49–73.

Young, James H. *The Medical Messiahs.* Princeton, N.J.: Princeton University Press, 1967.

Zirpins, Walter, and Terstegen, Otto. *Wirtschaftskriminalität.* Lübeck: M. Schmidt-Romhild, 1963.